REA's Test Prep Books Are The Best!

(a sample of the <u>hundreds of letters</u> REA receives each year)

" I used [*the REA study guide*] to study for the LAST and ATS-W tests —
and passed them both with *perfect* scores. This book provided
excellent preparation… "
Student, New York, NY

" The reviews in [the REA book] were outstanding... If it wasn't for your
excellent prep, I would not have stood a chance [of passing the NYSTCE]. "
Student, Elmira, New York

" Your book was such a better value and was so much more complete than
anything your competition has produced (and I have them all)! "
Teacher, Virginia Beach, VA

" Compared to the other books that my fellow students had, your book was
the most useful in helping me get a great score. "
Student, North Hollywood, CA

" Your book was responsible for my success on the exam, which helped me get
into the college of my choice... I will look for REA the next time I need help. "
Student, Chesterfield, MO

" Just a short note to say thanks for the great support your book gave me in
helping me pass the test... I'm on my way to a B.S. degree because of you! "
Student, Orlando, FL

(more on back page)

Research & Education Association

The Best Coaching & Study Guide for the

NYSTCE®
LAST · ATS-W · ATS-P
3rd Edition

**With CD-ROM for Windows®
REA's TESTware® for the NYSTCE**

Staff of
Research & Education Association

Visit our Educator Support Center at:
www.REA.com/teacher

Research & Education Association
61 Ethel Road West
Piscataway, New Jersey 08854
E-mail: info@rea.com

The Best Coaching and Study Guide for the
NYSTCE®: *LAST, ATS-W, and ATS-P*
with CD-ROM for Windows®

Year 2007 Printing

Copyright © 2005, 2002 by Research & Education Association, Inc. All rights reserved. No part of this book may be reproduced in any form without permission of the publisher.

Printed in the United States of America

Library of Congress Control Number 2005900957

International Standard Book Number 0-7386-0007-5

Windows® is a registered trademark of Microsoft Corporation.

E07-0101

About Research & Education Association

Founded in 1959, Research & Education Association (REA) is dedicated to publishing the finest and most effective educational materials—including software, study guides, and test preps—for students in middle school, high school, college, graduate school, and beyond.

REA's Test Preparation series includes books and software for all academic levels in almost all disciplines. Research & Education Association publishes test preps for students who have not yet entered high school, as well as high school students preparing to enter college. Students from countries around the world seeking to attend college in the United States will find the assistance they need in REA's publications. For college students seeking advanced degrees, REA publishes test preps for many major graduate school admission examinations in a wide variety of disciplines, including engineering, law, and medicine. Students at every level, in every field, with every ambition can find what they are looking for among REA's publications.

REA presents tests that accurately depict the official exams in both degree of difficulty and types of questions. REA's practice tests are always based upon the most recently administered exams, and include every type of question that can be expected on the actual exams.

REA's publications and educational materials are highly regarded and continually receive an unprecedented amount of praise from professionals, instructors, librarians, parents, and students. Our authors are as diverse as the fields represented in the books we publish. They are well known in their respective disciplines and serve on the faculties of prestigious high schools, colleges, and universities throughout the United States and Canada.

Today, REA's wide-ranging catalog is a leading resource for teachers, students, and professionals.

We invite you to visit us at *www.rea.com* to find out how "REA is making the world smarter."

Author & Staff Acknowledgments

Bruce Adams of Tonawanda (N.Y.) City High School for his authorship and technical editing of our humanities review and practice-test material; **Paul Babbitt** of Rutgers University, New Brunswick, N.J., **Niles Holt** of Illinois State University, Normal, Ill., and **Gary Land** of Andrews College, Berrien Springs, Mich., for their editorial contributions to our history and social science review and practice-test material; **Anita Price Davis** of Converse College, Spartanburg, S.C., for her editorial contributions to our communication skills and writing skills reviews and practice-test material; **Elizabeth Powell** and **Margaret Vezza** for their editorial contributions to the math and science sections; **Jacquelin Kovacs** of Cincinnatus (N.Y.) Central School for her editorial contributions; **Kathleen Velsor**, for her contributions to the practice tests. We would also like to thank **Larry B. Kling**, Vice President, Editorial, for his supervision of editorial production; **Pam Weston**, Vice President, Publishing, for setting the quality standards for production integrity and managing the publication to completion; **John Paul Cording**, Vice President, Technology, for coordinating the design and development of the TEST*ware*®; Technology Project Managers **Reena Shah** and **Dipen Patel** for software testing and design contributions; **Christine Saul** for the cover design; **Alice Leonard**, Senior Editor, for coordinating revisions; and **Rachel DiMatteo** for typesetting revisions.

CONTENTS

LAST/ATS-W

Chapter 1

Passing the LAST/ATS-W

Chapter 1

Passing the LAST/ATS-W

ABOUT THIS BOOK & TEST*ware*®

This book provides a complete and accurate representation of New York state's LAST/ATS-W (Liberal Arts and Sciences Test/Assessment of Teaching Skills-Written), part of one of the most broadly-based teacher certification programs used in the United States today. We include topical reviews correlating to each of the test sections on the LAST and ATS-W exams, along with a full-length practice test for each exam based on the current format of the New York State Teacher Certification Examinations, or NYSTCE. REA's practice tests contain every type of question that you can expect to encounter on the actual exam. We also present detailed explanations of each answer—as well as sample essays—to help you master the test material. The full-length practice exams are presented in two forms – in written form in the book and in our exclusive TEST*ware*® format on the enclosed CD. We strongly recommend you take the practice exams on CD first, to get the full benefit of enforced time conditions and instantaneous scoring.

ABOUT THE TEST

Who Takes the Test and What Is It Used for?

The LAST/ATS-W is taken by individuals seeking certification to teach in any of New York state's 704 public school districts. In most cases, candidates are beginning their teaching career or seeking additional certification.

While you're free to take the LAST or ATS-W at any time during college, most candidates find it best to attempt the former in their sophomore or junior year (after they have most basic liberal arts and sciences coursework behind them) and the latter after having completed pedagogical coursework and fieldwork (and in some cases even student teaching). Senior year is the time to consider taking the Content Specialty Test to help you peg what additional coursework will be required in your area of concentration. To do well on the Assessment of Teaching Skills-Performance, you should have at least two years of classroom experience under your belt.

Who Administers the Test?

The LAST/ATS-W is administered by National Evaluation Systems, Inc. (NES), in conjunction with the New York State Education Department. A comprehensive test development process was designed and implemented specifically to ensure that the content and difficulty level of the exam are appropriate. This process involved hundreds of teachers and teacher educators from across the state.

When and Where Is the Test Given?

The LAST/ATS-W is usually offered seven times a year at a number of locations throughout the state of New York. Selective administrations are offered in Puerto Rico as well. To receive information on upcoming test dates and locations, contact either of the following:

New York State Education Department
Office of Teaching
Room 5N Education Building
Albany, NY 12234
Website: http://www.highered.nysed.gov/tcert/
Phone: (518) 474-3852

NYSTCE
National Evaluation Systems, Inc.
P.O. Box 660
30 Gatehouse Road
Amherst, MA 01004-9008
Phone: (413) 256-2882 or (800) 309-5225
TTY for Deaf: (413) 256-8032
Website: www.nystce.nesinc.com

Registration information, as well as test dates and locations, is provided in the registration bulletin and on the NYSTCE website. Information regarding testing accommodations for candidates with special needs is also included.

Accommodations for Students with Disabilities

Alternative testing arrangements for students with both physical and learning disabilities are available for the NYSTCE exams. Please visit the NYSTCE website at *www.nystce.nesinc.com* for more information, including registration and documentation requirements.

Is There a Registration Fee?

You must pay a registration fee in order to take the LAST/ATS-W. A complete outline of registration fees is provided in your registration bulletin.

THE NYSTCE PROGRAM

The NYSTCE Program embraces six tests: the Liberal Arts and Sciences Test (LAST), the Assessment of Teaching Skills–Written (ATS-W), and the Assessment of Teaching Skills–Performance (ATS-P), along with the Content Specialty Test, English Language Proficiency Assessment, and Target Language Proficiency Assessment. This group of tests is designed to assess your knowledge of subject matter, as well as your ability to convey that knowledge to a student.

Format of the LAST

The Liberal Arts and Sciences Test is composed of roughly 80 multiple-choice questions and one essay. You will have four hours to complete the exam. The five subject areas it covers are as follows:

> Scientific, Mathematical and Technical Processes

> Historical and Social Scientific Awareness

> Artistic Expression and the Humanities

> Communication and Research Skills

> Written Analysis and Expression

The exact number of questions in each area *will* vary, as will the total number of questions on the exam and in each subarea. The test administrators often include a number of so-called pretest, or experimental, questions that do not count toward your score but are used to prepare future exams. In general, be prepared to make broad assessments and pick out underlying assumptions and inferences.

Format of the ATS-W

Like the LAST, the Assessment of Teaching Skills-Written is composed of roughly 80 multiple-choice questions and one essay. The test is offered in two versions: Elementary and Secondary. Candidates for K-12 Certification may elect to take either test. The number of questions may vary. The breakdown of the ATS-W subject matter is as follows:

> ➤ Student Development and Learning

> ➤ Instructional Planning, Assessment, and Delivery

> ➤ The Professional Environment

Format of the ATS-P

Unlike the LAST and the ATS-W, the Assessment of Teaching Skills–Performance is not a paper-and-pencil test. The ATS-P requires candidates to videotape themselves in the classroom environment. Our ATS-P review outlines the requirements of the 30-minute sample lesson and some suggestions on how to make your video place you in the best possible light.

SCORING THE NYSTCE

How Do I Score My Practice Test?

Each of the NYSTCE tests has a score range of 100–300 points. In each case (except, of course, for the ATS-P) you must achieve a minimum of 220 to pass the exam. Achieving a passing score on a particular test means you'll have satisfied that portion of the certification requirement. Your total score will derive from a combination of the number of multiple-choice questions that you answer correctly and your essay scores; the multiple-choice sections, however, account for a larger percentage of your overall score than your essays do.

In order to achieve a passing score on the practice tests, you need to answer at least 60% of the multiple-choice questions correctly and your essay grades can fall no lower than the middle of the scoring range (as set forth in our Detailed Explanations of Answers). It may be helpful to have a friend or colleague score your essays, since you will benefit from his or her ability to be more objective in judging the clarity and organization of your written responses.

When Will I Receive My Score Report?

Your score report should arrive about six weeks after you take the test. No scoring information will be given over the telephone. Unofficial scores may be viewed at the NYSTCE website approximately six weeks after the test date. For more information, see the registration bulletin or go online. Remember, your score report will show your *scaled* score, *not* the number of questions you answered correctly.

STUDYING FOR THE LAST/ATS-W

There is no one correct way to study for this exam. You must find the method that works best for you. Some candidates prefer to set aside a few hours every morning to study, while others prefer to study at night before going to sleep. Only you can determine when and where your study time will be most effective, but it is helpful to be consistent. You may retain more information if you study every day at roughly the same time. A study schedule appears at the end of this chapter to help you budget your time.

When taking the practice tests you should try to duplicate the actual testing conditions as closely as possible. A quiet, well-lit room, free from such distractions as the television or radio, is preferable. After you score the practice test, thoroughly review the explanations. Information that is wrong for one item may be correct for another, so it will be helpful for you to absorb as much data as possible.

HOW TO USE THIS BOOK & TEST*ware*®

When Should I Start Studying?

We provide a six-week study schedule on page 11 to assist you in preparing for the exam. Our schedule allows for a great deal of flexibility. If your test date is only three weeks away, you can halve the time allotted to each section—keep in mind, however, that this is not the most effective way to study. If you're fortunate enough to have several months before your test date, you may want to extend the time allotted to each section. Remember, the more time you spend studying, the better your chances of achieving a passing score.

About the Review Sections

By using our review material in conjunction with our practice tests, you should be well prepared for the actual exams. At some point in your educational experience, you have probably studied all the material that makes up the test. For most candidates, however, this was most likely some time ago. Our review material, while fact-rich, is not intended to have you memorize dates, names, and places. Rather, it's meant to provide the narrative thread to reinforce contextual memory. Because both the LAST and the ATS-W test sections contain an essay, the Writing Skills review included in the LAST section will be helpful in preparing for either test.

This book includes the best test preparation materials based on the latest information available from test administrators. The number and distribution of questions can vary from test to test. Accordingly, prospective examinees should pay strict attention to their strengths and weaknesses and not depend on specific proportions of any subject areas appearing on the actual exam.

LAST/ATS-W TEST-TAKING TIPS

Although you may have taken standardized tests like these before, it is crucial that you become familiar with the format and content of each section of the exam you'll be taking. This will help to alleviate any anxiety about your performance. Here are several ways to help you become accustomed to the test.

> *Become comfortable with the format of the test.* The exams cover a great deal of information, and the more comfortable you are with the format, the more confidence you will have when you take the actual exam. If you familiarize yourself with the requirements of each section individually, the whole test will be much less intimidating.

> *Read all of the possible answers.* Even if you believe you have found the correct answer, read all four options. Often answers that initially look right prove to be "magnet responses" meant to distract you from the correct choice.

> *Eliminate obviously incorrect answers.* In this way, even if you do not know the correct answer, you can make an educated guess.

> *Work quickly and steadily.* Remember, the final question on both the Liberal Arts and Sciences Test and the Assessment of Teaching Skills–Written is in essay form. You need more time to compose a clear, concise, well-constructed essay than you do to answer a multiple-choice question, so don't spend too much time on any one item. Pace yourself. If you feel that you are spending too much time on any one question, mark the answer choice that you think is most likely the correct one, circle the item number in your test booklet, and return to it if time allows. Timing yourself while you take the practice tests will help you learn to use your time wisely.

> *Be sure that the oval you are marking corresponds to the number of the question in the test booklet.* Multiple-choice tests like the NYSTCE are graded by a computer, which has no sympathy for clerical errors. One incorrectly placed response can upset your entire score.

THE DAY OF THE TEST

Try to get a good night's rest, and wake up early on the day of the test. You should have a good breakfast so you will not be distracted by hunger. Dress in layers that can be removed or applied as the conditions of the testing center require. Plan to arrive early. This will allow you to become familiar with your surroundings in the testing center, and minimize the possibility of distraction during the test.

Before you leave for the testing center, make sure you have any admissions material you may need, including photo identification. None of the mathematics items covered on the LAST test requires scientific functions, so a calculator is neither necessary nor permitted. Calculators, however, will be provided for any Content Specialty Tests for which they are required. No eating, drinking, or smoking will be permitted during the test.

LAST/ATS-W INDEPENDENT STUDY SCHEDULE

This study schedule allows for thorough preparation for the New York State Teacher Certification Examinations. It applies equally well whether you're taking the LAST, the ATS-W, or both. Although designed for six weeks, it can be condensed into a three-week course by collapsing each two-week block into a one-week period. If you are not enrolled in a structured course, be sure to set aside enough time—at least two or three hours each day—to study. No matter which study schedule works best for you, the more time you spend studying, the more prepared and relaxed you will feel on the day of the exam.

Week	Activity
1	Study REA's LAST/ATS-W review material and answer the drill questions provided. Highlight key terms and information. Take notes on the important theories and key concepts, since writing will aid in the retention of information.
2 and 3	Review your references and sources. Use any supplementary material that your education instructors recommend.
4	Condense your notes and findings. You should have a structured outline with specific facts. You may want to use index cards to help you memorize important facts and concepts.
5	Test yourself using the index cards. You may want to have a friend or colleague quiz you on key facts and items. Take the relevant practice exam on CD-ROM. Review the explanations for the items you answered incorrectly.
6	Study any areas where you've identified weaknesses. Use this book and any other relevant references and notes.

LAST/ATS-W

Chapter 2

Science and Mathematics Review

Chapter 2

Science and Mathematics Review

The Science and Mathematics section of the LAST focuses on the understanding of mathematical concepts necessary for teachers, as well as the ability to relate these concepts to others. The emphasis is on the candidate's ability to use logic and reason when solving problems.

The following reviews contain all the information you will need to do well on this portion of the LAST. There is probably nothing in this section that you have not studied before, so most of the topics should be familiar to you. Remember, the LAST focuses primarily on the *processes* involved in mathematics and science. Therefore, factual recall is less important than a general understanding of the material when taking the LAST.

ARITHMETIC

Integers

Integers are *signed numbers* preceded by either a "+" or a "−" sign. If no sign is given for the integer, one should infer that the integer is positive (e.g., 3 means +3). On a number line, integers to the *left of zero are negative* and integers to the *right of zero are positive*.

Natural or counting numbers are 1, 2, 3, …

Whole numbers are 0, 1, 2, 3, ...

Integers are ..., –2, –1, 0, 1, 2, ...

As shown below, a number line is often used to represent integers.

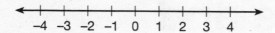

The *absolute value* of an integer is the measure of the distance of the integer from zero. Since the measure of distance is always positive, absolute value is always positive. The absolute value of the real number a is denoted by $|a|$ (e.g., $|-3| = 3$, $|3| = 3$).

Prime and Composite Numbers

When two whole numbers are multiplied, they yield a product. These two whole numbers can be called *factors* or *divisors* of the product. (An exception to this is 0. Zero can be a factor, but not a divisor, since division by 0 is undefined.)

A *prime number* is a whole number, greater than 1, that has only two different whole number factors, 1 and the number itself.

EXAMPLE

5 is a prime number, because it has only two different factors, 1 and 5.

A *composite number* is a whole number that has three or more whole number factors.

EXAMPLE

6 is a composite number, because it has four different factors, 1, 2, 3, and 6.

Arithmetic Operations and Integers

MULTIPLICATION

When multiplying two integers, the two integers are called *factors*, and the result is called the *product*, as illustrated in the following:

$$5 \quad \times \quad 3 \quad = \quad 15$$
$$\text{(factor)} \qquad \text{(factor)} \qquad \text{(product)}$$

When multiplying two integers, multiply the absolute values of the factors. If the factors have the *same sign*, the product is *positive;* if the factors have *different signs*, the product is *negative.* If either factor is zero, the product is zero.

EXAMPLE

$3 \times 5 = 15$ and $(-3) \times (-5) = 15$, but

$(-3) \times 5 = -15$ and $3 \times (-5) = -15$.

DIVISION

When dividing two integers, the number being divided is the *dividend,* the number being divided into another integer is the *divisor,* and the result is the *quotient,* as illustrated in the following:

$$10 \quad \div \quad 2 \quad = \quad 5$$
$$\text{(dividend)} \quad \text{(divisor)} \quad \text{(quotient)}$$

When dividing two integers, divide the absolute values of the dividend and divisor. The sign of the quotient can be obtained by following the same procedures given above in the multiplication section.

EXAMPLE

$10 \div 2 = 5$ and $(-10) \div (-2) = 5$, but

$(-10) \div 2 = (-5)$ and $10 \div (-2) = (-5)$.

Powers and Roots of Whole Numbers

EXPONENTS AND BASES

In the expression 5^3, 5 is called the *base* and 3 is called the *exponent*. The expression $5^3 = 5 \times 5 \times 5$. The base (5) represents the factor used in the expression and the exponent (3) represents the number of times the base is to be used as a factor.

EXAMPLE

$4^2 = 4 \times 4$

$3^5 = 3 \times 3 \times 3 \times 3 \times 3$

The Basic Laws of Exponents are

1) $b^m \times b^n = b^{m+n}$

2) $b^m \div b^n = b^{m-n}$

3) $(b^m)^n = b^{m \times n}$

ROOTS

Consider again the expression 5^3. If we carry out the implied multiplication, we get $5^3 = 5 \times 5 \times 5 = 125$. 5 is called the cube root of 125, since $5^3 = 125$. In general, when a base is raised to a power to produce a given result, the base is called the *root* of the given result.

If the power for the base is 2, the base is called the *square root*. If the power for the base is 3, the base is called the *cube root*. In general, if $b^n = p$, then b is the *n*th root of p.

EXAMPLE

Since $4^2 = 16$, 4 is the square root of 16.

Since $2^3 = 8$, 2 is the cube root of 8.

Since $3^5 = 243$, 3 is the 5th root of 243.

Common Fractions

A common fraction is a number that can be written in the form $\frac{a}{b}$ where a and b are whole numbers. In the expression $\frac{a}{b}$, the dividend a is called the *numerator* and the divisor b is called the *denominator.*

A common fraction may not have 0 as a denominator, since *division by 0 is undefined.*

A fraction is in *lowest terms* if the numerator and denominator have no common factors.

EXAMPLE

$\frac{1}{2}$, $\frac{3}{4}$, and $\frac{5}{6}$ are in lowest terms, since the numerator and denominator of each have no common factors.

$\frac{2}{4}$, $\frac{9}{21}$, and $\frac{20}{24}$ are *not* in lowest terms, since the numerator and denominator of each have common factors.

Fractions are *equivalent* if they represent the same number.

EXAMPLE

$\frac{8}{16}$, $\frac{4}{8}$, $\frac{2}{4}$, and $\frac{5}{10}$ are equivalent fractions, since each represents $\frac{1}{2}$.

A *mixed numeral* is a number that consists of an integer and a common fraction.

EXAMPLE

$5\frac{3}{4}$ is a mixed numeral since it consists of the integer 5 and the common fraction $\frac{3}{4}$.

An *improper fraction* is a common fraction whose numerator is larger than its denominator. A mixed numeral can be expressed as an improper fraction by multiplying the denominator of the common fraction part times the integer part and adding that product to the numerator of the common fraction part. The result is the numerator of the improper fraction. The denominator of the improper fraction is the same as the denominator in the mixed numeral.

EXAMPLE

$5\dfrac{3}{4} = \dfrac{23}{4}$ since $(4 \times 5) + 3 = 23$, and 4 was the denominator of the common fraction part. $\dfrac{23}{4}$ is an improper fraction, since the numerator, 23, is larger than the denominator, 4.

ADDITION AND SUBTRACTION

In order to *add* or *subtract* two fractions, the denominators of the fractions must be the same; when they are, they are called *common denominators*. The equivalent fractions with the smallest common denominator are said to have the *lowest common denominator*.

EXAMPLE

$\dfrac{3}{8} - \dfrac{2}{8} = \dfrac{1}{8},$ but $\dfrac{3}{8} - \dfrac{1}{4} = \dfrac{3}{8} - \dfrac{2}{8} = \dfrac{1}{8}$

In this example, 8 is the lowest common denominator.

MULTIPLICATION

To *multiply* two common fractions, simply find the product of the two numerators and divide it by the product of the two denominators. Reduce the resultant fraction to lowest terms.

EXAMPLE

$\dfrac{2}{3} \times \dfrac{9}{11} = \dfrac{18}{33} = \dfrac{6}{11}$

DIVISION

To find the *reciprocal* of a common fraction, exchange the numerator and the denominator.

EXAMPLE

The reciprocal of $\frac{2}{3}$ is $\frac{3}{2}$.

To *divide* two common fractions, multiply the fraction which is the dividend by the reciprocal of the fraction which is the divisor. Reduce the result to lowest terms.

EXAMPLE

$$\frac{4}{9} \div \frac{2}{3} = \frac{4}{9} \times \frac{3}{2} = \frac{12}{18} = \frac{2}{3}$$

Decimal Fractions

Another way to represent a fractional number is to write the number to include integer powers of ten. This allows us to represent *decimal fractions* as follows:

$$\frac{1}{10} = 10^{-1} = 0.1 \text{ (said "one-tenth")}$$

$$\frac{1}{100} = 10^{-2} = 0.01 \text{ (said "one-hundredth")}$$

$$\frac{1}{1,000} = 10^{-3} = 0.001 \text{ (said "one-thousandth"), and so forth.}$$

Percent

Percent is another way of expressing a fractional number. Percent always expresses a fractional number in terms of $\frac{1}{100}$'s or 0.01's. Percents use the "%" symbol.

EXAMPLE

$$100\% = \frac{100}{100} = 1.00, \text{ and}$$

$$25\% = \frac{25}{100} = 0.25$$

As shown in these examples, a percent is easily converted to a common fraction or a decimal fraction. To convert a percent to a common fraction, place the percent in the numerator and use 100 as the denominator (reduce as necessary). To convert a percent to a decimal fraction, divide the percent by 100, or move the decimal point two places to the left.

EXAMPLE

$$25\% = \frac{25}{100} = \frac{1}{4} \text{ and}$$

$$25\% = 0.25$$

To convert a common fraction to a percent, carry a division of the numerator by the denominator of the fraction out to three decimal places. Round the result to two places. To convert a decimal fraction to a percent, move the decimal point two places to the right (adding 0's as place holders, if needed) and round as necessary.

EXAMPLE

$$\frac{1}{4} = 1 \div 4 = 0.25 = 25\%, \text{ and}$$

$$\frac{2}{7} = 2 \div 7 = 0.28 = 28\%$$

If one wishes to find the *percentage* of a known quantity, change the percent to a common fraction or a decimal fraction and multiply the fraction times the quantity. The percentage is expressed in the same units as the known quantity.

EXAMPLE

To find 25% of 360 books, change 25% to 0.25 and multiply times 360, as follows: $0.25 \times 360 = 90$. The result is 90 books.

Elementary Statistics

MEAN

The average, or *mean*, of a set of numbers can be found by adding the set of numbers and dividing by the total number of elements in the set.

EXAMPLE

The mean of 15, 10, 25, 5, and 40 is

$$\frac{15+10+25+5+40}{5} = \frac{95}{5} = 19.$$

MEDIAN

If a given set of numbers is ordered from smallest to largest, the *median* is the "middle" number; that is, half of the numbers in the set of numbers are below the median and half of the numbers in the set are above the median.

EXAMPLE

To find the median of the set of whole numbers 15, 10, 25, 5, 40, first order the set of numbers to get 5, 10, 15, 25, 40. Since 15 is the middle number (half of the numbers are below 15, half are above 15), 15 is called the median of this set of whole numbers. If there is an even number of numbers in the set, the median is the mean of the middle two numbers.

MODE

The *mode* of a set of numbers is the number that appears most frequently in the set. There may be no mode or more than one mode for a set of numbers.

EXAMPLE

In the set 15, 10, 25, 10, 5, 40, 10, 15, the number 10 appears most frequently (three times); therefore, 10 is the mode of the given set of numbers.

RANGE

The *range* of a set of numbers is obtained by subtracting the smallest number in the set from the largest number in the set.

EXAMPLE

To find the range of 15, 10, 25, 5, 40, find the difference between the largest and the smallest elements of the set. This gives $40 - 5 = 35$. The range of the given set is 35.

ALGEBRA

Algebraic Expressions

An *algebraic expression* is an expression using letters, numbers, symbols, and arithmetic operations to represent a number or a relationship among numbers.

A *variable,* or unknown, is a letter that stands for a number in an algebraic expression. *Coefficients* are the numbers that precede the variable to give the quantity of the variable in the expression.

Algebraic expressions are comprised of *terms,* or groupings of variables and numbers.

An algebraic expression with one term is called a *monomial;* with two terms, a *binomial;* with three terms, a *trinomial.* Any algebraic expression with more than one term is called a *polynomial.*

EXAMPLES

$2ab - cd$ is a binomial algebraic expression with variables a, b, c, and d, and terms $2ab$ and $(-cd)$. 2 is the coefficient of ab and -1 is the coefficient of cd.

$x^2 + 3y - 1$ is a trinomial algebraic expression with variables x and y, and terms x^2, $3y$, and (-1). 1 is the coefficient of x^2 and 3 is the coefficient of y.

Simplifying Algebraic Expressions

Like terms are terms in an algebraic expression that are exactly the same; that is, they contain the same variables and the same powers.

EXAMPLES

The following are pairs of like terms:

x^2 and $(-3x^2)$, abc and $4abc$, $(x-1)$ and $(x-1)^2$.

The following are not pairs of like terms:

x and $(-3x^2)$, abc and $4a^2bc$, $(x-1)$ and (x^2-1).

To simplify an algebraic expression, combine like terms in the following order:

1) simplify all expressions within symbols of inclusion (e.g., ( ), [ ], { }) using steps 2–4 below;

2) carry out all exponentiation;

3) carry out all multiplication and division from left to right in the order in which they occur;

4) carry out all addition and subtraction from left to right in the order in which they occur.

Factoring Algebraic Expressions

In factoring algebraic expressions, first remove any monomial factors, then remove any binomial, trinomial, or other polynomial factors. Often, one may find other polynomial factors by inspecting for the sum and difference of two squares; that is, $x^2 - y^2 = (x + y)(x - y)$.

In factoring polynomials, one often uses what is called the *"FOIL" method (First, Outside, Inside, Last)*.

EXAMPLES

$x^2 + 3x - 10 = (x - 2)(x + 5)$

$6y^2 - y - 2 = (2y + 1)(3y - 2)$

$ab^2 - 3ab - 10a = a(b^2 - 3b - 10) = a(b + 2)(b - 5)$

Solving Linear Equations

To solve a linear equation, use the following procedures:

1)   isolate the variable; that is, group all the terms with the variable on one side of the equation (commonly the left side) and group all the constants on the other side of the equation (commonly the right side);

2)   combine like terms on each side of the equation;

3)   divide by the coefficient of the variable;

4)   check the result in the original equation.

EXAMPLE

Solve $3x + 2 = 5$ for x.

$3x + 2 = 5$ (add −2 to both sides)

$3x = 3$ (multiply by $\frac{1}{3}$)

$x = 1$

EXAMPLE

Solve $3(y - 2) + 5 = 3 + 5y$ for y.

$3(y - 2) + 5 = 3 + 5y$ (simplify)

$3y - 6 + 5 = 3 + 5y$ (combine like terms)

$3y - 1 = 3 + 5y$ (add 1 to both sides)

$3y = 4 + 5y$ (add −5y to both sides)

$-2y = 4$ (multiply by $-\frac{1}{2}$)

$y = -2$

Solving Inequalities

The following properties of inequalities should be noted:

If $x < y$ and $z > 0$, then $zx < zy$.

If $x > y$ and $z > 0$, then $zx > zy$.

If $x < y$ and $z < 0$, then $zx > zy$.

If $x > y$ and $z < 0$, then $zx < zy$.

Evaluating Formulas

Formulas are algebraic sentences that are frequently used in mathematics, science, or other fields. *To evaluate a formula*, replace each variable with the given values of the variables and solve for the unknown variable.

> **EXAMPLE**
>
> Since $A = l \times w$, if $l = 2$ ft. and $w = 3$ ft.,
>
> then $A = 2$ ft. $\times 3$ ft. $= 6$ sq. ft.

Algebra Word Problems

When taking the mathematics section of the LAST, translate the word problem into an algebraic sentence. Find a variable to represent the unknown in the problem. Look for key synonyms such as "is, are, were" for "=", "more, more than" for "+" "less, less than, fewer" for "−", and "of" for "x."

> **EXAMPLE**
>
> The sum of the ages of Bill and Paul is 32 years. Bill is 6 years older than Paul. Find the age of each.
>
> If $p =$ Paul's age, then Bill's age is $p + 6$. Therefore, $p + (p + 6) = 32$. Solve for p.

$$p + p + 6 = 32 \qquad \text{(combine like terms)}$$

$$2p + 6 = 32 \qquad \text{(add } -6 \text{ to both sides)}$$
$$2p = 26 \qquad \text{(multiply by } \frac{1}{2} \text{)}$$
$$p = 13$$

Since p = Paul's age, Paul is 13 years old. Bill is 13 + 6, which is 19 years old.

EXAMPLE

Julia drove from her home to her aunt's house in 3 hours and 30 minutes. The distance between the houses is 175 miles. Knowing that distance = rate × time, find the car's average speed.

As noted above, distance = rate × time. Since we know d = 175 mph and $t = 3\frac{1}{2}$ hr., then 175 mph = $r \times 3\frac{1}{2}$ hr. Solving for the rate (r), we get $r = 50$ mph.

(It is strongly suggested that individuals who feel they need additional practice in solving word problems seek out additional practice problems in a standard high school algebra textbook.)

GEOMETRY

Perimeter and Area

Perimeter refers to the measure of the distance around a figure. Perimeter is measured in linear units (e.g., inches, feet, meters). *Area* refers to the measure of the interior of a figure. Area is measured in square units (e.g., square inches, square feet, square meters).

Perimeter of Rectangles, Squares, and Triangles

The *perimeter of a rectangle* is represented by $P = 2l + 2w$, where l is the measure of the length and w is the measure of the width.

> **EXAMPLE**
>
> If a rectangle has $l = 10$ m and $w = 5$ m, then the perimeter of the rectangle is given by $P = 2(10$ m$) + 2(5$ m$) = 30$ m.

The *perimeter of a square* is represented by $P = 4s$, where s is the measure of a side of the square.

> **EXAMPLE**
>
> If a square has $s = 5$ ft., then the perimeter of the square is given by $P = 4(5$ ft.$) = 20$ ft.

The *perimeter of a triangle* is represented by $P = s_1 + s_2 + s_3$, where s_1, s_2, and s_3 are the measures of the sides of the triangle.

> **EXAMPLE**
>
> If a triangle has three sides measuring 3 in., 4 in., and 5 in., then the perimeter of the triangle is given by $P = 3$ in. $+ 4$ in. $+ 5$ in. $= 12$ in.

Area of Rectangles, Squares, and Triangles

The *area of a rectangle* is represented by $A = l \times w$, where l is the measure of the length and w is the measure of the width.

> **EXAMPLE**
>
> If a rectangle has $l = 10$ m and $w = 5$ m, then the area of the rectangle is given by $A = 10$ m $\times 5$ m $= 50$ m^2

The *area of a square* is represented by $A = s^2$, where s is the measure of a side.

> **EXAMPLE**
>
> If a square has $s = 5$ ft., then the area of the square is given by $A = (5 \text{ ft.})^2 = 25 \text{ ft}^2$.

The *area of a right triangle* is represented by $A = \frac{1}{2}bh$, where b is the base and h is the height.

> **EXAMPLE**
>
> If a triangle has a base of 3 in. and a height of 4 in., then the area of the triangle is given by
>
> $$A = \frac{1}{2}(3 \text{ in.} \times 4 \text{ in.}) = \frac{1}{2}(12 \text{ in.}^2) = 6 \text{ in.}^2$$

Circumference and Area of Circles

The *radius of a circle* is the distance from the center of the circle to the edge of the circle. The *diameter of a circle* is a line segment that passes through the center of the circle, the end points of which lie on the circle. The *measure of the diameter of a circle* is twice the measure of the radius.

The number π (approximately 3.14) is often used in computations involving circles.

The *circumference of a circle* is represented by $C = \pi \times d$, or $C = 2 \times \pi \times r$, where d is the diameter and r is the radius.

The *area of a circle* is represented by $A = \pi \times r^2$, where r is the radius.

> **EXAMPLE**
>
> If a circle has a radius of 5 cm, then
>
> $C = \pi \times 10 \text{ cm} \approx 3.14 \times 10 \text{ cm} = 31.4 \text{ cm}$, and
>
> $A = \pi \times (5 \text{ cm})^2 \approx 3.14 \times (5 \text{ cm})^2 = 78.50 \text{ cm}^2$

Volume of Cubes and Rectangular Solids

Volume refers to the measure of the interior of a three-dimensional figure.

A *rectangular solid* is a rectilinear (right-angled) figure that has length, width, and height. The volume of a rectangular solid is represented by $V = l \times w \times h$, where l is length, w is width, and h is height.

EXAMPLE

The volume of a rectangular solid with $l = 5$ cm, $w = 4$ cm, and $h = 3$ cm is given by

$$V = 5 \text{ cm} \times 4 \text{ cm} \times 3 \text{ cm} = 60 \text{ cm}^3.$$

A *cube* is a rectangular solid, the length, width, and height of which have the same measure. This measure is called the *edge of the cube*. The volume of a cube is represented by $V = e^3$, where e is edge.

EXAMPLE

The volume of a cube with $e = 5$ cm is given by $V = (5 \text{ cm})^3 = 125 \text{ cm}^3$.

Angle Measure

An *angle* consists of all the points in two noncollinear rays that have the same vertex. An angle is commonly thought of as two "arrows" joined at their bases.

Two angles are *adjacent* if they share a common vertex, share only one side, and one angle does not lie in the interior of the other.

Angles are usually measured in *degrees*. If the measures of two angles are the same, then the angles are said to be *congruent*.

An angle with a measure of 90° is called a *right angle*. Angles with measures less than 90° are called *acute*. Angles with measures more than 90° are called *obtuse*.

If the sum of the measures of two angles is 90°, the two angles are said to be *complementary*. If the sum of the measures of the two angles is 180°, the two angles are said to be *supplementary*.

If two lines intersect, they form two pairs of *vertical angles*. The measures of vertical angles are equivalent; that is, vertical angles are congruent.

Properties of Triangles

Triangles are three-sided polygons.

If the measures of two sides of a triangle are equal, then the triangle is called an *isosceles triangle*. If the measures of all sides of the triangle are equal, then the triangle is called an *equilateral triangle*. If no measures of the sides of a triangle are equal, then the triangle is called a *scalene triangle*.

The sum of the measures of the angles of a triangle is 180°.

The sum of the measures of any two sides of a triangle is greater than the measure of the third side.

EXAMPLE

Find the measures of the angles of a right triangle, if one of the angles measures 30°.

Since the triangle is a right triangle, a second angle of the triangle measures 90°. We know the sum of the measures of a triangle is 180°, so that $90° + 30° + x° = 180°$. Solving for $x°$, we get $x° = 60°$. The measures of the angles of the triangle are 90°, 60°, and 30°.

THE PYTHAGOREAN THEOREM

In a right triangle, the side opposite the 90° angle is called the *hypotenuse* and the other two sides are called the *legs*. If the hypotenuse has measure c and the legs have measures a and b, the relationship among the measures, known as the *Pythagorean Theorem*, is represented by

$$a^2 + b^2 = c^2$$

EXAMPLE

Find the length of the hypotenuse of a right triangle if the measure of one leg is 3 cm and the other leg is 4 cm.

By the Pythagorean Theorem, $(3 \text{ cm})^2 + (4 \text{ cm})^2 = c^2$ so that $9 \text{ cm}^2 + 16 \text{ cm}^2 = 25 \text{ cm}^2$. Taking the square root of both sides, we get $c = 5$ cm.

Properties of Parallel and Perpendicular Lines

If lines have a point or points in common, they are said to *intersect*.

Lines are *parallel* if they do not intersect.

Lines are *perpendicular* if they contain the sides of a right angle.

If a third line intersects two other lines, the intersecting line is called a *transversal*.

GENERAL SCIENCE

General Science, as its name implies, is a broad survey of the most important concepts from the three basic fields of science: life science, physical science, and Earth science.

Each of the basic science fields contains major specializations:

Life science—biology, ecology, human health

Physical science—measurement, chemistry, physics

Earth science—astronomy, geology, meteorology, oceanography

LIFE SCIENCE

Biology

Biology is the study of living things. Living things are differentiated from nonliving things by the ability to perform a particular group of life activities at some point in a normal life span.

Life Activity	Function
food getting	procurement of food through eating, absorption, or photosynthesis
respiration	exchange of gases
excretion	elimination of wastes
growth and repair	increase in size over part or all of a life span; repair of damaged tissue
movement	willful movement of a portion of a living thing's body, or channeling growth in a particular direction
response	reaction to events or things in the environment
secretion	production and distribution of chemicals that aid digestion, growth, metabolism, etc.
reproduction	the making of new living things similar to the parent organism(s)

It is important to note that living things *must*, during a typical life span, be able to perform all these activities. It is quite common for nonliving things to perform one or more of these activities (for example: robots—movement, response, repair; crystals—growth).

CELLS

Cells are the basic structure unit of living things. A cell is the smallest portion of a living thing that can, by itself, be considered living. Plant cells and animal cells, though generally similar, are distinctly different because of the unique plant structures, cell walls, and chloroplasts.

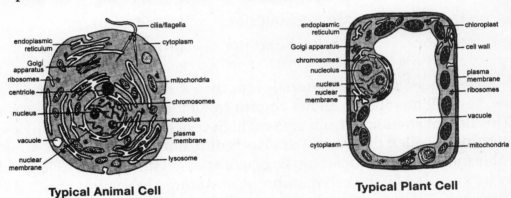

Typical Animal Cell   **Typical Plant Cell**

Cells are made of several smaller structures, called organelles, which are surrounded by cell fluid, or cytoplasm. The function of several cell structures is listed below.

Cell Structure	Function
cell membrane	controls movement of materials into and out of cells
cell wall	gives rigid structure to plant cells
chloroplast	contains chlorophyll, which enables green plants to make their own food
cytoplasm	jellylike substance inside a cell; comprises the cytosol and organelles but not the nucleus
mitochondria	liberate energy from glucose in cells for use in cellular activities
nucleus	directs cell activities; holds DNA (genetic material)
ribosome	makes proteins from amino acids
vacuole	stores materials in a cell

There are several processes cells perform to maintain essential life activities. Several of these processes, related to cell metabolism, are described below. Metabolism is the sum of chemical processes in living things.

Process	Organelle	Life Activity
diffusion	cell membrane	food getting, respiration, excretion
osmosis	cell membrane	food getting, excretion
phagocytosis	cell membrane	food getting
photosynthesis	chloroplasts	food getting
respiration (aerobic)	mitochondrion	provides energy
fermentation	mitochondrion	provides energy

Cells need to move materials into their structures to get energy and to grow. The cell membrane allows certain small molecules to flow freely across it. This flow of chemicals from areas of high concentration to areas of low concentration is called diffusion. Osmosis is diffusion of water across a semipermeable membrane. Particles too large to be passed through the cell membrane may be engulfed by the cell membrane and stored in vacuoles until they can be digested. This engulfing process is called phagocytosis.

All cells need energy to survive. Sunlight energy can be made biologically available by converting to chemical energy during photosynthesis. Photosynthesis is carried out in the chloroplasts of green cells. Chlorophyll, the pigment found in chloroplasts, catalyzes (causes or accelerates) the photosynthetic reaction that turns carbon dioxide and water into glucose (sugar) and oxygen. Sunlight and chlorophyll are needed for the reaction to occur. Chlorophyll, because it is a catalyst, is not consumed in the reaction and may be used repeatedly.

The term "respiration" has two distinct meanings in the field of biology. Respiration, the life activity, is the exchange of gases in living things. Respiration, the metabolic process, is the release of energy from sugars for use in life activities.

All living things get their energy from the digestion (respiration) of glucose (sugar). Respiration may occur with oxygen (aerobic respiration) or without oxygen (anaerobic respiration or fermentation). When respiration is referred to, it generally means aerobic respiration. Aerobic respiration occurs in most plant and animal cells. Fermentation occurs in yeast cells and other cells in the absence of oxygen. Fermentation by yeast produces the alcohol in alcoholic beverages and the gases that make yeast-raised breads light and fluffy.

CLASSIFICATION

All known living things are grouped in categories according to shared physical traits. The process of grouping organisms is called classification. Carl Linné, also known as Linnaeus, devised the classification system used in biology today. In the Linnaean system, all organisms are given a two-word name (binomial). The name consists of a genus (ex. Canis) and a species (ex. lupus) designation.

There exists just one binomial for each organism throughout the scientific community. Similar genera of organisms are grouped into families. Families are grouped into orders, orders are grouped into classes, classes are grouped into phyla, and phyla are grouped into kingdoms. The seven basic levels of classification, listed from the largest groupings to the smallest, are: kingdom, phylum, class, order, family, genus, species.

Most biologists recognize five biological kingdoms today: Animals, Plants, Fungi, Protists, and Monerans.

Animals are multicellular organisms that cannot make their own food but can move themselves about. The animal kingdom is divided into 26 phyla. Animals are categorized as either vertebrate (having a backbone) or invertebrate (having no backbone).

Most vertebrates are cold-blooded. Their bodies do not generate heat, so their body temperature is determined by their environment. Birds (Aves) and mammals, however, are warm-blooded. Their bodies generate heat. Birds and mammals can also sweat to lower body temperature.

Some examples of invertebrates are worms and jellyfish.

Plants are multicellular organisms that make their own food through photosynthesis.

Fungi (ex. molds, mushrooms, yeast) are many-celled decomposers that reproduce through spores. Yeast constitute an exception to the multicellular makeup of most fungi, in that they are single-celled and reproduce through budding.

Protists (ex. protozoa, single-celled algae) are single-celled organisms having cell nuclei.

Monerans (ex. bacteria, blue-green algae) are the simplest life forms known. They consist of single-celled organisms without a membrane-bound cell nucleus.

Ecology

Ecology is the study of the relationship between living things and their environment. An environment is all the living and nonliving things surrounding an organism.

POPULATIONS AND COMMUNITIES

A population is a group of similar organisms, like a herd of deer. A community is a group of populations that interact with one another. A pond community, for example, is made up of all the plants and animals in the pond. An ecosystem is a group of populations which share a common pool of resources and a common physical/geographical area.

Each population lives in a particular area and serves a special role in the community. This combination of defined role and living areas is the concept of niche. The niche of a pond snail, for example, is to decompose materials in ponds. The niche of a field mouse is to eat seeds in fields. When two populations try to fill the same niche, competition occurs. If one population replaces another in a niche, succession occurs. Succession is the orderly and predictable change of communities as a result of population replacement in niches.

FOOD AND ENERGY

Organisms that make their own food are called producers. Some animals get their food from eating plants or other animals; these are called consumers. Consumers that eat plants are herbivores; those that eat animals are carnivores; those that eat plants and animals are called omnivores. Organisms that get their food energy from dead plants or animals are called decomposers.

Many nutrients, such as nitrogen and phosphorous, are routinely cycled through the bodies of living things. These nutrient cycles are disrupted when humans remove parts of the ecosystem or add excess materials to an ecosystem.

Pollution is any material added to an ecosystem that disrupts its normal functioning. Typical pollutants are excess fertilizers and industrial emissions. Conservation is the practice of using natural areas without disrupting their ecosystems. Conservationists try to limit the amounts of pollution entering ecosystems.

Human Health

THE HUMAN BODY

A human is a very complex organism. It is made up of several systems.

The *skeletal system* is composed of bones, cartilage, and ligaments. The areas where two or more bones touch one another are called joints. Bone surfaces in joints are often covered with cartilage, which reduces friction in the joint. Ligaments hold bones together in a joint.

The *muscular system* controls movement of the skeleton and movement within organs. Three types of muscle exist: striated (voluntary), smooth (involuntary), and cardiac. Tendons attach muscles to bone. Skeletal muscles work in pairs. The alternate contraction of muscles within a pair causes movement in joints.

The *digestive system* receives and processes food. The digestive system includes the mouth, stomach, large intestine, and small intestine. Food is physically broken down by mastication, or chewing. Food is chemically broken down in the stomach. The small intestine absorbs nutrients from food and the large intestine absorbs water from solid food waste.

The *excretory system* eliminates wastes from the body. Excretory organs include the lungs, kidneys, bladder, large intestine, rectum, and the skin. The lungs excrete gaseous waste. The kidneys filter blood and excrete wastes, mostly in the form of urea. The bladder holds liquid wastes until they can be eliminated via the urethra. The large intestine absorbs water from solid food waste, and the rectum stores solid waste until it can be eliminated. The skin excretes waste through perspiration.

The *circulatory system* is responsible for internal transport in the body. It is composed of the heart, blood vessels, lymph vessels, blood, and lymph. The heart is a muscular four-chambered pump. The upper chambers are called atria and the lower chambers are called ventricles. Blood flows from the body to the right atrium, to the right ventricle, to the lungs, then to the left atrium, to the left ventricle, and back to the body.

The *respiratory system* exchanges oxygen for carbon dioxide. The respiratory system is composed of the nose, trachea, bronchi, lungs, and diaphragm. Air travels from the nose through the trachea and bronchi into the lungs. The air is drawn in by the contraction of the diaphragm, a muscle running across the body below the lungs, and is then pushed back toward the nose by relaxation of the diaphragm.

The *nervous system* controls the actions and processes of the body. The nervous system includes the brain, spinal cord, and nerves. Electrical impulses carry messages to and from the brain across the spinal cord and nerves. Nerves extend to every portion of the body. The spinal cord is protected by the vertebra, which comprise the spine.

The three principal regions of the brain are the cerebrum, cerebellum, and brain stem. The cerebrum occupies 80% of the brain's volume and is responsible for intelligence, memory, and thought. The cerebellum controls balance and coordination. The brain stem connects the brain to the spinal cord and is found at the lower central portion of the brain. The brain stem controls autonomic (involuntary) body functions and regulates hormones.

The *endocrine system* controls activities in the body through chemical agents called hormones. Hormones are produced in glands throughout the body and are excreted into the bloodstream. The brain controls production and release of hormones.

The *reproductive system* produces eggs and sperm which can combine to create an embryo. The female reproductive system includes the ovaries, fallopian tubes, uterus, and vagina. Each month, one egg is released from the ovaries and then travels down the fallopian tubes. If it is fertilized, it becomes implanted in the lining of the uterus, where a baby begins to form. When sufficiently grown, the baby leaves the uterus and its mother's body through the vagina, or birth canal.

The male reproductive system consists of the testicles, vas deferens, urethra, and penis. Sperm are produced in the testicles. They move through the vas deferens from the testicles to the urethra. During intercourse, sperm pass through the penis and into a woman's body. In a woman's body, sperm pass through the cervix into the uterus and up the fallopian tubes, where fertilization of an egg may take place.

NUTRITION

Nutrition is the study of how living things utilize food substances. Food provides energy and raw materials for growth, repair, and metabolism. Energy (calories) is derived chiefly from carbohydrates, but also from fats and proteins.

Listed below are several vitamins important to human health.

Vitamin	Principal Source	Deficiency Symptom(s)
A	green and yellow vegetables	night blindness; dry, brittle skin
B_1	cereals, yeast	beriberi (muscular atrophy and paralysis)
B_2	dairy products, eggs	eye problems
B_{12}	liver and meat	anemia
C	citrus fruits, tomatoes	scurvy
D	fortified milk, eggs	rickets (malformed bones)
E	meat, oils, vegetables	male sterility, muscular problems
K	green vegetables	impaired blood clotting

Foods can be placed in one of four basic food groups. These groups are listed below, in order of their need by the body.

Food Group	Importance	Examples
Grains and Cereals	starch (for energy), protein, fiber	bread, pasta
Fruits and Vegetables	fiber, minerals, vitamins	apples, carrots
Dairy	fats, calcium, protein	milk, cheese
Meat, Fish, and Eggs	protein	steak, trout

HUMAN GENETICS

Each of the cells in a living thing has a specific structure and role in the organism. The structure of a cell and its function are determined, to a large degree, by the genes within a cell. Genes are code units of chromosomes within the nucleus of a cell. Genes give information about the structure and function of a cell.

A fertilized human sex cell has 46 chromosomes, 23 from the mother and 23 from the father. This fertilized sex cell will multiply to form a new organism. The process of combining genetic materials from two parent organisms to form a unique offspring is called sexual reproduction.

During sexual reproduction, an organism receives two genes for each trait, one from each parent. Sometimes one trait will mask another, as is the case with eye color. If a person has one gene for brown eyes and one gene for blue eyes, the person will always have brown eyes. A genetic trait that masks another, like the gene for brown eyes, is called a dominant trait. A gene that can be masked, like the gene for blue eyes, is called a recessive trait.

Understanding dominance helps us to figure out the genetic configuration of an individual. An individual with blue eyes must have two genes for blue eyes, since it is a recessive trait. Recessive traits are shown by lowercase letters, so the genetic symbol for blue eyes is "bb." An individual with brown eyes must have at least one gene for brown eyes, which is dominant. Dominant genes are shown by uppercase letters, so the genetic symbol for brown eyes could be "Bb" or "BB."

When the genetic type of parents is known, the probability of the offspring showing particular traits can be predicted using the Punnett Square. A Punnett Square is a large square divided into four small boxes. The genetic symbol of each parent for a particular trait is written alongside the square, one parent along the top and one parent along the left side.

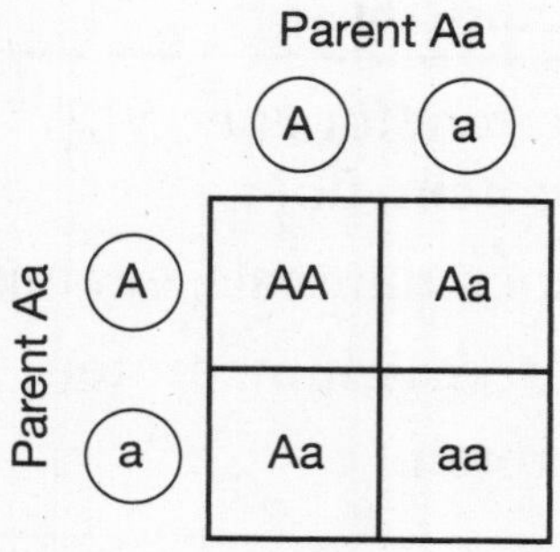

Parent Aa

	A	a
A	AA	Aa
a	Aa	aa

(left side labeled: Parent Aa)

Each gene symbol is written in both boxes below or to the right of it. This results in each box having two gene symbols in it. The genetic symbols in the boxes are all the possible genetic combinations for a particular trait of the offspring of these parents. Each box has a 25% probability of being the actual genetic representation for a given child.

Human sex type is determined by genetic material in sperm. The genetic sex code for human females is XX. The genetic sex code for human males is XY. Eggs carry only X genes. Sperm carry X or Y genes. The probability of a fertilized human egg being male, or XY, is 50%.

PHYSICAL SCIENCE

Measurement

The physical characteristics of an object are determined by measurements. Measured characteristics include mass, volume, length, temperature, time, and area. There are two common measurement systems, English and metric.

Characteristic	English System	Metric System
mass/weight	pound (weight)	kilogram (mass)
volume	quart	liter
length	foot	meter
temperature	°Fahrenheit	°Celsius

The English system, used most often in the United States, does not have a consistent system of conversion factors between units.

EXAMPLE

1 yard = 3 feet, 1 foot = 12 inches

The metric system, used most often in science, has conversion factors between units based on multiples of 10.

EXAMPLE

1 kilometer = 1000 meters,
1 meter = 100 centimeters = 1000 millimeters

Prefixes in the metric system indicate the number of multiples of the base units, so it is simple to determine the conversion factors between units.

Prefix	Multiplication Factor	Unit Symbols
kilo	× 1000	km, kg, kl
no prefix (base unit)	× 1	m, g, l
deci	× 0.1	dm, dg, dl
centi	× 0.01	cm, cg, cl
milli	× 0.001	mm, mg, ml

A third measurement system, the International System of Units, or Système International D'Unités (SI), is based on the metric system. SI differs from the metric system by using the Kelvin temperature scale. The size of a degree in the Celsius and Kelvin scales are the same, but "0°" is different. 0 Kelvin = –273°Celsius. 0 Kelvin, also known as absolute zero, is the temperature at which, theoretically, all molecular movement ceases.

To convert from °Celsius to °Fahrenheit, use the following equation:

$$°C = \frac{5}{9}(°F - 32).$$

To convert from °Celsius to Kelvin, use the following equation:

$$°C + 273 = K.$$

Chemistry

STATES OF MATTER

Matter is everything that has volume and mass. Water is matter because it takes up space; light is not matter because it does not take up space.

Matter exists in three states, as follows:

State	Properties	Example
solid	definite volume, definite shape	ice
liquid	definite volume, no definite shape	water
gas	no definite volume, no definite shape	water vapor or steam

Thermal energy, or heat, causes molecules or atoms to vibrate. As vibration of particles increases, a material may change to a different state; it may melt or boil. Decreasing energy in a material may cause condensation or freezing. For most materials, the boiling point and freezing point are important. The boiling point of water is 100°C, and its freezing point is 0°C.

STRUCTURE OF MATTER

Atoms are the basic building blocks of matter. Atoms are made up of three types of subatomic particles, which have mass and charge. Protons and neutrons are found in the nucleus, or solid center of an atom. Electrons are found in the outer portion of an atom. Under most conditions, atoms are indivisible. Atoms may be split or combined to form new atoms during atomic reactions. Atomic reactions occur deep inside the sun, in nuclear power reactors and nuclear bombs, and in radioactive decay.

Subatomic Particle	Mass	Charge	Location
proton	1 amu	+1	nucleus
neutron	1 amu	0	nucleus
electron	0 amu	−1	outside nucleus

A material made of just one type of atom is called an element. Atoms of an element are represented by symbols of one or two letters, such as C or Na. Two or more atoms may combine to form molecules.

Atoms of the same element have the same number of protons in their nucleus. An atom is the smallest particle of an element that retains the characteristics of that element. Each element is assigned an atomic number, which is equal to the number of protons in an atom of that element. The Periodic Table is an arrangement of all the elements in order according to their atomic number. The elements are grouped vertically in the Periodic Table according to their chemical properties. The Periodic Table is a reference tool used to summarize the atomic structure, mass, and reactive tendencies of elements.

THE PERIODIC TABLE

KEY

Group Classification →

4 IVA IVB
22
Ti
47.88

Atomic Number → 22
Symbol → Ti
Atomic Weight → 47.88

( ) indicates most stable or best known isotope

METALS — NONMETALS

TRANSITIONAL METALS

1 IA IA	2 IIA IIA	3 IIIA IIIB	4 IVA IVB	5 VA VB	6 VIA VIB	7 VIIA VIIB	8 VIIIA VIII	9 VIIIA VIII	10 VIIIA VIII	11 IB IB	12 IIB IIB	13 IIIB IIIA	14 IVB IVA	15 VB VA	16 VIB VIA	17 VIIB VIIA	18 VIII 0
1 H 1.008																	2 He 4.003
3 Li 6.941	4 Be 9.012											5 B 10.811	6 C 12.011	7 N 14.007	8 O 15.999	9 F 18.998	10 Ne 20.180
11 Na 22.990	12 Mg 24.305											13 Al 26.982	14 Si 28.086	15 P 30.974	16 S 32.066	17 Cl 35.453	18 Ar 39.948
19 K 39.098	20 Ca 40.078	21 Sc 44.956	22 Ti 47.88	23 V 50.942	24 Cr 51.996	25 Mn 54.938	26 Fe 55.847	27 Co 58.933	28 Ni 58.693	29 Cu 63.546	30 Zn 65.39	31 Ga 69.723	32 Ge 72.61	33 As 74.922	34 Se 78.96	35 Br 79.904	36 Kr 83.8
37 Rb 85.468	38 Sr 87.62	39 Y 88.906	40 Zr 91.224	41 Nb 92.906	42 Mo 95.94	43 Tc (97.907)	44 Ru 101.07	45 Rh 102.906	46 Pd 106.4	47 Ag 107.868	48 Cd 112.411	49 In 114.818	50 Sn 118.710	51 Sb 121.757	52 Te 127.60	53 I 126.905	54 Xe 131.29
55 Cs 132.905	56 Ba 137.327	57 La 138.906	72 Hf 178.49	73 Ta 180.948	74 W 183.84	75 Re 186.207	76 Os 190.23	77 Ir 192.22	78 Pt 195.08	79 Au 196.967	80 Hg 200.59	81 Tl 204.383	82 Pb 207.2	83 Bi 208.980	84 Po (208.982)	85 At (209.982)	86 Rn (222.018)
87 Fr (223.020)	88 Ra (226.025)	89 Ac (227.028)	104 Rf (261.108)	105 Db (262.114)	106 Sg (266.121)	107 Bh (264.124)	108 Hs (269.134)	109 Mt (268.138)	110 Uun (271.146)	111 Uuu (272.153)	112 Uub (277)		114 Uuq (289)		116 Uuh (289)		118 Uuo (293)

Alkali Metals — Alkaline Earth Metals — Halogens — Noble Gases

LANTHANIDE SERIES

58 Ce 140.115	59 Pr 140.908	60 Nd 144.24	61 Pm (144.913)	62 Sm 150.36	63 Eu 151.965	64 Gd 157.25	65 Tb 158.925	66 Dy 162.50	67 Ho 164.930	68 Er 167.26	69 Tm 168.934	70 Yb 173.04	71 Lu 174.967

ACTINIDE SERIES

90 Th 232.038	91 Pa 231.036	92 U 238.029	93 Np 237.048	94 Pu (244.064)	95 Am (243.061)	96 Cm (247.070)	97 Bk (247.070)	98 Cf (251.080)	99 Es (252.083)	100 Fm (257.095)	101 Md (258.1)	102 No (259.101)	103 Lr (262.11)

CHEMICAL REACTIONS

Matter may undergo chemical and physical changes. A physical change affects the size, form, or appearance of a material. These changes can include melting, bending, or cracking. Physical changes do not alter the molecular structure of a material. Chemical changes do alter the molecular structure of matter. Examples of chemical changes are burning, rusting, and digestion.

Under the right conditions, compounds may break apart, combine, or recombine to form new compounds. This process is called a chemical reaction. Chemical reactions are described by chemical equations, such as $NaOH + HCl \rightarrow NaCl + H_2O$. In a chemical equation, materials to the left of the arrow are called reactants and materials to the right of the arrow are called products. In a balanced chemical equation, the number of each type of atom is the same on both sides of the arrow.

unbalanced: $H_2 + O_2 \rightarrow H_2O$

balanced: $2H_2 + O_2 \rightarrow 2H_2O$

ACIDS AND BASES

Acid and *base* are terms used to describe solutions of differing pH. The concentration of hydrogen ion in a solution determines its pH, which is based on a logarithmic scale.

Solutions having pH 0–7 are called acids and have hydrogen ions (H+) present. Common acids include lemon juice, vinegar, and battery acid. Acids are corrosive and taste sour. Solutions having pH 7–14 are called bases (or alkaline) and have hydroxide ions (OH⁻) present. Bases are caustic and feel slippery in solution. Common bases include baking soda and lye. Solutions of pH 7 are called neutral and have both ions present in equal but small amounts.

Physics

MOTION

Moving objects can be measured for speed or momentum. Speed is the distance an object travels per unit of time.

$$\text{Speed} = \frac{\text{distance}}{\text{time}}$$

Momentum is the tendency of an object to continue in its direction of motion.

$$\text{Momentum} = \text{mass} \times \text{speed}$$

ENERGY

Energy is the ability to do work. Energy comes in many different forms, such as heat, light, and sound. All energy can be described as potential or kinetic. Potential energy is stored through chemical structure, position, or physical configuration. Kinetic energy is energy of motion. Light, sound, and heat are kinetic energy, as is the energy possessed by a moving object. Energy can be transformed from one type to another, but it never is created or destroyed.

WORK

Work occurs when a force (push or pull) is applied to an object, resulting in movement.

$$\text{Work} = \text{force} \times \text{distance}$$

The greater the force applied, or the longer the distance traveled, the greater the work done.

WAVE PHENOMENA

Sound and light are wave phenomena. Waves are characterized by wavelength, speed, and frequency. Wavelength is the distance between crests or troughs of waves.

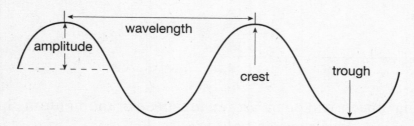

Sound is caused by the vibration of objects. This vibration creates waves of disturbance that can travel through air and most other materials. If these sound waves hit your eardrum, you perceive sound.

The speed of sound waves is related to their medium. Sound travels more quickly through more dense materials (solids, liquids) than less dense materials (gases). Sound does not travel through a vacuum.

Light travels much more quickly (300,000 km/sec) than sound does (330 m/sec). It can pass through a vacuum. As light passes through a material, it travels in a straight path. When light moves from one material to another, it may be transmitted, absorbed, reflected, or refracted.

Transparent materials (ex. water, glass) allow light to pass directly through them. This passing through is called transmission. Opaque objects (ex. wood) absorb light. No light comes out of them. Mirrors reflect light. They re-emit light into the medium it came from.

Refraction is the bending of light. Light may be refracted when it moves from one material to another (ex. air → water). Mirages are formed when light refracts while moving from cool air to warm air.

BASIC ELECTRICITY

Atoms may carry electrical charges. A neutral atom has an equal numbers of protons and electrons in it. The charges of the protons and electrons cancel each other, so the atom has no net charge. If an atom has more electrons than protons, the atom has a negative charge. If an atom has fewer electrons than protons, the atom has a positive charge.

If two objects are rubbed together, electrons—the lightest stable subatomic particles known—may move from one object to another, leaving both charged. Electrons may also flow through certain materials. The flow of electrons produces an electric current. Conductors are materials that let electrons flow freely (ex. metals, water). Insulators are materials that do not let electrons flow freely (ex. glass, rubber, air).

Circuits are the connections of electrical elements that form one or more complete paths through which current flows. Circuits may be described as being in series or in parallel. Series circuits are made of a single pathway through which all current must flow. If any part of a series circuit breaks, the circuit is "opened," and the flow of the current must stop. Some sets of Christmas tree lights are designed in series. If one bulb in the string of lights burns out, none of the lights in the string will work, because current is disrupted for the entire string.

Parallel circuits provide more than one pathway for current to flow. If one of the pathways is opened so that current cannot flow in it, the current will continue to move through the other paths. Most circuits (for example, those in our homes) are wired in parallel, so that burned-out light bulbs and turned-off television sets do not disrupt electricity used in other parts of our homes.

MAGNETISM

Magnets are solids that attract iron. Naturally occurring magnets are called lodestones. Magnetic forces make magnets attract or repel each other. Magnetic forces are created by regions in magnets called magnetic poles. All magnets have a north and a south pole. The north pole of one magnet will repel the north pole of another magnet; the same holds true for south poles. The south pole of one magnet will attract the north pole of another magnet.

A magnetic field is the area affected by magnetic force. A magnetic field surrounds both poles of a magnet and can be created by an electric current. Electromagnets create large magnetic fields with electric current. Similarly, if a wire is moved through a magnetic field, a current is produced.

The Earth has a magnetic field. Compasses are magnets that align themselves with Earth's magnetic field.

EARTH SCIENCE

Astronomy

Astronomy is the study of celestial bodies and their movements.

Earth is one of nine planets in our solar system. A solar system is composed of a star and the objects that move about it. The largest objects moving about a star are called planets. The planets in our solar system, beginning at the sun and moving away from it, are Mercury, Venus, Earth, Mars, Jupiter, Saturn, Uranus, Neptune, and Pluto (Neptune and Pluto sometimes switch order).

Many objects smaller than planets exist in our solar system. If one of these smaller objects collides with Earth, it is called a meteor or "shooting star." The glow of a meteor is caused by its burning as it passes through our atmosphere. Meteors that reach Earth's surface are called meteorites.

Earth's path around the sun is called its orbit. Earth's orbit around the sun, called a revolution, is completed in $365\frac{1}{4}$ days. An axis is an imaginary line passing through the poles of the Earth. The Earth spins on its axis, and each spin is called a rotation, which takes 24 hours. Rotation causes the alternation of day and night.

The moon is a satellite of Earth. It moves in orbit about Earth, and one revolution takes $27\frac{1}{3}$ days. The moon reflects sunlight, which causes it to glow. When the Earth blocks sunlight from reaching the moon, it creates a shadow on the moon's surface, known as a lunar eclipse. If the moon blocks sunlight from hitting the Earth, a solar eclipse is created. The moon has a gravitational pull on the Earth which causes tides, or periodic changes in depth of the ocean.

Geology

Geology is the study of the structure and composition of the Earth.

Earth is composed of three layers: the crust, mantle, and core. The core is at the center, and is made of solid iron and nickel. It is about 7,000 km in diameter. The mantle is the semi-molten layer between crust and core, and is about 3,000 km thick. The crust is the solid outermost layer, ranging from 5–40 km thick. It is composed of bedrock overlaid with mineral and/or organic sediment (soil).

Large sections of Earth's crust, called plates, move at times, creating earthquakes, volcanoes, faults, and mountains. The study of these movements is called plate tectonics. Faults are cracks in the crust formed when plates move. Earthquakes occur when plates slide past one another quickly. They may also be caused by volcanoes. Earthquakes are measured by a seismograph on the Richter scale.

Volcanoes form where plates move away from one another to let magma reach the crust's surface. Magma is molten rock beneath the Earth's crust. Lava is molten rock on the Earth's surface. Mountains are formed by volcanic activity or the collision of plates, which causes the crust to buckle upward.

Rocks are naturally occurring solids found on or below the Earth's surface. Rocks are made of one or more minerals. Minerals are pure substances made of just one element or chemical compound.

Rocks are divided into three groups, based on the way they are formed:

1. **Igneous**—rocks formed by the cooling of magma or lava (ex. granite, obsidian).

2. **Sedimentary**—rock formed from silt or deposited rock fragments by compaction at high pressures and/or cementation (ex. shale, limestone).

3. **Metamorphic**—rocks formed from igneous or sedimentary rock after exposure to high heat and pressure (ex. marble, slate).

Weathering is the breaking down of rock into small pieces. Rock is weathered by acid rain, freezing, wind abrasion, glacier scouring, and running water. Erosion is the transportation of rock or sediment to new areas. Agents of erosion include wind, running water, and glaciers.

Meteorology

Meteorology is the study of the atmosphere and its changes.

The atmosphere is a layer of air surrounding the earth. Air is a mixture of gases, the most common being nitrogen and oxygen.

The atmosphere can be divided into several layers. The troposphere is the layer closest to Earth. Almost all life and most weather is found there. The stratosphere is the chief thermally insulating layer of the atmosphere. It contains the ozone layer and jet stream. The stratosphere is the region where ozone is produced. The thermosphere causes meteors to burn up by friction as they pass through. This layer reflects radio waves. The exosphere is the outer layer of the atmosphere. It eventually blends into the vast region we call "space."

Weather is the local, short-term condition of the atmosphere. The two factors that affect weather most are the amounts of energy and water present.

Water covers about 70% of Earth's surface. As that water slowly evaporates, some of the vapor is held in the atmosphere. It is the water vapor in our atmosphere that causes humidity, fog, clouds, and precipitation.

An air mass is a huge area of air that has nearly uniform c̶
temperature and moisture. When two air masses meet, the bounda̶
them is called a front. Fronts are the location of most stormy weath̶

Clouds can be used to predict the weather. Three types of clo̶̶ are
stratus, cumulus, and cirrus.

Cloud Type	Appearance	Weather
stratus	flat, broad	light colored—stable weather conditions dark colored—rain expected soon
cumulus	fluffy, solid-looking	light colored—good weather dark colored—heavy rains, perhaps thunderstorms
cirrus	thin, wispy	changes in weather

Climate is the general atmospheric condition of a region over a long period of time.

Oceanography

Oceanography is the study of the ocean.

Sea water differs from fresh water in its salinity, or saltiness. Fresh water, the water we drink, has relatively few dissolved solids in it and has low salinity. Ocean water has a lot of dissolved material in it and therefore has a high salinity. Many materials are dissolved in sea water, but the most abundant dissolved material is common salt, sodium chloride.

Ocean waters move through tides, waves, and currents. Tides are periodic changes in ocean depth. They are caused by the gravitational pull of the moon on Earth. Most waves are caused by winds. Some ocean currents are caused by density differences in sea water. Currents are like rivers within the ocean. The swift-moving water in currents can transport material over large distances very quickly.

Drill Questions

Mathematics

1. $\sqrt{100} =$
     (A)   10
     (B)   50
     (C)   200
     (D)   500

2. $(2^2)^4 =$
     (A) $\sqrt{2}$
     (B) 2^6
     (C) 2^7
     (D) 2^8

3. $\dfrac{3}{4} \times \dfrac{8}{9} =$
     (A) $\dfrac{24}{9}$
     (B) $\dfrac{32}{3}$
     (C) $\dfrac{2}{3}$
     (D) $\dfrac{11}{13}$

4.   Change the fraction $\dfrac{7}{8}$ to a decimal.
     (A)   .666
     (B)   .75
     (C)   .777
     (D)   .875

5. $7.04 \times 2.5 =$
     (A)   17.6
     (B)   176
     (C)   9.25
     (D)   1.76

6. Forty-eight percent of the 1,200 students at Central High are males. How many male students are there at Central High?

   (A) 57
   (B) 576
   (C) 580
   (D) 600

7. $4x - 2 = 10$:   Solve for x.

   (A) −1
   (B) 2
   (C) 3
   (D) 4

8. John bought a $250 radio. The salesman gave him a 10% discount. How much did he pay for the radio?

   (A) $25
   (B) $125
   (C) $175
   (D) $225

9. Laura went cruising in her motor boat. She cruised for 2 hours and 20 minutes and found she had traveled 21 nautical miles. What was her speed to the nearest knot? (One knot = one nautical mile in one hour.)

   (A) 7 knots
   (B) $2\frac{1}{3}$ knots
   (C) 21 knots
   (D) 9 knots

10. When a number is multiplied by 6 and that product is subtracted from 70 the difference is 4. What is the number?

   (A) −11.
   (B) 10
   (C) 11
   (D) $12\frac{1}{3}$

Drill Questions

Science

1. Which statement best describes "Earth Science"?
    (A) The study of the planet Earth in comparison to other planets in the solar system.
    (B) The study of Earth's living organisms.
    (C) The study of Earth's natural sytems and structures.
    (D) The study of the structure and compositon of Earth.

2. The large intestine is part of the _____ system.
    (A) digestive
    (B) respiratory
    (C) endocrine
    (D) circulatory

3. The normal number of chromosomes in a human cell is
    (A) 52.
    (B) 108.
    (C) 30.
    (D) 46.

4. In an ecosystem, an example of a producer is a
    (A) fungus.
    (B) maple tree.
    (C) wolf.
    (D) rock.

5. An example of a fungus is
    (A) bacteria.
    (B) algae.
    (C) protozoa.
    (D) yeast.

6. The probability of parents' offspring showing particular traits can be predicted by using

   (A) the Linnaean System.

   (B) DNA tests.

   (C) the Punnett Square.

   (D) none of the above.

7. A material with definite volume but no definite shape is called a

   (A) plasma.

   (B) gas.

   (C) liquid.

   (D) solid.

8. An acidic solution can have a pH of

   (A) 20.

   (B) 10.

   (C) 7.

   (D) 5.

9. The intensity of an earthquake is measured by a(n)

   (A) thermograph.

   (B) seismograph.

   (C) telegraph.

   (D) oscilloscope.

10. _____ is the ability to do work.

    (A) Force

    (B) Energy

    (C) Speed

    (D) Distance

Answers to Drill Questions

Mathematics

1.	**(A)**	6.	**(B)**
2.	**(D)**	7.	**(C)**
3.	**(C)**	8.	**(D)**
4.	**(D)**	9.	**(D)**
5.	**(A)**	10.	**(C)**

Answers to Drill Questions

Science

1.	**(C)**	6.	**(C)**
2.	**(A)**	7.	**(C)**
3.	**(D)**	8.	**(D)**
4.	**(B)**	9.	**(B)**
5.	**(D)**	10.	**(B)**

LAST/ATS-W

Chapter 3

Historical and Social Scientific Awareness Review

Chapter 3

Historical and Social Scientific Awareness Review

The purpose of the Historical and Social Scientific Awareness section of the Liberal Arts and Sciences Test is to assess your understanding of the relationships that exist among historical, geographical, cultural, economic, political, and social issues and factors. It looks for an understanding of the principles and concepts underlying modern political and social concepts, arguments, and interpretations. The following review provides a comprehensive historical context for these skills, and concisely summarizes the information you will need to do well on this section of the exam.

WORLD HISTORY

Ancient and Medieval Times

THE APPEARANCE OF CIVILIZATION

Between 6000 and 3000 B.C.E., humans invented the plow, utilized the wheel, harnessed the wind, discovered how to smelt copper ores, and began to develop accurate solar calendars. Small villages gradually grew into populous cities. The invention of writing in 3500 B.C.E. in Mesopotamia marks the beginning of civilization and divides prehistoric from historic times.

MESOPOTAMIA

Sumer (4000 to 2000 B.C.E.) included the city of Ur. The Sumerians constructed dikes and reservoirs and established a loose confederation of city-states. They probably invented writing (called cuneiform because of its wedge-shaped letters).

After 538 B.C.E., the peoples of Mesopotamia, whose natural boundaries were insufficient to thwart invaders, were absorbed into other empires and dynasties.

EGYPT

During the end of the Archaic Period (5000–2685 B.C.E.), around 3200 B.C.E., Menes, or Narmer, probably unified Upper and Lower Egypt. The capital moved to Memphis during the Third Dynasty (ca. 2650 B.C.E.). The pyramids were built during the Fourth Dynasty (ca. 2613–2494 B.C.E.).

After 1085 B.C.E., in what is known as the Post-Empire Period, Egypt came under the successive control of the Assyrians, the Persians, Alexander the Great, and finally, in 30 B.C.E., the Roman Empire. The Egyptians developed papyrus and made many medical advances.

PALESTINE AND THE HEBREWS

Phoenicians settled along the present-day Lebanon coast (Sidon, Tyre, Beirut, Byblos) and established colonies at Carthage and in Spain. They spread Mesopotamian culture through their trade networks.

The Hebrews probably moved to Egypt around 1700 B.C.E. and were enslaved about 1500 B.C.E. The Hebrews fled Egypt under Moses and around 1200 B.C.E. returned to Palestine. Under King David (reigned ca. 1012–972 B.C.E.), the Philistines were defeated and a capital established at Jerusalem.

The poor and less attractive state of Judah continued until 586 B.C.E., when the Chaldeans transported the Jews to Chalden as advisors and slaves (Babylonian Captivity). When the Persians conquered Babylon in 539 B.C.E., the Jews were allowed to return to Palestine.

GREECE

In the Archaic Period (800–500 B.C.E.) Greek life was organized around the polis (city-state). Oligarchs controlled most of the polis until near the end of the sixth century, when individuals holding absolute power (tyrants) replaced them. By the end of the sixth century, democratic governments in turn replaced many tyrants.

THE CLASSICAL AGE

The fifth century was the high point of Greek civilization. It opened with the Persian Wars (560–479 B.C.E.), after which Athens organized the Delian League. Pericles (ca. 495–429 B.C.E.) used League money to rebuild Athens, including construction of the Parthenon and other buildings on the Acropolis hill. Athens' dominance spurred war with Sparta.

A revolution in philosophy occurred in classical Athens. The Sophists emphasized the individual and his attainment of excellence through rhetoric, grammar, music, and mathematics. Socrates (ca. 470–399 B.C.E.) criticized the Sophists' emphasis on rhetoric and emphasized a process of questioning, or dialogues, with his students. Like Socrates, Plato (ca. 428–348 B.C.E.) emphasized ethics.

Aristotle (ca. 384–322 B.C.E.) was Plato's pupil. He criticized Plato, arguing that ideas or forms did not exist outside of things. He contended that it was necessary to examine four factors in treating any object: its matter, its form, its cause of origin, and its end or purpose.

ROME

The traditional founding date for Rome is 753 B.C.E. Between 800 and 500 B.C.E., Greek tribes colonized southern Italy, bringing their alphabet and religious practices to Roman tribes. In the sixth and seventh centuries, the Etruscans expanded southward and conquered Rome.

In the early Republic, power was in the hands of the patricians (wealthy landowners).

During the 70s and 60s, Pompey (106–48 B.C.E.) and Julius Caesar (100–44 B.C.E.) emerged as the most powerful men.

In 60 B.C.E., Caesar convinced Pompey and Crassus (ca. 115–53 B.C.E.) to form the First Triumvirate. When Crassus died, Caesar and Pompey fought for leadership. In 47 B.C.E., the Senate proclaimed Caesar as dictator, and later named him consul for life. Brutus and Cassius believed that Caesar had destroyed the Republic. They formed a conspiracy, and on March 15, 44 B.C.E. (the Ides of March), Caesar was assassinated in the Roman Forum. His 18-year-old nephew and adopted son, Octavian, succeeded him.

THE ROMAN EMPIRE

After a period of struggle, Octavian (reigned 27 B.C.E.–14 C.E.), named as Caesar's heir, gained absolute control while maintaining the appearance of a republic. When he offered to relinquish his power in 27 B.C.E., the Senate gave him a vote of confidence and a new title, "Augustus." He introduced many reforms, including new coinage, new tax collection, fire and police protection, and land for settlers in the provinces.

By the first century, Christianity had spread throughout the Empire. Around 312 C.E., Emperor Constantine converted to Christianity and ordered toleration in the Edict of Milan (ca. 313 C.E.). In 391 C.E., Emperor Theodosius I (reigned 371–395 C.E.) proclaimed Christianity as the Empire's official religion.

THE BYZANTINE EMPIRE

Emperor Theodosius II (reigned 408–450 C.E.) divided his empire between his sons, one ruling the East, the other ruling the West. After the Vandals sacked Rome in 455 C.E., Constantinople was the undisputed leading city of the Empire. In 1453 C.E., Constantinople fell to the Ottoman Turks.

ISLAMIC CIVILIZATION IN THE MIDDLE AGES

Mohammed was born about 570 C.E. In 630 C.E., he marched into Mecca. The Sharia (code of law and theology) outlines five pillars of faith for Muslims to observe. The first pillar is the belief that there is one God and that Mohammed is his prophet. Second, the faithful must pray five times a day. Third, they must perform charitable acts. Fourth, they are required to fast from sunrise to sunset during the holy month of Ramadan. Finally, they must make a haj, or pilgrimage, to Mecca. The Koran, which consists of 114 suras (verses), contains Mohammed's teachings.

The Omayyad caliphs, based in Damascus, governed from 661–750 C.E. They called themselves Shiites and believed they were Mohammed's true successors. (Most Muslims were Sunnites, from the word "sunna," meaning oral traditions about the prophet.)

The Abbasid caliphs ruled from 750–1258 C.E. They moved the capital to Baghdad and treated Arab and non-Arab Muslims as equals. Genghis (or Chingis) Khan (reigned 1206–1227 C.E.) and his army invaded the Abbasids. In 1258 C.E., they seized Baghdad and murdered the last caliph.

FEUDALISM IN JAPAN

Feudalism in Japan began with the arrival of mounted nomadic warriors from throughout Asia during the Kofun Era (300–710 C.E.). Some members of these nomadic groups formed an elite class and became part of the court aristocracy in the capital city of Kyoto, in western Japan. During the Heian Era (794–1185 C.E.), a hereditary military aristocracy arose in the Japanese provinces, and by the late Heian Era, many of these formerly nomadic warriors had established themselves as independent landowners, or as managers of landed estates *(shoen)* owned by Kyoto aristocrats. These aristocrats depended on the warriors to defend their *shoen*, and in response to this need, the warriors organized into small groups called *bushidan*.

After victory in the Taira-Minamoto War (1180–1185 C.E.), Minamoto no Yorimoto forced the emperor to award him the title of *shogun,* which is short for "barbarian subduing generalissimo." He used this power to found the Kamakura Shogunate, which survived for 148 years.

By the fourteenth century, the *shugo* had augmented their power enough to become a threat to the Kamakura, and in 1333 C.E. led a rebellion that overthrew the shogunate.

The Tokugawa Shogunate was the final and most unified of the three shogunates. Under the Tokugawa, the *daimyo* were considered direct vassals of the shoguns, and were kept under strict control. The warriors were gradually transformed into scholars and bureaucrats under the *bushido,* or code of chivalry, and the principles of Neo-Confucianism. Under the Meji Restoration of 1868, power was restored to the emperor and all special privileges of the samurai class were abolished.

CHINESE AND INDIAN EMPIRES

In the third century B.C.E., the Indian kingdoms fell under the Mauryan Empire. The grandson of the founder of this empire, named Ashoka, opened a new era in the cultural history of India by believing in the Buddhist religion. Buddha had disregarded the Vedic gods and the institutions of caste and had preached a relatively simple ethical religion which had two levels of aspiration—a monastic life of renunciation of the world and a high, but not too difficult, morality for the layman. The two religions of Hinduism and Buddhism flourished together for centuries in a tolerant rivalry, and Buddhism virtually disappeared from India by the thirteenth century C.E.

Chinese civilization originated in the Yellow River Valley, only gradually extending to the southern regions. Three dynasties ruled early China: the Xia or Hsia, the Shang (ca. 1500 to 1122 B.C.E.), and the Zhou (ca. 1122 to 211 B.C.E.). After the Zhou fell, China welcomed the teachings of Confucius; warfare between states and philosophical speculation created circumstances ripe for such teachings. Confucius made the good order of society depend on an ethical ruler, who should be advised by scholar-moralists like Confucius himself.

In contrast to the Confucians, the Chinese Taoists professed a kind of anarchism; the best kind of government was none at all. The wise man did not concern himself with political affairs, but with mystical contemplation which identified him with the forces of nature.

AFRICAN KINGDOMS AND CULTURES

The Bantu peoples, numbering about 100,000,000, lived across large sections of Africa. Bantu societies lived in tiny chiefdoms, starting in the third millennium B.C.E., and each group developed its own version of the original Bantu language.

The Nok were a people that lived in the area now known as Nigeria. Artifacts indicate that they were peaceful farmers who built small communities consisting of houses of wattle and daub.

The Ghanaians lived about 500 miles from what we now call Ghana. Their kingdom fell to a Berber group in the late 11th century C.E., and Mali emerged as the next great kingdom in the 13th century.

The Malians lived in a huge kingdom that lay mostly on the savanna bordering the Sahara Desert. Timbuktu, built in the thirteenth century C.E., was a thriving city of culture where traders visited stone houses, shops, libraries, and mosques.

The Songhai lived near the Niger River and gained their independence from the Mali in the early 1400s. The major growth of the empire came after 1464 C.E. under the leadership of Sunni Ali, who devoted his reign to warfare and expansion of the empire.

CIVILIZATIONS OF THE AMERICAS

The great civilizations of early America were agricultural, and foremost of these was the Mayan, in Yucatan, Guatemala, and eastern Honduras.

Farther north in Mexico there arose a series of advanced cultures that derived much of their substance from the Maya. Peoples like the Zapotecs, Totonacs, Olmecs, and Toltecs evolved into a high level of civilization. By 500 B.C.E. agricultural peoples had begun to use a ceremonial calendar and had built stone pyramids on which they performed religious observances.

The Aztecs then took over Mexican culture, and a major feature of their culture was human sacrifice in repeated propitiation of their chief god. Aztec government was centralized, with an elective king and a large army.

Andean civilization was characterized by the evolution of beautifully made pottery, intricate fabrics, and flat-topped mounds called *huacas*.

The Inca, a tribe from the interior of South America who termed themselves "Children of the Sun," controlled an area stretching from Ecuador to central Chile. Sun worshippers, they believed themselves to be the vice-regents on earth of the sun god and to be all-powerful. Every person's place in society was fixed and immutable; the state and the army were supreme. They were at the apex of their power just before the Spanish conquest.

In the present-day southwestern United States and northern Mexico, two varieties of ancient culture can be identified. The Anasazi developed adobe architecture, worked the land extensively, had a highly developed system of irrigation, and made cloth and baskets. The Hohokam built separate stone and timber houses around a central plaza.

EUROPE IN ANTIQUITY

The Frankish Kingdom was the most important medieval Germanic state. Under Clovis I (reigned 481–511 C.E.), the Franks finished conquering France and the Gauls in 486 C.E. Clovis converted to Christianity and founded the Merovingian dynasty.

Charles the Great, or Charlemagne (reigned 768–814 C.E.), founded the Carolingian dynasty. In 800 C.E., Pope Leo III named Charlemagne Emperor of the Holy Roman Empire. In the Treaty of Aix-la-Chapelle (812 C.E.), the Byzantine emperor recognized Charles's authority in the West.

The Holy Roman Empire was intended to reestablish the Roman Empire in the West. Charles's son, Louis the Pious (reigned 814–840 C.E.), succeeded him. On Louis's death, his three sons vied for control of the Empire. The three eventually signed the Treaty of Verdun in 843 C.E. This gave Charles the Western Kingdom (France), Louis the Eastern Kingdom (Germany), and Lothair the Middle Kingdom, a narrow strip of land running from the North Sea to the Mediterranean.

Manorialism developed in this period. Manorialism refers to the economic system in which large estates, granted by the king to nobles, strove for self-sufficiency. Ownership was divided among the lord and his serfs (also called villeins).

The church was the only institution to survive the Germanic invasions intact. The power of the popes grew in this period. Gregory I (reigned 590–604 C.E.) was the first member of a monastic order to rise to the papacy. He advanced the ideas of penance and purgatory. He centralized church administration and was the first pope to rule as the secular head of Rome. Monasteries preserved the few remnants that survived the decline of Antiquity.

EUROPEAN HISTORY

High Middle Ages

The year 1050 marked the beginning of the High Middle Ages. Europe was poised to emerge from five centuries of decline. Between 1000 and 1350, the population grew from 38 million to 75 million. Agricultural productivity grew, aided by new technologies, such as heavy plows, and a slight temperature rise which produced a longer growing season.

THE HOLY ROMAN EMPIRE

Charlemagne's grandson, Louis the German, became Holy Roman Emperor under the Treaty of Verdun. Otto became Holy Roman Emperor in 962.

His descendants governed the Empire until 1024, when the Franconian dynasty assumed power, reigning until 1125.

Under the leadership of William the Conqueror (reigned 1066–1087), the Normans conquered England in 1066. William stripped the Anglo-Saxon nobility of its privileges and instituted feudalism. He ordered a survey of all property of the realm, which was recorded in the Domesday Book (1086).

William introduced Feudalism to England. Feudalism describes the decentralized political system of personal ties and obligations that bound vassals to their lords. Serfs were peasants who were bound to the land. They worked on the demesne, or lord's property, three or four days a week in return for the right to work their own land.

In 1215, the English barons forced King John I to sign the Magna Carta Libertatum, acknowledging their "ancient" privileges. The Magna Carta established the principle of a limited English monarchy.

In 710 to 711, the Moors conquered Spain from the Visigoths. Under the Moors, Spain enjoyed a stable, prosperous government. The caliphate of Córdoba became a center of scientific and intellectual activity.

The Reconquista (1085–1340) wrested control from the Moors. The fall of Córdoba in 1234 completed the Reconquista, except for the small state of Granada.

Most of Eastern Europe and Russia was never under Rome's control, and it was cut off from Western influence by the Germanic invasions.

In Russia, Vladimir I converted to Orthodox Christianity in 988. He established the basis of Kievian Russia. After 1054, Russia broke into competing principalities. The Mongols (Tatars) invaded in 1221. They completed their conquest in 1245 and cut Russia's contact with the West for almost a century.

The Crusades attempted to liberate the Holy Land from infidels. There were seven major crusades between 1096 and 1300. Urban II called Christians to the First Crusade (1096–1099) with the promise of a plenary indulgence (exemption from punishment in purgatory). Younger sons who would not inherit their fathers' lands were also attracted.

The Crusades helped to renew interest in the ancient world. However, thousands of Jews and Muslims were massacred as a result of the Crusades, and relations between Europe and the Byzantine Empire collapsed.

SCHOLASTICISM

Scholasticism was an effort to reconcile reason and faith and to instruct Christians on how to make sense of the pagan tradition.

The most influential proponent of this effort was Thomas Aquinas (ca. 1225–1274), who believed that there were two orders of truth. The lower, reason, could demonstrate propositions such as the existence of God, but the higher level necessitated that some of God's mysteries, such as the nature of the Trinity, must be accepted on faith. Aquinas viewed the universe as a great chain of being, with humans midway on the chain, between the material and the spiritual.

Late Middle Ages and the Renaissance

THE BLACK DEATH

Conditions in Europe encouraged the quick spread of disease. There was no urban sanitation, and streets were filled with refuse, excrement, and dead animals; living conditions were overcrowded, with families often sleeping in one room or one bed; poor nutrition was rampant; and there was also little personal cleanliness.

Carried by fleas on rats, the plague was brought from Asia by merchants, and arrived in Europe in 1347. By 1350, the plague had killed 25 to 40 percent of the European population.

LITERATURE, ART, AND SCHOLARSHIP

Humanists, as both orators and poets, were inspired by and imitated works of the classical past. The literature was more secular and wide-ranging than that of the Middle Ages.

Dante Alighieri (1265–1321) was a Florentine writer whose *Divine Comedy*, describing a journey through hell, purgatory, and heaven, shows that reason can only take people so far and that God's grace and revelation must be used.

Francesco Petrarch (1304–1374) encouraged the study of ancient Rome, collected and preserved work of ancient writers, and produced much work in the classical literary style.

Giovanni Boccaccio (1313–1375) wrote *The Decameron*, a collection of short stories in Italian, which were meant to amuse, not edify, the reader.

Artists also broke with the medieval past, in both technique and content. Renaissance art sometimes used religious topics, but often dealt with secular themes or portraits of individuals. Oil paints, chiaroscuro, and linear perspectives produced works of energy in three dimensions.

Leonardo da Vinci (1452–1519) produced numerous works, including *The Last Supper* and *Mona Lisa*. Raphael Santi (1483–1520), a master of Renaissance grace and style, theory, and technique, represented these skills in *The School of Athens*. Michelangelo Buonarroti(1475–1564) produced masterpieces in architecture, sculpture (*David*), and painting (the Sistine Chapel ceiling). His work was a bridge to a new, non-Renaissance style called Mannerism.

Renaissance scholars were more practical and secular than medieval ones. Manuscript collections enabled scholars to study the primary sources and to reject all traditions which had been built up since classical times. Also, scholars participated in the lives of their cities as active politicians.

Leonardo Bruni (1370–1444), a civic humanist, served as chancellor of Florence, where he used his rhetorical skills to rouse the citizens against external enemies.

Niccolo Machiavelli (1469–1527) wrote *The Prince*, which analyzed politics from the standpoint of expedience rising above morality in the name of maintaining political power.

THE REFORMATION

The Reformation destroyed Western Europe's religious unity and introduced new ideas about the relationships between God, the individual, and society. Its course was greatly influenced by politics and led, in most areas, to the subjection of the church to the political rulers.

MARTIN LUTHER

Martin Luther (1483–1546), to his personal distress, could not reconcile the sinfulness of humans with the justice of God. During his studies of the

Bible, Luther came to believe that personal efforts—good works such as a Christian life and attention to the sacraments of the church—could not "earn" the sinner salvation, but that belief and faith were the only way to obtain grace. By 1515 Luther believed that "justification by faith alone" was the road to salvation.

On October 31, 1517, Luther nailed 95 theses, or statements, about indulgences, the cancellation of a sin in return for money, to the door of the Wittenberg church and challenged the practice of selling them. At this time he was seeking to reform the church, not divide it.

In 1519 Luther presented various criticisms of the church and was driven to say that only the Bible, not religious traditions or papal statements, could determine correct religious practices and beliefs. In 1521 Pope Leo X excommunicated Luther for his beliefs.

CALVINISM

In 1536 John Calvin (1509–1564), a Frenchman, arrived in Geneva, a Swiss city-state which had adopted an anti-Catholic position. In 1540, Geneva became the center of the Reformation. Calvin's *Institutes of the Christian Religion* (1536), a strictly logical analysis of Christianity, had a universal appeal.

Calvin emphasized the doctrine of predestination (God knew who would obtain salvation before those people were born) and believed that church and state should be united.

Calvinism triumphed as the majority religion in Scotland, under the leadership of John Knox (ca. 1514–1572), and in the United Provinces of the Netherlands. Puritans in England and New England also accepted Calvinism.

THE THIRTY YEARS' WAR

Between 1618 and 1648, a series of wars was fought among the European powers. The reasons for these wars varied; religious, dynastic, commercial, and territorial rivalries all played a part. The battles were fought over most of Europe, and ended with the Treaty of Westphalia in 1648. The Thirty Years' War changed the boundaries of most European countries.

EXPLORATIONS AND CONQUESTS

In Portugal, Prince Henry the Navigator (1394–1460) supported exploration of the African coastline, largely in order to seek gold. Bartholomeu Dias (1450–1500) rounded the southern tip of Africa in 1487. Vasco da Gama (1460–1524) reached India in 1498 and, after some fighting, soon established trading ports at Goa and Calicut. Affonso de Albuquerque (1453–1515) helped establish an empire in the Spice Islands after 1510.

In Spain, Christopher Columbus (1451–1506), seeking a new route to the (East) Indies, "discovered" the Americas in 1492. Ferdinand Magellan (1480–1521) circumnavigated the globe. Conquests of the Aztecs by Hernando Cortes (1485–1547), and the Incas by Francisco Pizarro (ca. 1476–1541), enabled the Spanish to send much gold and silver back to Spain.

In the 1490s the Cabots, John (1450–1498) and Sebastian (ca. 1483–1557), explored North America, and after 1570 various other Englishmen, including Francis Drake (ca. 1540–1596), fought the Spanish around the world. Jacques Cartier (1491–1557) explored parts of North America for France in 1534.

Samuel de Champlain (1567–1635) and the French explored the St. Lawrence River, seeking furs to trade. The Dutch established settlements at New Amsterdam and in the Hudson River Valley. The Dutch founded trading centers in the East Indies, the West Indies, and southern Africa. Swedes settled on the Delaware River in 1638.

Revolution and the New World Order

THE SCIENTIFIC REVOLUTION

For the first time in human history, the eighteenth century saw the appearance of a secular worldview. This became known as the "Age of Enlightenment." The philosophical starting point for the Enlightenment was the belief in the autonomy of man's intellect apart from God. The most basic assumption was faith in reason rather than faith in revelation.

René Descartes (1596–1650) sought a basis for logic and thought he found it in man's ability to think. "I think; therefore, I am" was his most famous statement.

Benedict de Spinoza (1632–1677) developed a rational pantheism in which he equated God and nature. He denied all free will and ended up with an impersonal, mechanical universe.

Gottfried Wilhelm Leibniz (1646–1716) worked on symbolic logic and calculus, and invented a calculating machine. He, too, had a mechanistic world- and life-view and thought of God as a hypothetical abstraction rather than a persona.

John Locke (1632–1704) pioneered in the empiricist approach to knowledge and stressed the importance of environment in human development. He classified knowledge three ways: 1) according to reason, 2) contrary to reason, or 3) above reason. Locke thought reason and revelation were both complementary and from God.

David Hume (1711–1776) was a Scottish historian and philosopher who began by emphasizing the limitations of human reasoning and later became a dogmatic skeptic.

THE ENLIGHTENMENT'S EFFECT ON SOCIETY

The Enlightenment affected more than science and religion. New political and economic theories originated as well. John Locke and Jean Jacques Rousseau (1712–1778) believed that people were capable of governing themselves, either through a political (Locke) or social (Rousseau) contract forming the basis of society. However, most philosophes opposed democracy, preferring a limited monarchy that shared power with the nobility.

The assault on mercantilist economic theory was begun by the physiocrats in France, who proposed a "laissez-faire" (minimal governmental interference) attitude toward land usage which culminated in the theory of economic capitalism associated with Adam Smith (1723–1790) and his notions of free trade, free enterprise, and the law of supply and demand.

CAUSES OF THE FRENCH REVOLUTION

The rising expectations of "enlightened" society in France were demonstrated by the increased criticism directed toward government inefficiency and corruption, and toward the privileged classes. The remainder of the population (Third Estate) consisted of the middle class, urban workers, and the mass of peasants, who bore the entire burden of taxation and the imposition of feudal obligations.

Designed to represent the three estates of France, the Estates General had only met twice, once at its creation in 1302 and again in 1614. When the French parliaments insisted that any new taxes must be approved by this body, King Louis XVI reluctantly ordered it to assemble at Versailles by May 1789.

On May 5, 1789, the Estates General met and argued over whether to vote by estate or individually. Each estate was ordered to meet separately and vote as a unit. The Third Estate refused and insisted that the entire assembly stay together.

PHASES OF THE REVOLUTION

During the 1789 meeting of the Estates General, representatives of the Third Estate declared themselves the true National Assembly of France (June 17). Defections from the First and Second Estates caused the king to recognize the National Assembly (June 27) after dissolving the Estates General.

The Estates General was replaced by the Legislative Assembly, which was divided into competing political factions. The most important political clubs were republican groups such as the Jacobins (radical urban) and Girondins (moderate rural), while the Sans-culottes (working class, extremely radical) were a separate faction with an economic agenda.

The National Convention (1792–1795) abolished the monarchy and installed republicanism. The most notorious event of the French Revolution was the "Reign of Terror" (1793–1794), the government's campaign against its internal enemies and counterrevolutionaries. Louis XVI was charged with treason, found guilty, and executed on January 21, 1793. Later the same year, the queen, Marie Antoinette, met the same fate.

The Directory (1795–1799) was controlled by the middle class. It wanted peace in order to gain more wealth and to establish a society in which money and property would become the only requirements for prestige and power. Rising inflation and mass public dissatisfaction led to this government's downfall.

THE ERA OF NAPOLEON

The new government was installed on December 25, 1799, with a constitution which concentrated supreme power in the hands of Napoleon. Napoleon's domestic reforms and policies affected every aspect of society.

French-ruled peoples viewed Napoleon as a tyrant who repressed and exploited them for France's glory and advantage. Enlightened reformers believed Napoleon had betrayed the ideals of the Revolution. The downfall of Napoleon resulted from his inability to conquer England, economic distress caused by the Continental System (boycott of British goods), the Peninsular War with Spain, the German War of Liberation, and the invasion of Russia. The actual defeat of Napoleon occurred at the Battle of Waterloo in 1815.

THE INDUSTRIAL REVOLUTION

The term "Industrial Revolution" was intended to describe a time of transition when machines began to significantly displace human and animal power in methods of producing and distributing goods, and an agricultural and commercial society converted into an industrial one.

Roots of the Industrial Revolution can be found in the following: 1) the Commercial Revolution (1500–1700), which spurred the great economic growth of Europe and brought about the Age of Discovery and Exploration, which in turn helped to solidify the economic doctrines of mercantilism; 2) the effect of the Scientific Revolution, which produced the first wave of mechanical inventions and technological advances; 3) the increase in population in Europe from 140 million people in 1750 to 266 million people by the mid-part of the nineteenth century (more producers, more consumers); and 4) the political and social revolutions of the nineteenth century, which began the rise to power of the "middle class," and provided leadership for the economic revolution.

A transportation revolution ensued in order to distribute the productivity of machinery and deliver raw materials to the eager factories. This led to the growth of canal systems, the construction of hard-surfaced "macadam" roads, the commercial use of the steamboat [demonstrated by Robert Fulton (1765–1815)], and the railway locomotive [made commercially successful by George Stephenson (1781–1848)].

The Industrial Revolution created a unique new category of people who were dependent on their job alone for income, a job from which they might be dismissed without cause. Until 1850, workers as a whole did not share in the general wealth produced by the Industrial Revolution. Conditions improved as the century wore on, as union action combined with general prosperity and a developing social conscience to improve the working conditions, wages, and hours first of skilled labor, and later of unskilled labor.

SOCIALISM

The Utopian Socialists [from *Utopia*, Saint Thomas More's (1478–1535) book on a fictional ideal society] were the earliest writers to propose an equitable solution to improve the distribution of society's wealth. While they endorsed the productive capacity of industrialism, they denounced its mismanagement. Human society was to be organized as a community rather than a mixture of competing, selfish individuals. All the goods a person needed could be produced in one community.

Scientific Socialism, or Marxism, was the creation of Karl Marx (1818–1883), a German scholar who, with the help of Friedrich Engels (1820–1895), intended to replace utopian hopes and dreams with a militant blueprint for socialist working-class success. The principal works of this revolutionary school of socialism were *The Communist Manifesto* and *Das Kapital*.

Marxism consisted of a number of key propositions: 1) An economic interpretation of history, i.e., all human history has been determined by economic factors (mainly centered on who controls the means of production and distribution); 2) Class struggle, i.e., there has always been a class struggle between the rich and the poor (or the exploiters and the exploited); 3) Theory of surplus value, i.e., the true value of a product was labor, and since the worker received a small portion of his just labor price, the difference was surplus value, "stolen" from him by the capitalist; and 4) Socialism was inevitable, i.e., capitalism contained the seeds of its own destruction (overproduction, unemployment, etc.). The rich would grow richer and the poor would grow poorer until the gap between each class (proletariat and bourgeoisie) would become so great that the working classes would rise up in revolution and overthrow the elite bourgeoisie to install a "dictatorship of the proletariat." As modern capitalism was dismantled, the creation of a classless society guided by the principle "from each according to his abilities, to each according to his needs" would take place.

Realism and Materialism

THE CRIMEAN WAR

The Crimean War originated in the dispute between two differing groups of Christians and their protectors over privileges in the Holy Land. During the nineteenth century, Palestine was part of the Ottoman Turkish Empire. In 1852, the Turks negotiated an agreement with the French to provide enclaves in the Holy Land to Roman Catholic religious orders; this arrangement appeared to jeopardize already existing agreements which provided access to Greek Orthodox religious orders. Czar Nicholas I (reigned 1825–1855), unaware of the impact of his action, ordered Russian troops to occupy several Danubian principalities; his strategy was to withdraw from these areas once the Turks agreed to clarify and guarantee the rights of the Greek Orthodox orders. In October 1853, the Turks demanded that the Russians withdraw from the occupied principalities. The Russians failed to respond, and the Turks declared war. In 1854, Great Britain and France joined the Ottoman Turks and declared war on Russia. Russia was defeated in 1856 and agreed to settlements proposed by the Peace of Paris.

IMPERIAL RUSSIA

Fearing the transformation of Russian society from below, Alexander II instituted a series of reforms which altered the nature of the social contract in Russia. In 1861, Alexander II declared that serfdom was abolished. Further, he issued the following reforms: 1) The serf (peasant) would no longer be dependent upon the lord; 2) all people were to have freedom of movement and were free to change their means of livelihood; and 3) the serf could enter into contracts and could own property.

In the late 1870s and early 1880s, populist leaders such as Andrei Zheleabov and Sophie Perovsky became obsessed with the need to assassinate Alexander II. In March 1881, the czar was killed in St. Petersburg when his carriage was bombed. He was succeeded by Alexander III (reigned 1881–1894), who advocated a national policy based on "Orthodoxy, Autocracy, and Nationalism." Alexander III died in 1894 and was succeeded by the last of the Romanovs to hold power, Nicholas II (reigned 1894–1917). Nicholas II displayed a lack of intelligence, wit, and political acumen, and the absence of a firm will throughout his reign. From his ministers to his wife, Alexandra, to Rasputin (1872–1916), Nicholas was influenced by stronger personalities.

ORIGINS, MOTIVES, AND IMPLICATIONS OF THE NEW IMPERIALISM

By the 1870s, the European industrial economies required external markets to distribute products which could not be absorbed within their domestic economies. Further, excess capital was available and foreign investment, while risky, appeared to offer high returns. Finally, the need for additional sources of raw materials served as a rationale and stimulant for imperialism.

Britain's Benjamin Disraeli (1804–1881) was involved in the intrigue which would result in the British acquisition of the Suez Canal (1875), and Britain was victorious over the Zulus in the six-month Zulu War (1879) in eastern South Africa.

At about the same time, Belgium established its interest in the Congo. France, in addition to seizing Tunisia, extended its influence into French Equatorial Africa and Italy established small colonies in East Africa. During the 1880s Germany acquired several African colonies including German East Africa, the Cameroons, Togoland, and German South West Africa. The Berlin Conference (1884–1885) resulted in an agreement which specified the following: 1) The Congo would be under the control of Belgium through an International Association; 2) More liberal use would be made of the Niger and Congo rivers; 3) European powers could acquire African territory through first occupation and second notifying the other European states of their occupation and claim.

British movement north of the Cape of Good Hope involved Europeans fighting one another rather than a native African force. The Boers, descendants of Dutch settlers, had lived in South Africa since the beginning of the nineteenth century. With the discovery of gold (1882) in the Transvaal, many English Cape settlers moved into the region. The Boers, under the leadership of Paul Kruger, restricted the political and economic rights of the British settlers and developed alternative railroads through Mozambique which would lessen the Boer dependency on the Cape colony. The crisis mounted and, in 1899, the Boer War began. Until 1902, the British and Boers fought a war which was costly to both sides. Britain prevailed and by 1909, the Transvaal, Orange Free State, Natal, and the Cape of Good Hope were united into the Union of South Africa.

Another area of increased imperialist activity was the Pacific. While Britain, the Netherlands, and France demonstrated that they were interested in Pacific islands, the most active states in this region during the last 20 years of the nineteenth century were Germany and the United States. The United States acquired the Philippines in 1898. Germany gained part of New Guinea and the Marshall, Caroline, and Mariana island chains. The Western powers were also interested in the Asian mainland. Most powers agreed with the American Open Door Policy, which recognized the independence and integrity of China and provided economic access for all the powers. Rivalry between Russia and Japan for supremacy in Korea and China (Manchuria) led to the outbreak of the Russo-Japanese War in 1904.

World War I and Europe in Crisis

THE ORIGINS OF WORLD WAR I

The long-range roots of the origins of World War I can be traced to numerous factors, beginning with the creation of modern Germany in 1871. Achieved through a series of wars, the emergence of this new German state completely destroyed Europe's traditional balance of power, and forced its diplomatic and military planners back to their drawing boards to rethink their collective strategies.

From 1871 to 1890, balance of power was maintained through the network of alliances created by the German Chancellor, Otto von Bismarck (1815–1898), and centered around his *Dreikaiserbund* (League of the Three Emperors) that isolated France, and the Dual (Germany, Austria) and Triple (Germany, Austria, Italy) Alliances. Bismarck's fall in 1890 resulted in new policies that saw Germany move closer to Austria, while England and France (Entente Cordiale, 1904), and later Russia (Triple Entente, 1907), drew closer together.

Germany's dramatic defeat of France in 1870–1871, coupled with Kaiser William II's decision in 1890 to build up a navy comparable to that of Great Britain, created a reactive arms race. This, blended with European efforts to carve out colonial empires in Africa and Asia—plus a new spirit of nationalism and the growing romanticization of war—helped create an unstable international environment in the years before the outbreak of World War I.

THE OUTBREAK OF WAR

On June 28, 1914, the Archduke Franz Ferdinand (1863–1914), heir to the Austrian throne, was assassinated by Gavrilo Princip, a young Serbian nationalist. Austria consulted with the German government on July 6 and received a "blank check" to take whatever steps necessary to punish Serbia. On July 23, 1914, the Austrian government presented Serbia with a 10-point ultimatum that compelled Serbia—with the help of Austrian officials—to supress and punish all forms of anti-Austrian sentiment within its borders. On July 25, 1914, three hours after mobilizing its army, Serbia accepted most of Austria's terms; it asked only that Austria's unprecedented demand to participate in judicial proceedings against anti-Austrian agitators be adjudicated by the International Tribunal at The Hague.

Austria immediately broke official relations with Serbia and mobilized its army. On July 28, 1914, Austria went to war against Serbia, and began to bombard Belgrade the following day. At the same time, Russia gradually prepared for war against Austria and Germany, declaring full mobilization on July 30.

WORLD WAR I

The Western Front: After entering Belgium, the Germans attacked France on five fronts in an effort to encircle Paris rapidly. However, the unexpected Russian attack in East Prussia and Galicia from August 17 to 20 forced Germany to transfer important forces eastward to halt the Russian drive.

To halt a further German advance, the French army, aided by Belgian and English forces, counterattacked. In the Battle of the Marne (September 5–9), they stopped the German drive and forced small retreats. Mutual outflanking maneuvers by France and Germany created a battlefront that would determine the demarcation of the Western Front for the next four years. It ran, in uneven fashion, from the North Sea to Belgium and from northern France to Switzerland.

By the end of 1914, Allied fleets had gained control of the high seas, which caused Germany to lose control of its colonial empire. Germany's failure in 1914 to weaken British naval strength prompted German naval leaders to begin using the submarine as an offensive weapon to weaken the British. On February 4, Germany announced a war zone around the British Isles, and advised neutral powers to sail there at their own risk. On May 7, 1915, a German submarine sank the *Lusitania*, a British passenger vessel, because it was secretly carrying arms.

THE AMERICAN PRESENCE

The United States, which had originally hoped that it could simply supply the Allies with naval and economic support, made its naval presence known as soon as it entered the war on April 16, 1917. It helped Great Britain mount an extremely effective blockade of Germany and, through a convoy system, strengthened the shipment of goods across the Atlantic.

Stirred by the successes on the Marne, the Allies began their offensive against the Germans at Amiens on August 8, 1918. By September 3, the Germans retreated to the Hindenburg Line, which was taken by the allies on September 27.

Bulgaria, Turkey, and Austria-Hungary fell in rapid succession as the Allies strengthened their assault. Kaiser William II, pressured to abdicate, fled the country on November 9. On November 11, at 11 a.m., the war ended, with Germany accepting a harsh armistice.

THE PARIS PEACE CONFERENCE OF 1919–1920

The sudden, unexpected end of the war, combined with the growing threat of communist revolution throughout Europe, created an unsettling atmosphere at the conference. The "Big Four" of Woodrow Wilson (U.S.), Georges Clemenceau (France), David Lloyd-George (England), and Vittorio Orlando (Italy) took over the peace discussions. The delays, caused by uncertainty over the conference's direction, Wilson's insistence that the League of Nations be included in the settlement, and fear of European-wide revolution, resulted in a hastily prepared, dictated peace settlement.

THE TREATY OF VERSAILLES

The treaty's war-guilt statements were the justification for its harsh penalties. The former German emperor, William II, was accused of crimes against "international morality and the sanctity of treaties," while Germany took responsibility for itself and for its allies for all losses suffered by the Allied Powers and their supporters as a result of German and Central Power aggression.

THE RUSSIAN REVOLUTIONS OF 1917

The government's handling of the war prompted a new wave of civilian unrest. Estimates are that 1,140 riots and strikes swept Russia in January and February 1917. Military and police units ordered to move against the mobs either remained at their posts or joined them. On March 15, 1917, the czar was forced to abdicate.

THE BOLSHEVIK OCTOBER REVOLUTION

On October 23–24, 1917, Vladimir Lenin (1870–1924) returned from Finland to meet with the party's Central Committee to plan a coup. Though he met with strong resistance, the Committee agreed to create a Political Bureau (Politburo) to oversee the revolution.

At the Congress, it was announced that the government's new cabinet would include Lenin as Chairman, or head of government, Leon Trotsky (1879–1940) as Foreign Commissar, and Josef Stalin (1879–1953) as Commissar of Nationalities. The Second Congress issued two decrees on peace and land. The first called for immediate peace without any consideration of indemnities or annexations, while the second adopted the Socialist Revolutionary land program that abolished private ownership of land and decreed that a peasant could have only as much land as he could farm. Village councils would oversee distribution.

World War II

NAZI GERMANY

The Depression had a dramatic effect on the German economy and politics. By January 1932, 43 percent of the German work force were without jobs (compared to one-quarter of the work force in the U.S.).

In 1919, Adolf Hitler (1889–1945) joined the German Workers party (DAP), which he soon took over and renamed the National Socialist German Workers party (NAZI). In 1920, the party adopted a 25-point program that included treaty revision, anti-Semitism, and economic and other social changes. They also created a defense cadre of the *Sturmabteilung* (SA), "Storm Troopers," or "brown shirts," which was to help the party seize power.

In the midst of the country's severe economic crisis a march, known as the Beer Hall Putsch (1923), was stopped by police, and Hitler and his supporters were arrested. Though sentenced to five years' imprisonment, he was released after eight months. While incarcerated, he dictated *Mein Kampf* to Rudolf Hess.

In 1933, Hitler was appointed chancellor and head of a new coalition cabinet with three seats for the Nazis. Hitler dissolved the Reichstag and called for new elections on March 5. Using presidential decree powers, he initiated a violent anti-Communist campaign that included the lifting of certain press and civil freedoms.

On July 14, 1933, the Nazi party became the only legal party in Germany. In addition, non-Aryans and Nazi opponents were removed from the civil service, the court system, and higher education. Finally, the secret police, or Gestapo (*Geheime Staatspolizei*), was created on April 24, 1933, to deal with opponents and operate concentration camps.

From the inception of the Nazi state in 1933, anti-Semitism was a constant theme and practice in all nazification efforts. Illegal intimidation and harassment of Jews was coupled with rigid enforcement of civil service regulations that forbade employment of non-Aryans. This first wave of anti-Semitic activity culminated with the passage of the Nuremburg Laws, passed on September 15, 1935, that deprived Jews of German citizenship and outlawed sexual or marital relations between Jews and other Germans, thus effectively isolating them from the mainstream of German society.

THE COURSE OF EVENTS

The Spanish Civil War (1936–1939) is usually seen as a rehearsal for World War II because of outside intervention. Following an election victory by a popular front of republican and radical parties, right-wing generals in July began a military insurrection. Francisco Franco, stationed at the time in Spanish Morocco, emerged as the leader of this revolt, which became a devastating civil war lasting nearly three years.

The democracies, including the United States, followed a course of neutrality. Nazi Germany, Italy, and the U.S.S.R. did intervene despite non-intervention agreements negotiated by Britain and France. Spain became a battlefield for fascist and anti-fascist forces, with Franco winning by 1939 in what was seen as a serious defeat for anti-fascist forces everywhere. The Spanish Civil War was a factor in bringing together Italy's Benito Mussolini (1833–1945) and Hitler in a Rome-Berlin Axis. Already Germany and Japan had signed the Anti-Comintern Pact in 1936.

In 1938 Hitler renewed his compaign against Austria, which he had unsuccessfully tried to subvert in 1934. Hitler pressured the Austrian chancellor to make concessions. When this did not work, German troops annexed Austria (the *Anschluss*). Again, Britain and France took no effective action, and about six million Austrians were added to Germany.

Hitler turned next to Czechoslovakia. Britain and France, despite the French alliance with Czechoslovakia, put pressure on the Czech government to force it to comply with German demands. Hitler signed a treaty agreeing to this settlement as the limit of his ambitions.

In March 1939, Hitler annexed most of the Czech state while Hungary conquered Ruthenia. At almost the same time Germany annexed Memel from

Lithuania. In April, Mussolini, taking advantage of distractions created by Germany, landed an army in Albania and seized that Balkan state in a campaign lasting about one week.

Disillusioned by these continued aggressions, Britain and France made military preparations. Guarantees were given to Poland, Rumania, and Greece. On August 23, 1939, the world was stunned by the announcement of a Nazi-Soviet Treaty of friendship. Stalin agreed to remain neutral in any German war with Britain or France. World War II began with the German invasion of Poland on September 1, 1939, followed by British and French declarations of war against Germany on September 3.

THE GERMAN BLITZKRIEG

The German attack (known as the "blitzkrieg" or "lightning war") overwhelmed the poorly equipped Polish army, which could not resist German tanks and airplanes.

On May 10, 1940, the main German offensive was launched against France. Belgium and the Netherlands were simultaneously attacked. According to plan, British and French forces advanced to aid the Belgians. At this point the Germans departed from the World War I strategy by launching a surprise armored attack through Luxembourg and the Ardennes Forest (considered by the British and French to be impassable for tanks). The Dutch could offer no real resistance and collapsed in four days. Paris fell to the Germans in mid-June.

The German invasion of Russia began June 22, 1941. The Germans surrounded the city of Leningrad (although they never managed to actually capture it) and came within about 25 miles of Moscow. In November the enemy actually entered the suburbs, but then the long supply lines, early winter, and Russian resistance (strong despite heavy losses) brought the invasion to a halt. During the winter a Russian counterattack pushed the Germans back from Moscow and saved the capital.

THE ALLIED OFFENSIVE

The German forces launched a second offensive in the summer of 1942. At Stalingrad the Germans were stopped. On January 31, 1943, the German commander surrendered the remnants of his army. From then on the Russians were almost always on the offensive.

As the Americans (who entered the war in 1941), the British, and other Allied forces advanced into Germany, the Russians attacked from the east. While the Russian armies were fighting their way into Berlin, Hitler committed suicide in the ruins of the bunker where he had spent the last days of the war. On May 7, 1945, Germany surrendered.

On August 6, 1945, the atomic bomb was dropped by a single plane on Hiroshima and an entire city disappeared, with the instantaneous loss of 70,000 lives. In time many other persons died from radiation poisoning and other effects. Since no surrender was received, a second bomb was dropped on Nagasaki, obliterating that city. Even the most fanatical of the Japanese leaders saw what was happening and surrender came quickly.

PEACE CONFERENCES

At the Casablanca Conference (1943), Churchill and Roosevelt discussed the occupation and demilitarization of Germany. They also laid the foundation for a post-war organization—the United Nations—which like the earlier League of Nations was supposed to help regulate international relations, keep the peace, and ensure friendly cooperation among the nations of the world.

Arrangements for the United Nations were confirmed at the Yalta Conference (1945): the large powers (the United States, France, Great Britain, the Soviet Union, and China) would predominate in the Security Council, where they would have permanent seats together with six other powers elected from time to time from among the other members of the U.N. Consent of all the permanent members was necessary for any action to be taken by the Security Council (thus giving the large powers a veto). The General Assembly was to include all 50 members of the U.N.

The Cold War

NATO

In April 1949, the North Atlantic Treaty Organization was signed by the United States, Canada, Great Britain, and nine European nations. The signatories pledged that an attack against one would be considered an attack against all. The Soviets formed the Warsaw Treaty Organization in 1955 to counteract NATO.

THE FALL OF COMMUNISM

Joseph Stalin died in March 1953. Eventually a little-known party functionary, Nikita Khrushchev, became Communist Party General Secretary in 1954. Khrushchev's policy of relaxing the regime of terror and oppression of the Stalin years became known as "The Thaw," after the title of a novel by Ilya Ehrenburg.

Following the loss of face sustained by Russia as a result of the Cuban Missile Crisis and the failure of Khrushchev's domestic agricultural policies, he was forced out of the party leadership and lived in retirement in Moscow until his death in 1971.

Krushchev and his successors permitted somewhat greater freedom in literary and artistic matters and even allowed some political criticism. Controls were maintained, however, and sometimes were tightened. Anti-semitism was also still present, and Soviet Jews were long denied permission to emigrate to Israel.

Mikhail Gorbachev (General Secretary of the Communist Party of the Soviet Union, 1985–1991; President of the Soviet Union, 1990–1991) carried out a further relaxation of the internal regime. Gorbachev pushed disarmament and detente in foreign relations, and attempted a wide range of internal reforms known as *perestroika* ("restructuring").

Occupied with domestic economic concerns, Gorbachev de-emphasized Soviet concerns in eastern Europe. This was first felt in Poland which, because of the Solidarity labor union, already had an effective opposition movement. Poland became the first eastern European nation to shift from communism to democracy through free elections held in June 1989.

In August 1989, Hungary opened its borders with Austria, and the following October the Communists reorganized under the Socialist banner. Hungary then proclaimed itself a "free republic." The opening of its borders provided a route to the West for thousands of East Germans to cross into Hungary. On November 1, the East German government opened the border with Czechoslovakia and eight days later, on November 9, 1989, the Berlin Wall fell. On December 6, a non-Communist was elected head of state. Large demonstrations demanded reunification, and by October 1990 Germany was reunified.

Gorbachev resigned in 1991, and Boris Yeltsin assumed control over the collapsing Soviet Union, which would later become known as the Commonwealth of Independent States, with Yeltsin as Russia's President.

Change in Western Europe

THE EURO

The Treaty on European Union (1991), also known as the Maastricht Treaty, established the European Union out of the European Community to encourage a closer integration of Europe. Twelve member states in the European Union agreed to freeze the exchange rates on their currencies and tie their value to a new European-wide monetary unit, the "euro." However, the new monetary unit did not win universal acceptance, particularly after the value of the "euro" plummeted below that of the U.S. dollar. Several states claimed the right to "opt out" of using the new currency.

UNITED STATES HISTORY

The Colonial Period

THE AGE OF EXPLORATION

The Treaty of Tordesillas (1494) drew a line dividing the land in the New World between Spain and Portugal. Lands east of the line were Portuguese. As a result, Brazil eventually became a Portuguese colony, while Spain maintained claims to the rest of the Americas.

Spain administered its new holdings as an autocratic, rigidly controlled empire in which everything was to benefit the parent country. The Spaniards developed a system of large manors or estates (encomiendas), with Indian slaves ruthlessly managed for the benefit of the Spanish adventurers, known as conquistadores. The encomienda system was later replaced by the similar but somewhat milder hacienda system. As the Indian population died from overwork and European diseases, Spaniards began importing African slaves to supply their labor needs.

THE BEGINNINGS OF COLONIZATION

The Virginia Company of London settled Jamestown in 1607. It became the first permanent English settlement in North America. During the early years of Jamestown, the majority of the settlers died of starvation, various diseases, or hostile actions by Native Americans. The colony's survival remained in doubt for a number of years.

Impressed by the potential profits from tobacco growing, King James I was determined to have Virginia for himself. In 1624, he revoked the London Company's charter and made Virginia a royal colony. This pattern was followed throughout colonial history; both company colonies and proprietary colonies tended eventually to become royal colonies.

Many Englishmen came from England for religious reasons. For the most part, these fell into two groups, Puritans and Separatists. Though similar in many respects to the Puritans, the Separatists believed the Church of England was beyond saving and so felt they must separate from it.

Led by William Bradford, a group of Separatists departed in 1620, having obtained from the London Company a charter to settle just south of the Hudson River. Driven by storms, their ship, the *Mayflower*, made landfall at Cape Cod in Massachusetts. This, however, put them outside the jurisdiction of any established government; before going ashore they drew up and signed the Mayflower Compact, establishing a foundation for orderly government based on the consent of the governed. After a number of years of hard work, they were able to buy out the investors who had originally financed their voyage, and thus gain greater autonomy.

The Puritans were far more numerous than the Separatists. Charles I determined in 1629 to persecute the Puritans aggressively and to rule without the Puritan-dominated Parliament.

In 1629, they chartered a joint-stock company called the Massachusetts Bay Company. The charter neglected to specify where the company's headquarters should be located. Taking advantage of this unusual omission, the Puritans determined to make their headquarters in the colony itself, 3,000 miles from meddlesome royal officials.

Puritans saw their colony not as a place to do whatever might strike one's fancy, but as a place to serve God and build His kingdom. Dissidents would only be tolerated insofar as they did not interfere with the colony's mission. One such dissident was Roger Williams. When his activities became disruptive he was asked to leave the colony. He fled to the wilderness around

Narragansett Bay, bought land from the Indians, and founded the settlement of Providence in 1636. Another dissident was Anne Hutchinson, who openly taught things contrary to Puritan doctrine. She was banished from the colony. She also migrated to the area around Narragansett Bay and with her followers founded Portsmouth in 1638.

The American Revolution

THE COMING OF THE AMERICAN REVOLUTION

In 1764, George Grenville pushed through Parliament the Sugar Act (also known as the Revenue Act), which aimed at raising revenue by taxing goods imported by the Americans. The Stamp Act (1765) imposed a direct tax on Americans for the first time. It required Americans to purchase revenue stamps on everything from newspapers to legal documents, and would have created an impossible drain on hard currency in the colonies.

Americans reacted first with restrained and respectful petitions and pamphlets in which they pointed out that "taxation without representation is tyranny." From there, resistance progressed to stronger protests that eventually became violent. In October 1765, delegates from nine colonies met as the Stamp Act Congress, and passed moderate resolutions against the act, asserting that Americans could not be taxed without the consent of their representatives.

In March 1766 Parliament repealed the Stamp Act. At the same time, however, it passed the Declaratory Act, which claimed the power to tax or make laws for the Americans "in all cases whatsoever." In 1766, Parliament passed a program of taxes on items imported into the colonies. These taxes came to be known as the Townsend duties, named after Chancellor of the Exchequer, Charles Townsend.

American reaction was at first slow, but the sending of troops aroused them to resistance. Nonimportation was again instituted, and soon British merchants were calling on Parliament to repeal the acts. In March 1770, Parliament repealed all of the taxes except that on tea, which was retained to prove Parliament had the right to tax the colonies if it so desired.

A relative peace was brought to an end by the Tea Act of 1773. In desperate financial condition—partially because the Americans were buying smuggled Dutch tea rather than the taxed British product—the British East

India Company sought and obtained from Parliament concessions that allowed it to ship tea directly to the colonies rather than only by way of Britain. The result would be that East India Company tea, even with the tax, would be cheaper than smuggled Dutch tea. The colonists would thus, it was hoped, buy the tea, tax and all. The East India Company would be saved, and the Americans would be tacitly accepting Parliament's right to tax them. The Americans, however, proved resistant to this approach; rather than seem to admit Parliament's right to tax, they vigorously resisted the cheaper tea. Various methods, including tar and feathers, were used to prevent the collection of the tax on tea. In most ports, Americans did not allow the tea to be landed.

In Boston, however, pro-British Governor Thomas Hutchinson forced a confrontation by ordering Royal Navy vessels to prevent the tea ships from leaving the harbor. After 20 days, this would, by law, result in the cargoes being sold at auction and the tax paid. The night before the time was to expire, December 16, 1773, Bostonians thinly disguised as Native Americans boarded the ships and threw the tea into the harbor.

The British responded with four acts collectively titled the Coercive Acts (1774), in which they strengthened their control over the colonists. The First Continental Congress (1774) met in response to these acts. The Congress called for strict nonimportation and rigorous preparation of local militia companies.

THE WAR FOR INDEPENDENCE

British troops were sent to Massachusetts, which was officially declared to be in a state of rebellion. Orders were sent to General Gage to arrest the leaders of the resistance, or failing that, to provoke any sort of confrontation that would allow him to turn British military might loose on the Americans. The movement of his troops toward Concord was detected by the Americans, and the news was spread throughout the countryside by dispatch riders Paul Revere and William Dawes.

In Lexington, about 70 Minutemen (militiamen trained to respond at a moment's notice) awaited the British on the village green. A shot was fired (it is unknown what side fired first), and then the British opened fire and charged. Casualties occurred on both sides.

The following month the Americans tightened the noose around Boston by fortifying Breed's Hill (a spur of Bunker Hill). The British determined to remove them by a frontal attack. Twice the British were thrown back, but they finally succeeded when the Americans ran out of ammunition. Over a thousand British soldiers were killed or wounded in what turned out to be the bloodiest battle of the war (June 17, 1775), yet the British had gained very little and remained bottled up in Boston.

Congress put George Washington (1732–1799) in charge of the army, called for more troops, and adopted the "Olive Branch Petition," which pleaded with King George III to intercede with Parliament to restore peace. However, the king gave his approval to the Prohibitory Act, declaring the colonies in rebellion and no longer under his protection. Preparations were made for full-scale war against America.

In 1776, two committees were formed to establish independence and a national government. One was to work out a framework for a national government. The other was to draft a statement of the reasons for declaring independence. The statement, called the Declaration of Independence, was primarily the work of Thomas Jefferson (1743–1826) of Virginia. It was a restatement of political ideas by then commonplace in America and showed why the former colonists felt justified in separating from Great Britain. It was formally adopted by Congress on July 4, 1776.

The British landed that summer at New York City. Washington, who had anticipated this move, was waiting there for them. However, the undertrained, underequipped, and badly outnumbered American army was no match for the British. They were forced to retreat, and by December what was left of Washington's army had made it into Pennsylvania.

Washington, with his small army melting away as demoralized soldiers deserted, decided on a bold stroke. On Christmas night 1776, his army crossed the Delaware River and struck the Hessians at Trenton. The Hessians, still groggy from their hard-drinking Christmas party, were easily defeated. A few days later, Washington defeated a British force at Princeton. Much of New Jersey was regained from the British, and Washington's army was saved from disintegration.

Hoping to weaken Britain, France began making covert shipments of arms to the Americans early in the war. Shipments from France were vital for the Americans. The American victory at Saratoga convinced the French to join openly in the war against England. Eventually the Spanish (1779) and the Dutch (1780) joined as well.

The final agreement became known as the Treaty of Paris of 1783. Its terms stipulated the following: 1) The United States was recognized as an independent nation by the major European powers, including Britain; 2) Its western boundary was set at the Mississippi River; 3) Its southern boundary was set at 31° north latitude (the northern boundary of Florida); 4) Britain retained Canada, but had to surrender Florida to Spain; 5) Private British creditors would be free to collect any debts owed by United States citizens; 6) Congress was to recommend that the states restore confiscated loyalist property.

The Creation of New Governments

THE ARTICLES OF CONFEDERATION

The Articles of Confederation, adopted in 1777, provided for a unicameral Congress in which each state would have one vote, as had been the case in the Continental Congress. Executive authority under the articles would be vested in a committee of 13, with one member from each state. In order to amend the articles, the unanimous consent of all the states was required.

The Articles of Confederation government was empowered to make war, make treaties, determine the amount of troops and money each state should contribute to the war effort, settle disputes between states, admit new states to the Union, and borrow money. It was not empowered to levy taxes, raise troops, or regulate commerce.

THE UNITED STATES CONSTITUTION

As time went on, the inadequacy of the Articles of Confederation became increasingly apparent. It was decided in 1787 to call for a convention of all the states to meet in Philadelphia for the purpose of revising the Articles of Confederation. George Washington was unanimously elected to preside, and the enormous respect that he commanded helped hold the convention together through difficult times.

One major crisis involved the number of state representatives. The delegates finally adopted a proposal known as the "Great Compromise," which provided for a presidency, two senators per state, and a House of Representatives with representation according to population.

Another major crisis involved North-South disagreement over the issue of slavery. Here also a compromise was reached. Each slave was to count as three-fifths of a person for purposes of apportioning representation and direct taxation on the states (the Three-Fifths Compromise). The federal government was prohibited from stopping the importation of slaves prior to 1808.

The delegates were also forced to compromise upon the nature of the presidency. The result was a strong presidency with control of foreign policy and the power to veto Congress's legislation. Should the president commit an actual crime, Congress would have the power to impeach him. Otherwise, the president would serve for a term of four years and be reelectable without limit. As a check to the possible excesses of democracy, the president was to be elected by an electoral college, in which each state would have the same number of electors as it did senators and representatives combined.

The new Constitution was to take effect when nine states, through special state conventions, had ratified it. By June 21, 1788, the required nine states had ratified, but the crucial states of New York and Virginia still held out. Ultimately, the promise of the addition of a bill of rights helped win the final states. In March 1789, George Washington was inaugurated as the nation's first president.

The New Nation

THE FEDERALIST ERA

George Washington received virtually all the votes of the presidential electors, and John Adams (1735–1826) received the next highest number, thus becoming the vice president. After a triumphant journey from Mount Vernon, Washington was inaugurated in New York City, the temporary seat of government.

In order to oppose the anti-federalists, ten amendments were ratified by the states by the end of 1791 and became the Bill of Rights. The first nine spelled out specific guarantees of personal freedoms, and the Tenth Amendment reserved to the states all those powers not specifically withheld or granted to the federal government.

Alexander Hamilton (1757–1804) interpreted the Constitution as having vested extensive powers in the federal government. This "implied powers" stance claimed that the government was given all powers that were not expressly denied to it. This is the "broad" interpretation.

Jefferson and James Madison (1751–1836) held the view that any action not specifically permitted in the Constitution was thereby prohibited. This is the "strict" interpretation, and its adherents opposed the establishment of Hamilton's national bank based on this view of government. The Jeffersonian supporters, primarily under the guidance of James Madison, began to organize political groups in opposition to Hamilton's program. They called themselves Democratic-Republicans or Jeffersonians.

The Federalists, as Hamilton's supporters were called, received their strongest support from the business and financial groups in the commercial centers of the Northeast and from the port cities of the South. The strength of the Democratic-Republicans lay primarily in the rural and frontier areas of the South and West.

Federalist candidate John Adams won the election of 1796. The elections in 1798 increased the Federalists' majorities in both houses of Congress and they used their "mandate" to enact legislation to stifle foreign influences. The Alien Act raised new hurdles in the path of immigrants trying to obtain citizenship, and the Sedition Act widened the powers of the Adams administration to muzzle its newspaper critics. Democratic-Republicans were convinced that the Alien and Sedition Acts were unconstitutional, but the process of deciding on the constitutionality of federal laws was as yet undefined.

THE JEFFERSONIAN ERA

Thomas Jefferson and Aaron Burr ran for the presidency on the Democratic-Republican ticket, though not together, against John Adams and Charles Pinckney for the Federalists. Both Jefferson and Burr received the same number of electoral votes, so the election went to the House of Representatives. After a lengthy deadlock, Alexander Hamilton threw his support to Jefferson. Burr had to accept the vice presidency, the result obviously intended by the electorate.

The Twelfth Amendment was adopted and ratified in 1804, ensuring that a tie vote between candidates of the same party could not again cause the confusion of the Jefferson-Burr affair.

Following the Constitutional mandate, the importation of slaves was stopped by law in 1808.

An American delegation purchased the trans-Mississippi territory from Napoleon for $15 million in April 1803 (The Louisiana Purchase), even though they had no authority to buy more than the city of New Orleans.

THE WAR OF 1812

Democratic-Republican James Madison won the election of 1808 over Federalist Charles Pinckney, but the Federalists gained seats in both houses of the Congress.

The Native American tribes of the Northwest and the Mississippi Valley were resentful of the government's policy of pressured removal to the West, and the British authorities in Canada exploited their discontent by encouraging border raids against the American settlements.

At the same time, the British interfered with American transatlantic shipping, including impressing sailors and capturing ships. On June 1, 1812, President Madison asked for a declaration of war and Congress complied.

After three years of inconclusive war, the Treaty of Ghent (1815) was signed. It provided for the acceptance of the status quo that had existed at the beginning of hostilities, and both sides restored their wartime conquests to the other.

THE MONROE DOCTRINE

As Latin American nations began declaring independence, British and American leaders feared that European governments would try to restore the former New World colonies to their erstwhile royal owners. In December 1823, President James Monroe (1758–1831) included in his annual message to Congress a statement that the peoples of the American hemisphere were "henceforth not to be considered as subjects for future colonization by any European powers."

THE MARSHALL COURT

Chief Justice John Marshall (1755–1835) delivered the majority opinions in a number of critical decisions in the formative years of the U.S. Supreme Court. These decisions served to strengthen the power of the federal government (and of the court itself) and restrict the powers of state governments. These are two key examples:

Marbury v. Madison (1803): This case established the Supreme Court's power of judicial review over federal legislation.

Gibbons v. Ogden (1824): In a case involving competing steamboat companies, Marshall ruled that commerce included navigation, and that only Congress has the right to regulate commerce among states. Thus, the state-granted monopoly was voided.

THE MISSOURI COMPROMISE

The Missouri Territory, the first to be organized from the Louisiana Purchase, applied for statehood in 1819. Since the Senate membership was evenly divided between slaveholding and free states at that time, the admission of a new state would give the voting advantage either to the North or to the South.

As the debate dragged on, the northern territory of Massachusetts applied for admission as the state of Maine. The two admission bills were combined, with Maine coming in free and Missouri coming in as a slave state. To make the package palatable for the House, a provision was added that prohibited slavery in the remainder of the Louisiana Territory north of the southern boundary of Missouri (latitude 36°30').

JACKSONIAN DEMOCRACY

Andrew Jackson (1767–1845), the candidate of a faction of the emerging Democratic party, won the election of 1828. Jackson was popular with the common man. He seemed to be the prototype of the self-made westerner: rough-hewn, violent, vindictive, with few ideas but strong convictions. He ignored his appointed cabinet officers and relied instead on the counsel of his "Kitchen Cabinet," a group of partisan supporters. He exercised his veto power more than any other president before him.

Jackson supported the removal of all Native American tribes to the west of the Mississippi River. The Indian Removal Act in 1830 provided for the federal enforcement of that process. One of the results of this policy was the Trail of Tears, the forced march under United States Army escort of thousands of Cherokee Indians to the west. A quarter or more of them, mostly women and children, perished on the journey.

THE NATIONAL BANK

The Bank of the United States had operated under the direction of Nicholas Biddle since 1823. He was a cautious man, and his conservative economic policy enforced conservatism among the state and private banks—which many bankers resented. In 1832 Jackson vetoed the Bank's renewal, and it ceased being a federal institution in 1836.

THE ANTI-SLAVERY MOVEMENT

In 1831, William Lloyd Garrison started his paper, *The Liberator*, and began to advocate total and immediate emancipation. He founded the New England Anti-slavery Society in 1832 and the American Anti-slavery Society in 1833. Theodore Weld pursued the same goals, but advocated more gradual means.

The movement split into two wings: Garrison's radical followers, and the moderates who favored "moral suasion" and petitions to Congress. In 1840, the Liberty party, the first national antislavery party, fielded a presidential candidate on the platform of "free soil" (nonexpansion of slavery into the new western territories).

THE ROLE OF MINORITIES

The women's rights movement focused on social and legal discrimination, and women like Lucretia Mott and Sojourner Truth became well-known figures on the speakers' circuit.

By 1850, 200,000 free blacks lived in the North and West. Their lives were restricted everywhere by prejudice, and "Jim Crow" laws separated the races.

MANIFEST DESTINY AND WESTWARD EXPANSION

Although the term "Manifest Destiny" was not actually coined until 1844, the belief that the American nation was destined to eventually expand all the way to the Pacific Ocean, and to possibly embrace Canada and Mexico, had been voiced for years by many who believed that American liberty and ideals should be shared with everyone possible, by force if necessary.

In the 1830s, American missionaries followed the traders and trappers to the Oregon country. They began to publicize the richness and beauty of the land. The result was the "Oregon Fever" of the 1840s, as thousands of settlers trekked across the Great Plains and the Rocky Mountains to settle the new Shangri-la.

Texas had been a state in the Republic of Mexico since 1822, following the Mexican revolution against Spanish control. The new Mexican government invited immigration from the north by offering land grants to Stephen Austin and other Americans. By 1835, approximately 35,000 "gringos" were homesteading on Texas land. The Mexican officials saw their power base eroding as the foreigners flooded in, so they moved to tighten control through restrictions on immigration and through tax increases. The Texans responded in 1836 by proclaiming independence and establishing a new republic. In 1845, after a series of failed attempts at annexation, Texas was admitted to the Union.

THE MEXICAN WAR

Though Mexico broke diplomatic relations with the United States immediately upon Texas's admission to the Union, there was still hope of a peaceful settlement. In the fall of 1845, President James K. Polk (1795–1849) sent John Slidell to Mexico City with a proposal for a peaceful settlement. Nothing came of these attempts at negotiation. Racked by coup and counter-coup, the Mexican government refused even to receive him.

Polk thereupon sent United States troops into the disputed territory. On April 5, 1846, Mexican troops attacked an American patrol. When news of the clash reached Washington, Polk sought and received from Congress a declaration of war against Mexico. Negotiated peace came about when the Treaty of Guadalupe-Hidalgo (February 2, 1848) was signed. Under the terms of the treaty, Mexico ceded to the United States the southwestern territory from Texas to the California coast.

Sectional Conflict and the Causes of the Civil War

THE CRISIS OF 1850

The Mexican War had no more than started when, on August 8, 1846, freshman Democratic Congressman David Wilmot of Pennsylvania introduced his Wilmot Proviso as a proposed amendment to a war appropriations bill. It stipulated that "neither slavery nor involuntary servitude shall ever exist" in any territory to be acquired from Mexico. It was passed by the House, and though rejected by the Senate, it was reintroduced again and again amid increasingly acrimonious debate.

One compromise proposal called for the extension of the 36° 30' line of the Missouri Compromise westward through the Mexican Cession to the Pacific, with territory north of the line to be closed to slavery. Another compromise solution was known as "popular sovereignty." It held that the residents of each territory should be permitted to decide for themselves whether to allow slavery.

In September 1849, having more than the requisite population and being in need of better government, California petitioned for admission to the Union as a free state. Southerners were furious. Long outnumbered in the House of Representatives, the South would now find itself, should California be admitted as a free state, also outvoted in the Senate.

At this point, the aged Henry Clay proposed a compromise. For the North, California would be admitted as a free state; the land in dispute between Texas and New Mexico would go to New Mexico; the issue of slavery in the New Mexico and Utah territories (all of the Mexican Cession outside of California) would be decided by popular sovereignty; and the slave trade would be abolished in the District of Columbia. For the South, a tougher Fugitive Slave Law would be enacted; the federal government would pay Texas's $10 million preannexation debt; Congress would declare that it did not have jurisdiction over the interstate slave trade and would promise not to abolish slavery itself in the District of Columbia.

THE KANSAS-NEBRASKA ACT

All illusion of sectional peace ended abruptly in 1854 when Senator Stephen A. Douglas of Illinois introduced a bill in Congress to organize the area west of Missouri and Iowa as the territories of Kansas and Nebraska on the basis of popular sovereignty. The Kansas-Nebraska Act aroused a storm of outrage in the North, where its repeal of the Missouri Compromise was seen as the breaking of a solemn agreement. It hastened the disintegration of the Whig party and divided the Democratic party along North-South lines.

Springing to life almost overnight as a result of northern fury at the Kansas-Nebraska Act, the Republican party included diverse elements whose sole unifying principle was the firm belief that slavery should be banned from all of the nation's territories, confined to the states where it already existed, and allowed to spread no further.

THE DRED SCOTT DECISION

In *Dred Scott v. Sanford* (1857), the Supreme Court attempted to finally settle the slavery question. The case involved a Missouri slave, Dred Scott, who had been encouraged by abolitionists to sue for his freedom on the basis that his owner had taken him to a free state, Illinois, for several years and then to a free territory, Wisconsin.

The Court attempted to read the extreme southern position on slavery into the Constitution, ruling not only that Scott had no standing to sue in federal court, but also that temporary residence in a free state, even for several years, did not make a slave free, and that the Missouri Compromise (already a dead letter by that time) had been unconstitutional all along because Congress did not have the authority to exclude slavery from a territory, nor did territorial governments have the right to prohibit slavery.

THE ELECTION OF 1860

As the 1860 presidential election approached, the Republicans met in Chicago, confident of victory and determined to do nothing to jeopardize their favorable position. Accordingly, they rejected as too radical front-running New York Senator William H. Seward in favor of Illinois favorite son Abraham Lincoln (1809–1865). The platform called for federal support of a transcontinental railroad and for the containment of slavery.

On election day, the voting went along strictly sectional lines. Lincoln led in popular votes, and though he was short of a majority in that category, he did have the needed majority in electoral votes and was elected.

THE SECESSION CRISIS

On December 20, 1860, South Carolina, by vote of a special convention, seceded from the Union. By February 1, 1861, six more states (Alabama, Georgia, Florida, Mississippi, Louisiana, and Texas) had followed suit.

Representatives of the seceded states met in Montgomery, Alabama, in February 1861 and declared themselves to be the Confederate States of America. They elected former Secretary of War and United States senator Jefferson Davis (1808–1889) of Mississippi as president, and Alexander Stephens (1812–1883) of Georgia as vice president.

Civil War and Reconstruction

HOSTILITIES BEGIN

In his inaugural address, Lincoln urged southerners to reconsider their actions, but warned that the Union was perpetual, that states could not secede, and that he would therefore hold the federal forts and installations in the South. Only two remained in federal hands: Fort Pickens, off Pensacola, Florida; and Fort Sumter, in the harbor of Charleston, South Carolina. Lincoln soon received word from Major Robert Anderson, commander of the small garrison at Sumter, that supplies were running low. Desiring to send in the needed supplies, Lincoln informed the governor of South Carolina of his intention, but promised that no attempt would be made to send arms, ammunition, or reinforcements unless southerners initiated hostilities.

Confederate General P.G.T. Beauregard, acting on orders from President Davis, demanded Anderson's surrender. Anderson said he would surrender if not resupplied. Knowing supplies were on the way, the Confederates opened fire at 4:30 a.m. on April 12, 1861. The next day, the fort surrendered.

The day following Sumter's surrender, Lincoln declared an insurrection and called for the states to provide 75,000 volunteers to put it down. In response to this, Virginia, Tennessee, North Carolina, and Arkansas declared their secession. The remaining slave states—Delaware, Kentucky, Maryland, and Missouri—wavered, but stayed with the Union.

The North enjoyed many advantages over the South. It had the majority of wealth and was vastly superior in industry. The North also had an advantage of almost three to one in manpower; over one-third of the South's population was composed of slaves, whom Southerners would not use as soldiers. Unlike the South, the North received large numbers of immigrants during the war. The North retained control of the United States Navy, and thus could command the sea and be able to blockade the South. Finally, the North enjoyed a much superior system of railroads.

The South did, however, have some advantages. It was vast in size, making it difficult to conquer. In addition, its troops would be fighting on their own ground, a fact that would give them the advantage of familiarity with the terrain, as well as the added motivation of defending their homes and families.

THE HOMESTEAD ACT AND THE MORRILL LAND GRANT ACT

Congress in 1862 passed two highly important acts dealing with domestic affairs in the North. The Homestead Act granted 160 acres of government land free of charge to any person who would farm it for at least five years. Much of the West was eventually settled under the provisions of this act. The Morrill Land Grant Act offered large amounts of the federal government's land to states that would establish "agricultural and mechanical" colleges. Many of the nation's large state universities were later founded under the provisions of this act.

THE EMANCIPATION PROCLAMATION

By mid-1862, Lincoln, under pressure from radical elements of his own party and hoping to create a favorable impression on foreign public opinion, determined to issue the Emancipation Proclamation, which declared free all slaves in areas still in rebellion as of January 1, 1863. At Seward's recommendation, Lincoln waited to announce the proclamation until the North should win some sort of victory. This was provided by the Battle of Antietam (September 17, 1862).

NORTHERN VICTORY

Lincoln ran on the ticket of the National Union party, essentially the Republican party with loyal or "War" Democrats. His vice-presidential candidate was Andrew Johnson (1808–1875), a loyal Democrat from Tennessee.

In September 1864, word came that General William Sherman (1820–1891) had taken Atlanta. The capture of this vital southern rail and manufacturing center brought an enormous boost to northern morale. Along with other northern victories that summer and fall, it ensured a resounding election victory for Lincoln and the continuation of the war to complete victory for the North.

General Robert E. Lee (1807–1870) abandoned Richmond on April 3, 1865 and attempted to escape with what was left of his army. Pursued by Ulysses S. Grant (1822–1885), he was cornered and forced to surrender at Appomattox, Virginia on April 9, 1865. Other Confederate armies still holding out in various parts of the South surrendered over the next few weeks.

Lincoln did not live to receive news of the final surrenders. On April 14, 1865, he was shot in the back of the head while watching a play in Ford's Theater in Washington.

RECONSTRUCTION

In 1865, Congress created the Freedman's Bureau to provide food, clothing, and education, and generally look after the interests of former slaves. To restore legal governments in the seceded states, Lincoln developed a policy that made it relatively easy for southern states to enter the collateral process.

Congress passed a Civil Rights Act in 1866, declaring that all citizens born in the United States are, regardless of race, equal citizens under the law. It was later adopted as the Fourteenth Amendment to the Constitution.

President Andrew Johnson obeyed the letter but not the spirit of the Reconstruction acts, and Congress, angry at his refusal to cooperate, sought in vain for grounds to impeach him. In August 1867, in order to test its constitutionality, Johnson violated the Tenure of Office Act, which forbade the President from removing from office officials who had been approved by the Senate. The matter was not tested in the courts, however, but in Congress, where Johnson was impeached by the House of Representatives and came within one vote of being removed by the Senate.

THE FIFTEENTH AMENDMENT

In 1868, the Republicans nominated Ulysses S. Grant for president. His narrow victory prompted Republican leaders to decide that it would be politically expedient to give the vote to all blacks, Northern as well as Southern. For this purpose, the Fifteenth Amendment was drawn up and submitted to the states. Ironically, the idea was so unpopular in the North that it won the necessary three-fourths approval only with its ratification by southern states required to do so by Congress.

Industrialism, War, and the Progressive Era

THE ECONOMY

Captains of industry, such as John D. Rockefeller in oil, J. P. Morgan in banking, Gustavus Swift in meat processing, Andrew Carnegie in steel, and E. H. Harriman in railroads, put together major industrial empires.

In 1886, Samuel Gompers and Adolph Strasser put together a combination of national craft unions, called the American Federation of Labor, to represent labor's concerns with wages, hours, and safety conditions. Although militant in its use of the strike and in its demand for collective bargaining in labor contracts with large corporations, it did not promote violence or radicalism.

THE SPANISH-AMERICAN WAR

The Cuban revolt against Spain in 1895 threatened American business interests in Cuba. Sensational "yellow" journalism, and nationalistic statements from officials such as Assistant Secretary of the Navy Theodore Roosevelt (1858–1919), encouraged popular support for direct American military intervention on behalf of Cuban independence.

On March 27, 1897, President William McKinley (1843–1901) asked Spain to call an armistice, accept American mediation to end the war, and end the use of concentration camps in Cuba. Spain refused to comply. On April 21, Congress declared war on Spain with the objective of establishing Cuban independence (Teller Amendment). The first U.S. forces landed in Cuba on June 22, 1898 and by July 17 had defeated the Spanish forces. Spain ceded the Philippines, Puerto Rico, and Guam to the United States, in return for a payment of $20 million to Spain for the Philippines.

THEODORE ROOSEVELT AND PROGRESSIVE REFORMS

On September 6, 1901, while attending the Pan American Exposition in Buffalo, New York, President McKinley was shot by Leon Czolgosz, an anarchist. The president died on September 14. Theodore Roosevelt became the nation's 25th president, and at age 42, its youngest to date.

In accordance with the Antitrust Policy (1902), Roosevelt ordered the Justice Department to prosecute corporations pursuing monopolistic practices. Attorney General P. C. Knox first brought suit against the Northern Securities Company, a railroad holding corporation put together by J. P. Morgan, and then moved against Rockefeller's Standard Oil Company. By the time he left office in 1909, Roosevelt had indictments against 25 monopolies.

Roosevelt engineered the separation of Panama from Colombia and the recognition of Panama as an independent country. The Hay-Bunau-Varilla Treaty of 1903 granted the United States control of the canal zone in Panama for $10 million and an annual fee of $250,000, beginning nine years after ratification of the treaty by both parties. Construction of the Panama Canal began in 1904 and was completed in 1914.

In 1905, the African-American intellectual militant W.E.B. DuBois founded the Niagara Movement, which called for federal legislation to protect racial equality and for full rights of citizenship. The National Association for the Advancement of Colored People was organized in 1909.

A radical labor organization called the Industrial Workers of the World (I.W.W., or Wobblies; 1905–1924) was active in promoting violence and revolution. The I.W.W. organized effective strikes in the textile industry in 1912, and among a few western miners groups, but had little appeal to the average American worker. After the Red Scare of 1919, the government worked to smash the I.W.W. and deported many of its immigrant leaders and members.

THE WILSON PRESIDENCY

Democratic candidate Woodrow Wilson (1856–1924) was elected president in 1912. Before the outbreak of World War I in 1914, President Wilson, working with cooperative majorities in both houses of Congress, achieved much of the remaining progressive agenda, including lower tariff reform (Underwood-Simmons Act, 1913), the Sixteenth Amendment (graduated income tax, 1913), the Seventeenth Amendment (direct election of senators, 1913), the Federal Reserve banking system (which provided regulation and flexibility to monetary policy, 1913), the Federal Trade Commission (to investigate unfair business practices, 1914), and the Clayton Antitrust Act (improving the old Sherman Act and protecting labor unions and farm cooperatives from prosecution, 1914).

World War I

THE ROAD TO WAR IN EUROPE

When World War I broke out in Europe, Wilson issued a proclamation of American neutrality (August 4, 1914). The value of American trade with the Central Powers fell from $169 million in 1914 to almost nothing in 1916, but trade with the Allies rose from $825 million to $3.2 billion during the same period. In addition, the British and French had borrowed about $3.25 billion from American sources by 1917. The United States had become a major supplier of Allied munitions, food, and raw materials.

The sinking of the British liner *Lusitania* off the coast of Ireland on May 7, 1915, with the loss of 1,198 lives, including 128 Americans, brought strong protests from Wilson. Secretary of State William Jennings Bryan, who believed Americans should stay off belligerent ships, resigned rather than insist on questionable neutral rights and was replaced by Robert Lansing.

The British intercepted a secret message from the German foreign secretary, Arthur Zimmermann, to the German minister in Mexico, and turned it over to the United States on February 24, 1917. The Germans proposed that, in the event of a war between the United States and Germany, Mexico attack the United States. After the war, the "lost territories" of Texas, New Mexico, and Arizona would be returned to Mexico. When the telegram was released to the press on March 1, many Americans became convinced that war with Germany was necessary. A declaration of war against Germany was signed by Wilson on April 6.

MOBILIZING THE HOME FRONT

The Espionage Act of 1917 provided for fines and imprisonment for persons who made false statements which aided the enemy, incited rebellion in the military, or obstructed recruitment or the draft. Printed matter advocating treason or insurrection could be excluded from the mail. The Sedition Act of May 1918 forbade any criticism of the government, flag, or uniform, even if there were not detrimental consequences, and expanded the mail exclusion. The laws were applied in ways that trampled on civil liberties. The Espionage Act was upheld by the Supreme Court in the case of *Shenk v. United States* in 1919. The opinion, written by Justice Oliver Wendell Holmes, Jr., stated that Congress could limit free speech when the words represented a "clear and present danger," and that a person cannot cry "fire" in a crowded theater.

WILSON'S FOURTEEN POINTS

From the time of the American entry into the war, Wilson had maintained that the war would make the world safe for democracy. In an address to Congress on January 8, 1918, he presented his specific peace plan in the form of the Fourteen Points. The first five points called for open rather than secret peace treaties, freedom of the seas, free trade, arms reduction, and a fair adjustment of colonial claims. The next eight points were concerned with the national aspirations of various European peoples and the adjustment of boundaries. The fourteenth point, which he considered the most important and had espoused as early as 1916, called for a "general association of nations" to preserve the peace.

The Roaring Twenties

SOCIAL CONFLICTS

There had been calls for immigration restriction since the late nineteenth century, but the only major restriction imposed on immigration had been the Chinese Exclusion Act of 1882. Labor leaders believed that immigrants depressed wages and impeded unionization. Some progressives believed that they created social problems. In June 1917, Congress, over Wilson's veto, had imposed a literacy test for immigrants and excluded many Asian nationalities. In 1921, Congress passed the Emergency Quota Act. In practice, the law admitted about as many as wanted to come from such nations as Britain, Ireland, and Germany, while severely restricting Italians, Greeks, Poles, and eastern European Jews. It became effective in 1922 and reduced the number of immigrants annually to about 40 percent of the 1921 total. Congress then passed the National Origins Act of 1924, which further reduced the number of southern and eastern Europeans, and cut the annual immigration to 20 percent of the 1921 figure. In 1927, the annual maximum was reduced to 150,000.

On Thanksgiving Day in 1915, the Knights of the Ku Klux Klan was founded by William J. Simmons. Its purpose was to intimidate African Americans, who were experiencing an apparent rise in status during World War I. The Klan's methods of repression included cross burnings, tar and featherings, kidnappings, lynchings, and burnings. The Klan was not a political party, but it endorsed and opposed candidates and exerted considerable control over elections and politicians in at least nine states.

PROHIBITION

In 1920 the Eighteenth Amendment was passed; it prohibited the manufacture, transportation, and sale of alcoholic beverages in the United States. Speakeasies became popular, and bootlegging became a profitable underground business. Prohibition was repealed in 1933, with the ratification of the Twenty-First Amendment.

OTHER IMPORTANT ISSUES

Fundamentalist Protestants, under the leadership of William Jennings Bryan, began a campaign in 1921 to prohibit the teaching of evolution in the schools, and thus protect belief in the literal biblical account of creation. The idea was especially well received in the South.

The Nineteenth Amendment, providing for women's suffrage, which had been defeated in the Senate in 1918, was approved by Congress in 1919. It was ratified by the states in time for the election of 1920.

The Great Depression and the New Deal

THE CRASH

There were already signs of recession before the market crash in 1929. The farm economy, which involved almost 25 percent of the population, had been depressed throughout the decade. Coal, railroads, and New England textiles had not been prosperous. After 1927, new construction declined and auto sales began to sag. Many workers had been laid off before the crash of 1929.

Stock prices increased throughout the decade. The boom in prices and volume of sales was especially active after 1925, and was intensive during 1928–29. Careful investors, realizing that stocks were overpriced, began to sell to take their profits. During October 1929, prices declined as more stock was sold. On "Black Thursday," October 24, 1929, almost 13 million shares were traded; this was a large number for that time, and prices fell precipitously. Investment banks tried to boost the market by buying, but on October 29, "Black Tuesday," the market fell about 40 points, with 16.5 million shares traded.

HOOVER'S DEPRESSION POLICIES

Herbert Hoover (1874–1964) was elected to the presidency in 1928. The Agricultural Marketing Act, which created the Federal Farm Board, was passed in June 1929, before the market crash. It had a revolving fund of $500 million to lend agricultural cooperatives to buy commodities, such as wheat and cotton, and hold them for higher prices.

The Hawley-Smoot Tariff was passed in June 1930. It raised duties on both agricultural and manufactured imports.

The Reconstruction Finance Corporation was chartered by Congress in 1932, in order to loan money to railroads, banks, and other financial institutions. It prevented the failure of basic firms, on which many other elements of the economy depended, but was criticized by some as relief for the rich.

The Federal Home Loan Bank Act was passed in July 1932. It created home-loan banks, which made loans to building and loan associations, savings banks, and insurance companies to help them avoid foreclosures on homes.

THE FIRST NEW DEAL

Franklin D. Roosevelt (1882–1945), governor of New York, easily defeated Hoover in the election of 1932.

When Roosevelt was inaugurated on March 4, 1933, the American economic system seemed to be on the verge of collapse. Roosevelt assured the nation that "the only thing we have to fear is fear itself," called for a special session of Congress to convene on March 9, and asked for "broad executive powers to wage war against the emergency." Two days later, he closed all banks and forbade the export of gold or the redemption of currency in gold.

The special session of Congress, from March 9 to June 16, 1933, passed a great body of legislation which has left a lasting mark on the nation. The period has been referred to ever since as the "Hundred Days." Historians have divided Roosevelt's legislation into the First New Deal (1933–1935) and a new wave of programs beginning in 1935 called the Second New Deal.

The Emergency Banking Relief Act was passed on March 9, the first day of the special session. The law provided additional funds for banks from the RFC and the Federal Reserve, allowed the Treasury to open sound banks after 10 days and to merge or liquidate unsound ones, and forbade the hoarding or export of gold. Roosevelt, on March 12, assured the public of the soundness of the banks in the first of many "fireside chats," or radio addresses. People believed him, and most banks were soon open with more deposits than withdrawals.

The Banking Act of 1933, or the Glass-Steagall Act, established the Federal Deposit Insurance Corporation (FDIC) to insure individual deposits in commercial banks, and separated commercial banking from the more speculative activity of investment banking.

The Federal Emergency Relief Act appropriated $500 million for aid to the poor to be distributed by state and local governments. It also established the Federal Emergency Relief Administration under Harry Hopkins (1890–1946).

The Civilian Conservation Corps enrolled 250,000 young men aged 18 to 24 from families on relief to go to camps where they worked on flood control, soil conservation, and forest projects under the direction of the War Department.

The Public Works Administration had $3.3 billion to distribute to state and local governments for building projects such as schools, highways, and hospitals.

The Agricultural Adjustment Act of 1933 created the Agricultural Adjustment Administration (AAA). Farmers agreed to reduce production of principal farm commodities and were paid a subsidy in return. Farm prices increased, but tenants and sharecroppers were hurt when owners took land out of cultivation. The law was repealed in January 1936 on the grounds that the processing tax was not constitutional.

The National Industrial Recovery Act was viewed as the cornerstone of the recovery program. It sought to stabilize the economy by preventing extreme competition, labor-management conflicts, and overproduction. A board composed of industrial and labor leaders in each industry or business drew up a code for that industry which set minimum prices, minimum wages, maximum work hours, production limits, and quotas. The antitrust laws were temporarily suspended.

The economy improved but did not recover. The GNP, money supply, salaries, wages, and farm income rose. Unemployment dropped from about 25 percent of nonfarm workers in 1933 to about 20.1 percent, or 10.6 million, in 1935.

THE SECOND NEW DEAL

The Works Progress Administration (WPA) was started in May 1935, following the passage of the Emergency Relief Appropriations Act of April 1935. The WPA employed people from the relief rolls for 30 hours of work a week at pay double that of the relief payment but less than private employment.

The Rural Electrification Administration (REA) was created in May 1935 to provide loans and WPA labor to electric cooperatives so they could build lines into rural areas not served by private companies.

The Social Security Act was passed in August 1935. It established a retirement plan for persons over age 65, which was to be funded by a tax on wages paid equally by employee and employer. The first benefits, ranging from $10 to $85 per month, were paid in 1942. Another provision of the act forced the states to initiate unemployment insurance programs.

LABOR UNIONS

The passage of the National Labor Relations or Wagner Act in 1935 resulted in a massive growth of union membership, but at the expense of bitter conflict within the labor movement. The American Federation of Labor was made up primarily of craft unions. Some leaders wanted to unionize the mass-production industries, such as automobiles and rubber, with industrial unions. In November 1935, the Committee for Industrial Organization was formed to unionize basic industries, presumably within the AFL. President William Green of the AFL ordered the CIO to disband in January 1936. When the rebels refused, they were expelled by the AFL. The insurgents then reorganized the CIO as the independent Congress of Industrial Organizations.

World War II

THE AMERICAN RESPONSE TO THE WAR IN EUROPE

In August 1939, Roosevelt created the War Resources Board to develop a plan for industrial mobilization in the event of war. The next month, he established the Office of Emergency Management in the White House to centralize mobilization activities.

Roosevelt officially proclaimed the neutrality of the United States on September 5, 1939. The Democratic Congress, in a vote that followed party lines, passed a new Neutrality Act in November. It allowed the cash-and-carry sale of arms and short-term loans to belligerents, but forbade American ships to trade with belligerents or Americans to travel on belligerent ships.

Roosevelt determined that to aid Britain in every way possible was the best way to avoid war with Germany. In September 1940, he signed an agreement to give Britain 50 American destroyers in return for a 99-year lease on air and naval bases in British territories in Newfoundland, Bermuda, and the Caribbean.

THE ROAD TO PEARL HARBOR

In late July 1941, the United States placed an embargo on the export of aviation gasoline, lubricants, and scrap iron and steel to Japan, and granted an additional loan to China. In December, the embargo was extended to include iron ore and pig iron, some chemicals, machine tools, and other products.

In October 1941, a new military cabinet headed by General Hideki Tojo took control of Japan. The Japanese secretly decided to make a final effort to negotiate, and to go to war if no solution was found by November 25. A new round of talks followed in Washington, but neither side would make a substantive change in its position. The Japanese gave final approval on December 1 for an attack on the United States.

The Japanese planned a major offensive to take the Dutch East Indies, Malaya, and the Philippines in order to obtain the oil, metals, and other raw materials they needed. At the same time, they would attack Pearl Harbor in Hawaii to destroy the American Pacific fleet to keep it from interfering with their plans.

At 7:55 a.m. on Sunday, December 7, 1941, the first wave of Japanese carrier-based planes attacked the American fleet in Pearl Harbor. A second wave followed at 8:50 a.m. The United States suffered the loss of two battleships sunk, six damaged and out of action, three cruisers and three destroyers sunk or damaged, and a number of lesser vessels destroyed or damaged. All of the 150 aircraft at Pearl Harbor were destroyed on the ground. Worst of all, 2,323 American servicemen were killed and about 1,100 were wounded. The Japanese lost 29 planes, five midget submarines, and one fleet submarine.

DECLARED WAR BEGINS

On December 8, 1941, Congress declared war on Japan, with one dissenting vote. On December 11, Germany and Italy declared war on the United States. Great Britain and the United States then established the Combined Chiefs of Staff, headquartered in Washington, to direct Anglo-American military operations.

On January 1, 1942, representatives of 26 nations met in Washington, D.C., and signed the Declaration of the United Nations, pledging themselves to the principles of the Atlantic Charter and promising not to make a separate peace with their common enemies.

THE HOMEFRONT

In *Korematsu v. United States* (1944), the Supreme Court upheld President Roosevelt's 1942 order that Issei (Japanese-Americans who had emigrated from Japan) and Nisei (native born Japanese-Americans) be relocated to concentration camps. The camps were closed in March 1946.

Roosevelt died on April 12, 1945, at Warm Springs, Georgia. Harry S. Truman (1884–1972), formerly a senator from Missouri and vice president of the United States, became president on April 12, 1945.

THE ATOMIC BOMB

The Manhattan Engineering District was established by the army engineers in August 1942 for the purpose of developing an atomic bomb (it eventually became known as the Manhattan Project). J. Robert Oppenheimer directed the design and construction of a transportable atomic bomb at Los Alamos, New Mexico. On July 16, 1945, the first atomic bomb was exploded at Alamogordo, New Mexico.

The *Enola Gay* dropped an atomic bomb on Hiroshima, Japan, on August 6, 1945, killing about 78,000 persons and injuring 100,000 more. On August 9, a second bomb was dropped on Nagasaki, Japan.

Japan surrendered on August 14, 1945. The formal surrender was signed on September 2.

The Post-War Era

THE COLD WAR AND CONTAINMENT

In February 1947, Great Britain notified the United States that it could no longer aid the Greek government in its war against Communist insurgents. The next month President Truman asked Congress for $400 million in military and economic aid for Greece and Turkey. In what became known as the "Truman Doctrine," he argued that the United States must support free peoples who were resisting Communist domination.

Secretary of State George C. Marshall proposed in June 1947 that the United States provide economic aid to help rebuild Europe. The following March, Congress passed the European Recovery Program, popularly known as the Marshall Plan, which provided more than $12 billion in aid.

ANTICOMMUNISM

On February 9, 1950, Senator Joseph R. McCarthy of Wisconsin stated that he had a list of known Communists who were working in the State Department. He later expanded his attacks. After making charges against the army, he was censured and discredited by the Senate in 1954.

KOREAN WAR

On June 25, 1950, North Korea invaded South Korea. President Truman committed U.S. forces, commanded by General Douglas MacArthur, but under United Nations auspices. By October, the U.N. forces (mostly American) had driven north of the 38th parallel, which divided North and South Korea. Chinese troops attacked MacArthur's forces on November 26, pushing them south of the 38th parallel, but by spring 1951, the U.N. forces had recovered their offensive.

In June 1953, an armistice was signed, leaving Korea divided along virtually the same boundary that had existed prior to the war.

EISENHOWER-DULLES FOREIGN POLICY

Dwight D. Eisenhower (1890–1969), elected president in 1952, chose John

Foster Dulles as secretary of state. Dulles talked of a more aggressive foreign policy, calling for "massive retaliation" and "liberation" rather than containment. He wished to emphasize nuclear deterrents rather than conventional armed forces.

After several years of nationalist war against French occupation, France, Great Britain, the Soviet Union, and China signed the Geneva Accords in July 1954, dividing Vietnam along the 17th parallel. The North would be under Ho Chi Minh and the South under Emperor Bao Dai. Elections were scheduled for 1956 to unify the country, but Ngo Dinh Diem overthrew Bao Dai and prevented the elections from taking place. The United States supplied economic aid to South Vietnam.

In January 1959, Fidel Castro overthrew the dictator of Cuba. Castro soon began criticizing the United States and moved closer to the Soviet Union, signing a trade agreement with the Soviets in February 1960. The United States prohibited the importation of Cuban sugar in October 1960, and broke off diplomatic relations in January 1961.

SPACE EXPLORATION

The launching of the Soviet space satellite *Sputnik* on October 4, 1957, created fear that America was falling behind technologically. Although the United States launched *Explorer I* on January 31, 1958, the concern continued. In 1958, Congress established the National Aeronautics and Space Administration (NASA) to coordinate research and development, and passed the National Defense Education Act to provide grants and loans for education.

CIVIL RIGHTS

Eisenhower completed the formal integration of the armed forces, desegregated public services in Washington, D.C., naval yards, and veterans' hospitals, and appointed a Civil Rights Commission.

In *Brown v. Board of Education of Topeka* (1954), NAACP lawyer Thurgood Marshall challenged the doctrine of "separate but equal" (*Plessy v. Ferguson*, 1896). The Court declared that separate educational facilities were inherently unequal. In 1955, the Court ordered states to integrate "with all deliberate speed."

On December 11, 1955, in Montgomery, Alabama, Rosa Parks, a black woman, was arrested when she refused to give up her seat on a city bus to a white person. Under the leadership of Martin Luther King (1929–1968), an African-American pastor, African-Americans of Montgomery organized a bus boycott that lasted for a year, until, in December 1956, the Supreme Court refused to review a lower court ruling that stated that separate but equal was no longer legal.

In February 1960, four African-American students who had been denied service staged a sit-in at a segregated Woolworth lunch counter in Greensboro, North Carolina. This inspired sit-ins elsewhere in the South and led to the formation of the Student Nonviolent Coordinating Committee (SNCC), one of whose chief aims would be to end segregation in public accommodations.

The New Frontier, Vietnam, and Social Upheaval

KENNEDY'S "NEW FRONTIER"

Democratic Senator John F. Kennedy (1917–1963) won the election of 1960. The Justice Department, under Attorney General Robert F. Kennedy, began to push for civil rights, including desegregation of interstate transportation in the South, integration of schools, and supervision of elections. President Kennedy presented a comprehensive civil rights bill to Congress in 1963. With the bill held up in Congress, 200,000 people marched and demonstrated on its behalf, and Martin Luther King gave his "I Have a Dream" speech.

CUBAN MISSILE CRISIS

Under Eisenhower, the Central Intelligence Agency had begun training some 2,000 men for an invasion of Cuba to overthrow Fidel Castro. On April 19, 1961, this force invaded at the Bay of Pigs, but was pinned down and forced to surrender. Some 1,200 men were captured.

On October 14, 1962, a U-2 reconnaissance plane brought photographic evidence that missile sites were being built in Cuba. Kennedy, on October 22, announced a blockade of Cuba and called on Soviet Premier Nikita Khrushchev (1894–1971) to dismantle the missile bases and remove all weapons capable of attacking the United States from Cuba. Six days later, Khrushchev backed down, withdrew the missiles, and Kennedy lifted the blockade.

JOHNSON AND THE GREAT SOCIETY

On November 22, 1963, Kennedy was assassinated by Lee Harvey Oswald in Dallas, Texas; Oswald was killed two days later. Kennedy was succeeded by Lyndon B. Johnson (1908–1973).

The 1964 Civil Rights Act outlawed racial discrimination by employers and unions, created the Equal Employment Opportunity Commission to enforce the law, and eliminated the remaining restrictions on black voting.

Michael Harrington's *The Other America* (1962) showed that 20 to 25 percent of American families were living below the governmentally defined poverty line. The Economic Opportunity Act of 1964 sought to address the problem by establishing a Job Corps, community action programs, educational programs, work-study programs, job training, loans for small businesses and farmers, and Volunteers in Service to America (VISTA), a "domestic peace corps." The Office of Economic Opportunity administered many of these programs.

EMERGENCE OF BLACK POWER

In 1965, Martin Luther King announced a voter registration drive. With help from the federal courts, he dramatized his effort by leading a march from Selma to Montgomery, Alabama, between March 21 and 25. The Voting Rights Act of 1965 authorized the attorney general to appoint officials to register voters.

Seventy percent of African-Americans lived in city ghettos. In 1966, New York and Chicago experienced riots, and the following year there were riots in Newark and Detroit. The Kerner Commission, appointed to investigate the riots, concluded that they were directed at a social system that prevented African-Americans from getting good jobs and crowded them into ghettos.

On April 4, 1968, Martin Luther King was assassinated in Memphis by James Earl Ray (Ray, an escaped convict, pled guilty to the murder and was sentenced to 99 years). Riots in more than 100 cities followed.

VIETNAM

After the French defeat in 1954, the United States sent military advisors to South Vietnam to aid the government of Ngo Dinh Diem. The pro-Communist Vietcong forces gradually grew in strength, partly because Diem failed to follow through on promised reforms. They received support from North Vietnam, the Soviet Union, and China.

"Hawks" defended the president's policy and, drawing on the containment theory, said that the nation had the responsibility to resist aggression. If Vietnam should fall, it was said, all Southeast Asia would eventually go.

Antiwar demonstrations were attracting large crowds by 1967. "Doves" argued that the war was a civil war in which the United States should not meddle.

On January 31, 1968, the first day of the Vietnamese new year (Tet), the Vietcong attacked numerous cities and towns, American bases, and even Saigon. Although they suffered large losses, the Vietcong won a psychological victory, as American opinion began turning against the war.

THE NIXON CONSERVATIVE REACTION

Republican Richard M. Nixon (1913–1994), emphasizing stability and order, defeated Democratic nominee Hubert Humphrey by a margin of one percentage point.

The Nixon administration sought to block renewal of the Voting Rights Act and delay implementation of court-ordered school desegregation in Mississippi.

In 1969, Nixon appointed Warren E. Burger, a conservative, as chief justice. Although more conservative than the Warren court, the Burger court did declare the death penalty, as used at the time, unconstitutional in 1972, and struck down state antiabortion legislation in 1973.

The president turned to "Vietnamization," the effort to build up South Vietnamese forces while withdrawing American troops. In 1969, Nixon reduced American troop strength by 60,000, but at the same time ordered the bombing of Cambodia, a neutral country.

In the summer of 1972, negotiations between the United States and North Vietnam began in Paris. A few days before the 1972 presidential election, Henry Kissinger, the president's national security advisor, announced that "peace was at hand."

Nixon resumed the bombing of North Vietnam in December 1972, claiming that the North Vietnamese were not bargaining in good faith. In January 1973, the two sides reached a settlement in which the North Vietnamese retained control over large areas of the South and agreed to release American prisoners of war within 60 days. Nearly 60,000 Americans had been killed and 300,000 more wounded and the war had cost Americans $109 billion. On March 29, 1973, the last American combat troops left South Vietnam.

The North Vietnamese forces continued to push back the South Vietnamese, and in April 1975 Saigon fell to the North.

Watergate, Carter, and the New Conservatism

WATERGATE

Nixon, who had been renominated by the Republicans, won a landslide victory over the Democratic nominee, Senator George McGovern.

What became known as the Watergate crisis began during the 1972 presidential campaign. Early on the morning of June 17, a security officer for the Committee for the Re-election of the President, along with four other men, broke into Democratic headquarters at the Watergate apartment complex in Washington, D.C., and were caught while going through files and installing electronic eavesdropping devices.

In March 1974, a grand jury indicted some of Nixon's top aides and named Nixon an unindicted co-conspirator.

Meanwhile, the House Judiciary Committee televised its debate over impeachment. It charged the president with obstructing justice, misusing presidential power, and failing to obey the committee's subpoenas. Before the House began to debate impeachment, Nixon announced his resignation on August 8, 1974, to take effect at noon the following day. Gerald Ford (1913–) then became president.

Gerald Ford was in many respects the opposite of Nixon. Although a partisan Republican, he was well liked and free of any hint of scandal. Ford almost immediately encountered controversy when in September 1974 he offered to pardon Nixon. Nixon accepted the offer, although he admitted no wrongdoing and had not yet been charged with a crime.

CARTER'S MODERATE LIBERALISM

In 1976, the Democrats nominated James Earl Carter (1924–), formerly governor of Georgia, who ran on the basis of his integrity and lack of Washington connections. Carter narrowly defeated Ford in the election.

Carter offered amnesty to Americans who had fled the draft and gone to other countries during the Vietnam War. He established the Departments of Energy and Education and placed the civil service on a merit basis. He created a "superfund" for cleanup of chemical waste dumps, established controls over strip mining, and protected 100 million acres of Alaskan wilderness from development.

CARTER'S FOREIGN POLICY

Carter negotiated a controversial treaty with Panama, affirmed by the Senate in 1978, that provided for the transfer of ownership of the canal to Panama in 1999 and guaranteed its neutrality.

In 1978, Carter negotiated the Camp David Accords between Israel and Egypt. Israel promised to return occupied land in the Sinai to Egypt in exchange for Egyptian recognition, a process completed in 1982. An agreement to negotiate the Palestinian refugee problem proved ineffective.

THE IRANIAN CRISIS

In 1978, a revolution forced the shah of Iran to flee the country, replacing him with a religious leader, Ayatollah Ruhollah Khomeini (ca. 1900–1989). Because the United States had supported the shah with arms and money, the revolutionaries were strongly anti-American, calling the United States the "Great Satan."

After Carter allowed the exiled shah to come to the United States for medical treatment in October 1979, some 400 Iranians broke into the American embassy in Teheran on November 4, taking the occupants captive. They demanded that the shah be returned to Iran for trial and that his wealth be confiscated and given to Iran. Carter rejected these demands; instead, he froze Iranian assets in the United States and established a trade embargo against Iran.

After extensive negotiations with Iran, in which Algeria acted as an intermediary, the American hostages were freed on January 20, 1981.

ATTACKING BIG GOVERNMENT

Republican Ronald Reagan (1911–2004) defeated Carter by a large electoral majority in 1980.

Reagan placed priority on cutting taxes. His approach was based on "supply-side" economics, the idea that if government left more money in the hands of the people, they would invest rather then spend the excess on consumer goods. The results would be greater production, more jobs, and greater prosperity, and thus more income for the government despite lower tax rates. However, from a deficit of $59 billion in 1980, the federal budget was running $195 billion in the red by 1983.

Reagan ended ongoing antitrust suits against IBM and AT&T, thereby fulfilling his promise to reduce government interference with business.

IRAN-CONTRA

In 1985 and 1986, several Reagan officials sold arms to the Iranians in hopes of encouraging them to use their influence in getting American hostages in Lebanon released. Profits from these sales were then diverted to the Nicaraguan *contras*, i.e., militant opposition to the left-leaning elected government, in an attempt to get around congressional restrictions on funding the *contras*. The attorney general was forced to appoint a special prosecutor, and Congress held hearings on the affair in May 1987.

THE ELECTION OF 1988

Vice President George Bush (1924–) won the Republican nomination. Bush easily defeated Democrat Michael Dukakis, but the Republicans were unable to make any inroads in Congress.

OPERATION JUST CAUSE

Since coming to office, the Bush administration had been concerned that Panamanian dictator Manuel Noriega was providing an important link in the drug traffic between South America and the United States. After economic sanctions, diplomatic efforts, and an October 1989 coup failed to oust Noriega, Bush ordered 12,000 troops into Panama on December 20 for what became known as "Operation Just Cause." On January 3, 1990, Noriega surrendered to the Americans and was taken to the United States to stand trial on drug-trafficking charges. Found guilty in 1992, he was sentenced to 40 years.

PERSIAN GULF CRISIS

On August 2, 1990, Iraq invaded Kuwait, an act that Bush denounced as "naked aggression." The United States quickly banned most trade with Iraq, froze Iraq's and Kuwait's assets in the United States, and sent aircraft carriers to the Persian Gulf. On August 6, after the U.N. Security Council condemned the invasion, Bush ordered the deployment of air, sea, and land forces to Saudi Arabia, dubbing the operation "Desert Shield."

On February 23, the allied air assault began. Four days later, Bush announced that Kuwait had been liberated and he ordered offensive operations to cease. The United Nations established the terms for the cease-fire, which Iraq accepted on April 6.

Road to the Twenty-First Century

THE ELECTION OF 1992

William Jefferson Clinton (1946–) won 43 percent of the popular vote and 370 electoral votes while Bush won 37 percent of the popular vote and 168 electoral votes. Although he won no electoral votes, Independent candidate Ross Perot (1930–) gained 19 percent of the popular vote.

DOMESTIC AFFAIRS

The North American Free Trade Agreement (NAFTA), negotiated by the Bush administration, eliminated most tariffs and other trade barriers between the United States, Canada, and Mexico. Passed by Congress and signed by Clinton in 1993, NAFTA became law in January 1994.

In October 1993, the Clinton administration proposed legislation to reform the health care system, which included universal coverage with a guaranteed benefits package, managed competition through health care alliances which would bargain with insurance companies, and employer mandates to provide health insurance for employees. Opposed by most Republicans, small business, and insurance and medical-business interests, the Democrats dropped their attempt at compromise legislation in September 1994.

IMPEACHMENT AND ACQUITTAL

Clinton was criticized for alleged wrongdoing in connection with the Whitewater real estate development, in which he had been an investor with James B. and Susan McDougal, owners of a failed savings and loan institution, while governor of Arkansas. After Congress renewed the independent counsel law, a three-judge panel appointed Kenneth W. Starr to the new role of "independent prosecutor." The Starr investigation yielded massive findings in late 1998, roughly midway into Clinton's second term, including information on an adulterous affair that Clinton had had with Monica Lewinsky, a White House intern. It was on charges stemming from this report that Clinton was impeached by the House of Representatives in December 1998 for perjury and obstruction of justice. The Senate acquitted him in February 1999, with most Senators voting along party lines.

CONTINUING CRISIS IN THE BALKANS

During Clinton's second term, continued political unrest and civil war in the Balkans continued to be a major foreign policy challenge. In 1999, the Serbian government attacked ethnic Albanians in Kosovo, a province of Serbia. In response, NATO forces, led by the United States, bombed Serbia. Several weeks of bombing forced Serbian forces to withdraw from Kosovo.

THE ELECTION OF 2000

Pre-election polls indicated that the election would be close, and few ventured to predict the outcome. Indeed, the election outcome was much in doubt for several weeks after the election. Though Clinton's vice-president, Al Gore (1948–), won the popular vote, the Electoral College was very close, and Florida would be pivotal in deciding the election. George W. Bush (1946–), son of former president George H. W. Bush, appeared to win Florida, but by a very small margin, and a recount began. Then, controversy over how exactly to conduct the recount led to a series of court challenges, with the matter ultimately decided by the U.S. Supreme Court, which ruled in favor of Bush. George W. Bush thus became the forty-third President of the United States.

TERRORISM HITS HOME

The new president would soon face the grim task of dealing with a massive terrorist attack on major symbols of U.S. economic and military might. On the morning of September 11, 2001, hijackers deliberately crashed U.S. commercial jetliners into the World Trade Center in New York—toppling its 110-story twin towers—and the Pentagon, just outside Washington, D.C. Thousands were killed in the deadliest act of terrorism in American history. Though it wasn't immediately clear exactly who lay behind the attacks, Bush cast prime suspicion on Saudi exile Osama bin Laden, the alleged mastermind of the bombings of two U.S. embassies in 1998 and of a U.S. naval destroyer in 2000. The U.S. had earlier seen terrorism on its home soil carried out by Islamic militants in the 1993 bombing of the World Trade Center and by a member of the American militia movement in the bombing of the Oklahoma City federal building in 1995.

Presidents of the United States

	PRESIDENT	**VICE PRESIDENT**
1.	George Washington (1789-1797)	John Adams
2.	John Adams (1797-1801)	Thomas Jefferson
3.	Thomas Jefferson (1801-1809)	Aaron Burr, George Clinton
4.	James Madison (1809-1817)	George Clinton, Elbridge Gerry
5.	James Monroe (1817-1825)	Daniel D. Tompkins
6.	John Quincy Adams (1825-1829)	John C. Calhoun
7.	Andrew Jackson (1829-1837)	John C. Calhoun, Martin Van Buren
8.	Martin Van Buren (1837-1841)	Richard M. Johnson
9.	William Henry Harrison (1841)	John Tyler
10.	John Tyler (1841-1845)	
11.	James K. Polk (1845-1849)	George M. Dallas
12.	Zachary Taylor (1849-1850)	Millard Fillmore
13.	Millard Fillmore (1850-1853)	
14.	Franklin Pierce (1853-1857)	William King
15.	James Buchanan (1857-1861)	John C. Breckinridge
16.	Abraham Lincoln (1861-1865)	Hannibal Hamlin, Andrew Johnson
17.	Andrew Johnson (1865-1869)	
18.	Ulysses S. Grant (1869-1877)	Schuyler Colfax, Henry Wilson
19.	Rutherford B. Hayes (1877-1881)	William Wheeler
20.	James A. Garfield (1881)	Chester Arthur
21.	Chester Arthur (1881-1885)	
22.	Grover Cleveland (1885-1889)	Thomas Hendricks

23.	Benjamin Harrison (1889-1893)	Levi P. Morton
24.	Grover Cleveland (1893-1897)	Adlai E. Stevenson
25.	William McKinley (1897-1901)	Garret Hobart,
		Theodore Roosevelt
26.	Theodore Roosevelt (1901-1909)	Charles Fairbanks
27.	William Howard Taft (1909-1913)	James S. Sherman
28.	Woodrow Wilson (1913-1921)	Thomas R. Marshall
29.	Warren G. Harding (1921-1923)	Calvin Coolidge
30.	Calvin Coolidge (1923-1929)	Charles Dawes
31.	Herbert Hoover (1929-1933)	Charles Curtis
32.	Franklin D. Roosevelt (1933-1945)	John Nance Garner,
		Henry A. Wallace,
		Harry S. Truman
33.	Harry S. Truman (1945-1953)	Alben Barkley
34.	Dwight D. Eisenhower (1953-1961)	Richard M. Nixon
35.	John F. Kennedy (1961-1963)	Lyndon B. Johnson
36.	Lyndon B. Johnson (1963-1969)	Hubert Humphrey
37.	Richard M. Nixon (1969-1974)	Spiro Agnew,
		Gerald Ford
38.	Gerald R. Ford (1974-1977)	Nelson Rockefeller
39.	James Earl Carter (1977-1981)	Walter Mondale
40.	Ronald Reagan (1981-1989)	George H. W. Bush
41.	George H. W. Bush (1989-1993)	James Danforth Quayle
42.	William Jefferson Clinton (1993-2001)	Albert Gore, Jr.
43.	George W. Bush (2001-)	Richard Cheney

POLITICAL SCIENCE

United States Government

FUNDAMENTAL PRINCIPLES EMBODIED IN THE CONSTITUTION

The Founding Fathers drew upon a variety of sources to shape the government that was outlined in the Constitution. British documents such as the Magna Carta (1215), the Petition of Right (1628), and the Bill of Rights (1689), all of which promoted the concept of limited government, were influential in shaping the fundamental principles embodied in the Constitution. British philosopher John Locke, who wrote about the social contract concept of government and the right of people to alter or abolish a government that did not protect their interests, was a guiding force.

One of the most significant of the basic principles embodied in the Constitution is the concept of a federal system that divides the powers of government between the states and the national government. Local matters are handled on a local level, and those issues that affect all citizens are the responsibility of the federal government. Such a system was a natural outgrowth of the colonial relationship between the Americans and the mother country of England. It is clearly stated in the Tenth Amendment, which declares: "Those powers not delegated to the United States by the Constitution, nor prohibited by it to the States, are reserved to the States respectively, or to the people." The federal government and those of the separate states have powers that may in practice overlap, but in cases where they conflict, the federal government is supreme.

Another key principle is separation of powers. The national government is divided into three branches that have separate functions (legislative, executive, and judicial), but they are not entirely independent. These functions are outlined in Articles I, II, and III of the main body of the Constitution. Closely related to the concept of separation of powers is the system of checks and balances, in which each of the branches has the ability to limit the actions of the other branches. The legislative branch can check the executive by refusing to confirm the president's appointments or by passing laws over his veto (by a two-thirds majority in both houses). The executive can check the legislative branch by use of the veto and the judicial branch by appointing his choices to the federal bench. The judicial can check the other two branches by declaring laws to be unconstitutional.

Additional fundamental principles of the Constitution include:

1) the establishment of a representative government (a republic),

2) the belief in popular sovereignty or a government that derives its power from the people (the Preamble opens with the words, "We the People"), and

3) the enforcement of a government with limits, sometimes referred to as the "rule of law."

THE LEGISLATIVE BRANCH

Legislative power is vested in a bicameral Congress, which is the subject of Article I of the Constitution. The expressed or delegated powers are set forth in Section 8 and can be divided into several broad categories. Economic powers include:

1) to lay and collect taxes,

2) to borrow money,

3)   to regulate foreign and interstate commerce,

4)   to coin money and regulate its value, and

5)   to establish rules concerning bankruptcy.

Judicial powers are comprised of the following:

1)   to establish courts inferior to the Supreme Court,

2)   to provide punishment for counterfeiting, and

3)   to define and punish piracies and felonies committed on the high seas.

War powers of Congress are enumerated as follows:

1)   to declare war,

2)   to raise and support armies,

3)   to provide and maintain a navy, and

4)   to provide for organizing, arming, and calling forth the militia.

Other general peace powers include:

1)   to establish uniform rules on naturalization,

2)   to establish post offices and post roads,

3)   to promote science and the arts by issuing patents and copyrights, and

4)   to exercise jurisdiction over the seat of the federal government (District of Columbia).

The Constitution also grants Congress the power to discipline federal officials through impeachment and removal from office. The House of Representatives has the power to charge officials (impeach), and the Senate is empowered to conduct the trials. These powers have been invoked infrequently. More significant is the Senate's power to confirm presidential appointments (to the Cabinet, federal judiciary, and major bureaucracies) and to ratify treaties. Both houses are involved in choosing a president and vice-president if no majority is achieved in the Electoral College. The House of Representatives votes for the president from among the top three electoral candidates, with each state delegation casting one vote. The Senate votes for the vice-president. This power has been exercised only twice, in the disputed elections of 1800 and 1824.

THE EXECUTIVE BRANCH

Article II of the Constitution deals with the powers and duties of the president. The chief executive's constitutional responsibilities include the following:

1) to serve as Commander-in-Chief,

2) to negotiate treaties (with the approval of two-thirds of the Senate),

3) to appoint ambassadors, judges, and other high officials (with the consent of the Senate),

4) to grant pardons and reprieves for those convicted of federal crimes (except in impeachment cases),

5) to seek counsel of department heads (Cabinet secretaries),

6) to recommend legislation,

7) to meet with representatives of foreign states, and

8) to see that federal laws are "faithfully executed."

The president's powers with respect to foreign policy are paramount. Civilian control of the military is a fundamental concept embodied in the naming of the president as Commander-in-Chief; he is, in essence, the nation's leading general. As such, he can make battlefield decisions as well as shape military policy.

The president also has broad powers in domestic policy. The most significant domestic policy tool is the president's budget, which he submits to Congress. Though Congress must approve all spending, the president has a great deal of power in budget negotiations. The president can use considerable resources in persuading Congress to enact legislation, and he also has opportunities, such as the State of the Union Address, to reach out directly to the American People to convince them to support these presidential policies.

THE JUDICIAL BRANCH

Article III of the Constitution states that "the judicial power of the United States shall be vested in one Supreme Court, and in such inferior courts as the Congress may from time to time ordain and establish." Hence, the Supreme Court is the only court mentioned specifically in the document. Yet our contemporary judicial branch consists of thousands of courts and is, in essence, a dual system, with each state having its own judicial structure functioning simultaneously with a complete set of federal courts. The most significant piece of legislation with reference to establishing a federal court network was the Judiciary Act of 1789. This law organized the Supreme Court and set up the federal district courts (13) and the circuit (appeal) courts (3).

The Supreme Court today is made up of a Chief Justice and eight Associate Justices. They are appointed for life by the president with the approval of the Senate, and they are routinely, but not exclusively, drawn from the ranks of the federal judiciary. In recent years, the appointment of Supreme Court Justices has been the focus of intense scrutiny and in some cases, the center of heated political controversy.

Types of Government

Distribution of authority and responsibility between the federal and state governments are key variables in comparing government systems.

Confederation—a weak central government that delegates principal authority to smaller units, such as states. An example of this is the United States under the Articles of Confederation.

Federal—a division of sovereignty between a central government and those of its separate states. Contemporary examples of federal republics are Brazil, India, and the United States.

Unitary—the concentration of power and authority is held by a highly centralized government. Examples include France and Japan.

Separation of powers among branches of the federal government is another aspect of structure useful in comparing political systems.

Authoritarian—a government's central power is in a single or collective executive, with the legislative and judicial bodies having little input. Some examples of this include the former Soviet Union, the People's Republic of China, and Nazi Germany.

Parliamentary—the legislative and executive branches are combined, with a prime minister and cabinet selected from within the legislative body. They maintain control so long as the legislative assembly supports their major policies. Great Britain is an example of this form of government.

Presidential—the executive branch is clearly separated from the legislative and judicial branches. However, all three (particularly the executive and legislative branches) must cooperate in order for policy to be consistent and for government operations to be carried out smoothly. An example of this is the United States.

ECONOMICS

Economics is a social science that studies society's problem of choice among a limited amount of resources in its quest to attain the highest practical satisfaction of its unlimited wants. It is the allocation of scarce resources among competing ends.

Fundamentals of Economics

DEFINITION AND THEORY

Microeconomics focuses on problems specific to a household, firm, or industry, rather than those of a national or worldwide scale. Particular emphasis is placed on how these units make decisions and the consequences of these decisions. *Macroeconomics* is the study of the economy as a whole. Some of the topics considered include inflation, unemployment, and economic growth.

Economic Theory is an explanation of why certain economic phenomena occur. For example, there are theories explaining the rate of inflation, how many hours people choose to work, and the amount of goods and services a specific country will import. Economic theory is essentially a set of statements about cause and effect relationships in the economy.

SUPPLY AND DEMAND

Goods and services refer to anything that satisfy human needs, wants, or desires. Goods are tangible items, such as food, cars, and clothing, while services are intangible items such as education and health care. A market is referred to as the interaction between potential buyers and sellers of goods and services, where money is usually used as the medium of exchange. Supply of a good is the quantity of that good that producers offer at a certain price. The collection of all such points for every price is called the supply curve. Demand for a good is the quantity of a good that consumers are willing and able to purchase at a certain price. The demand curve is the combination of quantity and price, at all price levels.

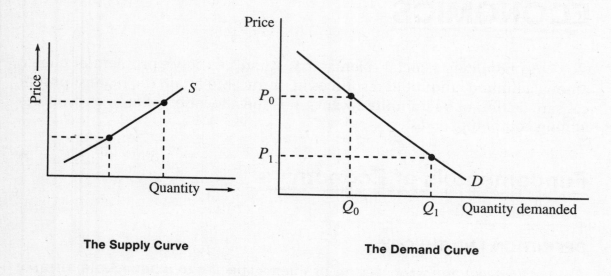

The Supply Curve   The Demand Curve

MONOPOLIES AND OLIGOPOLIES

Monopolies occur when one supplier dominates an industry. Monopolies arise due to conditions in the market in which a firm has complete control over its prices. A monopoly has the following properties: there is only one seller, there are no close substitutes for the company's product, the monopolist is the price setter, and there are barriers to enter the monopolist's market (i.e., the firm, and sometimes the government, prevent competition so as to stay the sole producer of the good).

An oligopoly is a market structure that is characterized by a few sellers of goods that are similar to each other. The price charged by one firm in the industry is considered by all other firms when they make their pricing decisions.

UNIVERSAL ECONOMIC GOALS AND ECONOMIC SYSTEMS

Allocative (Economic) Efficiency occurs when a society produces the types and quantities of goods and services that most satisfy its people. Failure to do so wastes resources. Technical Efficiency occurs when a society produces the greatest types and quantities of goods and services from its resources. Again, failure to do so wastes resources. Equity occurs when the distribution of goods and services conforms to a society's notions of "fairness." These goals often determine the type of economic system that a country has.

Traditional economies largely rely on custom to determine production and distribution issues. While not static, traditional systems are slow to change and are not well equipped to propel a society into sustained growth. Traditional systems are found in many of the poorer Third World countries. Command economies rely on a central authority to make decisions. The central authority may be a dictator or a democratically constituted government. Market economies have no central authority and custom plays very little role. Every consumer makes buying decisions based on his or her own needs, desires, and income; individual self-interest rules. Every producer decides for him- or herself what goods or services to produce, what price to charge, what resources to employ, and what production methods to use; producers are motivated solely by profit considerations. There is vigorous competition in a market economy.

A mixed economy contains elements of each of the three systems defined above. All real world economies are mixed economies, although the mixture of tradition, command, and market differs greatly. In the United States, greater emphasis is usually placed on the market, although there is a large and active government (command) sector as well. The Soviet economy relies mainly on the government to direct economic activity, although there is a small market sector as well.

Capitalist economies produce resources that are owned by individuals, while socialist economies produce resources that are owned collectively by society. In a socialist economy, these resources are under the control of the government.

ADAM SMITH AND "THE WEALTH OF NATIONS"

Adam Smith (1723–1790) was a Scottish economist whose writing can be said to have inaugurated the modern era of economic analysis. Published in 1776, *The Wealth of Nations* can be read as an analysis of a market economy. It was Smith's belief that a market economy was a superior form of organization from the standpoint of both economic progress and human liberty. Smith acknowledged that self-interest was a dominant motivating force in a market economy, yet this self-interest, he said, was ultimately consistent with the public interest. Market participants were guided by an "invisible hand" to act in ways that promoted the public interest. Firms may only be concerned with profits, but profits are only earned by firms that satisfy consumer demand and keep costs down.

 Drill Questions

1. In 1215, English barons forced King John I to sign the _____, acknowledging their "ancient privileges."

    (A) Treaty of Barons Religion

    (B) Domesday Book

    (C) Institutes of the Christian Religion

    (D) Magna Carta

2. A basic assumption of the Age of Enlightenment was

    (A) faith in reason rather than faith in revelation.

    (B) the arts were more important than the sciences.

    (C) religious dissidents should not be tolerated.

    (D) man's intellect does not exist apart from God.

3.   During the 18th century in France, the "third estate" consisted of

   (A)   wealthy landowners.

   (B)   the middle class, urban workers, and peasants.

   (C)   members of the aristocracy.

   (D)   members of the clergy and other appointed officials.

4.   Reasons for the Industrial Revolution include

   (A)   mechanical inventions and technical advances that resulted from the Enlightenment.

   (B)   economic and political instability following the French Revolution.

   (C)   constant war between England and France, which required more advanced weapons and machinery.

   (D)   None of the above.

5.   Karl Marx believed that

   (A)   capitalism could not be destroyed without the help of outside forces.

   (B)   class struggle did not begin until the Industrial Revolution.

   (C)   socialism was inevitable.

   (D)   All of the above.

6.   In 1861, Alexander II instituted a series of reforms, including

   (A)   serfs would no longer be dependent on the lord.

   (B)   all people were to have freedom of movement and were free to change their means of livelihood.

   (C)   serfs could enter into contracts and could own their own property.

   (D)   All of the above.

7. **During the European conflicts of the 1930s, France and Britain**

(A) intervened despite signing non-intervention treaties.

(B) intervened only to settle disputes.

(C) followed a course of neutrality.

(D) intervened in the beginning, but then moved towards neutrality.

8. **The general pattern throughout American colonial history was**

(A) proprietary colonies eventually became either company colonies or royal colonies.

(B) company colonies and proprietary colonies both eventually became royal colonies.

(C) royal colonies often became company colonies.

(D) the ownership of the colonies did not change.

9. **Which of the following was a direct response to the Townshend Acts?**

(A) The Battle of Lexington

(B) The nonimportation of British goods

(C) The Boston Massacre

(D) A tax on all British imports except for tea

10. **The Treaty of Paris of 1783, which granted American independence, stipulated the following:**

(A) America's western boundary was set at the Mississippi River.

(B) Britain retained Canada, but had to surrender Florida to Spain.

(C) private British creditors would be free to collect any debts owed by United States citizens.

(D) All of the above.

11. The Bill of Rights was added to the Constitution in order to appease

    (A) Anti-Federalists   (C) Republicans

    (B) Whigs   (D) Federalists

12. The statement that the peoples of the American hemisphere were "henceforth not to be considered as subjects for future colonization by any European powers" was issued by what president?

    (A) James Madison

    (B) Andrew Jackson

    (C) James Monroe

    (D) Thomas Jefferson

13. The term "Manifest Destiny" describes the belief that

    (A) Americans were destined for greatness.

    (B) orderly government could only be established with the consent of the governed.

    (C) the American nation was destined to eventually expand to the Pacific Ocean.

    (D) people should serve God and build His kingdom.

14. In *Dred Scott v. Sanford*, the Supreme Court ruled that

    (A) Scott had no standing to sue in federal court.

    (B) Scott should be free because he had lived for many years in both a free state and a free territory.

    (C) Congress had the authority to exclude slavery from territories.

    (D) territorial governments had the right to exclude slavery from territories.

15. The Eighteenth Amendment to the United States Constitution
    (A) prohibited the sale of alcoholic beverages.
    (B) provided for women's right to vote.
    (C) established the federal income tax.
    (D) established the direct election of United States senators.

16. Lyndon Johnson's "Great Society" program was aimed primarily at
    (A) spurring advances in American science and technical education and increasing funding to high-tech research facilities.
    (B) sending American volunteers to impoverished foreign nations to help educate their people and build their economic base.
    (C) securing civil rights for all Americans and eliminating poverty.
    (D) providing minimum wage jobs for all unemployed Americans.

17. Among the sources drawn upon for establishing an American constitution were the
    (A) Magna Carta
    (B) Petition of Right
    (C) Bill of Rights
    (D) All of the above.

18. The type of government in which the concentration of power and authority is held by a highly centralized government is called
    (A) Federal
    (B) Presidential
    (C) Unitary
    (D) Confederation

19. Powers of the Legislative Branch include the
    (A) declaration of war.
    (B) appointment of ambassadors, judges, and other high officials.
    (C) granting of pardons and reprieves for those convicted of federal crimes.
    (D) authority to declare laws and executive actions to be unconstitutional.

20. What type of economy relies largely on custom to determine production and distribution issues?
    (A) Command
    (B) Traditional
    (C) Market
    (D) Mixed

Answers to Drill Questions

1. (D)	6. (D)	11. (A)	16. (C)
2. (A)	7. (C)	12. (C)	17. (D)
3. (B)	8. (B)	13. (C)	18. (C)
4. (A)	9. (B)	14. (A)	19. (A)
5. (C)	10. (D)	15. (A)	20. (B)

LAST/ATS-W

Chapter 4

Artistic Expression
and the
Humanities Review

Chapter 4

Artistic Expression and the Humanities Review

The Artistic Expression and the Humanities section of the LAST is designed to assess your ability to comprehend, interpret, and contextualize works of art. You will be expected to understand basic elements of form and content in the visual and performing arts from various time periods and cultures. You should be able to respond to themes and motifs in literature and the arts, as well as analyze religious and philosophical ideas and their significance in shaping various cultures. Again, remember that the LAST focuses primarily on the processes involved in understanding the subject matter. Therefore, factual recall is less important than a general understanding of the material.

AESTHETIC PERCEPTION AND CREATIVE EXPRESSION

Visual and Performing Arts

Beginning with the first great civilized society (the Sumerians in Mesopotamia more than 5,000 years ago), the peoples of the world have continued on a consistent path in the area of fine, applied, and performing arts.

The visual and performing arts basically encompass the categories of sculpture, painting and graphics, architecture, dance, music, and theater.

Sculpture is concerned with three-dimensional forms. Sculptures may be cast by pouring molten metals into molds to create cast-bronze figures. They may also be carved (from wood, stone, or marble), shaped from clay, or welded together from metal pieces.

Painting is two-dimensional. Surfaces have traditionally been walls, wooden panels, canvas, paper and parchment, and even decorative objects such as vases. Paint is usually applied with a brush, using pigments mixed with media such as linseed oil or water. For frescoes, pigments are applied directly over wet plaster to seal in the art on a wall or ceiling. Other two-dimensional art includes *drawing* and *printmaking*. In etching, woodcuts, lithographs, and the many variations on these methods, multiple copies of a drawing are made by creating either a raised or recessed surface (metal, wood, or stone) that takes ink and pressing paper against the surface.

Architecture is the design of structures for living, working, worshipping, or for other residential or civic needs. Gothic cathedrals, for example, soar to the heavens with massive vertical elements to reflect the religious devotion of medieval Europe. The simple designs of many twentieth-century buildings reveal a fascination with using such materials as glass, steel, and concrete.

Dance is an art form based on physical movement and expression—by humans singly, or in couples or groups. Folk and tribal dancing are often related to communal celebration or religious ritual. Dance created to entertain an audience may be choreographed and worked out in strict steps and gestures, such as in ballet or musical theater.

Music is the arrangement of sounds for voice and musical instruments and, like dance and visual art, requires training and repetitive practice. For most of history, music has been an outgrowth of a community's or an ethnic group's need to celebrate, and has often been linked to story-telling or poetry. In Europe, a system of musical notation developed during the Middle Ages, and the use of notation (written symbolic indications of pitch and duration of tones) is a convenient way to distinguish "art" (or classical, or complexly composed) music from folk music.

Theater is the performance, for the sake of an audience's education or entertainment, of a story, usually of drama, comedy, or some combination thereof. The West's tradition of theater originated chiefly with the ancient Greeks and many feel reached its high point in the late sixteenth and early seventeenth centuries in England with the plays of William Shakespeare. Theater requires vocal declamation, acting, costumes, sometimes masks, usually a scenic backdrop or constructed set, and poetic expression. Theater may be said to encompass all the art forms, since a theatrical production of ballet, opera, or musical drama/comedy can include all the disciplines, employing set decoration, costuming, dance, song, and instrumental music.

Historical Survey

VISUAL ARTS

Paleolithic people in Europe painted animal pictures on the cave walls at Lascaux and Altimira about 15,000–13,000 B.C.E. Some examples of even older art, dating from 30,000 to 20,000 B.C.E., are the various "Venuses"—small stylized stone carvings of women as symbols of fertility, found in modern Europe. The artists of the ancient civilizations of Sumer, Babylon, and Assyria carved narratives of battles and historical records. Egyptian statues, like their architectural monuments the pyramids, were often of colossal size, to further exalt the power of the society's leaders and gods. The art of ancient Greece has its roots in the Minoan civilization on the island of Crete, which flourished about 2500–1400 B.C.E. This is evident in the palace at Knossos, which is known for characteristic wall paintings revealing a people enamored of games, leisure, and the beauty of the sea. The ancient Greeks of the classical period were fascinated by physical beauty. Their Olympian gods were fashioned in an idealized human image, and a universe of perfection, guided by a master plan, was re-created in their idealized and gracefully proportioned sculptures, architecture, and paintings. In the Hellenistic period, these various objects came to be appreciated as art, for their beauty alone.

The ancient Romans adopted much of the classical style of the Greeks. They also built temples, roads, bath complexes, civic buildings, palaces, and aqueducts. One of the greatest of their artistic and engineering accomplishments was the massive-domed temple of all the gods, the Pantheon, which is today one of the most perfectly preserved of all classical-period buildings.

The early Christian era borrowed the basilica form of Roman architecture for its churches. The seventh-century church of San Vitale echoes the mosaic mastery of the eastern Roman, or Byzantine, empire in Constantinople (which flourished as a center of civilization for a thousand years after the decline of Rome).

The Romanesque style of art and architecture was preeminent from about 800 to 1200. By then many local styles, including the decorative arts of the Byzantines, the Near East, and the German and Celtic tribes, were contributing to European culture. Common features of Romanesque churches are round arches, vaulted ceilings, and heavy walls that are profusely decorated.

Gothic art flourished in Europe for the next 300 years. The cathedrals in this style are some of the purest expressions of an age. They combine a continued search for engineering and structural improvement with stylistic features that convey a relentless verticality, a reach toward heaven, and the unbridled adoration of God. Soaring and airy, these cathedrals were constructed using such elements as flying buttresses and pointed arches and vaults, and were decorated by a profusion of sculptures and stained-glass windows.

The Italian Renaissance's roots are found as early as the 1300s, when the painter Giotto di Bondone began to compose his figures into groups and depict expressive human gestures. During the fifteenth century, art, architecture, literature, and music were invigorated. Renaissance artists developed new forms and revived classical styles and values, with the belief in the importance of human experience on Earth. Great sculptors approached true human characterization and realism.

Architecture revived the Greek elements and took a scientific, ordered approach, one similarly expressed in painting, with the emphasis on the calculated composition of figures in space known as perspective. The Renaissance artists sought to produce works of perfect beauty and engaged in a constant search for knowledge, most often portraying religious subjects and wealthy patrons.

Color and movement were heightened, compositions were more vigorous, and there were increased references to classical iconography and the pleasures of an idyllic golden age. These aspects can be seen in Michelangelo Buonarroti's magnificent Sistine Chapel frescoes and his powerful sculptures of *David* and *Moses*, Leonardo da Vinci's *Mona Lisa*, Raphael Santi's *School of Athens* fresco, and the increasingly dramatic and colorful works of the Venetian and northern Italian masters. The northern European Renaissance also emphasized a renewed interest in the visible world, and works of the time reveal an emphasis on the symbolism of minutely observed details and accurate realism based on observation of reality.

The baroque period of the seventeenth century produced artists who added heightened drama to the forms of Renaissance art. Artists such as Peter Paul Rubens portrayed figures in constant motion, draperies of agitated angles, and effects of lighting and shadow that amplified emotional impact and mystery.

In this spirit followed such painters of court life and middle-class portraiture as Diego Velazquez, Rembrandt van Rijn, Anthony Van Dyck, and Frans Hals. Rembrandt used expressive brushwork and mysterious light contrasts and sections of his compositions glow with a mysterious inner light often unrelated to realistic effects.

The art of the early eighteenth century is often called rococo. Painters turned the agitated drama of the baroque into light, pastel-toned, swirling compositions that seem placed in an idyllic land of a golden age. In the seventeenth and eighteenth centuries, European artists also responded to middle-class life and everyday objects and created genre paintings.

In the nineteenth century, narrative art combined with romantic literature—Johann Goethe, Lord George Byron, Percy Bysshe Shelley, Sir Walter Scott, William Wordsworth, and others—and political events to produce works with a political point of view or a story to tell. Jacques-Louis David used a severe classical sculptural style (neoclassical) in his paintings to revive classical art and ennoble images of the French Revolution and Napoleon's empire. Neoclassical sculpture revived the aloof severity and perfection of form of ancient art.

In the first half of the nineteenth century, landscape painting in England reached a zenith with the works of John Constable and Joseph Turner. Turner's awe-inspiring landscapes form a bridge between the spirit of romanticism and the expressionistic brushwork and realism of the Barbizon School in France. Beginning with Barbizon, the French painters of the nineteenth century concentrated more and more on the reporterlike depiction of everyday life and the natural environment in a free, painterly (gesture and brushwork) style.

The realist pioneers were Gustave Courbet, Jean-Francois Millet, and Honoré Daumier. Renowned as a political caricaturist, Daumier's chief medium was the lithograph and paved the way for the stylistic and subject innovations of the Impressionists. In Impressionism, traditional means of composing a picture, color relations, and accurate and exact rendering of people and objects, were rejected in favor of an art that emphasized quickly observed and sketched moments from life, the relation of shapes and forms and colors, the effects of light, and the act of painting itself.

Beginning with Edouard Manet in the 1860s, French artists continually blurred the boundaries of realism and abstraction, and the landscapes and everyday-life paintings of such Impressionist artists as Claude Monet, Camille Pissarro, Auguste Renoir, Alfred Sisley, and Edgar Degas gave way to the more experimental arrangements of form and color of the great Post-impressionists—Paul Gauguin, Vincent van Gogh, Georges Seurat, and Toulouse-Lautrec.

Greatly influenced by Japanese art and particularly the flattened space, distinctive shapes, and strong colors of Japanese woodblock prints, artists used paintings, pastels, and lithography to further break down the boundaries between representational art and abstraction. The new, freer form of art—centered around the personality of the artist and celebrating personal style and the manipulation of form and color—evolved in a number of directions.

Some artists turned inward to explore mystical, symbolic, and psychological truths: Symbolists, Expressionists, and exponents of art nouveau. Others pursued formal innovations, among them Paul Cézanne, Henri Matisse, and Pablo Picasso. Picasso's cubism seemed the most direct call for the total destruction of realistic depiction; his use of African and Oceanic tribal art, and his emphasis on taking objects apart and reassembling them, led to similar experiments by Fernand Leger, Marcel Duchamp, the sculptors Alexander Archipenko and Jacques Lipchitz, and the Italian Futurist Umberto Boccioni.

Pure abstraction, with little or no relation to the outside world, was approached in the more emotional, expressionistic, and color-oriented paintings of Wassily Kandinsky, Roger Delauney, and Paul Klee. More cerebral arrangements of abstract geometrical shapes and colors were the mark of Kasimir Malevich, Piet Mondrian, and the Bauhaus School of Design in Germany, whose stripped-down, simplified, and usually geometrically-oriented aesthetic influenced architecture, industrial and commercial design, sculpture, and the graphic arts for half a century.

In architecture can be seen the most obvious results of this new tradition, from the simplified, sleek structures of Charles Le Corbusier and Walter Gropius to the boxlike glass skyscrapers of Philip Johnson. The pioneering giant of twentieth-century architecture was Frank Lloyd Wright. Wright's buildings exhibited a personal and bold originality, based on a philosophy of "organic architecture," a belief that the form of a structure should be dictated by its natural surroundings, purpose, and building materials.

Inspired by the psychoanalytic writings of Sigmund Freud and Carl Jung, the subconscious and the metaphysical became another important element in art, especially in the work of the Surrealist artists Salvador Dali, René Magritte, and Juan Miro. Sculptors manipulated abstract shapes and were influenced by tribal arts in the twentieth century. Artists such as Louise Nevelson made constructions and wall sculptures from scraps of everyday objects.

The muralists and social realists between the world wars created art that was physically interesting, and whose subjects were accessible to the average person. John Sloan, George Bellows, Edward Hopper, Thomas Hart Benton, Grant Wood, and John Stuart Curry were among those who celebrated the American scene in paintings. The great Mexican muralists, who usually concentrated on political themes—Diego Rivera and Clemente Orozco—brought their work to the public both in Mexico and in the United States. The icons of American popular culture found their way, in the movement known as Pop Art, into canvases by Andy Warhol, Robert Indiana, Larry Rivers, Jasper Johns, Roy Lichtenstein, and Robert Rauschenberg.

MUSIC

The ancient Greeks accompanied the recitation of poetry with the stringed lyre, and choral songs were heard between recited passages. In the early Christian era, plainsong, or unaccompanied religious chant, was codified and arranged with early forms of music notation by Pope Gregory the Great (late sixth century). This is the origin of Gregorian chant. By the twelfth and thirteenth centuries, the important form of polyphony, upon which the distinctive art music of the West is based, enabled supportive melodies to be added to the main chant. Throughout the later Middle Ages, both religious and secular polyphonic music was composed and melodies and rhythms became more diversified.

During the Renaissance, the spirit of humanism and rationalism pervaded polyphonic music, and music began to be seen as a mark of culture. Emphasis was placed upon secular music and dance and instrumental music ensembles.

Baroque music of the seventeenth and early eighteenth centuries employed a greater complexity of contrapuntal, or multimelodic, form, and the beginnings of harmony, the use of colorful instrumental ensembles, and great drama and emotion. Other innovative forms included the oratorio, the cantata, the sonata, the suite, the concerto, and the fugue. The great works of baroque music were composed by Antonio Vivaldi and Johann Sebastian Bach.

The greatest composers of the classical period of the latter half of the eighteenth century, marked by clarity of form, logical thematic development, and strict adherence to sonata form, were Franz Joseph Haydn and Wolfgang Amadeus Mozart. Mozart's structurally exquisite works approach perfection of form while adding to music inventive melodic diversity. The German composer Ludwig van Beethoven ushered in the romantic school of symphonic music. His symphonies and piano sonatas, concertos, and string quartets explode with dramatic passion, expressive melodies and harmonies, and complex thematic development.

Romantic composers included Frédéric Chopin, Hector Berlioz, Franz Liszt, Richard Strauss, and Felix Mendelssohn. Other important symphonic composers of the nineteenth century were Robert Schumann, Johannes Brahms, Peter Ilyich Tchaikovsky, and Gustav Mahler.

Other important influences in nineteenth-century music include the use of ethnic influences or folk melodies and music of a nationalistic vein, as well as of popular song (often linked to composers who were outstanding melodists and harmonic innovators).

The concert music of the twentieth century increasingly endeavored to enlarge the boundaries of rhythm, form, and harmony, seemingly parallel to the direction in the visual arts away from traditional structure and melodic-harmonic connections with listeners and toward more personal or intellectual experiments in abstraction.

Ethnic and popular influences continued to exert an important pull in the creation of twentieth-century music. Ragtime, blues, jazz, and other popular folk, dance, and commercial music provided material for some of the most innovative and exciting work in twentieth-century music. Composers after World War II experimented with tape-recorded sound (Edgard Varese) and conceptual music based on indeterminacy or chance (John Cage).

DANCE, OPERA, AND ETHNIC/FOLK TRADITIONS

Many tribal peoples believe that through imitative dance they can gain knowledge of the mysterious powers of nature and influence the unseen world. But even the pharaohs of ancient Egypt enjoyed dancing as spectacle, and the ancient Greeks held dancing in high esteem, establishing many different styles for different purposes.

During the Middle Ages, the common folk enjoyed dancing, much of it related to fertility or seasonal rituals such as Maypole and wedding dances. Secular dance with more formalized steps and forms became important among the upper classes after the Renaissance period.

Among Western and non-Western cultures alike, the folk traditions of the performing arts often link the disciplines of dance, theater, and music.

Ethnic dance with the longest and most sophisticated tradition is the classical dance of India. Indian dance has exerted great influence over the court and temple dances of Asia.

Dance is primarily linked with theatrical entertainments in China and Japan. Japanese Kabuki theater employs masks, singing, and dancing in a highly stylized manner, and the Noh plays of Japan are dance-dramas with stylized scenery and acting. Native American tribal dances are essentially ritualistic (such as the ghost dance of the Paiutes), but the hoop and eagle dances of the western Indian peoples are theatrical and intricate.

Folk dancing for pure recreation is also an important tradition. Popular American social dancing in the twentieth century has adopted many Latin American dances, including the rhumba, mambo, and tango.

Ballet has origins in both the ancient Roman pantomime and the Italian *commedia dell'arte*. France led the way in establishing the essentials of the classical ballet, beginning with the founding of the Royal Academy of Dancing in Paris in 1661. France created a theatrical tradition of opera ballets, and dance rules and steps were strictly formalized.

THEATRE

Music and theater have always been linked, and the traditions of opera, operetta, and musical comedy/drama in Europe and America have produced enduring theatrical masterpieces, most notably the operas of George Gershwin and the operettas of Sir William Gilbert and Sir Arthur Sullivan.

Drama and comedy have sought without music to portray humanity's deepest passions and most universal concerns, and simply to amuse or entertain. Medieval drama was primarily religious and often presented in cathedrals and monasteries. Most theatrical performances in Europe until the sixteenth century took place in booths or courtyards or an outside open area. The great plays of Shakespeare and his contemporaries were presented in theaters, but these were merely stages set against the side of a building with spectators gathered around the stage on three sides in the yard or in galleries, with no provisions for scenery. Over the next hundred years, theaters were gradually enclosed and a separated stage, demarcated by a proscenium opening, hosted theatricals with elaborate scenery and even indoor lighting.

Similar plays, with somewhat more realism and characters reflecting the interests and values of the middle class, were written in the nineteenth century. Drama became more psychological and sought to reveal truths about real people and their inner and interpersonal conflicts.

Prose

GENERAL RULES AND IDEAS

Students are sometimes confused as to what exactly prose is. Basically, prose is *not* poetry. Prose is what we write and speak most of the time in our everyday intercourse: unmetered, unrhymed language. This is not to say that prose does not have its own rhythms—language, whether written or spoken, has cadence and balance. Prose can have instances of rhyme or assonance, alliteration or onomatopoeia.

Furthermore, prose may be either *fiction* or *non-fiction*. A novel (like a short story) is fiction; an autobiography is non-fiction. While a novel (or short story) may have autobiographical elements, an autobiography is presumed to be entirely factual. Essays are usually described in other terms: expository, argumentative, persuasive, critical, narrative. Essays may have elements of either fiction or non-fiction, but are generally classed as a separate subgenre.

These subgenres require from the reader a different kind of involvement than does the essay. The essay, rather than presenting a story from which the reader may discern meaning through the skillful analysis of character, plot, symbol, and language, presents a relatively straightforward account of the writer's opinion(s) on an endless array of topics. Depending upon the type of essay, the reader may become informed (expository), provoked (argumentative), persuaded or enlightened (critical), or, in the case of the narrative essay, better acquainted with the writer who wishes to illustrate a point with his or her story, whether it is autobiographical or fictitious.

READING NOVELS

Most literary handbooks will define a novel as an extended fictional prose narrative. The novel has, over some 600 years, developed into many special forms which are classified by subject matter: detective novel, psychological novel, historical novel, Gothic novel, and so on. Furthermore, depending on the conventions of the author's time period, his style, and his outlook on life, his *mode* may be termed *realism, romanticism, impressionism, expressionism, naturalism,* or *neo-classicism.*

The works generally included on the LAST are those which have stood the test of time in significance, literary merit, and reader popularity.

Analyzing novels is a bit like asking the journalist's five questions: what? who? why? where? how? Students may be familiar with Freytag's Pyramid, originally designed to describe the structure of a five-act drama but now widely used to analyze fiction as well. The stages generally specified are *introduction* or *exposition, complication, rising action, climax, falling action,* and *denouement* or *conclusion.* There are many events in a long narrative but generally only one set of events comprises the "real" or "significant" story.

Sometimes an author divides the novel into chapters. Some writers, such as John Steinbeck in *The Grapes of Wrath,* use intercalary chapters, alternating between the "real" story (the Joads) and peripheral or parallel stories (the Okies and migrants in general). Look for the pattern of such organization and try to see the interrelationships of these alternating chapters.

We describe major characters in novels as *protagonists* or *antagonists.* Built into those two terms is the Greek word *agon,* meaning "struggle." The *pro*tagonist struggles toward or for someone or something; the *ant(i)*agonist struggles against someone or something. The possible conflicts are usually cited as man against himself, man against man, man against society, and man against nature.

Characters often serve as *foils* for other characters, enabling us to see one or more of them better. A classic example is in Harper Lee's *To Kill a Mockingbird.* Scout is the naive observer of events which her brother Jem, four years older, comes to understand from the perspective of the adult world.

Sometimes characters are *allegorical,* standing for qualities or concepts rather than for actual personages. For instance, Jim Casey (initials "J.C.") in *The Grapes of Wrath* is often regarded as a Christ figure, pure and self-sacrificing in his aims for the migrant workers.

Other characters are fully three-dimensional, "rounded," "mimetic" of humans in all their virtue, vice, hope, despair, strength and weakness.

The interplay of plot and characters determines in large part the *theme* of the story. First of all, the difference between a mere topic and a genuine theme or thesis must be distinguished, followed by the difference between a theme and contributing *motifs.* A *topic* is a phrase, such as "man's inhumanity to man" or "the fickle nature of fate." A *theme,* however, turns a phrase into a statement: "Man's inhumanity to man is barely concealed by 'civilization.'"

Skilled writers often employ *motifs* to help unify their works. A motif is a detail or element of the story which is repeated throughout, and which may even become symbolic.

Motifs in the hands of a skillful writer are valuable devices. For example, when wise Piggy, in William Golding's *Lord of the Flies,* is reduced to one lens in his specs, and finally to no specs at all, we see the loss of insight and wisdom on the island, and chaos follows.

READING SHORT STORIES

The modern short story differs from earlier short fiction such as the parable, fable, and tale, in its emphasis on character development through scenes rather than summary. Furthermore, the characters are human with recognizable human motivations, both social and psychological. Setting—time and place—is realistic rather than fantastic. And, as Edgar Allan Poe stipulated, the elements of plot, character, setting, style, point of view, and theme all work toward a single *unified* effect.

However, some modern writers have stretched these boundaries and have mixed in elements of nonrealism—such as the supernatural and the fantastic—sometimes switching back and forth between realism and nonrealism, and confusing the reader who is expecting conventional fiction.

READING ESSAYS

Essays fall into four rough categories: *speculative, argumentative, narrative,* and *expository.* Depending on the writer's purpose, his essay will fit into one of these groupings.

The *speculative* essay is so named because, as its Latin root suggests, it *looks* at ideas; it explores them rather than explains them. While the speculative essay may be said to be *meditative,* it often makes one or more points. But the thesis may not be as obvious or clear-cut as that in an expository or argumentative essay.

The purposes of the *argumentative* essay are always clear: to present a point and provide evidence, which may be factual or anecdotal, and to support it. The structure is usually very formal, as in a debate, with counterpositions and counterarguments.

Narrative and expository essays have elements of both the speculative and argumentative modes. The *narrative* essay may recount an incident or a series of incidents and is almost always autobiographical, in order to make a point. The informality of the storytelling makes the narrative essay less insistent than the argumentative essay, but more directed than the speculative essay.

Students are probably most familiar with the *expository* essay, the primary purpose of which is to explain and clarify ideas. While the expository essay may have narrative elements, that aspect is minor and subservient to that of explanation. Furthermore, while nearly all essays have some element of persuasion, argumentation is incidental in the expository essay. In any event, the four categories—speculative, argumentative, narrative, and expository— are neither exhaustive nor mutually exclusive.

As non-fiction, essays have a different set of elements from novels and short stories: *voice, style, structure*, and *thought*.

Voice in non-fiction is similar to the narrator's tone in fiction but the major difference is in who is "speaking." In fiction, the author is not the speaker—the narrator is the speaker. In an essay, however, the author speaks directly to the reader.

Style in non-fiction derives from the same elements as style in fiction: word choice, syntax, balance between dialogue and narration, voice, and use of description.

Structure and thought, the final elements of essays, are so intertwined as to be inextricable. We must be aware that to change the *structure* of an essay will alter its meaning. Writers signal structural shifts with alterations in focus, as well as with visual cues (spacing), verbal cues (*but, therefore, however*), or shifts in the kind of information being presented (personal, scientific, etc.).

Thought is perhaps the single element which most distinguishes non-fiction from fiction. The essayist chooses this form not to tell a story but to present an idea. It is this idea which we are after when we analyze an essay.

READING SATIRE

Satire is a *mode* which may be employed by writers of various genres: poetry, drama, fiction, and non-fiction. It is more a perspective than a product.

Satire mainly exposes, ridicules, derides, and denounces vice, folly, evil, and stupidity as these qualities manifest themselves in persons, groups of persons, ideas, institutions, customs, or beliefs. There are basically only two types of satire: gentle or harsh, depending on the author's intent, audience, and methods.

The satirist's techniques include *irony, parody, reversal* or *inversion, hyperbole, understatement, sarcasm, wit,* and *invective.* By exaggerating characteristics, saying the opposite of what he or she means, or using cleverness to make cutting or even cruel remarks at the expense of the subject, the writer of satire can call the reader's attention to those things he or she believes are repulsive, despicable, or destructive.

Irony is perhaps the satirist's most powerful weapon. The basis of irony is inversion or reversal, doing or saying the opposite or the unexpected. Shakespeare's famous sonnet beginning "My mistress' eyes are nothing like the sun..." is an ironic tribute to the speaker's beloved, who, he finally declares is "as rare/As any she belied with false compare." At the same time, Shakespeare is poking fun at the sonnet form as it was used by his contemporaries—himself included—to extol the virtues of their ladies. By selecting a woman who, by his own description, is physically unattractive in every way imaginable, and using the conventions of the love sonnet to present her many flaws, he has inverted the sonnet tradition. Then by asserting that she compares favorably with any of the other ladies whose poet-lovers have lied about their virtues, he presents us with the unexpected twist. Thus, he satirizes both the love sonnet form and its subject by using irony.

Satire in drama is also common; Oscar Wilde's "The Importance of Being Earnest" is wonderfully funny in its constant word play (notably on the name *Earnest*) and its relentless ridiculing of the superficiality which Wilde saw as characteristic of British gentry.

Classic novels that employ satire include Jonathan Swift's *Gulliver's Travels* and Francois-Marie Voltaire's *Candide,* both of which fairly vigorously attack aspects of the religions, governments, and prevailing intellectual beliefs of their respective societies. A modern novel which uses satire is Joseph Heller's *Catch-22,* which is an attack on war and the government's bureaucratic bungling of men and material, specifically in WWII.

Poetry

VERSE AND METER

The word *verse* strictly refers to a line of poetry, perhaps from the original Latin word "versus," meaning a row or a line, and the notion of turning, "vertere," meaning to turn or move to a new idea. In modern use we refer to verse with the connotation of rhyme, rhythm and meter, but we still recognize verse because of the positioning of lines on the page.

A *stanza* is a grouping of lines with a metrical order and an often repeated rhyme, which we know as the *rhyme scheme*. Such a scheme is shown by letters to represent the repeating sounds. Byron's "Stanzas" will help you see the use of a definite rhyme and how to mark it:

"Stanzas"

(When a man hath no freedom to fight for at home)
When a man hath no freedom to fight for at home,   *a*
Let him combat for that of his neighbors;   *b*
Let him think of the glories of Greece and of Rome,   *a*
And get knocked on the head for his labors.   *b*

The rhyme scheme is simple: *abab*.

Certain types of rhyme are worth learning. The most common is the *end rhyme*, which has the rhyming word at the end of the line, bringing the line to a definite stop but setting up for a rhyming word in another line later on, as in "Stanzas": home… Rome, a perfect rhyme. *Internal rhyme* includes at least one rhyming word within the line, often for the purpose of speeding the rhythm or making it linger. Look at the effect of Byron's internal rhymes mixed with half-rhymes: "combat… for that." *Slant rhyme*, sometimes referred to as half, off, near or approximate rhyme, often jolts a reader who expects a perfect rhyme; poets thus use such a rhyme to express disappointment or a deliberate let-down. *Masculine rhyme* uses one-syllable words or stresses the final syllable of polysyllabic words, giving the feeling of strength and impact. *Feminine rhyme* uses a rhyme of two or more syllables, the stress not falling upon the last syllable, giving a feeling of softness and lightness.

Meter simply means the pattern or measure of stressed or accented words within a line of verse. When studying meter a student should note where stresses fall on syllables; if an absence of stressed syllables occurs there is always an explanation why. Usually, we use a rising and falling rhythm, known as *iambic rhythm*. A line of poetry that alternates stressed and unstressed syllables is said to have *iambic meter*. A line of poetry with ten syllables of rising and falling stresses is known as *iambic pentameter*, best used by Shakespeare and John Milton in their blank verse. The basic measuring unit in a line of poetry is called a *foot*. An iambic foot has one unstressed syllable followed by a stressed syllable; it is marked by ∪ /. Pentameter means "five-measure." Therefore iambic pentameter has five groups of two syllables, or ten beats, to the line.

TYPES OF POETRY

The pattern or design of a poem is known as *form*, and even the strangest, most experimental poetry will have some type of form to it. Allen Ginsberg's "A Supermarket in California" caused a stir because it didn't read like poetry, but on the page there is a certain form to it. *Closed form* will be immediately recognizable because lines can be counted and its shape determined. The poet must keep to the recognized form, in number of lines, rhyme scheme, and/or meter. *Open form* developed from "vers libre"; it gives a freedom of pattern to the poet.

The most easily recognized closed form of poetry is the *sonnet*, sometimes referred to as a *fixed form*. The sonnet always has fourteen lines. There are two types of sonnets, the Petrarchan or Italian, and the Shakespearean or English. The Petrarchan sonnet is organized into two groups of eight lines and six: the *octave* and the *sestet*. The Shakespearean sonnet organizes the lines into three groups of four lines: *quatrains* and a *couplet*, which has two rhyming lines.

The couplet, mentioned earlier, leads us to a closed form of poetry that is very useful for the poet. It is a two-line stanza that usually contains an end rhyme. If the couplet is firmly end-stopped and written in iambic pentameter it is known as *heroic couplet*, after the use was made of it in the English translations of the great classical, heroic epics such as *The Iliad* and *The Odyssey*.

A simpler type of poem is the *ballad*. The stories—a ballad is a story in a song—revolve around themes such as love, hate, lust, murder, rejected lovers, knights, and the supernatural. The form gave rise to the *ballad stanza*, four lines rhyming abcb with lines 1 and 3 having 8 syllables and lines 2 and 4 having 6. Poets who later wrote what are known as *literary ballads* kept the same pattern.

The *elegy* is a lament for someone's death or the passing of a love or concept. One of the most famous is Thomas Gray's "Elegy Written in a Country Churchyard," which mourns not only the passing of individuals but of a past age and the wasted potential within every human being, no matter how humble. Often *ode* and elegy become synonymous, but an ode is usually longer, dealing with more profound areas of human life than simply death. John Keats' odes are perhaps the most famous and most beloved in English poetry.

FIGURATIVE LANGUAGE AND POETIC DEVICES

Perhaps what most distinguishes poetry from any other genre is the use of figurative language, used through the ages to convey the poet's own particular world-view in a unique way. Words have *connotation* and *denotation*, *figurative* and *literal* meanings. A simple example involves the word "home." If we free-associated among a group of twenty students we would find a number of connotations for the word, depending on what home means to each person: comforting, scary, lonely, dark, creepy, safety, haven, hell, etc. However, the denotation is straightforward: a home is a dwelling that provides shelter for an individual or family.

The most important poetic devices are the *metaphor* and the *simile*. Metaphors compare two unlike things, feelings, or objects. Similes also compare two dissimilar things but always use the words "as if" (for a clause) or "like" (for a word or phrase). Metaphors suggest the meaning is implicit. An easy way to distinguish between the two is the example of the camel.

Metaphor: The camel is the ship of the desert.

Simile: A camel is like a ship in the desert.

Both conjure up a camel almost sliding across the desert, and the notion of the vastness of the desert parallels the sea.

Personification is usually easier than metaphor to detect in poetry. Usually the object that is being personified—referred to as a human or possessing human attributes—is capitalized.

Samuel Coleridge employs a visual personification in "Rime of the Ancient Mariner":

> ...the Sun (was) flecked with bars
> (Heaven's Mother send us grace!)
> As if through a dungeon-grate he peered
> With broad and burning face.

We can see the prisoner behind the bars, and this particular prisoner has a broad and burning face... of course, because he is the sun! The personification brings us that flash of recognition when we can say "Yes, I see that!"

Image is another important aspect of figurative language. Although it is not a figure of speech in itself, the image plays a large role in poetry because the reader is expected to imagine what the poet is evoking. The image can be literal, wherein the reader has little adjustment to make to see or touch or taste the image, or figurative, which demands more from readers. For example, the second stanza of Keats' "Ode to a Nightingale" sets up the taste imagery of a

> …draught of vintage that hath been
> Cooled a long age in the deep-delvéd earth,
> Tasting of Flora and the country green,
> Dance, and Provençal song, and sunburnt mirth!
> O for a beaker of the warm South,
> Full of the true, the blushful Hippocrene,
> With beaded bubbles winking at the brim,
> And purple-stainéd mouth

Even though Flora and Hippocrene are not names we are readily familiar with, the image of the cool wine, the taste, the look, and the feeling evoked of the South and warmth, all come rushing into our minds as we enter the poet's imagination and find images in common.

Image in figurative language inevitably leads to symbolism. When an object, image, or feeling takes on a larger meaning outside of itself, then a poet is employing a symbol, something which stands for something greater. Many symbols have become stock or conventional, such as the rose standing for love and the flag standing for patriotism.

Literary Terms

Following are some more terms that will be useful to know when you take the LAST.

Alliteration—the repetition of consonants at the beginning of words that are next door or close by to each other. Gerard Hopkins' "The Caged Skylark" provides some fine examples: "<u>s</u>kylark <u>s</u>canted"; "<u>M</u>an's <u>m</u>ounting… <u>m</u>ean house"; "<u>f</u>ree <u>f</u>ells"; "<u>d</u>rudgery, <u>d</u>ay-<u>l</u>abouring-out <u>l</u>ife's age."

Apostrophe—the direct address of someone or something that is not present. Many odes, such as Keats' "Ode on a Grecian Urn," begin this way: "Thou still unravished bride of quietness."

Assonance—the repetition of vowel sounds usually internally rather than initially. "Her goodly <u>eyes</u> like sapph<u>i</u>res sh<u>i</u>ning br<u>i</u>ght."

Bathos—deliberate anticlimax to make a definite point or draw attention to a falseness. The most famous example is from Alexander Pope's "Rape of the

Lock": "Here thou, great Anna! whom three realms obey, /Dost sometimes counsel take—and sometimes tea."

Consonance—similar to slant rhyme—the repetition of consonant sounds without the vowel sound repeated. Hopkins again frequently uses this, as in "Pied Beauty": "All things counter, original, spare, strange;… adazzle, dim."

Diction—the style of word usage. Is the poet using formal or informal language? Does the poetry hinge on slang or a dialect? Are the words "highfalutin" or low-brow?

Enjambment—the running-on of one line of poetry into another. Usually the endings of lines are rhymed so there is an end-stop. In more modern poetry, without rhyme, run-on lines often occur to give a speedier flow, the sound of the speaking voice, or a conversational tone.

Hyperbole—refers to large overstatement often used to draw attention to a mark of beauty or a virtue or an action that the poet disagrees with.

Onomatopoeia—a device in which the word captures the sound. In many poems the words are those in general use: the whiz of fireworks; the crashing of waves on the shore; the booming of water in a underground sea-cave.

Oxymoron—a form of paradox in which contradictory words are used next to each other: "painful pleasure," "sweet sorrow."

Paradox—a situation or action or feeling that appears to be contradictory but on inspection turns out to be true or at least make sense. "The pen is mightier than the sword" at first glance is a contradiction of reality. One can hardly die by being stabbed by a pen, but in the larger world view the words of men, the signing of death warrants, etc., have killed.

Pun—a play on words, often for humorous or sarcastic effect; many of Shakespeare's comedies draw on punning.

Sarcasm—when verbal irony is too harsh it moves into the sarcastic realm. It has been termed the "lowest form of wit" but can be used to good effect in the tone of a poem.

Syntax—the ordering of words into a particular pattern.

Tone—the voice or attitude of the speaker. Remember that the voice need not be that of the poet's. He or she may be adopting a particular tone for a purpose. Your task is to analyze if the tone is angry, sad, conversational, abrupt, wheedling, cynical, affected, satiric, etc.

Drill Questions

1. **The pose of the horse in the sculpture pictured below serves to express**

Flying Horse. 2nd century Han. Wuwie Tomb, Gansu.

(A) **physical aging and decay.**   (C) **lightness and motion.**

(B) **massiveness and stability.**   (D) **military prowess.**

Questions 2–4 refer to the following poem.

> My mistress' eyes are nothing like the sun;
> Coral is far more red than her lips' red;
> If snow be white, why then her breasts are dun;
> If hairs be wires, black wires grow on her head.

I have seen roses damasked, red and white,
But no such roses see I in her cheeks;
And in some perfumes is there more delight
Than in the breath that from my mistress reeks.
I love to hear her speak, yet well I know
That music hath a far more pleasing sound;
I grant I never saw a goddess go;
My mistress, when she walks treads on the ground.
And yet, by heaven, I think my love as rare
As any she belied with false compare.

2.   **This poem is different from other sonnets in that**
   (A)   it is Shakespearean.
   (B)   it is Italian.
   (C)   it describes the appearance of a beloved woman.
   (D)   it does not describe the woman as beautiful.

3.   **The last two lines of the poem**
   (A)   reaffirm the argument held throughout the poem.
   (B)   start a new topic.
   (C)   refute the argument held throughout the poem.
   (D)   are a continuation of the ideas introduced in the poem.

4.   **The poem can best be described as**
   (A)   witty and satirical.   **(C)   sarcastic.**
   (B)   intense.   **(D)   brooding.**

Questions 5–7 refer to the following excerpts.

(A)   For shade to shade will come too drowsily,
       And drown the wakeful anguish of the soul.

(B)   Rocks, caves, lakes, fens, bogs, dens, and shades of death.

(C)   ... yet from these flames
       No light, but rather darkness visible

(D)   Because I could not stop for Death—
       He kindly stopped for me—

5.   Which passage contains an oxymoron?

6.   Which passage uses personification?

7.   Which passage is written in iambic pentameter?

8.   Which of the following describes the design of structures for living, working, worshipping, or other residential or civic needs?
      (A) Architecture
      (B) Painting
      (C) Dance
      (D) Sculpture

Questions 9–10 refer to the following passage.

Creating an English garden on a mountainside in the Ouachita Mountains in central Arkansas may sound like an impossible endeavor, but after two years the dream is becoming reality. Digging up the rocks and replacing them with bags of top soil, humus, and peat, the persistent gardener now has sprouts that are not all weeds. Gravel paths meander through the beds of shasta daisies, marigolds, lavender, valerian, iris, day lilies, Mexican heather, and other flowers. Ornamental grasses, dogwood trees, and shrubs back up the flowers. Along the periodic waterway created by an underground spring, swamp hibiscus, helenium, hosta, and umbrella plants display their colorful and seasonal blooms. The flower beds are outlined by large rocks dug up by a pickax. Blistered hands are worth the effort when people stop by to view the mountainside beauty.

9.　**The point of view of this passage is**
　　(A)　first person.
　　(B)　second person.
　　(C)　third person.
　　(D)　first and third person.

10.　**The purpose of this essay is**
　　(A)　speculative.
　　(B)　argumentative.
　　(C)　narrative.
　　(D)　expository.

Answers to Drill Questions

1. **(C)**　　　6. **(D)**

2. **(D)**　　　7. **(A)**

3. **(C)**　　　8. **(A)**

4. **(A)**　　　9. **(C)**

5. **(C)**　　　10. **(C)**

LAST/ATS-W

Chapter 5

Communication Skills Review

Chapter 5

Communication Skills Review

This review was developed to prepare you for the Communication Skills Section of the LAST. You will be guided through a step-by-step approach to attacking reading passages and questions. Also included are tips to help you quickly and accurately answer the questions which will appear in this section. By studying our review, you will greatly increase your chances of achieving a passing score on the Communication Skills Section of the LAST.

A FOUR-STEP APPROACH

When you read passages in the Communication Skills section of the LAST, you will have four tasks:

Step 1: preview,

Step 2: read actively,

Step 3: review the passage, and

Step 4: answer the questions.

Step 1: Preview

Before beginning to read the passage, you should take about 30 seconds to look over the passage and questions. An effective way to preview the passage is to read quickly the first sentence of each paragraph, the concluding

ce of the passage, and the questions—but not the answers—following
passage. Practice previewing the following passage and questions.

PASSAGE

That the area of obscenity and pornography is a difficult one for the Supreme Court is well documented. The Court's numerous attempts to define obscenity have proven unworkable and left the decision to the subjective preferences of the justices. Perhaps Justice Stewart put it best when, after refusing to define obscenity, he declared, "But I know it when I see it." Does the Court literally have to see it to know it? Specifically, what role does the fact-pattern, including the materials' medium, play in the Court's decision?

Several recent studies employ fact-pattern analysis in modeling the Court's decision making. These studies examine the fact-pattern or case characteristics, often with ideological and attitudinal factors, as a determinant of the decision reached by the Court. In broad terms, these studies owe their theoretical underpinnings to attitude theory. As the name suggests, attitude theory views the Court's attitudes as an explanation of its decisions.

These attitudes, however, do not operate in a vacuum. As Spaeth explains, "the activation of an attitude involves both an object and the situation in which that object is encountered." The objects to which the court directs its attitudes are litigants. The situation—the subject matter of the case—can be defined in broad or narrow terms. One may define the situation as an entire area of the law (e.g., civil liberties issues). On an even broader scale the situation may be defined as the decision to grant certiorari or whether to defect from a minimum-winning coalition.

Defining the situation with such broad strokes, however, does not allow one to control for case content. In many specific issue areas, the cases present strikingly similar patterns. In examining the Court's search and seizure decisions, Segal found that a relatively small number of situational and case characteristic variables explain a high proportion of the Court's decisions.

Despite Segal's success, verification of the applicability of fact-pattern analysis in other issue areas has been slow in forthcoming. Renewed interest in obscenity and pornography by federal and state governments, the academic community, and numerous antipornography interest groups indicates the Court's decisions in this area deserve closer examination.

The Court's obscenity and pornography decisions also present an opportunity to study the Court's behavior in an area where the Court has granted significant decision-making authority to the states. In *Miller v. California* (1973) the Court announced the importance of local community standards in obscenity determinations. The Court's subsequent behavior may suggest how the Court will react in other areas where it has chosen to defer to the states (e.g., abortion).

QUESTIONS

1.   The main idea of the passage is best stated in which of the following sentences?

   (A)   The Supreme Court has difficulty convicting those who violate obscenity laws.

   (B)   The current definitions for obscenity and pornography provided by the Supreme Court are unworkable.

   (C)   Fact-pattern analysis is insufficient for determining the attitude of the Court toward the issues of obscenity and pornography.

   (D)   Despite the difficulties presented by fact-pattern analysis, Justice Segal found the solution in the patterns of search and seizure decisions.

2.   The main purpose of the writer in this passage is to

   (A)   convince the reader that the Supreme Court is making decisions about obscenity based on their subjective views only.

   (B)   explain to the reader how fact-pattern analysis works with respect to cases of obscenity and pornography.

   (C)   define obscenity and pornography for the layperson.

   (D)   demonstrate the role fact-pattern analysis plays in determining the Supreme Court's attitude about cases in obscenity and pornography.

3.   Of the following, which fact best supports the writer's contention that the Court's decisions in the areas of obscenity and pornography deserve closer scrutiny?

(A)   The fact that a Supreme Court Justice said, "I know it when I see it."

(B)   The fact that recent studies employ fact-pattern analysis in modeling the Court's decision-making process.

(C)   The fact that attitudes do not operate in a vacuum.

(D)   The fact that federal and state governments, interest groups, and the academic community show renewed interest in the obscenity and pornography decisions by the Supreme Court.

4.   Among the following statements, which states an opinion expressed by the writer rather than a fact?

(A)   That the area of obscenity and pornography is a difficult one for the Supreme Court is well documented.

(B)   The objects to which a court directs its attitudes are the litigants.

(C)   In many specific issue areas, the cases present strikingly similar patterns.

(D)   The Court's subsequent behavior may suggest how the Court will react in other legal areas.

5.   The list of topics below that best reflects the organization of the topics of the passage is

(A)   I.   The difficulties of the Supreme Court

II.   Several recent studies

III. Spaeth's definition of "attitude"

IV.   The similar patterns of cases

V.   Other issue areas

VI.   The case of *Miller v. California*

(B)   I   The Supreme Court, obscenity, and fact-pattern analysis

II.   Fact-pattern analyses and attitude theory

III. The definition of "attitude" for the Court

IV. The definition of "situation"

V. The breakdown in fact-pattern analysis

VI. Studying Court behavior

(C) I. Justice Stewart's view of pornography

II. Theoretical underpinnings

III. A minimum-winning coalition

IV. Search and seizure decisions

V. Renewed interest in obscenity and pornography

VI. The importance of local community standards

(D) I. The Court's numerous attempts to define obscenity

II. Case characteristics

III. The subject matter of cases

IV. The Court's proportion of decisions

V. Broad-based factors

VI. Obscenity determination

6. Which paragraph below is the best summary of the passage?

(A) The Supreme Court's decision-making process with respect to obscenity and pornography has become too subjective. Fact-pattern analyses, used to determine the overall attitude of the Court, reveal only broad-based attitudes on the part of the Court toward the situations of obscenity cases. But these patterns cannot fully account for the Court's attitudes toward case content. Research is not conclusive that fact-pattern analyses work when applied to legal areas. Renewed public and local interest suggests continued study and close examination of how the Court makes decisions. Delegating authority to the states may reflect patterns for Court decisions in other socially sensitive areas.

(B) Though subjective, the Supreme Court decisions are well documented. Fact-pattern analyses reveal the attitude of the Supreme Court toward its decisions in cases. Spaeth explains that an attitude involves both an object and a situation. For the Court, the situation may be defined as the decision to grant certiorari. Cases present strikingly similar patterns, and a small number of variables explain a high proportion of the Court's decisions. Segal has made an effort to verify the applicability of fact-pattern analysis with some success. The Court's decisions on obscenity and pornography suggest weak Court behavior, such as in *Miller v. California*.

(C) To determine what obscenity and pornography mean to the Supreme Court, we must use fact-pattern analysis. Fact-pattern analysis reveals the ideas that the Court uses to operate in a vacuum. The litigants and the subject matter of cases is defined in broad terms (such as an entire area of law) to reveal the Court's decision-making process. Search and seizure cases reveal strikingly similar patterns, leaving the Court open to grant certiorari effectively. Renewed public interest in the Court's decisions proves how the Court will react in the future.

(D) Supreme Court decisions about pornography and obscenity are under examination and are out of control. The Court has to see the case to know it. Fact-pattern analyses reveal that the Court can only define cases in narrow terms, thus revealing individual egotism on the part of the Justices. As a result of strikingly similar patterns in search and seizure cases, the Court should be studied further for its weakness in delegating authority to state courts, as in the case of *Miller v. California*.

7. Based on the passage, the rationale for fact-pattern analyses arises out of what theoretical groundwork?

(A) Subjectivity theory

(B) The study of cultural norms

(C) Attitude theory

(D) Cybernetics

8. Based on data in the passage, what would most likely be the major cause for the difficulty in pinning down the Supreme Court's attitude toward cases of obscenity and pornography?

(A) The personal opinions of the Court Justices

(B) The broad nature of the situations of the cases

(C) The ineffective logistics of certiorari

(D)   The inability of the Court to resolve the variables presented by individual case content

9.   In the context of the passage, *subjective* might be most nearly defined as

(A)   personal.

(B)   wrong.

(C)   focused.

(D)   objective.

As you begin to examine the passage, you should first determine the main idea and underline it so that you can easily refer back to it if a question requires you to do so. The main idea should be found in the first paragraph of the passage, and may even be the first sentence. From what you have read thus far, you now know that the main idea of this passage is that the Supreme Court has difficulty in making obscenity and pornography decisions.

In addition, you know that recent studies have used fact-pattern analysis in modeling the Court's decision. You have learned also that attitudes do not operate independently and that case content is important. The feasibility of using fact-pattern analysis in other issue areas has not been quickly verified. To study the behavior of the Court in an area in which it has granted significant decision-making authority to the states, one has only to consider the obscenity and pornography decisions. In summary, the author suggests that the Court's subsequent behavior may suggest how the Court will react in those other areas in which decision-making authority has previously been granted to the states. As you can see, having this information will make the reading of the passage much easier.

You should have also looked at the stem of the question when you previewed the passage. You do not need to spend time reading the answers to each question. The stem alone can help to guide you as you read.

Step 2: Read Actively

After you preview, you should read actively. This means that as you read you should identify—and even underline—important words, topic sentences, main ideas, and words that express tone.

Read carefully the first sentence of each paragraph because this often contains the topic of the paragraph. You may wish to underline each topic sentence.

One of the question stems may ask you to determine *the purpose* of the writing. Use the following questions to hep you determine an author's intent:

- What is the writer's overall primary goal or objective?

- Is the writer trying primarily to persuade you by proving or using facts to make a case for an idea?

- Is the writer trying primarily to inform and enlighten you about an idea, object, or event?

- Is the writer attempting primarily to amuse you? Keep you fascinated? Laughing?

Make sure you examine all of the facts that the author uses to support the main idea. This will help you decide whether the writer has made a case, and what sort of purpose he or she supports. Note the supporting details: facts, examples, illustrations, testimony, and the research of experts. You may want to label each supporting detail to help you locate it easily when answering questions.

Step 3: Review the Passage

After you finish reading actively, take 10 or 20 seconds to look over the main idea, the topic sentences that you have underlined, and the key words and phrases you have marked. Now you are ready to go to Step 4 and answer the questions.

Step 4: Answer the Questions

In Step 2, you gathered enough information from the passage to answer questions dealing with main idea, purpose, support, fact vs. opinion, organization, and summarization. Refer to the previous passage and questions on the Supreme Court as you read.

MAIN IDEA QUESTIONS

Looking back at the questions which follow the passage, you see that Question 1 is a "main idea" question.

In answering the question, you see that answer choice (C) is correct. The writer uses the second, third, fourth, and fifth paragraphs to show how fact-pattern analysis is an ineffective determinant of the Court's attitude toward obscenity and pornography.

Answer (A) is incorrect. There is no reference to "convicting" persons accused of obscenity; it is only stated that the Court has difficulty defining it.

Choice (B) is also incorrect. Though it is stated as a fact by the writer, it is couched only as an effect that leads the writer to examine how fact-pattern analysis does or does not work to reveal the "cause" or attitude of the Court toward obscenity and pornography.

Finally, answer choice (D) is incorrect. The statement is contrary to what Segal found when he examined search and seizure cases.

PURPOSE QUESTIONS

Question 2 requires you to determine the writer's purpose.

(D) is correct. Though the writer never states it directly, he or she summons data consistently to show that fact-pattern analysis gives us only part of the picture. It cannot account for the attitude toward individual cases.

Choice (A) is incorrect. The writer does not try to convince us of this fact, but merely states it as an opinion resulting from the evidence derived from the "well-documented" background to the problem.

(B) is also incorrect. The writer does more than just explain the role of fact-pattern analysis, but rather shows how it cannot fully apply.

The passage is about the Court's, not the public's, difficulty in defining these terms. Nowhere do definitions for these terms appear. Therefore, choice (C) is incorrect.

SUPPORT QUESTIONS

Question 3 requires you to analyze the author's supporting details.

Choice (D) must be correct. In the fifth paragraph, the writer states that the "renewed interest"—a real and observable fact—from these groups "indicates the Court's decisions . . . deserve closer examination," another way of saying scrutiny.

Answer (A) is incorrect. The writer uses this remark to show how the Court cannot effectively define obscenity and pornography, and relies on "subjective preferences" to resolve issues.

In addition, choice (B) is incorrect because the writer points to the data in (D), not fact-pattern analyses, to prove this.

(C), too, is incorrect. Although it is true, the writer makes this point to show how fact-pattern analysis doesn't help clear up the real-world "situation" in which the Court must make its decisions.

FACT VS. OPINION QUESTIONS

Question 4 requires you to know the difference between fact and opinion.

An opinion is something that cannot be proven to hold true in all circumstances; therefore, choice (D) is correct. It is the only statement among the four for which the evidence is yet to be gathered. It is the writer's opinion that this may be a way to predict the Court's attitudes.

(A), (B), and (C) are all taken from data or documentation already in existence and are, therefore, incorrect.

ORGANIZATION QUESTIONS

Question 5 asks you to arrange given topics to reflect the organization of the passage.

Examination shows that choice (B) is the correct response. These topical areas lead directly to the implied thesis that the "role" of fact-pattern analysis is insufficient for determining the attitude of the Supreme Court in the areas of obscenity and pornography.

Answer (A) is incorrect. The first topic stated in the list is too global to be the topic of the first paragraph. The first paragraph is about the difficulties the Court has with defining obscenity and how fact-pattern analysis might be used to determine the Court's attitude and clear up the problem.

(C) is incorrect because each of the items listed in this topic list is supporting evidence or data for the real topic of each paragraph. [See the list in (B) for correct topics.] For example, Justice Stewart's statement about pornography is cited only to indicate the nature of the problem with obscenity for the Court. It is not the focus of the paragraph itself.

Finally, (D) is incorrect. As with choice (C), these are all incidental pieces of information or data used to make broader points.

SUMMARIZATION QUESTIONS

Question 6 focuses on summarizing.

The paragraph that best and most accurately reports what the writer demonstrated based on the implied thesis is answer choice (C).

Choice (A) is incorrect. It reflects some of the evidence presented in the passage, but the passage does not imply that all Court decisions are subjective—just the ones about pornography and obscenity.

Response (B) is also incorrect. The writer summons information over and over to show how fact-pattern analysis cannot pin down the Court's attitude toward case content. Similarly, the writer does not suggest that delegating authority to the states, as in *Miller v. California,* is a sign of some weakness, but merely that it is worthy of study as a tool for predicting or identifying the Court attitude.

(D) is incorrect. Nowhere does the writer say or suggest that the justice system is "out of control" or that the justices are "egotists." The writer implies only that they are liable to make "subjective" decisions rather than decisions based on an identifiable shared standard.

RECALL QUESTIONS

To answer Question 7, you must be able to recall information from the passage.

The easiest way to answer this question is to refer to the passage. In the second paragraph, the writer states that recent studies using fact-pattern analyses "owe their theoretical underpinnings to attitude theory." Therefore, we can conclude that response (C) is correct.

Answer choices (A), (B), and (D) are incorrect; they are never discussed or mentioned by the writer.

CAUSE/EFFECT QUESTIONS

Question 8 requires you to analyze a cause-and-effect relationship.

Choice (D) is correct; it is precisely what fact-pattern analyses cannot resolve.

Response (A) is incorrect because no evidence is presented for this. It is stated that they do make personal decisions, but not how these decisions cause difficulty.

Answer choice (B) is incorrect because this is one way in which fact-pattern analysis can be helpful.

Finally, (C) is only a statement about certiorari being difficult to administer, but this was never claimed by the writer.

DEFINITION QUESTIONS

Question 9 requires you to know the definition of *subjective*.

The passage refers to individual, rather than institutional, ideas. Therefore choice (A), personal, is the correct answer.

Answer (B) is incorrect. Nothing is implied or stated about the rightness or wrongness of the decisions themselves. Rather, it is the definition of obscenity that seems "unworkable."

(C) is incorrect because the Court's focus is already in place: on obscenity and pornography.

(D) is also incorrect. *Objective* is the direct opposite of *subjective*. Reasoning based on the object of study (objective) is the opposite of reasoning based upon the beliefs, opinions, or ideas of the one viewing the object (subjective).

VOCABULARY ENHANCER

It is important to understand the meanings of all words—not just the ones you are asked to define. A good vocabulary is a strength that can help you perform well on all sections of this test. The following information will build your skills in determining the meanings of words.

Similar Forms and Sounds

The complex nature of language sometimes makes reading difficult. Words often become confusing when they have similar forms and sounds. In fact, the author may have a correct meaning in mind, but an incorrect word choice can alter the meaning of the sentence or even make it totally illogical.

NO: Martha was always part of that cliché.

YES: Martha was always part of that clique.

(A *cliché* is a trite or hackneyed expression; a *clique* is an exclusive group of people.)

NO: The minister spoke of the soul's immorality.

YES: The minister spoke of the soul's immortality.

(*Immorality* means wickedness; *immortality* means imperishable or unending life.)

NO: Where is the nearest stationary store?

YES: Where is the nearest stationery store?

(*Stationary* means immovable; *stationery* is paper used for writing.)

Below are groups of words that are often confused because of their similar forms and sounds.

---

accent—*v.* – to stress or emphasize (You must *accent* the last syllable.)

ascent—*n.* – a climb or rise (John's *ascent* of the mountain was dangerous.)

assent—*n.* – consent; compliance (We need your *assent* before we can go ahead with the plans.)

---

accept—*v.* – to take something offered (She *accepted* the gift.)

except—*prep.* – other than; but (Everyone was included in the plans *except* him.)

---

advice—*n.* – opinion given as to what to do or how to handle a situation (Her sister gave her *advice* on what to say at the interview.)

advise—*v.* – to counsel (John's guidance counselor will *advise* him on where he should apply to college.)

affect—*v.* – to influence (Mary's suggestion did not *affect* me.)

effect—*v.* 1. – to cause to happen (The plan was *effected* with great success.); *n.* 2. – result (The *effect* of the medicine is excellent.)

allusion—*n.* – indirect reference (In the poem, there are many Biblical *allusions.*)

illusion—*n.* – false idea or conception; belief or opinion not in accord with the facts (Greg was under the *illusion* that he could win the race after missing three weeks of practice.)

all ready—*adv. + adj.* – prepared (The family was *all ready* to leave on vacation.)

already—*adv.* – previously (I had *already* read that novel.)

altar—*n.* – table or stand used in religious rites (The priest stood at the *altar.*)

alter—*v.* – to change (Their plans were *altered* during the strike.)

capital—*n.* 1. – a city where the government meets (The senators had a meeting in Albany, the *capital* of New York.); 2. money used in business (They had enough *capital* to develop the industry.)

capitol—*n.* – building in which the legislature meets (Senator Brown gave a speech at the *capitol* in Washington.)

choose—*v.* – to select (Which camera did you *choose*?)

chose—*v.* – past tense of *choose* (Susan *chose* to stay home.)

cite—*v.* – to quote (The student *cited* evidence from the text.)

site—*n.* – location (They chose the *site* where the house would be built.)

clothes—*n.* – garments (Because she got caught in the rain, her *clothes* were wet.)

cloths—*n.* – pieces of material (The *cloths* were used to wash the windows.)

coarse—*adj.* – rough; unrefined (Sandpaper is *coarse.*)

course—*n.* 1. – path of action (She did not know what *course* would solve the problem.); 2. passage (We took the long *course* to the lake.); 3. series of studies (We both enrolled in the physics *course.*); 4. part of a meal (She served a five-*course* meal.)

consul—*n.* – a person appointed by the government to live in a foreign city and represent the citizenry and business interests of his or her native country there (The *consul* was appointed to Naples, Italy.)

council—*n.* – a group used for discussion, advisement (The *council* decided to accept his letter of resignation.)

counsel—*v.* – to advise (Tom *counsels* Jerry on tax matters.)

decent—*adj.* – proper; respectable (He was very *decent* about the entire matter.)

descent—*n.* 1. – moving down (In Dante's *Inferno*, the *descent* into Hell was depicted graphically.); 2. ancestry (He is of Irish *descent*.)

device—*n.* 1. – plan; scheme (The *device* helped her win the race.); 2. invention (We bought a *device* that opens the garage door automatically.)

devise—*v.* – to contrive (He *devised* a plan so John could not win.)

emigrate—*v.* – to go away from a country (Many Japanese *emigrated* from Japan in the late 1800s.)

immigrate—*v.* – to come into a country (Her relatives *immigrated* to the United States after World War I.)

eminent—*n.* – prominent (He is an *eminent* member of the community.)

imminent—*adj.* – impending (The decision is *imminent*.)

immanent—*adj.* – existing within (Maggie believed that religious spirit is *immanent* in human beings.)

fair—*adj.* 1. – beautiful (She was a *fair* maiden.); 2. just (She tried to be *fair*.); *n.* 3. – festival (There were many games at the *fair*.)

fare—*n.* – amount of money paid for transportation (The city proposed that the subway *fare* be raised.)

forth—*adv.* – onward (The soldiers moved *forth* in the blinding snow.)

fourth—*n., adj.* – 4th (She was the *fourth* runner-up in the beauty contest.)

its—possessive form of *it* (Our town must improve *its* roads.)

it's—contraction of *it is* (*It's* time to leave the party.)

later—*adj., adv.* – at a subsequent date (We will take a vacation *later* this year.)

latter—*n.* – second of the two (Susan can visit Monday or Tuesday. The *latter,* however, is preferable.)

lead—*n.* 1. – [led] a metal (The handgun was made of *lead.*); *v.* 2. – [leed] to show the way (The camp counselor *leads* the way to the picnic grounds.)

led—*v.* – past tense of *lead* (#2 above) (The dog *led* the way.)

loose—*adj.* – free; unrestricted (The dog was let *loose* by accident.)

lose—*v.* – to suffer the loss of (He was afraid he would *lose* the race.)

moral—*n.* 1. – lesson taught by a story, incident, etc. (Most fables end with a *moral.*); *adj.* 2. – virtuous (She is a *moral* woman with high ethical standards.)

morale—*n.* – mental condition (After the team lost the game, their *morale* was low.)

of—*prep.* – from (She is *of* French descent.)

off—*adj.* – away; at a distance (The television fell *off* the table.)

passed—*v.* – to have satisfied some requirement (He *passed* the test.)

past—*adj.* 1. – gone by or elapsed in time (His *past* deeds got him in trouble.); *n.* 2. – a period of time gone by (His *past* was shady.); *prep.* 3. – beyond (She ran *past* the house.)

personal—*adj.* – private (Jack was unwilling to discuss his childhood; it was too *personal.*)

personnel—*n.* – staff (The *personnel* at the department store was primarily young adults.)

principal—*adj.* 1. – first or highest in rank or value (Her *principal* reason for leaving was boredom.); *n.* 2. – head of a school (The *principal* addressed the graduating class.)

principle—n. – the ultimate source, origin, or cause of something; a law, truth (The *principles* of physics were reviewed in class today.)

prophecy—*n.* – prediction of the future (His *prophecy* that he would become a doctor came true.)

prophesy—*v.* – to declare or predict (He *prophesied* that we would win the lottery.)

quiet—*adj.* – still; calm (At night all is *quiet.*)

quite—*adv.* – really; truly (She is *quite* a good singer.)

quit—*v.* – to free oneself (Peter had little time to spare so he *quit* the chorus.)

respectfully—*adv.* – with respect, honor, esteem (He declined the offer *respectfully.*)

respectively—*adv.* – in the order mentioned (Jack, Susan, and Jim, who are members of the club, were elected president, vice president, and secretary, *respectively.*)

straight—*adj.* – not curved (The road was *straight.*)

strait—*adj.* 1. – restricted; narrow; confined (The patient was put in a *strait* jacket.); *n.* 2. – narrow waterway (He sailed through the *Strait* of Magellan.)

than—*conj.* – used most commonly in comparisons (Maggie is older *than* I.)

then—*adv.* – soon afterward (We lived in Boston; *then* we moved to New York.)

their—possessive form of *they* (That is *their* house on Tenafly Drive.)

there—*adv.* – at that place (Who is standing *there* under the tree?)

they're—contraction of *they are* (*They're* leaving for California next week.)

to—*prep.* – in the direction of; toward; as (She made a turn *to* the right on Norman Street.)

too—*adv.* 1. – more than enough (She served *too* much for dinner.); 2. also (He is going to Maine, *too.*)

two—*n.* 1. – the number 2; one plus one (The total number of guests is *two.*); *adj.* 2. – amounting to more than one (We have *two* pet rabbits.)

weather—*n.* – the general condition of the atmosphere (The *weather* is expected to be clear on Sunday.)

whether—*conj.* – if it be a case or fact (We don't know *whether* the trains are late.)

who's—contraction of *who is* or *who has* (*Who's* willing to volunteer for the night shift?)

whose—possessive form of *who* (*Whose* book is this?)

your—possessive form of *you* (Is this *your* seat?)

you're—contraction of *you are* (I know *you're* going to do well on the test.)

Multiple Meanings

In addition to words that sound alike, you must be careful when dealing with words that have multiple meanings. For example:

The boy was thrilled that his mother gave him a piece of chewing *gum*.

Dentists advise people to floss their teeth to help prevent *gum* disease.

As you can see, one word can have different meanings depending on the context in which it is used.

VOCABULARY BUILDER

Although the context in which a word appears can help you determine the meaning of the word, one sure-fire way to know a definition is to learn it. By studying the following lists of words and memorizing their definition(s), you will be better equipped to answer Communication Skills questions that deal with word meanings.

abstract—*adj.* – not easy to understand; theoretical

acclaim—*n.* – loud approval; applause

acquiesce—*v.* – to agree or consent to an opinion

adamant—*adj.* – not yielding; firm

adversary—*n.* – an enemy; foe

advocate—*v.* 1. – to plead in favor of; *n.* 2. – supporter; defender

aesthetic—*adj.* – showing good taste; artistic

alleviate—*v.* – to lessen or make easier

aloof—*adj.* – distant in interest; reserved; cool

altercation—*n.* – controversy; dispute

altruistic—*adj.* – unselfish

amass—*v.* – to collect together; to accumulate

ambiguous—*adj.* – not clear; uncertain; vague

ambivalent—*adj.* – undecided

ameliorate—*v.* – to make better; to improve

amiable—*adj.* – friendly

amorphous—*adj.* – having no determinate form

anarchist—*n.* – one who believes that a formal government is unnecessary

antagonism—*n.* – hostility; opposition

apathy—*n.* – lack of emotion or interest

appease—*v.* – to make quiet; to calm

apprehensive—*adj.* – fearful; aware; conscious

arbitrary—*adj.* – based on one's preference or whim

arrogant—*adj.* – acting superior to others; conceited

articulate—*v.* 1. – to speak distinctly; 2. to hinge; to connect; 3. to convey; to express effectively; *adj.* 4. – eloquent; fluent; 5. capable of speech

assess—*v.* – to estimate the value of

astute—*adj.* – cunning; sly; crafty

atrophy—*v.* – to waste away through lack of nutrition

audacious—*adj.* – fearless; bold

augment—*v.* – to increase or add to; to make larger

austere—*adj.* – harsh; severe; strict

authentic—*adj.* – real; genuine; trustworthy

authoritarian—*adj.* – acting as a dictator; demanding obedience

banal—*adj.* – common; petty; ordinary

belittle—*v.* – to make small; to think lightly of

benefactor—*n.* – one who helps others; a donor

benevolent—*adj.* – kind; generous

benign—*adj.* – mild; harmless

biased—*adj.* – prejudiced; influenced; not neutral

blasphemous—*adj.* – irreligious; away from acceptable standards

blithe—*adj.* – happy; cheery; merry

brevity—*n.* – briefness; shortness

candid—*adj.* – honest; truthful; sincere

capricious—*adj.* – changeable; fickle

caustic—*adj.* – burning; sarcastic; harsh

censor—*v.* – to examine and delete objectionable material

censure—*v.* – to criticize or disapprove of

charlatan—*n.* – an imposter; fake

coalesce—*v.* – to combine; to come together

collaborate—*v.* – to work together; to cooperate

compatible—*adj.* – in agreement; harmonious

complacent—*adj.* – content; self-satisfied; smug

compliant—*adj.* – yielding; obedient

comprehensive—*adj.* – all-inclusive; complete; thorough

compromise—*v.* – to settle by mutual adjustment

concede—*v.* 1. – to acknowledge; to admit; 2. to surrender; to abandon one's position

concise—*adj.* – in few words; brief; condensed

condescend—*v.* – to come down from one's position or dignity

condone—*v.* – to overlook; to forgive

conspicuous—*adj.* – easy to see; noticeable

consternation—*n.* – amazement or terror that causes confusion

consummation—*n.* – the completion; finish

contemporary—*adj.* – living or happening at the same time; modern contempt—*n.* – scorn; disrespect

contrite—*adj.* – regretful; sorrowful

conventional—*adj.* – traditional; common; routine

cower—*v.* – to crouch down in fear or shame

defamation—*n.* – any harm to a name or reputation; slander

deference—*n.* – a yielding to the opinion of another

deliberate—*v.* 1. – to consider carefully; to weigh in the mind; *adj.* 2. – intentional

denounce—*v.* – to speak out against; to condemn

depict—*v.* – to portray in words; to present a visual image

deplete—*v.* – to reduce; to empty

depravity—*n.* – moral corruption; badness

deride—*v.* – to ridicule; to laugh at with scorn

desecrate—*v.* – to violate a holy place or sanctuary

detached—*adj.* – separated; not interested; standing alone

deter—*v.* – to prevent; to discourage; to hinder

didactic—*adj.* 1. – instructive; 2. dogmatic; preachy

digress—*v.* – to stray from the subject; to wander from topic

diligence—*n.* – hard work

discerning—*adj.* – distinguishing one thing from another

discord—*n.* – disagreement; lack of harmony

discriminate—*v.* 1. – to distinguish one thing from another; 2. – to demonstrate bias; *adj.* 3. – able to distinguish

disdain—*v.* 1. – to look down upon; to scorn; *n.* 2. – intense dislike

disparage—*v.* – to belittle; to undervalue

disparity—*n.* – difference in form, character, or degree

dispassionate—*adj.* – lack of feeling; impartial

disperse—*v.* – to scatter; to separate

disseminate—*v.* – to circulate; to scatter

dissent—*v.* – to disagree; to differ in opinion

dissonance—*n.* – harsh contradiction

diverse—*adj.* – different; dissimilar

document—*v.* 1. – to support; to substantiate; to verify; *n.* 2. – official paper containing information

dogmatic—*adj.* – stubborn; biased; opinionated

dubious—*adj.* – doubtful; uncertain; skeptical; suspicious

eccentric—*adj.* – odd; peculiar; strange

efface—*v.* – to wipe out; to erase

effervescence—*n.* 1. – liveliness; spirit; enthusiasm; 2. bubbliness

egocentric—*adj.* – self-centered

elaboration—*n.* – act of clarifying; adding details

eloquence—*n.* – the ability to speak well

elusive—*adj.* – hard to catch; difficult to understand

emulate—*v.* – to imitate; to copy; to mimic

endorse—*v.* – to support; to approve of; to recommend

engender—*v.* – to create; to bring about

enhance—*v.* – to improve; to compliment; to make more attractive

enigma—*n.* – mystery; secret; perplexity

ephemeral—*adj.* – temporary; brief; short-lived

equivocal—*adj.* – doubtful; uncertain

erratic—*adj.* – unpredictable; strange

erroneous—*adj.* – untrue; inaccurate; not correct

esoteric—*adj.* – incomprehensible; obscure

euphony—*n.* – pleasant sound

execute—*v.* 1. – to put to death; to kill; 2. to carry out; to fulfill

exemplary—*adj.* – serving as an example; outstanding

exhaustive—*adj.* – thorough; complete

expedient—*adj.* – advisable; convenient; makeshift

expedite—*v.* – to speed up

explicit—*adj.* – specific; definite

extol—*v.* – to praise; to commend

extraneous—*adj.* – irrelevant; not related; not essential

facilitate—*v.* – to make easier; to simplify

fallacious—*adj.* – misleading

fanatic—*n.* – enthusiast; extremist

fastidious—*adj.* – fussy; hard to please

fervor—*n.* – passion; intensity

fickle—*adj.* – changeable; unpredictable

fortuitous—*adj.* – accidental; happening by chance; lucky

frivolity—*n.* – giddiness; lack of seriousness

fundamental—*adj.* – basic; necessary

furtive—*adj.* – secretive; sly

futile—*adj.* – worthless; unprofitable

glutton—*n.* – overeater

grandiose—*adj.* – extravagant; flamboyant

gravity—*n.* – seriousness

guile—*n.* – slyness; deceit

gullible—*adj.* – easily fooled

hackneyed—*adj.* – commonplace; trite

hamper—*v.* – to interfere with; to hinder

haphazard—*adj.* – disorganized; random

hedonistic—*adj.* – pleasure seeking

heed—*v.* – to obey; to yield to

heresy—*n.* – opinion contrary to popular belief

hindrance—*n.* – blockage; obstacle

humility—*n.* – lack of pride; modesty

hypocritical—*adj.* – two-faced; deceptive

hypothetical—*adj.* – assumed; uncertain

illuminate—*v.* – to make understandable

illusory—*adj.* – unreal; false; deceptive

immune—*adj.* – protected; unthreatened by

immutable—*adj.* – unchangeable; permanent

impartial—*adj.* – unbiased; fair

impetuous—*adj.* 1. – rash; impulsive; 2. forcible; violent

implication—*n.* – suggestion; inference

inadvertent—*adj.* – not on purpose; unintentional

incessant—*adj.* – constant; continual

incidental—*adj.* – extraneous; unexpected

inclined—*adj.* 1. – apt to; likely to; 2. angled

incoherent—*adj.* – illogical; rambling

incompatible—*adj.* – disagreeing; disharmonious

incredulous—*adj.* – unwilling to believe; skeptical

indifferent—*adj.* – unconcerned

indolent—*adj.* – lazy; inactive

indulgent—*adj.* – lenient; patient

inevitable—*adj.* – sure to happen; unavoidable

infamous—*adj.* – having a bad reputation; notorious

infer—*v.* – to form an opinion; to conclude

initiate—*v.* 1. – to begin; to admit into a group; *n.* 2. – a person who is in the process of being admitted into a group

innate—*adj.* – natural; inborn

innocuous—*adj.* – harmless; innocent

innovate—*v.* – to introduce a change; to depart from the old

insipid—*adj.* – uninteresting; bland

instigate—*v.* – to start; to provoke

intangible—*adj.* – incapable of being touched; immaterial

ironic—*adj.* – contradictory; inconsistent; sarcastic

irrational—*adj.* – not logical

jeopardy—*n.* – danger

kindle—*v.* – to ignite; to arouse

languid—*adj.* – weak; fatigued

laud—*v.* – to praise

lax—*adj.* – careless; irresponsible

lethargic—*adj.* – lazy; passive

levity—*n.* – silliness; lack of seriousness

lucid—*adj.* 1. – shining; 2. easily understood

magnanimous—*adj.* – forgiving; unselfish

malicious—*adj.* – spiteful; vindictive

marred—*adj.* – damaged

meander—*v.* – to wind on a course; to go aimlessly

melancholy—*n.* – depression; gloom

meticulous—*adj.* – exacting; precise

minute—*adj.* – extremely small; tiny

miser—*n.* – penny pincher; stingy person

mitigate—*v.* – to alleviate; to lessen; to soothe

morose—*adj.* – moody; despondent

negligence—*n.* – carelessness

nostalgic—*adj.* – longing for the past; filled with bittersweet memories

novel—*adj.* – new

nullify—*v.* – to cancel; to invalidate

objective—*n.* 1. – goal; *adj.* 2. – open-minded; impartial

obscure—*adj.* – not easily understood; dark

obsolete—*adj.* – out of date; passe

ominous—*adj.* – threatening

optimist—*n.* – person who hopes for the best; sees the good side

orthodox—*adj.* – traditional; accepted

pagan—*n.* 1. – polytheist; *adj.* 2. – polytheistic

partisan—*n.* 1. – supporter; follower; *adj.* 2. – biased; one sided

perceptive—*adj.* – full of insight; aware

peripheral—*adj.* – marginal; outer

pernicious—*adj.* – dangerous; harmful

pessimism—*n.* – seeing only the gloomy side; hopelessness

phenomenon—*n.* 1. – miracle; 2. occurrence

philanthropy—*n.* – charity; unselfishness

pious—*adj.* – religious; devout; dedicated

placate—*v.* – to pacify

plausible—*adj.* – probable; feasible

pragmatic—*adj.* – matter-of-fact; practical

preclude—*v.* – to inhibit; to make impossible

predecessor—*n.* – one who has occupied an office before another

prodigal—*adj.* – wasteful; lavish

prodigious—*adj.* – exceptional; tremendous

profound—*adj.* – deep; knowledgeable; thorough

profusion—*n.* – great amount; abundance

prosaic—*adj.* – tiresome; ordinary

provincial—*adj.* – regional; unsophisticated

provocative—*adj.* 1. – tempting; 2. irritating

prudent—*adj.* – wise; careful; prepared

qualified—*adj.* – experienced; indefinite

rectify—*v.* – to correct

redundant—*adj.* – repetitious; unnecessary

refute—*v.* – to challenge; to disprove

relegate—*v.* – to banish; to put to a lower position

relevant—*adj.* – of concern; significant

remorse—*n.* – guilt; sorrow

reprehensible—*adj.* – wicked; disgraceful

repudiate—*v.* – to reject; to cancel

rescind—*v.* – to retract; to discard

resignation—*n.* 1. – quitting; 2. submission

resolution—*n.* – proposal; promise; determination

respite—*n.* – recess; rest period

reticent—*adj.* – silent; reserved; shy

reverent—*adj.* – respectful

rhetorical—*adj.* – having to do with verbal communication

rigor—*n.* – severity

sagacious—*adj.* – wise; cunning

sanguine—*adj.* 1. – optimistic; cheerful; 2. red

saturate—*v.* – to soak thoroughly; to drench

scanty—*adj.* – inadequate; sparse

scrupulous—*adj.* – honorable; exact

scrutinize—*v.* – to examine closely; to study

servile—*adj.* – slavish; groveling

skeptic—*n.* – doubter

slander—*v.* – to defame; to maliciously misrepresent

solemnity—*n.* – seriousness

solicit—*v.* – to ask; to seek

stagnant—*adj.* – motionless; uncirculating

stanza—*n.* – group of lines in a poem having a definite pattern

static—*adj.* – inactive; changeless

stoic—*adj.* – detached; unruffled; calm

subtlety—*n.* 1. – understatement; 2. propensity for understatement; 3. sophistication; 4. cunning

superficial—*adj.* – on the surface; narrow-minded; lacking depth

superfluous—*adj.* – unnecessary; extra

surpass—*v.* – to go beyond; to outdo

sycophant—*n.* – flatterer

symmetry—*n.* – correspondence of parts; harmony

taciturn—*adj.* – reserved; quiet; secretive

tedious—*adj.* – time-consuming; burdensome; uninteresting

temper—*v.* – to soften; to pacify; to compose

tentative—*adj.* – not confirmed; indefinite

thrifty—*adj.* – economical; pennywise

tranquility—*n.* – peace; stillness; harmony

trepidation—*n.* – apprehension; uneasiness

trivial—*adj.* – unimportant; small; worthless

tumid—*adj.* – swollen; inflated

undermine—*v.* – to weaken; to ruin

uniform—*adj.* – consistent; unvaried; unchanging

universal—*adj.* – concerning everyone; existing everywhere

unobtrusive—*adj.* – inconspicuous; reserved

unprecedented—*adj.* – unheard of; exceptional

unpretentious—*adj.* – simple; plain; modest

vacillation—*n.* – fluctuation

valid—*adj.* – acceptable; legal

vehement—*adj.* – intense; excited; enthusiastic

venerate—*v.* – to revere

verbose—*adj.* – wordy; talkative

viable—*adj.* 1. – capable of maintaining life; 2. possible; attainable

vigor—*n.* – energy; forcefulness

vilify—*v.* – to slander

virtuoso—*n.* – highly skilled artist

virulent—*adj.* – deadly; harmful; malicious

vital—*adj.* – important; spirited

volatile—*adj.* – changeable; undependable

vulnerable—*adj.* – open to attack; unprotected

wane—*v.* – to grow gradually smaller

whimsical—*adj.* – fanciful; amusing

wither—*v.* – to wilt; to shrivel; to humiliate; to cut down

zealot—*n.* – believer; enthusiast; fan

zenith—*n.* – point directly overhead in the sky

 ## Drill Questions

Match each word in the left column with the word in the right column that is most opposite *in meaning.*

Word		Match	
1. ____ articulate	6. ____ furtive	(A) placid	(F) changeable
2. ____ deter	7. ____ ephemeral	(B) jovial	(G) pessimistic
3. ____ volatile	8. ____ prodigious	(C) minute	(H) eternal
4. ____ immutable	9. ____ euphony	(D) dissonance	(I) candid
5. ____ sanguine	10. ____ morose	(E) assist	(J) incoherent

Questions 11–15 refer to the following passage.

> We laymen have always been intensely curious to know—like the   1
> cardinal who put a similar question to Ariosto—from what sources
> that strange being, the creative writer, draws his material, and how
> he manages to make such an impression on us with it and to arouse
> in us emotions of which, perhaps, we had not even thought our-   5
> selves capable. Our interest is only heightened the more by the fact
> that, if we ask him, the writer himself gives us no explanation, or

none that is satisfactory, and it is not at all weakened by our knowledge that not even the clearest insight into the determinants of his choice of material and into the nature of the art of creating imaginative form will ever help to make creative writers of us. 10

If we could at least discover in ourselves or in people like ourselves an activity which was in some way akin to creative writing! An examination of it would then give us a hope of obtaining the beginnings of an explanation of the creative work of writers. And, indeed, 15 there is some prospect of this being possible. After all, creative writers themselves like to lessen the distance between their kind and the common run of humanity; they so often assure us that every man is a poet at heart and that the last poet will not perish till the last man does. 20

Should we not look for the first traces of imaginative activity as early as in childhood? The child's best-loved and most intense occupation is with his play or games. Might we not say that every child at play behaves like a creative writer, in that he creates a world of his own, or, rather, rearranges the things of his world in a new way which 25 pleases him? It would be wrong to think he does not take that world seriously; on the contrary, he takes play very seriously and he expends large amounts of emotion on it. The opposite of play is not what is serious but what is real. In spite of all the emotion with which he cathects his world of play, the child distinguishes it quite 30 well from reality; and he likes to link his imagined objects and situations to the tangible and visible things of the real world. This linking is all that differentiates the child's "play" from "fantasying."

11. **What is the effect of the speaker's use of "we"?**

    (A) **It separates the speaker and his or her colleagues from the reader.**

    (B) **It involves the reader in the search for, yet distinguishes him or her from, the creative writer.**

    (C) **It creates a royal and authoritative persona for the speaker.**

    (D) **It makes the speaker the stand-in for all men.**

12. **What is the antecedent of "it" (line 8)?**

    (A) **"explanation"**   (C) **"interest"**

    (B) **"fact"**   (D) **"impression"**

13. Which of the following statements would the speaker be most likely to DISAGREE with?

(A) A lay person cannot become a creative writer by studying the writer's methods.

(B) All men are writers at heart.

(C) Creative writers are fundamentally different from nonwriters.

(D) Children understand the distinction between imagination and reality.

14. "Cathects" (line 28) can best be defined as

(A) constructs.

(B) distances.

(C) fantasizes.

(D) discourages.

15. It can be inferred that the speaker believes that creative writing is

(A) an opposite of childhood play.

(B) unrelated to childhood play.

(C) a continuation of childhood play.

(D) similar to the fantasizing of childhood play.

Answers to Drill Questions

1. (J)	6. (I)	11. (B)
2. (E)	7. (H)	12. (C)
3. (A)	8. (C)	13. (C)
4. (F)	9. (D)	14. (A)
5. (G)	10. (B)	15. (D)

Chapter 6

Writing Skills Review

Chapter 6

Writing Skills Review

The LAST does not require you to memorize grammatical terms. However, it is important to understand grammatical concepts in order to write and revise text. It is not necessary to memorize all of the following rules, but if you have problems with certain areas of your writing, be sure to study the appropriate review sections.

GRAMMAR AND USAGE

The requirements for informal spoken English are much more relaxed than the rigid rules for "standard written English." While slang, colloquialisms, and other informal expressions are acceptable and sometimes very appropriate in casual speech, they are inappropriate in academic and business writing.

You should watch for errors in grammar, spelling, punctuation, capitalization, sentence structure, and word choice. Remember that this is a test of written language skills; therefore, your responses should be based on what you know to be correct for written work, not what you know to be appropriate for a casual conversation.

Sentence Structure Skills

PARALLELISM

Parallel structure is used to express matching ideas. It refers to the grammatical balance of a series of any of the following:

Phrases

The squirrel ran *along the fence*, *up the tree*, and *into his burrow* with a mouthful of acorns.

Adjectives

The job market is flooded with *very talented*, *highly motivated*, and *well-educated* young people.

Nouns

You will need a *notebook*, *pencil*, and *dictionary* for the test.

Clauses

The children were told to decide *which toy they would* keep and *which toy they would* give away.

Verbs

The farmer *plowed*, *planted*, and *harvested* his corn in record time.

Verbals

Reading, *writing*, and *calculating* are fundamental skills that all of us should possess.

Correlative conjunctions

Either you will do your homework *or* you will fail.

Repetition of structural signals

(such as articles, auxiliaries, prepositions, and conjunctions)

INCORRECT: I have quit my job, enrolled in school, and am looking for a reliable babysitter.

CORRECT: I *have quit* my job, *have enrolled* in school, and *am looking* for a reliable babysitter.

Note: Repetition of prepositions is considered formal and is not necessary.

MISPLACED AND DANGLING MODIFIERS

A misplaced modifier is one that is in the wrong place in the sentence. Misplaced modifiers come in all forms—words, phrases, and clauses. Sentences containing misplaced modifiers are often very comical: *Mom made me eat the spinach instead of my brother*. Misplaced modifiers, like the one in this sentence, are usually too far away from the word or words they modify. This sentence should read: *Mom made me, instead of my brother, eat the spinach*.

Modifiers like *only*, *nearly*, and *almost* should be placed next to the word they modify and not in front of some other word, especially a verb, that they are not intended to modify.

A modifier is misplaced if it appears to modify the wrong part of the sentence or if we cannot be certain what part of the sentence the writer intended it to modify. To correct a misplaced modifier, move the modifier next to the word it describes.

INCORRECT: She served hamburgers to the men on paper plates.

CORRECT: She served hamburgers on paper plates to the men.

A squinting modifier is one that may refer to either a preceding or a following word, leaving the reader uncertain about what it is intended to modify. Correct a squinting modifier by moving it next to the word it is intended to modify.

INCORRECT: Snipers who fired on the soldiers often escaped capture.

CORRECT: Snipers who often fired on the soldiers escaped capture.

OR: Snipers who fired on the soldiers escaped capture often.

A dangling modifier is a modifier or verb in search of a subject. The modifying phrase appears to modify the wrong word or has nothing to modify. It is literally dangling at the beginning or the end of a sentence. The sentences often look and sound correct: *To be a student government officer, your grades must be above average*. However, the verbal modifier has nothing to describe. Who is *to be a student government officer*? Your grades?

To correct a dangling modifier, reword the sentence by either: 1) changing the modifying phrase to a clause with a subject, or 2) changing the subject of the sentence to the word that should be modified.

INCORRECT: Shortly after leaving home, the accident occurred.

(Who is <u>leaving home</u>, the accident?)

CORRECT: Shortly after we left home, the accident occurred.

FRAGMENTS

A fragment is an incomplete construction, which may or may not have a subject and a verb. Specifically, a fragment is a group of words pretending to be a sentence. Not all fragments appear as separate sentences, however. Often, fragments are separated by semicolons.

INCORRECT: Traffic was stalled for ten miles on the freeway. Because repairs were being made on potholes.

CORRECT: Traffic was stalled for ten miles on the freeway because repairs were being made on potholes.

RUN-ON/FUSED SENTENCES

A run-on/fused sentence is not necessarily a long sentence or a sentence that the reader considers too long; in fact, a run-on may be two short sentences: *Dry ice does not melt it evaporates.* A run-on results when the writer fuses or runs together two separate sentences without using any correct mark of punctuation to separate them.

INCORRECT: Knowing how to use a dictionary is no problem each dictionary has a section in the front of the book telling how to use it.

CORRECT: Knowing how to use a dictionary is no problem. Each dictionary has a section in the front of the book telling how to use it.

Even if one or both of the fused sentences contains internal punctuation, the sentence is still a run-on.

COMMA SPLICES

A comma splice is the use of only a comma to combine what really is two separate sentences.

INCORRECT: One common error in writing is incorrect spelling, the other is the occasional use of faulty diction.

CORRECT: One common error in writing is incorrect spelling; the other is the occasional use of faulty diction.

SUBORDINATION, COORDINATION, AND PREDICATION

Suppose you want to combine the information in these two sentences to create one statement:

I studied a foreign language. I found English quite easy.

How you decide to combine this information should be determined by the relationship you'd like to show between the two facts. *I studied a foreign language, and I found English quite easy* seems rather illogical. The *coordination* of the two ideas (connecting them with the coordinating conjunction *and*) is ineffective. Using *subordination* (connecting the sentences with a subordinating conjunction) instead clearly shows the degree of relative importance between the expressed ideas:

After I studied a foreign language, I found English quite easy.

When using a conjunction, keep in mind the following rules.

While is most widely used and most precisely applied in reference to time; exercise care in writing it in its other senses: *although, and*, or *but*.

To denote simultaneity: He wrote the script *while* I assembled the slides.

To denote undertaking: He wrote the script, *while* I assembled the slides.

Note the addition of a comma. The ambiguity remains, however, if the sentence is spoken. Thus, it might be preferable to write:

He wrote the script and I assembled the slides.

Where refers to time and should not be used as a substitute for *that*.

INCORRECT: We read in the paper *where* they are making great strides in DNA research.

CORRECT: We read in the paper *that* they are making great strides in DNA research.

After words like reason and explanation, use *that*, not *because*.

INCORRECT: His explanation for his tardiness was *because* his alarm did not go off.

CORRECT: His explanation for his tardiness was *that* his alarm did not go off.

Verbs

VERB TENSES

Tense sequence indicates a logical time sequence.

Use Present Tense

in statements about the present:

I *am* tired.

in statements about habitual conditions:

I *go* to bed at 10:30 every night.

in statements of universal truth:

I learned that the sun *is* 93 million miles from the earth.

in statements about the contents of literature and other published works:

In this book Sandy *becomes* a nun and *writes* a book on psychology.

Use Past Tense

in statements of the finished past:

He *wrote* his first book in 1949, and it *was published* in 1952.

Use Future Tense

to indicate an action or condition expected in the future:

I *will* graduate next year.

Use Present Perfect Tense

for an action that began in the past but continues into the future:

I *have lived* here all my life.

Use Past Perfect Tense

for an earlier action that is mentioned in a later action:

Cindy ate the apple that she *had picked*.

(First she picked it, then she ate it.)

Use Future Perfect Tense

for an action that will have been completed at a specific future time:

By May I *shall have graduated*.

Use a Present Participle

for action that occurs at the same time as the verb:

Speeding down the interstate, I saw a cop's flashing lights.

Use a Perfect Participle

for action that occurred before the main verb:

Having read the directions, I started the test.

Use the Subjunctive Mood

to express a wish or state a condition contrary to fact:

If it were not raining, we could have a picnic.

in *that* clauses after verbs like *request, recommend, suggest, ask, require,* and *insist* and after such expressions as *it is important* and *it is necessary*:

It is necessary that all papers *be* submitted on time.

Pronouns

PRONOUN CASE

Appropriate pronoun case is essential to effective, understandable essay writing. Pronoun case can either be nominative or objective.

Nominative Case		Objective Case	
I	we	me	us
he	they	him	them
she	who	her	whom

Use the nominative case (subject pronouns)

for the subject of a sentence:

We students studied until early morning for the final.

for pronouns in apposition to the subject:

Only two students, Alex and *I*, were asked to report on the meeting.

for the subject of an elliptical clause:

Molly is more experienced than *he*.

for the subject of a subordinate clause:

Robert is the driver *who* reported the accident.

for the complement of an infinitive with no expressed subject:

I would not want to be *he*.

Use the objective case (object pronouns)

for the direct object of a sentence:

Mary invited *us* to her party.

for the object of a preposition:

Just between you and *me*, I'm bored.

for the indirect object of a sentence:

Walter gave a dozen red roses to *her*.

for the appositive of a direct object:

The committee elected two delegates, Barbara and *me*.

for the object of an infinitive:

The young boy wanted to help *us* paint the fence.

for the object of a gerund:

Enlisting *him* was surprisingly easy.

for the object of a past participle:

Having called the other students and *us*, the secretary went home for the day.

for a pronoun that precedes an infinitive (the subject of an infinitive):

The supervisor told *him* to work late.

When a conjunction connects two pronouns or a pronoun and a noun, remove the "and" and the other pronoun or noun to determine the correct pronoun form:

Mom gave ~~Tom and~~ myself a piece of cake.

Mom gave ~~Tom and~~ I a piece of cake

Mom gave ~~Tom and~~ me a piece of cake.

Removal of these words reveals what the correct pronoun should be:

Mom gave *me* a piece of cake.

The only pronouns that are acceptable after prepositions are *me, her, him, them,* and *whom.* When deciding between *who* and *whom,* try substituting *he* for *who* and *him* for *whom;* then follow these easy transformation steps:

1. Isolate the *who* clause or the *whom* clause:

    whom we can trust

2. Invert the word order, if necessary:

    we can trust whom

3. Read the final form with the *he* or *him* inserted:

    We can trust ~~whom~~ him.

When a pronoun follows a comparative conjunction like *than* or *as,* complete the elliptical construction to help you determine which pronoun is correct.

EX: She has more credit hours than me [do].

She has more credit hours than I [do].

PRONOUN-ANTECEDENT AGREEMENT

Using the appropriate pronoun antecedent is very important to the effective essay. Pronouns must agree with their antecedent in number, gender and person. An antecedent is a noun or pronoun to which another noun or pronoun refers.

Here are the two basic rules for pronoun reference-antecedent agreement:

1. Every pronoun must have a conspicuous antecedent.

2. Every pronoun must agree with its antecedent in number, gender, and person.

When an antecedent is one of dual gender like *student, singer, artist, person, citizen,* etc., use *his* or *her*. Some careful writers change the antecedent to a plural noun to avoid using the sexist, singular masculine pronoun *his*:

INCORRECT: Everyone hopes that he will win the lottery.

CORRECT: Most people hope that they will win the lottery.

Ordinarily, the relative pronoun *who* is used to refer to people, *which* and *that* to refer to things and places, and *where* to refer to places. The distinction between *that* and *which* is a grammatical distinction. When differentiating something from a larger class of which it is a member, use *that*. When the subject is not being distinguished from a larger class, use *which*.

EX: I bought the sweater *that* was on sale.

EX: There were many sweaters, all of *which* were on sale.

Many writers prefer to use *that* to refer to collective nouns.

EX: A family *that* traces its lineage is usually proud of its roots.

Adjectives and Adverbs

CORRECT USAGE

Adjectives are words that modify nouns or pronouns by defining, describing, limiting, or qualifying those nouns or pronouns.

Adverbs are words that modify verbs, adjectives, or other adverbs and that express such ideas as time, place, manner, cause, and degree. Use adjectives as subject complements with linking verbs; use adverbs with action verbs.

The old man's speech was *eloquent*.	ADJECTIVE
Mr. Brown speaks *eloquently*.	ADVERB
Please be *careful*.	ADJECTIVE
Please drive *carefully*.	ADVERB

Good or Well

Good is an adjective; its use as an adverb is colloquial and nonstandard.

INCORRECT: He plays *good*.

CORRECT: He looks *good* for an octogenarian.

Well may be either an adverb or an adjective. As an adjective, *well* means "in good health."

| CORRECT: | He plays *well*. | ADVERB |
| | My mother is not *well*. | ADJECTIVE |

Bad or Badly

Bad is an adjective used after sense verbs (*look, smell, taste, feel*, or *sound*) or after linking verbs (*is, am, are, was, were*).

INCORRECT: I feel *badly* about the delay.

CORRECT: I feel *bad* about the delay.

Badly is an adverb used after all other verbs.

INCORRECT: It doesn't hurt very *bad*

CORRECT: It doesn't hurt very *badly*.

Real or Really

Real is an adjective; its use as an adverb is colloquial and nonstandard. It means "genuine."

INCORRECT: He writes *real* well.

CORRECT: This is *real* leather.

Really is an adverb meaning "very."

INCORRECT: This is *really* diamond.

CORRECT: Have a *really* nice day.

Sort of and Kind of

Sort of and *kind of* are often misused in written English by writers who actually mean *rather* or *somewhat*.

INCORRECT: Jan was *kind of* saddened by the results of the test.

CORRECT: Jan was *somewhat* saddened by the results of the test.

FAULTY COMPARISONS

Sentences containing a faulty comparison often sound correct because their problem is not one of grammar but of logic. Make sure that like things are being compared, that the comparisons are complete, and that the comparisons are logical.

When comparing two persons or things, use the comparative, not the superlative, form of an adjective or an adverb. Use the superlative form for comparison of more than two persons or things. Use *any*, *other*, or *else* when comparing one thing or person with a group of which it, he, or she is a part.

Most one- and two-syllable words form their comparative and superlative degrees with *-er* and *-est* suffixes. Adjectives and adverbs of more than two syllables form their comparative and superlative degrees with the addition of *more* and *most*.

Positive	Comparative	Superlative
good	better	best
old	older	oldest
friendly	friendlier	friendliest
lonely	lonelier	loneliest
talented	more talented	most talented
beautiful	more beautiful	most beautiful

Punctuation

COMMAS

Commas should be placed according to standard rules of punctuation for purpose, clarity, and effect. The proper use of commas is explained in the following rules and examples:

Series

When more than one adjective describes a noun, use a comma to separate and emphasize each adjective. The comma takes the place of the word *and* in the series.

the long, dark passageway

an elaborate, complex, brilliant plan

Some adjective-noun combinations are thought of as one word. In these cases, the adjective in front of the adjective-noun combination needs no comma. If you inserted *and* between the adjective-noun combination, it would not make sense.

a stately oak tree

a china dinner plate

The comma is also used to separate words, phrases, and whole ideas (clauses); it still takes the place of *and* when used this way.

She lowered the shade, closed the curtain, turned off the light, and went to bed.

The only question that exists about the use of commas in a series is whether to use one before the final item. It is standard usage to do so, although many newspapers and magazines have stopped using the final comma. Occasionally, the omission of the comma can be confusing.

INCORRECT: We planned the trip with Mary and Harold, Susan, Dick and Joan, Gregory and Jean and Charles.

CORRECT: We planned the trip with Mary and Harold, Susan, Dick and Joan, Gregory and Jean, and Charles.

Long introductory phrase

Usually if a phrase of more than five or six words or a dependent clause precedes the subject at the beginning of a sentence, a comma is used to set it off.

After last night's fiasco at the disco, she couldn't bear the thought of looking at him again.

Whenever I try to talk about politics, my wife leaves the room.

If an introductory phrase includes a verb form that is being used as another part of speech (a *verbal*), it must be followed by a comma.

INCORRECT: When eating Mary never looked up from her plate.

CORRECT: When eating, Mary never looked up from her plate.

Separating sentences with two main ideas

When a sentence contains more than two subjects and verbs (clauses) and the two clauses are joined by a conjunction (*and, but, or, nor, for, yet*), use a comma before the conjunction to show that another clause is coming.

I thought I knew the poem by heart, but he showed me three lines I had forgotten.

If the two parts of the sentence are short and closely related, it is not necessary to use a comma.

Jane played the piano and Michael danced.

Be careful not to confuse a sentence that has a compound verb and a single subject with a compound sentence. If the subject is the same for both verbs, there is no need for a comma.

Charles sent some flowers and wrote a long letter explaining why he had not been able to attend.

In general, words and phrases that stop the flow of the sentence or are unnecessary for the main idea are set off by commas.

Nonrestrictive elements

Parts of a sentence that modify other parts are sometimes essential to the meaning of the sentence and sometimes not. When a modifying word or group of words is not vital to the meaning of the sentence, it is set off by commas and is called "nonrestrictive." Modifiers that are essential to the meaning of the sentence are called "restrictive" and are not set off by commas.

ESSENTIAL: The girl *who wrote the story* is my sister.

NONESSENTIAL: My sister, *the girl who wrote the story*, has always loved to write.

Commas should also be used in the following circumstances.

Abbreviations after names

Did you invite John Paul, Jr., and his sister?

Interjections (an exclamation without added grammatical connection)

Oh, I'm so glad to see you.

Direct address

Roy, won't you open the door for the dog?

Tag questions

I'm really hungry, aren't you?

Geographical names and addresses

The letter was addressed to Mrs. Marion Heartwell, 1881 Pine Lane, Palo Alto, California 95824.

(Note: No comma is needed before the ZIP code because it is already clearly set off from the state name.)

Transitional words and phrases

You'll find, therefore, that no one is more loyal than I am.

Parenthetical words and phrases

The Mannes affair was, to put it mildly, a surprise.

Unusual word order

The dress, new and crisp, hung in the closet.

Direct quotations

"I won't know what to do," said Michael, "if you leave me."

Note: Commas always go inside the closing quotation mark, even if the comma is not part of the material being quoted.

Contrasting elements

It was a reasonable, though not appealing, idea.

Dates

Both forms of the date are acceptable.

He left on 5 December 1980.

On October 22, 1992, Frank and Julie were married.

SEMICOLONS

Semicolons are often followed by conjunctive adverbs. Usually, a comma follows the conjunctive adverb. Note that a period can be used to separate two sentences joined by a conjunctive adverb. Some common conjunctive adverbs are:

accordingly	nevertheless	besides
next	consequently	nonetheless
finally	now	furthermore
on the other hand	however	otherwise
indeed	perhaps	in fact
still	moreover	therefore

Then is also used as a conjunctive adverb, but it is not usually followed by a comma.

Use the semicolon

to separate independent clauses which are not joined by a coordinating conjunction:

I understand how to use commas; the semicolon I have not yet mastered.

to separate two independent clauses connected by a conjunctive adverb:

He took great care with his work; *therefore*, he was very successful.

to combine two independent clauses connected by a coordinating conjunction if either or both of the clauses contain other internal punctuation:

Success in college, some maintain, requires intelligence, industry, and perseverance; *but* others, fewer in number, assert that only personality is important.

to separate items in a series when each item has internal punctuation:

Call our customer service line for assistance: Arizona, 1-800-555-6020; New Mexico, 1-800-555-5050; California, 1-800-555-3140; or Nevada, 1-800-555-3214.

COLONS

Although it is true that a colon precedes a list, one must also make sure that a complete sentence precedes the colon. The colon signals the reader that a list, explanation, or restatement of the preceding will follow. The difference between the colon and the period is that the colon is an introductory mark, not a terminal mark. Look at the following examples:

The Constitution provides for a separation of powers among the three branches of government.

government.	The period signals a new sentence.
government;	The semicolon signals an interrelated sentence.
government,	The comma signals a coordinating conjunction followed by another independent clause.
government:	The colon signals a list.

The Constitution provides for a separation of powers among the three branches of *government*: executive, legislative, and judicial.

Use the colon

to introduce a list; one item may constitute a list:

I hate this one course: English.

to introduce a list preceded by *as follows* or *the following*:

The reasons he cited for his success are as follows: integrity, honesty, industry, and a pleasant disposition.

to separate two independent clauses, when the second clause is a restatement or explanation of the first:

All of my high school teachers said one thing in particular: college is going to be difficult.

to introduce a word or word group which is a restatement, explanation, or summary of the first sentence:

These two things he loved: an honest man and a beautiful woman.

to introduce a formal appositive:

I am positive there is one appeal which you can't overlook: money.

to separate the introductory words from a quotation which follows if the quotation is formal, long, or paragraphed separately:

The actor then stated: "I would rather be able to adequately play the part of Hamlet than to perform a miraculous operation, deliver a great lecture, or build a magnificent skyscraper."

APOSTROPHES

Apostrophes are required to make a noun possessive, not plural. Remember the following rules when considering how to show possession.

Add *'s* to singular nouns and indefinite pronouns:

Tiffany's flowers

a dog's bark

Add *'s* to singular nouns ending in *s*, unless this distorts the pronunciation:

the boss's pen

Dr. Evans's office OR Dr. Evans' office

Add *an apostrophe* to plural nouns ending in *s* or *es*:

two cents' worth

ladies' night

Add *'s* to plural nouns not ending in *s:*

men's room

children's toys

Add *'s* to the last word in compound words or groups:

brother-in-law's car

someone else's paper

Add *'s* to the last name when indicating joint ownership:

Joe and Edna's home

women and children's clinic

Add *'s* to both names if you intend to show ownership by each person:

Joe's and Edna's trucks

Julie's and Kathy's pies

Possessive pronouns change their forms *without* the addition of an apostrophe:

her, hers

their, theirs

it, its

Use the possessive form of a noun preceding a gerund:

My bowling a strike irritated him.

Do you mind our stopping by?

Add *'s* to letters, numbers, words referred to as words, and abbreviations with periods to show that they are plural:

no *if's*, *and's*, or *but's*

Ph.D.'s are granted by universities.

Add *s* to decades, symbols, and abbreviations without periods to show that they are plural:

VCRs

the 1800s

QUOTATION MARKS

The most common use of double quotation marks (") is to set off quoted words, phrases, and sentences.

"Then you would say what you mean," the March Hare went on.

"I do," Alice hastily replied: "at least—at least I mean what I say—that's the same thing, you know."

—from Lewis Carroll's *Alice in Wonderland*

Single quotation marks are used to set off quoted material within a quote.

"Shall I bring 'Rime of the Ancient Mariner' along with us?" she asked her brother.

Mrs. Green said, "The doctor told me, 'Go immediately to bed when you get home!'"

Use quotation marks to enclose words used as words. (Sometimes italics are used for this purpose.)

"Horse and buggy" and "bread and butter" can be used either as adjectives or as nouns.

If slang is used within more formal writing, the slang words or phrases should be set off with quotation marks.

Harrison's decision to leave the conference and to "stick his neck out" by flying to Jamaica was applauded by the rest of the conference attendees.

When words are meant to have an unusual or specific significance to the reader, for instance irony or humor, they are sometimes placed in quotation marks.

The "conversation" resulted in one black eye and a broken nose.

To set off titles of TV shows, poems, stories, and book chapters, use quotation marks. (Book, motion picture, newspaper, and magazine titles are underlined when handwritten and italicized when typed.)

You will find Keats' "Ode on a Grecian Urn" in Chapter 3, "The Romantic Era," in Lastly's *Selections from Great English Poets.*

Capitalization

When a word is capitalized, it calls attention to itself. This attention should be for a good reason. There are standard uses for capital letters. In general, capitalize (1) all proper nouns, (2) the first word of a sentence, and (3) the first word of a direct quotation.

You should capitalize

names of ships, aircraft, spacecraft, and trains:

Apollo 13	DC-10
S.S. *United States*	Boeing 707

names of deities:

Allah	Holy Ghost
Venus	Jehovah

geological periods:

Neolithic age	Cenozoic era
late Pleistocene times	Ice Age

names of astronomical bodies:

Mercury	Halley's comet
Ursa Major	North Star

personifications:

Reliable Nature brought her promised Spring.

Bring on Melancholy in his sad might.

historical periods:

Middle Ages	Reign of Terror
Great Depression	Renaissance

organizations, associations, and institutions:

Girl Scouts	Kiwanis Club
League of Women Voters	Smithsonian Institution

government and judicial groups:

United States Court of Appeals	Senate
Committee on Foreign Affairs	Peace Corps

A general term that accompanies a specific name is capitalized only if it follows the specific name. If it stands alone or comes before the specific name, it is put in lowercase. This rule does *not* apply, however, when the general term directly precedes a person's name, thus acting as part of his or her title.

Washington State	the state of Washington
Central Park	the park
Mississippi River	the river
Pope John XXIII	the pope

Use a capital to start a sentence:

Our car would not start.

When will you leave? I need to know right away.

When a sentence appears within a sentence, start it with a capital letter:

We had only one concern: When would we eat?

He answered, "We can only stay a few minutes."

The most important words of titles are capitalized. Those words not capitalized are conjunctions (*and, or, but*) and short prepositions (*of, on, by, for*). The first and last word of a title must always be capitalized:

Of Mice and Men	*Rise of the West*
"Rubaiyat of Omar Khayyam"	"All in the Family"

Capitalize newspaper and magazine titles:

U.S. News & World Report	*National Geographic*
The New York Times	*The Washington Post*

Capitalize radio and TV station call letters:

KNX-AM	KQED-FM
WNEW	WBOP

Do not capitalize compass directions or seasons:

east	south
autumn	summer

Capitalize regions:

the South	the Northeast
the West	Eastern Europe

BUT :

the south of France

the eastern part of town

Capitalize specific military units:

U.S. Army

1st Infantry Division

Capitalize political groups and philosophies:

Democratic party	Communist party
Libertarian party	Transcendentalism

BUT do not capitalize systems of government or individual adherents to a philosophy:

democracy	communist
fascist	agnostic

Spelling

RULES TO REMEMBER

This section reviews spelling tips and rules to help you spot incorrect spellings. Problems such as the distinction between *to* and *too* and *lead* and *led* are covered in the Vocabulary Enhancer section of the Communication Skills Review.

- Remember, *i* before *e* except after *c*, or when sounded as "a" as in *neighbor* and *weigh*.

- There are only three words in the English language that end in -*ceed*:

  proceed, succeed, exceed

- There are several words that end in -*cede*:

  secede, recede, concede, precede

- There is only one word in the English language that ends in -*sede*:

  supersede

Many people learn to read English phonetically; that is, by sounding out the letters of the words. However, many English words are not pronounced the way they are spelled; people who try to spell English words phonetically often make spelling errors. It is better to memorize the correct spelling of English words rather than to rely on phonetics to spell correctly.

FREQUENTLY MISSPELLED WORDS

The following words are frequently misspelled. Study the spelling of each word by having a friend or teacher drill you on the words. Then mark down the words that you misspelled and study those select ones again. (The words appear in their most popular spellings.)

a lot	accident	ache
ability	accommodate	achieve
absence	accompanied	achievement
absent	accomplish	acknowledge
abundance	accumulation	acquaintance
accept	accuse	acquainted
acceptable	accustomed	acquire

across
address
addressed
adequate
advantage
advantageous
advertise
advertisement
advice
advisable
advise
advisor
aerial
affect
affectionate
again
against
aggravate
aggressive
agree
aisle
all right
almost
already
although
altogether
always
amateur
American
among
amount
analysis
analyze
angel
angle
annual
another
answer
antiseptic
anxious
apologize
apparatus
apparent
appear
appearance
appetite
application

apply
appreciate
appreciation
approach
appropriate
approval
approve
approximate
argue
arguing
argument
arouse
arrange
arrangement
article
artificial
ascend
assistance
assistant
associate
association
attempt
attendance
attention
audience
August
author
automobile
autumn
auxiliary
available
avenue
awful
awkward
bachelor
balance
balloon
bargain
basic
beautiful
because
become
before
beginning
being
believe
benefit

benefited
between
bicycle
board
bored
borrow
bottle
bottom
boundary
brake
breadth
breath
breathe
brilliant
building
bulletin
bureau
burial
buried
bury
bushes
business
cafeteria
calculator
calendar
campaign
capital
capitol
captain
career
careful
careless
carriage
carrying
category
ceiling
cemetery
cereal
certain
changeable
characteristic
charity
chief
choose
chose
cigarette
circumstance

citizen
clothes
clothing
coarse
coffee
collect
college
column
comedy
comfortable
commitment
committed
committee
communicate
company
comparative
compel
competent
competition
compliment
conceal
conceit
conceivable
conceive
concentration
conception
condition
conference
confident
congratulate
conquer
conscience
conscientious
conscious
consequence
consequently
considerable
consistency
consistent
continual
continuous
controlled
controversy
convenience
convenient
conversation
corporal

corroborate
council
counsel
counselor
courage
courageous
course
courteous
courtesy
criticism
criticize
crystal
curiosity
cylinder
daily
daughter
daybreak
death
deceive
December
deception
decide
decision
decisive
deed
definite
delicious
dependent
deposit
derelict
descend
descent
describe
description
desert
desirable
despair
desperate
dessert
destruction
determine
develop
development
device
dictator
died
difference

different
dilemma
dinner
direction
disappear
disappoint
disappointment
disapproval
disapprove
disastrous
discipline
discover
discriminate
disease
dissatisfied
dissection
dissipate
distance
distinction
division
doctor
dollar
doubt
dozen
earnest
easy
ecstasy
ecstatic
education
effect
efficiency
efficient
eight
either
eligibility
eligible
eliminate
embarrass
embarrassment
emergency
emphasis
emphasize
enclosure
encouraging
endeavor
engineer
English

enormous
enough
entrance
envelope
environment
equipment
equipped
especially
essential
evening
evident
exaggerate
exaggeration
examine
exceed
excellent
except
exceptional
exercise
exhausted
exhaustion
exhilaration
existence
exorbitant
expense
experience
experiment
explanation
extreme
facility
factory
familiar
fascinate
fascinating
fatigue
February
financial
financier
flourish
forcibly
forehead
foreign
formal
former
fortunate
fourteen
fourth

frequent
friend
frightening
fundamental
further
gallon
garden
gardener
general
genius
government
governor
grammar
grateful
great
grievance
grievous
grocery
guarantee
guess
guidance
half
hammer
handkerchief
happiness
healthy
heard
heavy
height
heroes
heroine
hideous
himself
hoarse
holiday
hopeless
hospital
humorous
hurried
hurrying
ignorance
imaginary
imbecile
imitation
immediately
immigrant
incidental

increase
independence
independent
indispensable
inevitable
influence
influential
initiate
innocence
inoculate
inquiry
insistent
instead
instinct
integrity
intellectual
intelligence
intercede
interest
interfere
interference
interpreted
interrupt
invitation
irrelevant
irresistible
irritable
island
its
it's
itself
January
jealous
journal
judgment
kindergarten
kitchen
knew
knock
know
knowledge
labor
laboratory
laid
language
later
latter

laugh
leisure
length
lesson
library
license
light
lightning
likelihood
likely
literal
literature
livelihood
loaf
loneliness
loose
lose
losing
loyal
loyalty
magazine
maintenance
maneuver
marriage
married
marry
match
material
mathematics
measure
medicine
million
miniature
minimum
miracle
miscellaneous
mischief
mischievous
misspelled
mistake
momentous
monkey
monotonous
moral
morale
mortgage
mountain

mournful
muscle
mysterious
mystery
narrative
natural
necessary
needle
negligence
neighbor
neither
newspaper
newsstand
niece
noticeable
o'clock
obedient
obstacle
occasion
occasional
occur
occurred
occurrence
ocean
offer
often
omission
omit
once
operate
opinion
opportune
opportunity
optimist
optimistic
origin
original
oscillate
ought
ounce
overcoat
paid
pamphlet
panicky
parallel
parallelism
particular

partner
pastime
patience
peace
peaceable
pear
peculiar
pencil
people
perceive
perception
perfect
perform
performance
perhaps
period
permanence
permanent
perpendicular
perseverance
persevere
persistent
personal
personality
personnel
persuade
persuasion
pertain
picture
piece
plain
playwright
pleasant
please
pleasure
pocket
poison
policeman
political
population
portrayal
positive
possess
possession
possessive
possible
post office

potatoes
practical
prairie
precede
preceding
precise
predictable
prefer
preference
preferential
preferred
prejudice
preparation
prepare
prescription
presence
president
prevalent
primitive
principal
principle
privilege
probably
procedure
proceed
produce
professional
professor
profitable
prominent
promise
pronounce
pronunciation
propeller
prophet
prospect
psychology
pursue
pursuit
quality
quantity
quarreling
quart
quarter
quiet
quite
raise

realistic
realize
reason
rebellion
recede
receipt
receive
recipe
recognize
recommend
recuperate
referred
rehearsal
reign
relevant
relieve
remedy
renovate
repeat
repetition
representative
requirements
resemblance
resistance
resource
respectability
responsibility
restaurant
rhythm
rhythmical
ridiculous
right
role
roll
roommate
sandwich
Saturday
scarcely
scene
schedule
science
scientific
scissors
season
secretary
seize
seminar

sense
separate
service
several
severely
shepherd
sheriff
shining
shoulder
shriek
siege
sight
signal
significance
significant
similar
similarity
sincerely
site
soldier
solemn
sophomore
soul
source
souvenir
special
specified
specimen
speech
stationary
stationery
statue
stockings
stomach
straight
strength
strenuous
stretch
striking
studying
substantial
succeed
successful
sudden
superintendent
suppress
surely

surprise	tragedy	vicinity
suspense	transferred	vicious
sweat	treasury	view
sweet	tremendous	village
syllable	tries	villain
symmetrical	truly	visitor
sympathy	twelfth	voice
synonym	twelve	volume
technical	tyranny	waist
telegram	undoubtedly	weak
telephone	United States	wear
temperament	university	weather
temperature	unnecessary	Wednesday
tenant	unusual	week
tendency	useful	weigh
tenement	usual	weird
therefore	vacuum	whether
thorough	valley	which
through	valuable	while
title	variety	whole
together	vegetable	wholly
tomorrow	vein	whose
tongue	vengeance	wretched
toward	versatile	

WRITTEN COMPOSITION

The NYSTCE contains two writing exercises: one in the LAST and one in the ATS-W. You must pace yourself on the multiple choice sections so that you will have enough time to produce an adequate essay.

Writing under pressure can be frustrating, but studying this review will give you a chance to practice and polish your essay skills. With a realistic sense of what to expect, you can turn problems into possibilities. This review will show you how to plan and write a logical, coherent, and interesting essay.

Pre-Writing/Planning

Before you begin to write, there are certain preliminary steps you need to take. A few minutes spent planning pays off; your final essay will be more focused, better developed, and clearer.

UNDERSTAND THE QUESTION

Read the essay question very carefully and ask yourself the following questions:

- What is the meaning of the topic statement?

- Is the question asking me to persuade the reader of the validity of a certain opinion?

- Do I agree or disagree with the statement? What will be my thesis (main idea)?

- What kinds of examples can I use to support my thesis? Explore personal experiences, historical evidence, current events, and literary subjects.

CONSIDER YOUR AUDIENCE

Essays would be pointless without an audience. Why write an essay if no one wants or needs to read it? Why add evidence, organize your ideas, or correct bad grammar? The reason to do any of these things is because someone out there needs to understand what you mean.

What does the audience need to know to believe you or to come over to your position? Imagine someone you know listening to you declare your position or opinion and then saying, "Oh, yeah? Prove it!" This is your audience—write to them. Ask yourself the following questions so that you will know what to say to a person who says, "Prove it!"

- What evidence do I need to prove my idea to this skeptic?

- What would he or she disagree with me about?

- What does he or she share with me as common knowledge? What do I need to tell the reader?

Writing Your Essay

Once you have considered your position on the topic and thought of several examples to support it, you are ready to begin writing.

Decide how many paragraphs you will write. In a 300-600 word exercise, you will probably be able to write no more than four or five paragraphs.

In such a format, the first paragraph will be the introduction, the next two or three will develop your thesis with specific examples, and the final paragraph should present a strong conclusion.

INTRODUCTION

The focus of your introduction should be the thesis statement. This statement allows your reader to understand the point and direction of your essay. The statement should identify the central idea of your essay and clearly state your attitude about the subject. It should also dictate the basic content and organization of your essay. If you do not state your thesis clearly, your essay will suffer.

The thesis must be something that can be argued, not just an accepted fact. For example, "Animals are used every day in cosmetic and medical testing," is a fact; it needs no proof. However, if the writer says, "Using animals for cosmetic and medical testing is cruel and should be stopped," we have a point that must be supported and defended by the writer.

The thesis can be placed in any paragraph of the essay, but in a short essay, especially one written for evaluative exam purposes, the thesis is most effective when placed in the opening paragraph.

Consider the following sample question:

ESSAY TOPIC:

"That government is best which governs least."

ASSIGNMENT: Do you agree or disagree with this statement? Choose a specific example from current events, personal experience, or your reading to support your position.

After reading the topic statement, decide if you agree or disagree. If you agree with this statement, your thesis could be the following:

"Government has the right to protect individuals from interference but no right to extend its powers and activities beyond this function."

This statement clearly states the writer's opinion in a direct manner. It also serves as a blueprint for the essay. The remainder of the introduction should give two or three brief examples that support your thesis.

SUPPORTING PARAGRAPHS

The next two or three paragraphs of your essay will elaborate on the supporting examples you gave in your introduction. Each paragraph should discuss only one idea. Like the introduction, each paragraph should be coherently organized, with a topic sentence and supporting details.

The topic sentence is to each paragraph what the thesis statement is to the essay as a whole. It tells the reader what you plan to discuss in that paragraph. It has a specific subject and is neither too broad nor too narrow. It also establishes the author's attitude and gives the reader a sense of the direction in which the writer is going.

Although it may occur in the middle or at the end of the paragraph, the topic sentence usually appears at the beginning. Placing it at the beginning is advantageous because it helps you stay focused on the main idea.

The remainder of each paragraph should support the topic sentence with examples and illustrations. Each sentence should progress logically from the previous one and be centrally connected to your topic sentence. Do not include any extraneous material that does not serve to develop your thesis.

CONCLUSION

Your conclusion should briefly restate your thesis and explain how you have shown it to be true. Since you want to end your essay on a strong note, your conclusion should be concise and effective. Make sure your conclusion is clearly on the topic and represents your perspective; there should be no confusion about what you really mean and believe.

PROOFREADING

Make sure to leave yourself enough time at the end to proofread your essay. Consider the following:

- Are all your sentences really sentences? Have you written any fragments or run-on sentences?

- Are you using vocabulary correctly?

- Did you leave out any punctuation? Did you capitalize correctly?

- Are there any misspellings, especially of difficult words?

Effective Use of Language

Clear organization, sentence structure, and parts of speech, are not the only factors that will be considered in scoring your essay. How you use this language to express your thoughts will also play a role in the grading process.

POINT-OF-VIEW

Depending on the audience, essays may be written from one of three points of view:

1. *First Person* Point of View:

   "I believe cars are more trouble than they are worth."

2. *Second Person* Point of View

   "If *you* own a car, *you* will soon find out that it is more trouble than it is worth."

3. *Third Person* Point of View (focuses on the idea, not what "I" think of it):

   "The writer presents her views concisely."

It is very important to maintain a consistent point of view throughout your essay. If you begin writing in the first-person ("I"), do not shift to the second- or third-person in the middle of the essay. Such inconsistency is confusing to your reader and will be penalized.

USE YOUR OWN VOCABULARY

Is it a good idea to use big words that sound good in the dictionary or thesaurus, but that you don't normally use or understand? No. So whose vocabulary should you use? Your own. You will be most comfortable with your own level of vocabulary.

AVOID THE PASSIVE VOICE

In writing, the active voice is preferable because it is emphatic and direct. A weak passive verb leaves the doer unknown or seemingly unimportant. However, the passive voice is essential when the action of the verb is more important than the doer, when the doer is unknown, or when the writer wishes to place the emphasis on the receiver of the action rather than on the doer.

Active: She kicked the winning field goal.

In this case, the active construction is directly and clearly communicated to the reader.

Passive: The winning field goal was kicked by her.

This passive construction is awkward and wordy.

 Drill Questions

Choose the correct replacement for the underlined words.

1. If you <u>had been concerned</u> about Marilyn, you <u>would have went</u> to greater lengths to ensure her safety.

    (A) had been concern . . . would have gone

    (B) was concerned . . . would have gone

    (C) had been concerned . . . would have gone

    (D) No change is necessary.

2. Alcohol and tobacco are harmful to <u>whomever</u> consumes them.

    (A) whom   (C) whoever

    (B) who   (D) No change is necessary.

3. His <u>principal</u> reasons for resigning were his <u>principles</u> of right and wrong.

    (A) principal . . . principals   (C) principle . . . principles

    (B) principle . . . principals   (D) No change is necessary.

4. He did <u>very well</u> on the test although his writing skills are not <u>good</u>.

    (A) real well . . . good   (C) good . . . great

    (B) very good . . . good   (D) No change is necessary.

5. Students must pay a penalty for overdue library <u>books, however, there</u> is a grace period.

    (A) books; however, there   (C) books: however, there
    (B) books however, there   (D) No change is necessary.

6. The fall of the <u>Berlin wall</u> was an important symbol of the collapse of <u>Communism</u>.

    (A) berlin Wall . . . communism
    (B) Berlin Wall . . . communism
    (C) berlin wall . . . Communism
    (D) No change is necessary.

7. <u>Preceding</u> the <u>business</u> session, lunch will be served in a <u>separate</u> room.

    (A) preceeding . . . business . . . seperate
    (B) proceeding . . . bussiness . . . seperate
    (C) proceeding . . . business . . . seperite
    (D) No change is necessary.

8. Although the band performed <u>badly</u>, I feel <u>real bad</u> about missing the concert.

    (A) badly . . . real badly   (C) badly . . . very bad
    (B) bad . . . badly   (D) No change is necessary.

9. Indianola, <u>Mississippi, where B.B. King and my father grew up,</u> has a population of less than 50,000 people.

    (A) Mississippi where, B.B. King and my father grew up,
    (B) Mississippi where B.B. King and my father grew up,
    (C) Mississippi; where B.B. King and my father grew up,
    (D) No change is necessary.

10. Rosa Lee's parents discovered that it was <u>her who</u> wrecked the family car.

   (A) she who
   (B) she whom
   (C) her whom
   (D) No change is necessary.

11. Every man, woman, and child <u>were given</u> a life preserver.

   (A) have been given
   (B) had gave
   (C) was given
   (D) No change is necessary.

12. Every car owner should be sure that <u>their</u> automobile insurance is adequate.

   (A) your
   (B) his or her
   (C) its
   (D) No change is necessary.

13. Among the states that seceded from the Union to join the Confederacy in 1860-1861 <u>were:</u> Mississippi, Florida, and Alabama.

   (A) were;
   (B) were
   (C) were,
   (D) No change is necessary.

14. The bakery's specialty <u>are</u> wedding cakes.

   (A) is
   (B) were
   (C) be
   (D) No change is necessary.

15. A photograph of <u>mars</u> was printed in <u>*the New York Times*</u>.

   (A) Mars . . . *The New York Times*
   (B) Mars . . . *the New York times*
   (C) mars . . . *The New York Times*
   (D) No change is necessary

Answers to Drill Questions

1. **(C)**	6. **(B)**	11. **(C)**
2. **(C)**	7. **(D)**	12. **(B)**
3. **(D)**	8. **(C)**	13. **(B)**
4. **(D)**	9. **(D)**	14. **(A)**
5. **(A)**	10. **(A)**	15. **(A)**

LAST/ATS-W

Chapter 7

Knowledge
of the Learner

Chapter 7

Knowledge of the Learner

In order for teachers to successfully teach students of all ages and in all disciplines, they need to understand the learning process. Benjamin Bloom (1976) has suggested that students' cognitive entry skills and intelligence (or IQ) account for about 50 percent of what students achieve academically; 25 percent can be attributed to the quality of instruction students receive; 25 percent can be attributed to affective characteristics of the students. Those affective characteristics include such things as the learner's personality, self-concept, locus of control, attitudes, level of anxiety, and study habits. Therefore, although it is important that teachers acquire and utilize effective teaching techniques and provide quality instruction to students, it can be argued that it is even more important in terms of educational outcomes that teachers understand cognitive and affective factors which influence student performance.

Educators recognize that students bring to the classroom an array of personal characteristics and experiences upon which they base their present knowledge. Those characteristics and experiences may or may not be congruent with the teacher's background; nonetheless, they constitute a knowledge base for the learner. Therefore, the teacher's role is to activate the learner's prior knowledge and help the student connect new information with what is known already. Thus, in today's educational model, the student is seen as an active learner who brings much to the classroom.

It is important that teachers appreciate a dynamic and interactive view of human development. People exist in an environment which—friendly or unfriendly, supportive or nonsupportive—evokes and provokes reactions from individuals. People also act in certain ways to shape and form their environment. There is a constant interaction or interplay between people and their environments. Thus, effective teachers must be sensitive to and knowledgeable of both personal characteristics of students and characteristics of their environment.

STUDENT DEVELOPMENT AND MATURATION

Physiological changes play a significant role in the development of children as they increase their control of bodily movements and functions and refine their motor skills. Their ability to engage in simple to complex classroom and playground activities becomes more sophisticated as they develop. Classroom and playground activities must be adjusted and adapted in order to be developmentally appropriate for the skill levels of the children.

As students enter junior high or begin their secondary education, they again experience important physiological changes with the onset of puberty. With puberty comes changes in primary sexual characteristics and the emergence of secondary sexual characteristics. In addition to bodily characteristics, there is a change in bodily feelings, and there is an increase in sex drive.

Girls, on average, reach maturational milestones before boys. Physical changes may cause embarrassment to both females and males when they draw unwelcome attention; moreover, these changes almost always create some discomfort as adolescents find the body they were familiar and comfortable with to be quite different, sometimes seemingly overnight.

David Elkind has noted two developmental characteristics of adolescence which share a relationship to the physiological changes accompanying maturation. These two characteristics are the *imaginary audience* and the *personal fable*. First, adolescents, preoccupied with their own physiological changes, often assume that others are equally intrigued by these changes in appearance and behavior; they may feel that others are staring at them, watching their every move, scrutinizing their behavior for one misstep or their appearance for any flaws. If everyone is watching, then it's imperative to be, to act, and to look just right. In today's culture, that means wearing the right clothes and having all the right brand names and status symbols. Because of adolescents' sensitivity to attention (especially the wrong kind of attention, that is, not fitting in, not being "right"), it is especially important that teachers of this age group be aware of the *imaginary audience* phenomenon and be sensitive to social interactions in the classroom. It, indeed, is important that teachers not contribute to creating unwanted attention or to stigmatizing or stereotyping students.

Personal fable refers to the belief that "My life is different from everyone else's; therefore, no one can understand how I feel or what I think. No one has ever felt or thought what I feel and think." This out-of-focus view tends to support both a feeling of isolation (which may be precipitated by the changing sensations from a body that is undergoing biological changes) and a willingness to engage in risky behaviors (thinking that only others have car accidents when they drive dangerously—"It won't happen to me"—or, only other girls get pregnant when they have unprotected sexual relations—"It won't happen to me.").

In sum, these two characteristics of adolescence are examples of how physical changes accompany and, perhaps even evoke, emotional and cognitive changes as individuals grow and mature. Both phenomena of *imaginary audience* and *personal fable* have emotional features (fear of rejection, fear of isolation, fear of difference, shame, guilt from increased sexual feelings, frustration, and so forth) and both describe a feature of adolescent cognitive ability: the ability to think about one's self as an object of one's own and of other's thought. The developmental epistemologist Jean Piaget explained that this way of thinking represents the cognitive stage of formal operations.

THEORIES OF COGNITIVE DEVELOPMENT

Cognition is a term commonly used to refer to all the processes whereby knowledge is acquired; the term can be used to cover very basic perceptual processes, such as smell, touch, sound, and so forth, to very advanced operations, such as analysis, synthesis, and critical thinking.

Until his death in 1980, Jean Piaget was a predominant figure in the field of cognitive psychology. His theory of cognitive development is based on the notion that cognitive abilities are developed as individuals mature physiologically and have opportunities to interact with their environment. Piaget described these interactions as the *equilibration* of *accommodation* and *assimilation* cycles or processes. In other words, when individuals (who, according to Piaget, are innately endowed with certain cognitive predispositions and capabilities) encounter a new stimulus, they are brought into a state of *disequilibrium*.

That is a way of saying that they are thrown off balance; they do not know or understand that which is new or unfamiliar. However, through the complementary processes of *accommodation* (or adjusting prior knowledge gained through former experiences and interactions) and *assimilation* (fitting together the new information with what has been previously known or understood), individuals come to know or understand that which is new. Individuals are returned to a state of *equilibrium,* where they remain until the next encounter with an unfamiliar something. For Piaget, this is how learners learn.

Piaget also predicted that certain behaviors and ways of thinking characterize individuals at different ages. For this reason, his theory is considered a *stage* theory. *Stage* theories share the common tenet that certain characteristics will occur in predictable sequences and at certain times in the life of the individual.

According to Piaget, there are four stages of cognitive development, beginning with the *sensorimotor* stage describing individuals from birth to around the age of two. The second stage, *preoperational* (describing cognitive behavior between the ages of two and seven), is characterized by egocentrism, rigidity of thought, semilogical reasoning, and limited social cognition; some cognitive psychologists have observed that this stage seems to describe how individuals think more in terms of what they can't do than what they can do. This stage describes the way that children in preschool and kindergarten go about problem-solving; also, many children in the primary grades may be at this stage in their cognitive development.

The next two stages, however, may be most important for elementary and secondary school teachers because they describe cognitive development during the times that most students are in school. The third stage, *concrete operations,* is the beginning of operational thinking and describes the thinking of children between the ages of 7 and 11. Learners at this age begin to decenter. They are able to take into consideration viewpoints other than their own. They can perform transformations, meaning that they can understand reversibility, inversion, reciprocity, and conservation. They can group items into categories. They can make inferences about reality and engage in inductive reasoning; they increase their quantitative skills, and they can manipulate symbols if they are given concrete examples with which to work. This stage of cognitive development is the threshold to higher-level learning for students.

Finally, *formal operations* is the last stage of cognitive development and opens the door for higher-ordered, critical thinking. This stage describes the way of thinking for learners between the ages of 11 and 15 (it also describes adult thinking). Learners at this stage of cognitive development can engage in logical, abstract, and hypothetical thought; they can use the scientific method, meaning they can formulate hypotheses, isolate influences, and identify cause-and-effect relationships. They can plan and anticipate verbal cues. They can engage in both deductive and inductive reasoning, and they can operate on verbal statements exclusive of concrete experiences or examples. These cognitive abilities characterize the highest levels of thought.

Another theoretical approach to understanding human development is offered by Erik Erikson, who described psychosocial development. For each of eight stages, he identified a developmental task explained in terms of two polarities. For the purposes of this discussion, only those stages describing school-age individuals will be included.

According to Erikson, preschoolers and primary-school aged children must be able to function in the outside world independently of parents; when children are able to do this, they achieve a sense of *initiative*; when children are not able to move away from total parental attachment and control, they experience a sense of *guilt*. Thus, this stage of psychosocial development is the stage of initiative versus guilt. The child's first venture away from home and into the world of school has considerable significance when viewed in light of this theory; it is imperative that teachers assist students in their first experiences on their own, away from parental control.

Erikson's next stage of development is one involving a tension between *industry* and *inferiority*. For example, if the child who enters school (thus achieving initiative) acquires the skills (including academic skills such as reading, writing, and computation, as well as social skills in playing with others, communicating with others, forming friendships, and so forth) which enable her or him to be successful in school, then the child achieves a sense of *industry*; failure to achieve these skills leads to a sense of *inferiority*.

Identity Achievement and Diffusion

Around the time students enter junior high, they begin the developmental task of achieving *identity*. According to Erikson, the struggle to achieve identity is one of the most important developmental tasks and one which creates serious psychosocial problems for adolescents. For example, even the individual who has successfully achieved all the important developmental milestones (such as initiative and industry) now finds him- or herself in a state of flux: Everything (body, feelings, thoughts) is changing. The adolescent starts to question, "Who am I?" Erikson believed that if adolescents find out what they believe in, what their goals, ideas, and values are, then they attain identity achievement; failure to discover these things leads to identity diffusion.

By the time many students reach high school, they are entering a stage of young adulthood, which for Erikson is a psychosocial stage characterized by the polarities of *intimacy* and *isolation.* Individuals at this stage of development begin to think about forming lasting friendships, even marital unions. Erikson would argue that many psychosocial problems experienced by young adults have their origin in the individual's failure to achieve identity during the preceding stage; the young man or woman who does not know who he or she really is cannot achieve true intimacy.

For the classroom teacher, knowledge of psychosocial stages of human development can result in greater effectiveness. For example, the effective teacher realizes the importance of helping students to achieve skills necessary to accomplish crucial developmental tasks. According to Erikson's theory, teachers of elementary school-aged learners would do well to focus on teaching academic and social skills, helping students to gain proficiency in skills that will enable learners to be productive members of society. On the other hand, secondary school teachers would do well to keep in mind, as they engage students in higher-ordered thinking activities appropriate to their stage of cognitive development, that students have pressing psychological and social needs in their struggle to achieve identity and to attain intimacy.

By understanding key principles of human development in its multiple dimensions, effective teachers provide students with both age-appropriate and developmentally-appropriate instruction. This, in sum, is the best instruction. It is instruction that addresses all the needs of students—physical, emotional, and social, as well as cognitive (or intellectual).

Maslow's Hierarchy of Needs

Abraham Maslow's hierarchy of human needs is a model applicable to many diverse fields, including education, business and industry, health and medical professions, and more. Maslow identified different levels of individuals' needs in a hierarchical sequence, meaning that lower level needs must be satisfied before individuals could ascend to higher levels of achievement. He identified the fulfillment of basic physiological needs as fundamental to individuals' sense of well-being and their ability to engage in any meaningful activity. Simply stated, students' physiological needs (to have hunger and thirst satisfied, to have sleep needs met, to be adequately warm, and so forth) must be met before students can perform school tasks. Today's schools provide students with breakfast and lunch when needed, and great effort and expense is often directed towards heating and cooling school buildings.

Maslow's second level of need concerned safety. Again, students must feel safe from harm and danger before they are ready to learn. Today, schools often are equipped with metal detectors to increase students' sense of safety. In some schools, guards and security officers patrol the halls.

The third level of need, according to Maslow's theory, is the need for affiliation or the need to belong and to be accepted by others. Although this need may, at first glance, seem less related to the student's environment, it does, indeed, refer to the student's social environment. Students need the opportunity to develop social relationships and to establish friendships among their peers. In essence, Maslow, through his theory, determined that environmental factors are important in education.

Another significant principle of human development arises from a long debate between those experts who believed that innate characteristics (those the individual is born with) play the most important role in determining who the individual will become and what he or she will do versus those who believed that environmental characteristics are most important. This argument is referred to in the literature as the *nature* versus *nurture* debate.

Nature and Nurture

After experts on both sides of the argument stated their positions, the conclusion seemed to be that both *nature* (the internal variables) and *nurture* (the environment) play equally important roles in determining the outcome of individuals' growth and maturation. Again, it is important to remember the interaction of the individual with her or his environment, recalling that this view is the *dynamic* view of human development.

Before proceeding, teachers would do well to understand that perception plays an important role for learners to the extent that perception creates our individual reality. The world as we know it is a result of our selective perception. We cannot attend to all events and variables in our environment. We select certain events and variables to notice and attend to, and these phenomena which we observe form our perceptions; thus, we create our own reality. External and internal phenomena grab our attention and shape reality for each of us.

Thus, it is one thing for teachers to be aware of and sensitive to the students' environment; it is, however, impossible for teachers to see, feel, and understand the individual's environment in exactly the same way that it is seen, felt, and understood by the student.

Carol Tavris, a social psychologist and author of the book *Anger the Misunderstood Emotion*, notes that emotion plays a significant role in students' perceptions. For example, guilt is an emotion aroused by thoughts such as, "I should study or my parents will be disappointed in me." This is easily contrasted with the emotion of fear generated by the thought, "I should study or I will be a failure in life." Furthermore, guilt and fear can be compared to the emotion of anger, which is prompted by thoughts such as, "Why should I study when my teacher is out to get me?" Today's student often sees the teacher as an enemy, not as an authority figure or a friend. Tavris has identified anger as a primary emotion experienced by many students today and one which plays a significant role in shaping their academic perceptions which, in turn, form their reality of classroom experiences.

Explaining further, Tavris observes that unfulfilled expectations lead to anger. For example, if a student is led to believe (by teachers, school administrators, their peers, or by parents and siblings) that attending class is somehow irrelevant to academic achievement, then the student who is frequently absent still has the expectation of being successful. The student's perception is that absenteeism is compatible with academic achievement. If, because of absenteeism, the student fails to master essential elements of the curriculum and does not succeed, then the student will feel anger, the appropriate and anticipated emotion.

Anger, however, can be diffused by addressing perceptions, correcting false impressions, and establishing appropriate and realistic expectations. To illustrate, if all those significant individuals to the student emphasize the importance of class attendance, then students acquire the correct perception (in this case) that attendance is important for academic achievement and that absenteeism leads to academic failure.

For the sake of illustration only, let's consider what might happen if the teacher stresses attendance and the parents do not. In this case, the best route for the teacher to take is to show empathy for the student's dilemma. The teacher can acknowledge how difficult it is for the student to attend class when the parents are not supporting attendance, but the teacher also must seek to empower the student to make choices and to take responsibility for her or his own behavior.

In the situation described here, the student undergoes stress because of conflicting messages, and stress is faced by students and faculty alike. In fact, in the above example, the teacher is stressed too in facing the dilemma between supporting the parents of the student and supporting that which is in the best educational interests of the student.

Stress is the product of any change; both negative and positive changes produce stress. Environmental factors such as noise, air pollution, and crowding create stress; physiological factors such as sickness and physical injuries create stress; and, finally, psychological factors such as self-deprecating thoughts and negative self-image cause stress. In addition to the normal stressors that everyone experiences, some students are living in dysfunctional families; some students are dealing with substance abuse and addictions; some are experiencing sexual abuse. There are numerous sources of stress in the lives of students.

Since life is a stressful process, it is important that students and faculty learn acceptable ways to cope with stress. The first step in coping with stress is to recognize the role that stress plays in our lives. A teacher might lead a class through a brainstorming activity to help the students become aware of the various sources of stress affecting them. Next, the teacher could identify positive ways of coping with stress such as the importance of positive self-talk, physical exercise, proper nutrition, adequate sleep, balanced activities, time-management techniques, good study habits, and relaxation exercises.

Students who are stressed often experience a wide range of emotions. They may be sad, depressed, frustrated, or afraid, and on the positive side, happy and surprised. Effective teachers realize that students' emotions, as explained in this section and the preceding section on human development, play a significant role in students' classroom performance and achievement. Thus, effective teachers seek to create a classroom environment supportive of students' emotional needs. They have appropriate empathy and compassion for the emotional conflicts facing students, yet their concern is tempered by a realistic awareness of the importance of students attaining crucial academic and social skills that will grant them some control over their environment as they become increasingly independent and, eventually, must be prepared to be productive citizens.

Effective teachers recognize the effects of students' perceptions on the learning process and the effects of many environmental factors; as a result, they plan instruction to enhance students' self-esteem and to promote realistic expectations. It is important that teachers be able to differentiate positive and negative environmental factors, maximizing the positive variables and minimizing the negative ones. The teacher has the primary responsibility of creating a classroom environment that recognizes the different environmental factors affecting each student and that encourages each learner to excel, to achieve her or his personal best. Effective teachers work hard at creating learning environments in which all students are ready to learn—where students feel safe, accepted, competent, and productive.

DIVERSITY IN THE CLASSROOM

Effective teachers realize that students bring to the classroom a variety of characteristics, both personal and social, that create within the classroom a microcosm reflective of American society at large. Indeed, America has long held to the notion of being a "melting pot" whereby members of various racial, ethnic, religious, and national origin groups have contributed to the wealth of our culture.

Ethnocentrism is a sociological term used to describe the natural tendency of viewing one's own cultural or familial way of doing things as the right, correct, or best way. Because ethnocentrism is a natural tendency, all people are likely to engage in ethnocentric thinking and behaviors at times.

Many social critics have pointed out that ethnocentrism has played a notable role in American education. They assert that educational institutions often have been guilty of assuming a Eurocentric viewpoint, that is, recognizing the contributions of European writers, artists, scientists, philosophers, and so forth, at the expense of those from other cultures. These critics have also noted that the contributions of men often are disproportionately recognized over like achievements of women (Sadker & Sadker, 1994).

Moreover, David and Myra Sadker (1994) have found that teachers, both male and female, at all grade levels, are more likely to call on male than female students, are more likely to give positive reinforcement to males' correct responses than to those of females, and to provide coaching or instructional help to males when their responses are incorrect than to females. Their research has led them to conclude that teachers are usually unaware of gender bias in their teaching, but that such bias is pervasive in American schools. Their research also has persuaded them that bias can be eliminated once teachers become sensitive to its debilitating effects on students.

The point made here is that ethnocentrism, in any form, can be damaging because it is exclusive rather than inclusive. Eurocentric, Afrocentric, and other ethnocentric perspectives are equally limited in that they narrowly focus attention on one set of ideas at the neglect of others. Therefore, effective teachers will wisely expend a degree of effort in avoiding ethnocentric thinking and behaviors. Effective teachers will attempt to include all students in all classroom activities. The race, ethnicity, religion, national origin, and gender of learners will be viewed as strengths which enable students to learn with and from each other.

Historically speaking, educational experiments have demonstrated the importance of teachers' avoiding bias and ethnocentric thinking. The *Hawthorne effect,* or the phenomenon whereby what's expected becomes reality, was demonstrated when teachers were told that some students in their classes were extremely intelligent whereas others were extremely slow or even mentally retarded. In fact, all students had normal-range intelligence. Nonetheless, at the end of the experiment, students who had been identified to the teachers as being extremely intelligent all had made significant academic progress and were not only at the top of their class, but also performing at the top on national achievement tests. Those students who had been identified as retarded had made no progress at all; in fact, they had lost previously-made gains. Thus, it was demonstrated that teachers' expectations for students often become self-fulfilling prophecies.

In today's society, there is considerable reference to multiculturalism. Multiculturalism, if it serves merely to separate and distinguish the accomplishments of select cultural and ethnic groups, has the potential of separating and alienating Americans. To view multiculturalism in a positive light is to acknowledge a kind of multiculturalism which embraces the accomplishments of all cultural and ethnic groups, thereby strengthening our country and society, and promoting a sense of unity in the classroom.

Because multiculturalism and/or cultural diversity can be a controversial issue with many sides to consider, another approach to diversity for the classroom teacher is to acknowledge both cultural diversity and learning diversity and to focus on diversity in learning. This approach transcends cultural boundaries and recognizes that all people have distinct learning preferences and tendencies. Furthermore, this approach acknowledges that all preferences and tendencies are equally valid and that each style of learning has strengths. The teacher who understands learning styles can validate all students in the class.

Environmental Factors

Many factors play a role in determining a student's learning style. Among those most often cited in the research literature on learning style are environmental, emotional, sociological, physiological, and psychological factors (Dunn & Dunn, 1993). Although there are several different models for understanding learning differences and many good instruments for assessing learning styles, the Dunn & Dunn (1993) model is one widely used in public schools with versions suitable for students in elementary and secondary classrooms. It will serve as the basis for the following discussion.

Environmental factors include students' reactions to such stimuli as sound, light, temperature, and room design. Do students prefer to study and learn with or without sound, with bright or soft lights, in warm or cool rooms, with standard classroom furniture or alternative seating? Classroom teachers observe that some students are easily distracted by any noise and require absolute quiet when studying or working on assignments. On the other hand, some students seem to learn best when they can listen to music. Some researchers have found evidence that students who prefer sound learn best when classical or instrumental music is played in the background.

Light is another environmental factor with students' preferences for light appearing to be basically inherited, with family members often exhibiting the same preference. Some students prefer bright, direct illumination while others prefer dim, indirect lighting.

Temperature and design are two other environmental factors affecting learning style. Some students will prefer warmer temperatures whereas others will prefer cooler temperatures. Finally, some students will prefer to sit in straight-backed chairs at desks while others may prefer to sit on soft, comfy chairs or to sit or recline on the floor.

Although traditional classrooms are structured to provide quiet, brightly illuminated study and work areas with straight-backed chairs and desks, classroom teachers will observe that this environment meets the needs of only some of the learners in the class. An effective teacher will take into consideration the learning styles of all students and experiment with different room designs, study centers, and creating different environments in the classroom. Although classroom temperature may seem to be beyond the control of the teacher, students can be advised to dress in layers so that they can remove outer garments when they are too warm and put on more layers when they are too cool.

Emotional Factors

According to Rita and Kenneth Dunn, emotional factors include motivation, persistence, responsibility, and structure. To explain, some students are motivated intrinsically: they undertake and complete tasks because they see the value in doing so. Other students are motivated extrinsically: They undertake and complete tasks because they desire to please others or to earn good marks. In regard to persistence, some students, when they undertake assignments, become totally and completely engaged in their work; they seem to lose track of time and can work for long periods without interruption or without feeling fatigued. Other students seem to work in short spurts of energy, needing to take frequent breaks.

When it comes to responsibility, some students are nonconforming, always doing the unexpected (and sometimes unwanted), whereas other students are conforming, always following the rules. Structure refers to whether or not students need detailed and precise instructions. Some students have lots of questions about how assignments should be done, and they desire detailed, step-by-step instructions on each phase of the assignment. Other students, however, seem to work from general concepts and are usually eager to begin assignments, often beginning their work before the directions have been given.

Sociological factors include whether or not students are social learners—preferring to work in pairs or in groups—or whether they are independent learners—preferring to work alone. Another sociological factor is whether or not students work best under the close guidance and supervision of an authority figure, be it teacher or parent, or whether they work best with a minimum of adult guidance and are best left primarily on their own to do their work.

Physiological factors include students' preferences for food or drink while they study, what time of day they learn best, their mobility needs, and their perceptual strengths. Briefly, some students may need to eat or drink in order to effectively and efficiently learn. Rita Dunn says that to make sure that students do not abuse this privilege, she allows them to eat only carrot or celery sticks (cooked so that the snacks will not crunch when eaten by students) and to drink water. This way, she is certain that only students who really need intake when they are learning will take advantage of this concession.

Some students may learn best early in the morning, some later in the morning, some in early afternoon, and some later in the afternoon. Researchers have found that merely manipulating the time of day that certain students take tests can significantly affect their test performance.

Mobility needs refer to the fact that some students need to move around when they study, whereas other students can sit still for longer periods of time. Although all of these factors are important, and a growing body of literature tends to support the idea that these factors play a significant role in increasing students' performance and in increasing teachers' effectiveness with students, perhaps one of the most important elements in understanding learning style is to identify students' perceptual strengths. Perceptual strengths refer to students' learning modalities, such as whether they are visual, auditory, tactile, or kinesthetic learners. Basically, these perceptual modalities refer to whether students learn best by seeing, hearing, or doing.

Some students can be given a book or handout to read and then perform a task well based on what they have read. These students tend to have visual (iconic or semantic) perceptual strength. Other students are visual learners, too, but they tend to learn best from images. These are the students who seem to recall every event, even minor details, from films, videos, or classroom demonstrations.

Although evidence indicates that less than 15 percent of the school-age population is auditory (Dunn, 1993), much of the classroom instruction takes the form of teachers telling students information. Most students do not learn auditorially. Therefore, these students must be taught how to listen and learn from oral instructions and lecture.

Teachers who rely on telling students the information that is important would do well to remember that females are more likely to learn auditorially than males. Teachers should also keep in mind that whether or not students benefit from lectures is likely to depend on several other elements as well as whether or not the students are auditory learners, such as whether or not the students like the teacher, whether or not they think the information being presented is important, or whether or not they think that listening to the teacher will help them to achieve their goals (Baxter-Magolda, 1992).

On the other hand, there are students who do not seem to benefit much from lectures, textbook assignments, or visual aids. These students' perceptual strengths are tactile and kinesthetic. They learn from movement and motion, from being able to touch, handle, and manipulate objects. Often these students may have been identified as having learning disabilities. Sometimes they have been relegated to shop or cooking classes or have found their success in athletics, music, or art. Interestingly, many of the "hands on" skills that often identify a student for a career as an auto mechanic are also important skills for mechanical engineers and surgeons.

Learning Styles

The obvious benefit of knowing whether or not students are auditory, visual, tactile, or kinesthetic learners is not simply to cater to the learners' preferences or strengths. The significance is that once strengths are identified, then teachers can teach students to use those strengths in situations which are not easy or natural. For example, students who are not auditory learners (but tactile and kinesthetic) must learn responsibility for their own learning; they must learn to become involved in lecture classes. Becoming involved means that they learn to take copious notes, participate in class discussions, ask questions, and answer questions posed by the teacher.

Visual learners must sit where they can see what's going on in class, where they can see the teacher and the board. They need opportunities to draw pictures, to diagram, to take good notes, to create mind maps, and to use flashcards. They must be taught how to visualize the abstract concepts they are being taught, and they need opportunities to practice all these techniques.

For visual learners who learn best by reading, teachers can provide adequate opportunities to read in class. Students need to learn specific note-taking methods, and reading and comprehension strategies. They also can be taught to use supplemental readings, to use the library effectively, and to use workbooks.

Auditory learners need to learn attention-directing activities. They can learn to use audio cassettes as learning aids. They can learn to ask questions in class and to participate in class discussions. They must be taught how to summarize and paraphrase—especially how to state in their own words the concepts they are trying to master. They may need the teacher to repeat or to restate ideas. Students must learn to pay close attention to verbal cues such as voice tone and inflection. Reciting what they have heard (or read) is an important strategy for auditory learners as is finding someone to whom they can explain ideas they have acquired. It may be helpful for auditory learners to work on some assignments with students who are visual learners (Nolting, 1993).

Tactile, kinesthetic learners may benefit from study groups, discussion groups, role-playing situations, lab settings, computer activities, learning games, and using flashcards and other manipulatives. They must get involved in class by asking questions and participating in discussions. They learn best when they can convert what they are learning into real-life, concrete experiences; for example, they may learn fractions by cutting a pizza into slices. Often, they need to work math problems immediately after being shown examples to check their understanding. They often need to move around while they are studying, reviewing ideas while exercising, or doing chores. Many times, they do their best work when they are using tools such as computers, calculators, or even their fingers.

When classroom teachers assess students' learning styles and then begin to teach to empower students to learn more effectively and perform tasks with greater proficiency, the result is that students also learn a tremendous lesson about diversity. They learn that not everyone learns in the same way, but that everyone can achieve. The products of learning can meet the same high standards although the processes for learning may be different for different students.

UNDERSTANDING LEARNERS

It is one thing for teachers to have command of their subject matter. After all, it is a given that English teachers will be able to write well, that math teachers will be able to compute and calculate, that science teachers will know and understand science, and so forth. However, it is something else—and something at least as important—that teachers know how to teach.

When teachers understand learners—that is, when they understand developmental processes common to all learners, and how environmental features and learning styles affect learning—they are better able to design and deliver effective instruction. Although there may be some intuitive aspects to teaching (and it does seem that some people were born to teach), teaching skills can be acquired through processes of introspection, observation, direct instruction, self-evaluation, and experimentation.

How teachers teach should be directly related to how learners learn. Theories of cognitive development describe how learners learn new information and acquire new skills. There are many theories of cognitive development, two of which will be included in this review; they are (a) the Piagetian (or Neo-Piagetian) theory, and (b) information processing theory.

Piagetian theory describes learning in discrete and predictable stages. Therefore, teachers who understand this theory can provide students with de-

velopmentally-appropriate instruction. This the͏
moving from simpler ways of thinking to more con͏
ing and thinking. For teachers, there are many im͏
theoretical perspective. For example, teachers m͏
ments that present learners with multiple opport͏
unfamiliar stimuli—be they objects or ideas. Tea͏
ers with opportunities to engage in extended di͏
to Piaget's theory, conversational interactions ͏
nent in cognitive development, especially the acquisition of formal o͏
(or higher-ordered thinking skills). Moreover, it is important that adults (and
teachers in particular) model desired behaviors; teachers must reveal their own
complex ways of thinking and solving problems to students.

On the other hand, information processing theories of human development take a different approach to describing and understanding how learners
learn. Based on a computer metaphor and borrowing computer imagery to
describe how people learn, information processing theories begin by determining the processing demands of a particular cognitive challenge (or problem to solve) necessitating a detailed task-analysis of how the human mind
changes external objects or events into a useful form according to certain, pre-
cisely-specified rules or strategies, similar to the way a computer programmer
programs a computer to perform a function. Thus, information processing
theories focus on the process, how the learner arrives at a response or answer.

A brief analysis of one information processing theory will serve to illustrate this point. Sternberg's (1985) triarchic theory of intelligence is a theory
taking into account three features of learning. Those three features are (a) the
mechanics or components of intelligence (including both higher-ordered
thinking processes, such as planning, decision making and problem solving,
and lower-ordered processes, such as making inferences, mapping, selectively
encoding information, retaining information in memory, transferring new information in memory, and so forth); (b) the learner's experiences; and (c) the
learner's context (including the adaptation to and the shaping and selecting
of environments).

According to Sternberg, learners' use of the mechanics of intelligence is
influenced by learners' experiences. To illustrate, some cognitive processes
(such as those required in reading) become automatized as a result of continued exposure to and practice of those skills. Learners who come from homes
where parents read and where there are lots of different reading materials tend
to be more proficient readers; certainly, learners who read a lot become more
proficient readers. Those learners who are exposed to reading activities and

...mple opportunities to practice reading have greater skill and ex-
... reading; and in a cyclical manner, students who have skills in read-
... to read. Conversely, those who lack reading skills don't like to read.
...ents who don't like to read, don't read; thus, their reading skills, lacking
...actice, fail to improve.

An information processing approach acknowledges that not only are individuals influenced by their environments and adapt to those environments, individuals also are active in shaping their own environments. In other words, a child who wants to read but who has no books at home may ask parents to buy books, or may go to the library to read, or check out books to read at home.

Information processing theory is of interest to educators because of its insistence on the idea that intelligent performance can be facilitated through instruction and direct training. In sum, intelligent thinking can be taught. Sternberg has urged teachers to identify the mental processes that academic tasks require and to teach learners those processes; he challenges teachers to teach learners what processes to use, when and how to use them, and how to combine them into strategies for solving problems and accomplishing assignments.

Teachers who wish to follow Sternberg's advice might choose to begin teaching by identifying *instructional objectives*, that is, what should students be able to do as a result of instruction. Second, teachers would analyze the objectives in terms of identifying the *instructional outcomes*, those being the tasks or assignments that students can perform as a result of achieving the instructional objectives. Third, teachers would analyze instructional outcomes in terms of the *cognitive skills* or mental processes required to perform those tasks or assignments. After following these three steps and identifying instructional objectives, instructional outcomes, and cognitive skills involved, the teacher is ready to conduct a *preassessment* (or pretest) to determine what students already know.

Instruction is then based on the results of the preassessment with teachers focusing on teaching directly the cognitive skills needed in order for students to perform the task(s). Following instruction, teachers would conduct a *post-assessment* (or post-test) to evaluate the results of instruction. Further instruction would be based on the results of the post-assessment, that is, whether or not students had achieved expected outcomes and whether or not teachers had achieved instructional objectives.

Regardless of which theoretical perspective is adopted by teachers, and, at times, teachers may find themselves taking a rather eclectic approach and borrowing elements from several theoretical bases, it is helpful for teachers to consider if they are structuring their classrooms to satisfy learners' needs or merely their own needs as teachers. Furthermore, if the teachers' goal is to increase teaching effectiveness by facilitating learners' knowledge and skill acquisition, then teachers will engage continuously in a process of self-examination and self-evaluation.

Metacognition

Self-examination and self-evaluation are both types of *metacognitive* thinking. *Metacognition* is a term used to describe what, how, and why people know what they know when they know it. In short, it is thinking about thinking and knowing about knowing. Cognitive psychologists describe metacognition as a characteristic of higher-ordered, mature, and sophisticated thinking. Generally speaking, as learners achieve higher levels of cognitive skills, they also increase their metacognitive skills. Therefore, not only should teachers engage in metacognitive thinking, they should model that thinking for their students, and encourage their students to develop metacognitive skills.

Metacognition can be understood in terms of (a) metacognitive knowledge and (b) metacognitive control (Flavell, 1987). Basically, metacognitive knowledge is what learners need to know and metacognitive control is what learners need to do. Metacognitive control, therefore, is in the hands of the learner. Teachers cannot control learners' behavior although they can encourage and admonish. The best that teachers can do is help learners expand their metacognitive awareness and knowledge.

Awareness can be increased by talking about metacognition. Flavell has explained that there are three kinds of metacognitive knowledge; they are (a) person knowledge, (b) task knowledge, and (c) strategy knowledge.

Person knowledge falls into one of three categories: (a) intraindividual knowledge, (b) interindividual knowledge, and (c) universal knowledge. First, intraindividual knowledge is what the learner knows or understands about him- or herself. Therefore, it is important that learners have opportunities to learn about themselves, about their interests, abilities, propensities, and so forth. For this reason (among others), it is important that learners have opportunities to learn about their own learning style and their perceptual strengths. It is also helpful for them to have opportunities to examine their personalities, values, and goals.

Furthermore, in a model that recognizes the dynamic nature of instruction, that is, one which recognizes that the learner also knows certain things and can contribute to the classroom, the teacher realizes that she or he is a learner, too. Teachers, then, can benefit from examining their own learning style, perceptual strengths, personalities, values, and goals. Moreover, it can be extremely beneficial for teachers to consider their own instructional style.

Instructional Style Assessment

One instrument that assesses instructional style, the Instructional Style Inventory (Canfield & Canfield, 1988), identifies instructional styles in four general categories (although there also can be combinations of different styles). The four categories are *social*, *independent*, *applied*, and *conceptual*. Briefly stated, the social style is one which describes the teacher who values classroom interactions, who stresses teamwork and group work; the independent style describes the teacher who emphasizes working alone and is likely to rely on self-paced, individualized, and programmed instruction; the applied style is one which stresses real-world experiences and avoids lecture and preparatory reading, but focuses on practicums and site visits, and so forth; finally, the conceptual style is one describing the teacher who is language-oriented and likes highly organized materials and tends to depend on lectures and readings.

Returning to the discussion on metacognitive knowledge, the second kind of person knowledge is interindividual knowledge, how learners are alike and how they are different. Again, this is another reason why the recognition of diversity brought about by studying learning styles can inform learners and improve their cognitive performance. As they learn about their own learning style, learners also observe that their classmates have some similarities and some differences when it comes to the various elements or factors in determining learning style. Interindividual knowledge is increased as students realize that there are many different ways to learn.

Finally, the third kind of personal knowledge is universal knowledge, the knowledge that there are degrees of understanding. Examples are the realization that short-term memory is fallible and has limited capacity, that people can make mistakes, that it is easier to remember things if they are written down, that memory work requires repetition, and so forth. To examine students' understanding of universal knowledge, teachers might ask students to identify what they know about learning. They might, for example, ask students to write down on notecards what they know about how people learn things or by brainstorming the question in class.

The second broad category of metacognitive knowledge, according to Flavell, is task knowledge. Task knowledge includes several different variables, such as whether information is interesting or boring, or if it is new or familiar, or if it is easy or difficult. Task knowledge enables learners to plan appropriately for undertaking tasks (for example, if something is hard to learn, then it may take more time, more concentration, and more effort) and tells them how to go about accomplishing the task (for example, if the task requires memory, then a memory strategy is needed).

Specific tasks relevant to academic disciplines can be identified by classroom teachers; however, there are academic tasks that are generally applicable to all content areas. These academic tasks include what are broadly referred to as study skills, which are foundational skills for all learning. They include such tasks as time management, directing attention, processing information, finding main ideas, studying, and taking tests, among others (Weinstein, Schulte, & Palmer, 1988).

Flavell's final category of metacognitive knowledge is strategy knowledge, which takes into account how learners can best accomplish particular tasks and how they can be reasonably certain that they have reached their cognitive goals. Strategy knowledge also equips learners to monitor their cognitive activities and to gain confidence in their abilities. To illustrate, if the task is to find main ideas, then learners need strategies for finding main ideas. Strategies for this task include learning (a) to preview or survey reading assignments (reading headings, words in bold print; looking at illustrations and graphic aids); (b) to ask questions (What is this about? Who is this about? When did it happen? Where did it happen? How did it happen? Why did it happen?); and (c) to read the first and last sentences in each paragraph (knowing that the first and last sentences in paragraphs are most likely to be topic sentences).

Study Strategies

If the task is to study, then learners need specific strategies for studying. These strategies can include, among others, (a) outlining, mapping, or summarizing text (from books or notes); (b) marking text (using margins for notetaking and summarizing); (c) participating in group review sessions; (d) comparing notes with a friend, tutor, or teacher; (e) getting extra help (from a tutor, teacher, or parent); and, (f) going to the library (to get additional information from alternative sources). Of course, strategies such as outlining can be further delineated into specific steps for various kinds of outlines.

Obviously, there is an interaction between person, task, and strategy knowledge. For example, if the task is studying, then a visual learner who learns well by reading (individual characteristic) might choose to go to the library to find an alternative source of information (strategy characteristic); in this example, there is a three-way interaction involving task, individual, and strategy.

Although teachers willingly expend considerable energy teaching students about tasks, they often erroneously assume that students will automatically or tacitly acquire learning strategies. However, the fact is that many students do not acquire these strategies and that even those who may learn some strategies would benefit from direct instruction in the use of specific learning strategies. The research literature indicates that the use of think-aloud protocols, spontaneous private speech, skimming, rereading, context clues, error-detection, grouping skills, examination/evaluation skills (distinguishing between conceptual versus superficial features, or between major themes and minor details and between decoding and comprehension, between verbatim recall and recall for gist) can significantly enhance learners' performance.

Teachers who incorporate an understanding of the role played by metacognition (especially in teaching middle-school and older students) into their instruction will find that they are preparing their students well for a lifetime of learning. Flavell (1979) explained that metacognition is necessary for the oral communication of information, oral persuasion, oral comprehension, reading comprehension, writing, language acquisition, attention, memory, problem-solving, social cognition, self-control, and self-instruction. It is hard to imagine a task that one might do that wouldn't require metacognition.

A recent critique of education in America includes the observation that the movement to teach basic academic skills in America's schools may have resulted in more students performing well on tests of basic skills; however, thinking skills, not just basic skills, are needed in the real world of jobs, families, and citizenship. To better prepare students for the real world, teachers need to focus on the *process* of learning, teaching students *how to think and learn*. Teaching metacognitive awareness and fostering the development of metacognitive knowledge are steps in the right direction.

MOTIVATING STUDENTS

Students often say that they like teachers who can motivate students when, in fact, teachers are not responsible for students' motivation. Motivation is a student's responsibility; motivation comes from within the student. However, effective teachers will help students develop self-discipline, self-control, and self-motivation. These skills of self-management can be taught, yet they require a great deal of effort and practice in order for students to gain true proficiency.

One researcher has offered three principles to guide teachers that will lead to greater effectiveness in the classroom (Baxter-Magolda, 1992). Interestingly, each of these principles leads to empowering students and, thus, are motivational in nature.

The first principle is to *validate students as knowers*. This principle is based on the idea of the active learner who brings much to the classroom (the dynamic view of human development). How can teachers validate students? Baxter-Magolda suggests that teachers display a caring attitude towards students. This means that it's appropriate for teachers to take an interest in students, to learn about their likes and dislikes, their interests and hobbies, both in school and outside school. This also means that it's okay for teachers to show enthusiasm and excitement for their classes, not only the subject-matter they teach, but the students they teach as well. It also means, as Carol Tavris (1994) noted, that it's good for teachers to show empathy for students' emotional needs.

Baxter-Magolda also recommends that teachers question authority by example and let students know that they, as teachers, can also be questioned. This means that teachers model critical thinking skills in the classroom. Teachers can question authority when they examine and evaluate readings—whether from textbooks or other sources. Teachers can question authorities when they teach propaganda techniques, exposing advertising claims and gimmicks. Teachers can question authority when they discuss the media and how so-called news sources shape and form public opinion. There are numerous opportunities for teachers in dealing with current affairs and public opinion to question authority and inculcate in their students, critical thinking and higher-ordered reasoning skills.

Also, when teachers allow students to question them, teachers are acknowledging that everyone is a learner. Everyone should participate in a life-long process of continuous learning. It is no shame or disgrace for the teacher to admit that sometimes he or she doesn't know the answer to every question. This gives the teacher the opportunity to show students how adults think, how they have a level of awareness (metacognition) when they don't know something, and about how they go about finding answers to their questions. Teachers who admit that they don't have all the answers thus have the opportunity to show students how answers can be found and/or to reveal to students that there are no easy answers to some of life's most difficult questions.

Third, to validate students as knowers, teachers can value students' opinions, ideas, and comments. Teachers' affirmations include smiles and nods of approval, positive comments (such as, "That's a good answer."), and encouraging cues (such as, "That may seem like a reasonable answer, but can you think of a better answer?" or "Can you explain what you mean by that answer?"). Validating students as knowers also means supporting students' voices, that is, giving them ample opportunities to express their own ideas, to share their opinions, to make their own contributions to the classroom. These opportunities can include times of oral discussion as well as written assignments.

Jointly Constructed Meaning

Another principle in Baxter-Magolda's guidelines for teaching effectiveness is for teachers and students to recognize that learning is *a process of jointly-constructing meaning*. To explain, Baxter-Magolda says that it is important for teachers to dialogue with students (also an important concept in Piagetian theory) and that teachers emphasize mutual learning. Also in agreement with Piagetian principles, Baxter-Magolda recommends that teachers reveal their own thinking processes as they approach subjects and as they analyze and understand new subjects and as they solve problems and reach decisions. She further advises that teachers share leadership and promote collegial learning (group work), acknowledging that individual achievement is not the sole purpose or focus for learning. By allowing students to collaborate, they also will learn significant lessons directly applicable to work situations where most accomplishments are the result of team efforts, not the sole efforts of individuals.

Baxter-Magolda's final principle for teachers is to *situate learning in the students' own experiences*. She suggests that this be done by letting students know that they are wanted in class, by using inclusive language (avoiding ethnic and cultural bias and stereotyping, instead using gender-neutral and inclusive language), and focusing on activities. Activities are important for motivation because they give learners things to do, to become actively involved in, arousing their attention and interest, and giving them an outlet for their physical and mental energy. Activities can have an additional positive benefit in that they can serve to connect students to each other, especially when students are given opportunities to participate in collaborative learning (the way things happen in the "real world") and to work in groups. Finally, in situating learning in students' own experiences, it is important to consider the use of personal stories in class, as appropriate (that is, without violating anyone's right to privacy and confidentiality). Moreover, teachers can share personal stories which allow them to connect with students in a deeper and more personal way.

When students assume responsibility for their own motivation, they are learning a lesson of personal empowerment. Unfortunately, although personal empowerment is probably one of the most important lessons anyone ever learns, it is a lesson infrequently taught in classrooms across the country.

Empowerment has many components, one of which is *self-esteem*. A good definition of self-esteem is that it is my opinion of me, your opinion of you. It is what we think and believe to be true about ourselves, not what we think about others and not what they think about us. Self-esteem appears to be a combination of self-efficacy and self-respect as seen against a background of self-knowledge.

Self-efficacy, simply stated, is one's confidence in one's own ability to cope with life's challenges. Self-efficacy refers to having a sense of control over life or, better, over one's responses to life. Experts say that ideas about self-efficacy get established by the time children reach the age of four. Because of this early establishment of either a feeling of control or no control, classroom teachers may find that even primary grade students believe that they have no control over their life, that it makes no difference what they do or how they act. Therefore, it is all the more important that teachers attempt to help all students achieve coping skills and a sense of self-efficacy.

Control, in this definition of self-efficacy, can be examined in regard to external or internal motivators. For example, external motivators include such things as luck and the roles played by others in influencing outcomes. Internal motivators are variables within the individual. To explain, if a student does well on a test and is asked, "How did you do so well on that test?," a student who relies on external motivators might reply, "Well, I just got lucky," or "The teacher likes me." A student who relies on internal motivators and who does well on a test may explain, "I am smart and always do well on tests," or "I studied hard and that's why I did well." On the other hand, even the student who relies on internal motivators can do poorly on tests and then may explain, "I'm dumb and that's why I don't do well," or "I didn't think the test was important and I didn't try very hard." Even though students have similar experiences, in regard to issues of control, what is important is how students explain their experiences. If students have external motivators, they are likely to either dismiss their performance (success or failure) as matters of luck or to credit or blame the influence of others. If students have internal motivators, then they are likely to attribute their performance to either their intelligence and skills or their effort.

Students who have external motivators need help understanding how their behavior contributes to and influences outcomes in school. Students need clarification as to how grades are determined and precise information about how their work is evaluated. Students who have internal motivators but low self-esteem (such as thinking, "I'm dumb") need help identifying their strengths and assets (something that can be accomplished when students are given information about learning styles). Self-efficacy can be enhanced.

Another factor in empowerment is *self-respect*. Self-respect is believing that one deserves happiness, achievement, and love. Self-respect is treating one's self at least as nicely as one treats other people. Many students are not aware of their internal voices (which are established at an early age). Internal voices are constantly sending messages, either positive or negative. Psychologists say that most of us have either a generally positive outlook on life, which causes our inner voice to send positive messages ("You're okay," "People like you," "Things will be all right," and so forth) or a generally negative outlook on life, which causes our inner voice to send negative messages ("You're not okay," "You're too fat, skinny, ugly, stupid," and so forth).

Two tools which can help students to "reprogram" their inner voice are affirmations and visualizations (Ellis, 1991). Affirmations are statements describing what students want. Affirmations must be personal, positive, and written in the present tense. What makes affirmations effective are details. For example, instead of saying, "I am stupid," students can be encouraged to say, "I am capable. I do well in school because I am organized, I study daily, I get all my work completed on time, and I take my school work seriously." Affirmations must be repeated until they can be said with total conviction.

Visualizations are images students can create whereby they see themselves the way they want to be. For example, if a student wants to improve his or her typing skills, then the student evaluates what it would look like, sound like, and feel like to be a better typist. Once the student identifies the image, then the student has to rehearse that image in her or his mind, including as many details and sensations as possible. Both visualization and affirmation can restructure attitudes and behaviors. They can be tools for students to use to increase their motivation.

The final component of empowerment is *self-knowledge.* Self-knowledge refers to an individual's strengths and weaknesses, assets and liabilities; self-knowledge comes about as a result of a realistic self-appraisal (and can be achieved by an examination of learning styles). Achieving self-knowledge also requires that students have opportunities to explore their goals and values.

Students who know what their goals and values are can more easily see how education will enable them to achieve those goals and values. Conversely, students cannot be motivated when they do not have goals and values, or when they do not know what their goals and values are. In other words, without self-knowledge, motivation is impossible. Therefore, teachers who follow Baxter-Magolda's guidelines for effective instruction and who teach their students about personal empowerment are teachers who realize the importance of motivation and who set the stage for students to claim responsibility for their own successes and failures. Such teachers help students to become motivated to make changes and to accomplish more.

Drill Questions

1. Rueben Stein is a middle-school teacher who wants to teach his class about the classification system in the animal kingdom. He decides to introduce this unit to his class by having the students engage in general classification activities. He brings to class a paper bag filled with 30 household items. He dumps the contents of the bag onto a table and then asks the students, in groups of three or four, to put like items into piles and then to justify or explain why they placed certain items into a particular pile.

    By assigning this task to his students, Mr. Stein is providing his students with a developmentally-appropriate task because

    (A) middle-school students like to work in groups.

    (B) the items in the bag are household items with which most students will be familiar.

(C)   the assignment gives students the opportunity to practice their skills at categorizing.

(D)   the assignment will give students a task to perform while the teacher finishes grading papers.

2.   Maria Smith is a high school English teacher who is concerned about a student who is failing her junior English class. The student has not turned in any outside assignments, and Ms. Smith has noticed a definite decline in the quality of work the student completes in class. Ms. Smith also has observed that the student has great difficulty staying awake in class and that she seems irritable and distracted most of the time.

In her efforts to help the student, Ms. Smith decides to ask the student

(A)   if she has been having family problems.

(B)   if she realizes that the quality of her classwork is suffering and if she knows of any reasons for the decline.

(C)   to work on better time-management skills.

(D)   to start coming in early or to stay after class to receive extra help with her work.

3.   Elva Rodriguez teaches fourth grade. She has structured her class so that students can spend thirty minutes daily, after lunch, in sustained, silent reading activities with books and reading materials of their own choosing.

In order to maximize this reading opportunity and to recognize differences among learners, Ms. Rodriguez

(A)   allows some students to sit quietly at their desks while others are allowed to move to a reading area where they sit on floor cushions or recline on floor mats.

(B)   makes sure that all students have selected appropriate reading materials.

(C) plays classical music on a tape player to enhance student learning.

(D) dims the lights in the classroom in order to increase students' reading comprehension.

4. Karla Dixon is a second-grade teacher who has selected a book to read to her class after lunch. She shows the students the picture on the cover of the book and reads the title of the book to them. She then asks, "What do you think this book is about?"

By asking this question, Ms. Dixon is

(A) learning which students are interested in reading strategies.

(B) trying to keep the students awake since she knows they usually get sleepy after lunch.

(C) encouraging students to make a prediction, a precursor of hypothetical thinking.

(D) finding out which students are good readers.

5. Ben Douglas is a high school history teacher. His class is studying the Korean Conflict when a student brings up a question about the morality of the war in Vietnam. This is not a subject that Mr. Douglas is prepared to teach at the time.

In response to the student's question, Mr. Douglas

(A) tells the student that the day's topic is the Korean Conflict and suggests that the student bring up the question later on in the term.

(B) invites the class to respond to the student's question.

(C) gives the student a cursory response, eliminating the need for any further discussion.

(D) disciplines the student for not paying attention to the topic under discussion.

Answers to Drill Questions

1.   **(C)**   According to Piaget's theory of cognitive development, students in middle school would be at the stage of *concrete operational* thought. Students at this stage of cognitive development would be able to categorize items. Choice (A) is a false statement. Although some students will like to work in groups, some students will prefer to work alone—at this and at any age group or cognitive stage. Preferring to learn in groups (or socially) or to learn alone (or independently) is a characteristic of learning style or preference, not a characteristic of cognitive or affective development. Choice (B) is irrelevant to the teacher's intent in assigning the task. Students could just as easily work with unfamiliar items, grouping them by observable features independent of their use or function. Choice (D) is not a good choice under any circumstances. Teachers should assiduously avoid giving students assignments merely to keep them busy while the teacher does something else. All assignments should have an instructional purpose.

2.   **(B)**   This question opens the door for dialogue with the student about a range of possible problems. This response shows that the teacher is concerned about the student and her welfare without making assumptions, jumping to conclusions, and/or intruding into the private affairs of the student. Choice (A) presumes that the source of all problems lies with the family. Although the student may be having family-related difficulties, there are other possibilities to consider as well. The student may have taken a job that is taking too much of her time away from her studies or the student may be having health problems. It is unwise for the teacher to conclude that the student is having family problems. Choice (C) is inappropriate because it too narrowly identifies one possible coping mechanism as the solution to the student's problem. Although the student may benefit from acquiring better time-management skills, it also is possible that the student's present problems have little or nothing to do with time-management. Choice (D) is equally inappropriate in that it demands that the student devote even more time to school, even though she currently is having trouble with present demands. If the student is unwell, then certainly spending more time at school is not the solution to her problem. Clearly, choice (B) is the best alternative to helping the student identify her problem(s) and find a solution.

3.   **(A)**   Only choice (A) takes into account differences among learners by giving them options as to how and where they will read. Choice (B) violates the students' freedom to select reading materials which they find interesting and wish to read. When students are allowed to choose their own reading materials, it may seem that some students select materials beyond their present reading comprehension. However, reading research indicates that students can comprehend more difficult material when their interest level is high.

Therefore, any efforts by the teacher to interfere with students' selection of their own reading material would be ill-advised. Choices (C) and (D) are equally poor in that they both describe a concession to only one group of learners. For example, with choice (C), while some students may prefer to read with music playing in the background, other students will find music distracting. The best action for the teacher to take would be for her to allow some students to listen to music on earphones while others read in quiet. In regard to choice (D), some students will prefer bright illumination just as some students will read better with the lights dimmed. Ms. Rodriguez would do well to attempt to accommodate various learner needs by having one area of the room more brightly illuminated than the other.

4.   **(C)**   The teacher is encouraging students to become actively engaged in the learning process by making a prediction based on limited information given in the book title and cover illustration. When students can generate their own predictions or formulate hypotheses about possible outcomes on the basis of available (although limited) data, they are gaining preparatory skills for formal operations (or abstract thinking). Although second-grade students would not be expected to be at the level of cognitive development characterized by formal operations, Piagetian theory would indicate that teachers who model appropriate behaviors and who give students opportunities to reach or stretch for new cognitive skills are fostering students' cognitive growth. Choice (A) is a poor choice because students' responses to this one question posed by the teacher cannot be used to assess adequately their interest in reading activities. Choice (B), likewise, is a poor choice in that it implies no instructional intent for asking the question. Choice (D) is incorrect because students' responses to a single question cannot allow the instructor to determine which students are good readers and which ones are not.

5.   **(B)**   This is the best answer because it acknowledges the student's curiosity and legitimizes the student's right to pursue information by asking questions. It gives approval and recognition to the student's voice of inquiry, *and* it allows other students to voice their opinions and/or to make relevant comments. The teacher does not have to have a ready answer to every question, and this answer choice recognizes that also. The other three choices, (A), (C), and (D), all have the opposite effect of ignoring students' voices and missing an opportunity for students to become active learners, learning something about which they may be genuinely interested. All three of the incorrect choices reflect an autocratic attitude towards teaching which is the opposite of what Baxter-Magolda recommends for teaching effectiveness.

References

Baxter-Magolda, M. B. (1992). *Knowing and reasoning in college: Gender-related patterns in students' intellectual development.* San Francisco: Jossey Bass.

Bloom, B. (1976). *Human characteristics and school learning.* New York: McGraw-Hill.

Canfield, A. A. & Canfield, J. S. (1988). Instructional styles inventory. Los Angeles: Western Psychological Services.

Coles, R. (1993). Point of view: When earnest volunteers are solely tested. *Chronicle of Higher Education,* May 5, A52.

Dunn, R. (1993). Presentation on the Productivity Environmental Preferences Scale (PEPS) at Learning Styles Institute, Lubbock, Texas, June 5-9. (Sponsored by Education Service Center, Region XVII.)

Dunn, R., & Dunn, K. (1993). Presentation on Using Learning Styles Information to Enhance Teaching Effectiveness at Learning Styles Institute, Lubbock, Texas, June 5-9. (Sponsored by Education Service Center, Region XVII.)

Elkind, D. (1967). Egocentrism in adolescence. *Child Development,* 38, 1025-34.

Ellis, D. (1991). *Becoming a master student.* Rapid City, SD: College Survival.

Erikson, E. (1963). *Childhood and society.* New York: Horton.

Flavell, J. H. (1979). Metacognition and cognitive monitoring: A new area of cognitive-developmental inquiry. *American Psychologist,* 34, 906-911.

Flavell, J. H. (1987). Speculations about the nature and development of metacognition. In R. H. Kluwe & F. E. Weinert (Eds.), *Metacognition, motivation, and learning* (pp. 21-30). Hillsdale, NJ: Erlbaum.

Maslow, A. (1968). *Toward a psychology of being.* New York: Van Nostrand Reinhold.

Nolting, P. (1993). Presentation on Meeting Learners' Special Needs at West Texas Regional TASP Workshop, Lubbock, Texas, August 7. (Sponsored by Texas Tech University.)

Piaget, J. (1950). *The psychology of intelligence.* London: Routledge and Kegan Paul.

Sadker, M., & Sadker, D. (1994). *Failing at fairness: How America's schools cheat girls.* New York: Charles Scribner's Sons.

Sternberg, R. J. (1985). *Beyond IQ: A triarchic theory of human intelligence.* Cambridge: Cambridge University Press.

Tavris, C. (1994). Presentation on Coping with Student Conflict Inside and Outside the Classroom at Texas Junior College Teachers Conference, San Antonio, February 25.

Weinstein, C. E., Schulte, A.C., & Palmer, D. R. (1988). The learning and study strategies inventory. Clearwater, FL: H & H Publishing.

LAST/ATS-W

Chapter 8

Instructional Planning, Delivery, and Assessment

Chapter 8

Instructional Planning, Delivery, and Assessment

Teachers are responsible for creating a classroom environment that is conducive to learning. Although students must make their own commitment to learning, professional educators must make the commitment to do everything in their power to ensure that all students learn what they need to learn. Teachers are responsible for making classes interesting instead of dull, appropriate instead of irrelevant, and challenging instead of boring. If students aren't learning, then no teaching has occurred, no matter how many lectures and activities are provided.

The professional educator is responsible for careful planning, alone or with others, so the class has purpose and direction. He or she also teaches students how to set their own goals so they can become self-directed learners. Although students may provide suggestions and make plans for classroom activities, the teacher is ultimately responsible for what goes on in the classroom. The teacher must be an effective communicator, using both spoken and written language to convey ideas and serve as a model for student communication. Knowing how to ask questions and what questions to ask is essential. Skillful questioning can draw out from students more ideas and work than they ever thought possible.

The professional educator must use a variety of teaching methods, choosing different methods for different goals. His or her repertoire must be expanded to include a wide variety of methods, including cooperative learning, inquiry or discovery, discussion, synectics, and other deductive and inductive methods. Today's educator must use all available resources in order to meet a variety of learning styles. He or she must be able to use computers to enhance instruction in a variety of ways.

Assessment must be authentic, that is, appropriate to the learning task and reflective of what the student has actually learned or accomplished. Essay questions, portfolios, projects, and peer and self-assessment are usually more authentic measures than true/false or multiple-choice tests.

The professional educator must also master the art of organizing a classroom so that maximum use is made of available time and resources. He or she must use classroom rules, consequences, and procedures which enforce consistency. Although he may allow students suggestions about rules, the educator is responsible for seeing that no one interferes with another's learning.

In short, in order to enhance each student's achievement to their full potential, the professional educator must be a master planner, communicator, teacher, facilitator, organizer, guide, and role model.

OUTCOME-ORIENTED LEARNING

In outcome-oriented learning, teachers define outcomes, or what they want students to know, do, and be when they complete a required course of study. The teachers set high but realistic goals and objectives for their students, then plan instructional activities which will assist students in achieving these goals.

The key to effective outcome-oriented planning is to consider what outcomes must be achieved, then determine which teacher behaviors and which student behaviors will improve the probability that students will achieve the outcomes.

Outcome-based planning starts with the end product—what must be learned or accomplished in a particular course or grade level. For example, an algebra teacher may decide that the final outcome of his or her algebra course would be that students use quadratic equations to solve problems. He or she then works "backward" to determine prerequisite knowledge and skills students need to have in order to accomplish this outcome. By continuing to ask these questions about each set of prerequisites, the teacher finds a starting point for the subject or course, then develops goals and objectives. The outcomes should be important enough to be required of all students.

An outcome-oriented system means that students are given sufficient time and practice to acquire the knowledge and skills. It also means that teachers take into account students' various learning styles and time required for learning and make adaptations by providing a variety of educational opportunities.

SOURCES OF DATA

Information about what outcomes are important for students comes from several sources. Ralph Tyler has defined three basic sources of needs: students, society, and content area. Consideration of these sources leads to a draft of outcomes, which are further refined by screening them through our philosophy and through what we know about educational psychology. Society makes ever-changing demands upon the educational system. Businesses are focusing more on workers who can solve problems. Other national issues—health problems, environmental concerns, etc.—can provide data for educators.

A look at student needs determines the current level of achievement through a study of evaluation results, whether teacher-made, district-developed, or standardized. Comparing where students are, with where they need to be, will show teachers where to start. A consideration of student needs also involves understanding their diverse learning styles, developmental levels, achievement levels, and special adaptations for learning-disabled students. This understanding assists the effective teacher in planning a variety of activities to meet these diverse needs.

Considering content area needs involves reading current research to determine trends in the subject areas. For example, science teachers are heavily involved in providing hands-on experiences in labs. English teachers have moved in the direction of whole-language activities at all levels and an integrated approach to composition and grammar. National and state curriculum committees in mathematics have endorsed a problem-solving approach for all math classes.

PLANNING PROCESSES

Madeline Hunter describes a planning model which requires teacher decisions about content, teacher behavior, and student behavior. The three parts of this model overlap and are related to each other; a decision in one category influences a decision in another. Decisions about content are often made at the state or district level. Teachers use frameworks from the state, curriculum documents developed by the district, and materials from district-chosen textbooks as bases for planning lessons.

A teacher using this model would make decisions about content, including goals and objectives for a lesson or unit, length of lesson/unit, emphasis of lesson, textbooks, and additional resource materials.

Decisions about his or her own behavior include teaching strategies, accommodations for various learning styles, types of activities, sizes of groups, uses of technology and other resources, and room arrangements.

Decisions about their students' behavior include individual or group responses, format of responses, ways students will demonstrate learning, and products of activities.

Robert Gagné delineates nine external events which are important in planning an appropriate sequence of instruction. They are: gaining attention, informing students of the lesson objectives, stimulating recall of previous learning, presenting stimuli with distinctive features, guiding learning, eliciting student performance, providing informative feedback, assessing student performance, and enhancing the retention and transfer of learning.

The term lesson cycle has been applied to processes of lesson planning developed by a variety of people. Planning is cyclical because the process repeats itself continually. These planning processes usually include the development of objectives and a focus for attention, a design for instructional input, constant monitoring of student understanding, provision for rehearsal and practice of knowledge, and opportunities for enrichment or follow-up.

Teachers choose objectives for a lesson from a curriculum guide or develop their own from their knowledge of their subject area and the needs of students. These objectives are clearly communicated to the students in terms of what they will learn (not activities they will do) during the lesson. In a deductive lesson, these objectives are explained to students at the beginning; in an inductive lesson, objectives are clarified at the end of the lesson. Teachers develop a focus or introduction to the lesson (called anticipatory set by Hunter) which should hook the students' interest and focus attention toward the upcoming activities. Instruction may take a variety of forms. The teacher provides instructional activities which will produce the desired outcomes in the students. A wide variety of instructional methods may be used for input, from mastery lectures or labs to cooperative learning or several different types of inductive strategies. The teacher is constantly monitoring student behavior, checking for understanding, and modifying the instruction as necessary.

After or during instructional input, the students rehearse or apply what they've learned. In guided practice, the teacher watches carefully to make sure students have grasped the material correctly. Because the teacher is on hand to assess student responses, she is able to provide correction or additional input if necessary. During independent practice, students work independently. At the end of each lesson (or at the end of the class), the teacher or students summarize or review what has been learned. An additional feature is enrichment, which should be for all students, not only the faster ones. Enrichment means that students either delve deeper into a subject they've been studying or broaden their understanding of the general topic. For example, students who have been studying the stock market could research the history of its development, or they could study the market in other countries.

Self-Directed Learning

Effective teachers not only set goals for their students, but also teach students to set and accomplish their own goals, both individually and in groups. The teacher explains how he or she develops goals and objectives for the class. One way of encouraging students to set goals is to ask students to set a performance standard for themselves in regard to time needed to complete a project. For example, students might determine they will need 15 minutes to answer five questions, writing one paragraph of at least five sentences for each question. In order to accomplish this goal, the students must focus their attention very carefully and limit themselves to about three minutes per question. The teacher should then ask questions to help students determine whether their goal was realistic, and if not, what adjustments they need to make.

Other steps could be to ask students to develop their own questions about material to be learned or to plan activities to accomplish the goals of the lesson. The highest level is to have students determine the goals for their own learning. For example, a science teacher might introduce the topic of earthquakes, then help students determine what they need to know about earthquakes and the activities and resources which will help them learn.

Students also need to develop plans for products which will show that they have met their goals.

Collaborative Learning

Collaborative or cooperative learning strategies provide important ways for students to learn to work and plan together. David and Roger Johnson and Robert Slavin are three of several educators who have researched cooperative learning and have developed strategies, materials, and resources to assist teachers and students in learning how to work together.

Cooperative groups are formed heterogeneously, so that students of various achievement levels can learn from each other. Lower-achieving students are challenged to keep up with and contribute to their groups; advanced students gain a deeper understanding when they discuss concepts with others. The groups vary in size from three to five members, who usually work with each other for several months in order to develop profitable relationships.

There are five basic elements associated with collaborative learning. The first is *face-to-face interaction*. Group members should be sitting very close to each other so they can look each other in the eye while they discuss. It is important that students begin to form working relationships with their peers.

Another element is *positive interdependence*, which means that students must learn to depend on each other to complete a project or achieve a goal. This is often achieved by providing only one set of resources or one answer sheet. Another is to provide *incentives*, such as five extra points on individual tests if everyone in the group makes at least 80 percent. This encourages students to help each other learn so that all will do well on the assessment.

The third element is *individual accountability*. This means that each student in the group is held accountable for everything that is to be learned. One way of encouraging this is to give individual tests. Although students work and study together, each must pass a test for himself. Another method is to give the same grade to each person in the group. This encourages interdependence because students hold each other accountable for learning and performing the assigned part. It encourages individual accountability because the group is successful only if all members perform well. A common error teachers make with this element is neglecting to make sure that all students do their part. Success of the group should not depend on one diligent student or be undermined because of one lazy student.

The next element is *social skills*. The effective teacher has two types of objectives for collaborative learning: cognitive and affective. The cognitive objectives relate to the content which students must understand and master; the affective objectives relate to social skills which are necessary for students to be able to function in their groups. Examples of social skills include listening actively to others, listening without interrupting, encouraging each other, and using polite language and manners. In addition, teachers assign roles to each member of the group. For example, one student may have the role of group recorder, responsible for writing and turning in any papers or products. Another may have the role of resource clerk, responsible for obtaining and returning materials. Each group member should have a different role; the effective teacher rotates role assignments so that each member has an opportunity to become proficient in each role.

The final element is very important, but it is often omitted. During *group processing*, students reflect on how well their group worked together. They also determine what they can do to function more effectively during the next group assignment. Students learn to set goals for their collaborative groups, in terms of achievement and products. They learn to evaluate their own performance so they can improve it during future projects. The effective teacher helps students set their goals, then monitors to make sure they are making progress. If they are, the teacher will positively reinforce their goal-oriented behavior; if they are not, he or she will steer them back on course, usually by asking questions which lead students to decide what they need to do next.

Thematic Curriculum

The effective teacher knows how to collaborate with peers to plan instruction. Collaboration may be as simple as planning and sharing ideas, or as complex as developing a multidisciplinary thematic unit in which teachers of several subject areas will teach around a common theme.

Planning thematic curriculum often involves teachers from several areas, such as math, English, history, science, and health, although an individual teacher could plan thematic units for her own class. Based on a system developed by Sandra Kaplan, the team of teachers develops a one-word universal theme which is applied in all areas, e.g., survival, conflict, traditions, frontiers, or changes. The team lists a series of key words associated with universal themes, e.g., significance, relationships, types, functions, origins, value, or causes. They develop a generalization for the unit, then each teacher plans outcomes for his or her subject area and class. For example, for the theme "Conflict," the team may choose as the generalization, "Conflict is an inherent part of life." The English teacher then develops a literature and composition unit which encourages students to describe conflicts and how they are solved in literature.

The history teacher might focus on conditions which tend to lead to conflict or the effects of conflict. A science unit could explore conflicts between people and the environment. The math teacher might focus on research methods which attempt to resolve conflicts. The health teacher could address constructive ways of solving conflict between good health practices and unhealthy life-styles.

Effective communication is an obvious mark of an effective teacher. Communication occurs only when someone sends a message and another person receives it. Teachers may "teach" and think they're sending a message, but if students aren't listening, there has been no communication because the receivers are not tuned in.

PRINCIPLES OF VERBAL COMMUNICATION

There are several principles which apply to written and oral messages in the classroom.

The message must be accurate. As Mark Twain said, "The difference between the right word and the almost right word is the difference between lightning and the lightning bug." Teachers in particular must be careful to use very specific words that carry the appropriate denotation (literal meaning) as well as connotation (feelings, associations, and emotions associated with the word). Content teachers must carefully teach vocabulary related to the subject area.

It is possible to be completely accurate, however, without being clear. At times a teacher may use an excessive amount of jargon from his or her subject area. While students must learn vocabulary related to the subject area, the teacher must ensure that she teaches the words and then reviews them so the students have practice using them. At other times a teacher may assume that students understand difficult words. Many students are hesitant to ask what a word means; teachers must be alert to nonverbal signs that students don't understand a word (confused looks, pauses in writing a word down, failure to answer a question containing the word, etc.). Taking a couple of seconds to ask students to define a word will help them understand the larger content area concepts.

Words should also be specific or concrete. The more abstract a word, the more ambiguous it will be. For example, "physical activity" is very general; "Little League baseball" is much more specific. Although students need to learn abstract words, explaining them in a concrete manner will increase their understanding.

A teacher's communications must also be organized. Students will not be able to follow directions which are given in jumbled order, interrupted with, "Oh, I forgot to tell you." Effective teachers plan their directions carefully, writing them down for the students or making notes for themselves so they will give directions or explain concepts in appropriate order.

Other communication strategies include monitoring the effects of a message, or making sure that the audience actually received and understood the message. A teacher may encourage students to be active and reflective listeners by having each student summarize what another has said before making his or her own contribution.

NONVERBAL COMMUNICATION

Even when the verbal or written message is accurate, clear, specific, and organized, nonverbal communication can confuse the message. Sometimes the nonverbal aspect of communication can carry more weight than the verbal. Nonverbal messages can be sent by the way teachers dress, the way they use their facial expressions, and the way they use their voice. Experienced educators realize that students respond better when teachers dress professionally. Most people find it easier to take seriously someone dressed in neat, clean clothes than someone in wrinkled, ill-fitting clothing. Also, students behave better when they themselves are dressed better.

Facial expressions communicate a world of emotions and ideas. Teachers use many voluntary facial expressions. All students have seen "the look" from a teacher, usually when a student does something out of order. A frown or raised eyebrows can also be very effective. Although positive involuntary expressions such as smiles and laughter are appropriate, teachers should guard against involuntary negative facial expressions that convey contempt, anger, or dislike to a student.

Eye contact can be used to control interactions. Teachers often look directly at students to encourage them to speak, and look away to discourage them from speaking. "The stare" can be part of "the look" which teachers use for discipline reasons. Making eye contact with students is important when the teacher is giving instructions, sharing information, or answering questions. Many people make a habit of scanning the room with their eyes, pausing briefly to meet the gaze of many members of an audience. However, eye contact should last about four seconds to assure the person in the audience (or classroom) that the speaker has actually made contact.

Students also use their eyes, making contact with the teacher when they want to answer a question, but often looking at the floor or ceiling when they want to avoid being called on. However, teachers must be careful in making assumptions about eye contact. Research has revealed that students who are visually oriented tend to look upward while they are thinking about a response; kinesthetic learners tend to look down while they are thinking; auditory learners may look to the side. The teacher who says to a student, "The answer's not written on the floor!" may not understand the student's mode of thinking. Effective teachers who are encouraging higher-level thinking may find a classroom filled with eyes that look in various directions.

Cultural factors may also contribute to confusion about eye contact. Many cultures teach children that it is very disrespectful to look an adult in the eye; therefore, these students may stand or sit with downcast eyes as a gesture of respect. Forcing the issue only makes the students and teacher uncomfortable and actually hinders communication.

Body language can also convey feelings and emotions to students. A teacher can emphasize points and generalizations by gesturing or tapping something on the chalkboard. If a teacher gestures too often or too wildly, students find it difficult to determine what the teacher is trying to emphasize. Too many gestures can also cause the students to watch the gestures instead of attending to the information.

Beginning teachers especially need to convey a relaxed but formal body posture, which denotes strength, openness, and friendliness. Hiding behind the desk or crossing the arms indicate timidity or even fear. A teacher who meets students at the door with a smile and even a handshake shows students he or she is confident and in control.

The way a teacher uses the voice conveys prejudices, feelings, and emotions. When a teacher's words convey one meaning and her tone of voice conveys another, the students will believe the tone rather than the meaning.

Students immediately know the difference between "That's a great idea" said in a low voice with a shrug, and "That's a great idea!" said with energy and a smile. Messages can be modified by varying the loudness or softness, by varying the tone, by using high or low pitch, and by changing the quality of speech.

A teacher's expectations for student behavior can be revealed through a combination of verbal and nonverbal communication. Jere Brophy and others have researched the relationship between teacher expectations and student behavior. This research shows that teachers often communicate differently when dealing with high-achievers and low-achievers. This behavior is not always deliberate or conscious on the part of the teacher, but it can communicate negative expectations. When dealing with high-achievers as opposed to low-achievers, teachers tend to listen more carefully, give them more time to answer, prompt or assist them more, call on them more often, give more feedback, and look more interested. The effective communicator will be careful not to differentiate communication based on a student's achievement level.

QUESTIONING

There are many ways that teachers can ask questions that elicit different levels of thinking, although studies of teachers' skills in questioning often reveal frequent use of lower-level questions and infrequent use of higher-level ones.

A simple method is to divide questions into two types: closed and open. An example of a closed question is, "What was the main character's name?" There is usually only one right answer to a closed question. Often students can point to a phrase or sentence in a book to answer a closed question.

An open-ended question requires students to think carefully about the answer. There may be more than one appropriate answer to an open-ended question. An example is, "What do you think was the most important contribution of Pascal to the field of mathematics?" Teachers who ask open-ended questions are not looking for one specific answer; rather, they are looking for well-supported responses. Asking an open-ended question but requiring one specific answer will discourage rather than encourage thinking.

There are other ways to categorize questions. Benjamin Bloom, et al., developed a taxonomy of educational objectives for the cognitive domain.

Teachers have used this taxonomy for a variety of purposes in addition to writing objectives, including categorizing questions and activities.

THE SIX LEVELS OF TAXONOMY

There are six levels in the taxonomy, each one building on the previous level. The first level is knowledge. This is similar to the closed question, with one right answer which should be obvious to students who have read or studied. Words which often elicit recall or memory answers include who, what, when, and where. Examples of knowledge-level questions include: Who developed the first microscope? What were the names of Columbus' ships? In what year was South Carolina first settled? Where is Tokyo?

The next level is comprehension, which also elicits lower-level thinking and answers. The primary difference from the first level is that students must show that they understand a concept, perhaps by explaining in their own words. The question "What does obfuscate mean?" would be answered on a knowledge level if students repeat a memorized definition from the dictionary and on a comprehension level if students explain the term in their own words.

The first higher-level category is application. Students take what they've learned and use this knowledge in a different way or in a different situation. A simple example of this level is using mathematics operations—add, subtract, multiply, and divide—to solve problems. Another example is translating an English sentence into Spanish, or applying what the students have learned about Spanish vocabulary and grammar to develop an appropriate and correct response. Another form of application is changing the format of information, e.g., create a graph from a narrative description of a survey. The key to this level is the use or application of knowledge and skills in a similar but new situation.

The next level is analysis, which involves taking something apart, looking at all the pieces, and then making a response. An example of an analytical question is, "How are these two characters alike and how are they different?" This question requires students to examine facts and characteristics of each individual, then put the information together in an understandable comparison. Other examples might be, "What are the advantages and disadvantages of each of these two proposals?" and, "Compare the wolves in *The Three Little Pigs* and *Little Red Riding Hood*."

The next level is synthesis, which involves putting information together in a new, creative way. Developing a new way of solving problems, writing a short story, designing an experiment—these are all creative ways of synthesizing knowledge. For example, fourth-grade science students may develop and conduct research on food waste in the cafeteria and make recommendations for changes. An example of a synthesis question is, "What do you predict will happen if we combine these two chemicals?" This question assumes students will have factual knowledge. Their predictions must be reasonable and based on prior reading and/or discussion.

The highest level is evaluation. This level involves making value judgments and very often involves the question "Why?" or a request to "Justify your answer." For example, students may be asked to use their analysis of two possible solutions to a problem to determine which is the better solution. Their response must be reasonable and well-supported.

Evaluation-level activities must build on previous levels. Skipping from knowledge-level to evaluation-level questions will result in ill-conceived and poorly-supported responses. Although teachers might use an evaluation question to provoke interest in a topic, they should make sure that students have opportunities to work at other levels as they develop their responses.

Classroom Climate

All of the elements of effective communication can be used to promote an atmosphere of active inquiry in the classroom. Teachers can present an idea to students, ask a real question that they are interested in, then guide exploration, using effective communication skills to encourage and lead the students.

Effective teachers also teach students to use the elements of communication so they can work together to explore concepts and then make effective presentations to the rest of the class (or other classrooms). Structured cooperative learning activities can promote collaborative learning and effective communication. The elements of communication are social skills which can be addressed during cooperative activities.

METHODS OF ENHANCEMENT

Effective teachers use not one but many methods and strategies to enhance student learning. Teachers choose different strategies to meet different purposes that are both content- and student-driven. If the purpose is to provide a foundation for future investigations, the teacher might choose to use a short mastery lecture with questions. If the purpose is to encourage creative thinking, the teacher might choose a synectic strategy. If the purpose is to encourage expression of a variety of viewpoints about a topic, the teacher might choose structured discussion. If the purpose is to investigate current problems without specific answers, the teacher might choose an inquiry lesson.

Deductive Strategies

Methods can be divided into two categories: deductive and inductive. Deductive methods are those in which teachers present material through mastery lecture, or students teach each other through presentations. In deductive lessons, the generalizations or rules are taught from the beginning, then examples and elaboration are developed which support the generalizations or rules. Deductive thinking often requires students to make assessments based on specific criteria which they or others develop. Inductive methods are those in which teachers encourage students to study, research, and analyze data they collect, then develop generalizations and rules based on their findings.

During inductive lessons, a hypothesis or concept is introduced at the beginning, but generalizations are developed later in the lesson and are based on inferences from data.

The lecture is a deductive method, whereby information is presented to students by the teacher. New teachers are especially attuned to lecture because that is the usual mode of instruction in college classes. An advantage of lecture is that large amounts of information can be presented in an efficient manner; however, effective teachers avoid dumping loads of information through lectures. Mastery lectures should be short, usually no more than 10 or 15 minutes at a time, and constantly interrupted with questions to and from students. The effective teacher uses both lower- and higher-level questions during lectures.

Information sessions must also be supplemented with an array of visual materials that will appeal to visual learners as well as auditory ones. Putting words or outlines on the board or a transparency is very helpful; however, this is still basically a verbal strategy. Drawings, diagrams, cartoons, pictures, caricatures, and graphs are visual aids for lectures. Teacher drawings need not be highly artistic, merely memorable. Often a rough or humorous sketch will be more firmly etched in students' minds than elaborate drawings. Using a very simple sketch provides a better means of teaching the critical attributes than a complicated one. The major points stand out in a simple sketch; details can be added once students understand the basic concepts.

Teachers should also be careful to include instruction on how to take notes while listening to a speaker, a skill that will be useful during every student's career, whether educational or professional. One way a teacher can do this is to show students notes or an outline from the mini-lecture he or she is about to present or to write notes or an outline on the board or overhead while she is presenting the information. This activity requires careful planning by the teacher and will result in a more organized lecture. This type of structure is especially helpful for sequential learners, who like organization. It will also help random learners develop organizational skills. A web or map or cluster is a more right-brained method of connecting important points in a lecture or a chapter. The effective teacher will use both systems and teach both to students, so they have a choice of strategies.

Inductive Strategies

Inquiry or discovery lessons are inductive in nature. Inquiry lessons start with a thought-provoking question for which students are interested in finding an explanation. The question can be followed by brainstorming a list of what the students already know about the topic, then categorizing the information. The categories can then be used as topics for group or individual research. Deductive presentations by students of their research can follow.

Some advantages of inductive lessons are that they generally require higher-level thinking by both teacher and students, and they usually result in higher student motivation, interest, and retention. They are also more interesting to the teacher, who deals with the same concepts year after year. Disadvantages include the need for additional preparation by the teacher, the need for access to a large number of resources, and additional time for students to research the concepts. The teacher spends a great amount of time in planning the lessons, then acts as facilitator during classes.

Generally, the greater the amount of planning and prediction by the teacher, the greater the success of the students. This does not mean that the activity must be tightly structured or set in concrete, but the effective teacher tries to predict student responses and his or her reactions to them. The need for purchasing additional resources has been moderated by computerized bibliographic services, interlibrary loan, and CD-ROMs with all types of information. Because inductive, research-oriented units require more class time, subject-area teachers must work together to determine what concepts are essential for students to understand; other nonessential concepts are omitted.

Discussion Strategies

Discussions are often thought of as unstructured talk by students sitting around in a circle, answering the basic question, "What do you think about _____?" However, profitable discussions are carefully planned, with specific objectives leading to understanding of specific concepts.

Discussion lessons may be deductive or inductive, depending on the emphasis. Deductive lessons will be more structured, often with clear answers which the teacher expects and leads the students to provide. Inductive lessons will be less structured, but very well planned. Teachers ask open-ended questions and accept a variety of answers which are well supported by information or inferences from the text. The effective teacher plans a variety of questions, with learner outcomes in mind, and leads the discussion without dominating it. She also will make certain that all students participate and have an opportunity to contribute. Students may also plan and lead discussions, with careful assistance from the teacher.

Comparison/Contrast

An important higher-order thinking skill is the ability to compare and contrast two things or concepts which are dissimilar on the surface. Thomas Gordon has described a process of synectics, whereby students are forced to make an analogy between something that is familiar and something that is new; the concepts seem to be completely different, but through a series of steps, students discover underlying similarities. For example, a biology teacher might plan an analogy between a cell (new concept) and a city government (familiar concept). Although they seem impossibly different, they both have systems for transportation, disposal of unwanted materials, and parts that govern these systems. By comparing something new with something familiar, students have a "hook" for the new information which will help them remember it as well as better understand it. In this example, students trying to remember functions of a cell would be assisted by remembering parts of the city government.

Teacher and Student Roles

An effective teacher plays many roles in the classroom. Teachers who use lecture are in the role of an instructor who provides information. Students who listen to lectures are usually in a passive, often inattentive, role of listener. Teachers who use cooperative strategies take on the roles of a coach, who encourages his or her students to work together, and a facilitator, who helps activities proceed smoothly and provides resources. Students in a collaborative role must learn social and group roles as well as content in order to accomplish learning tasks. Teachers who use inquiry strategies take the role of a facilitator who plans outcomes and provides resources for students as they work. Students in an inquirer role must take more responsibility for their own learning by planning, carrying out, and presenting research and projects. Teachers who listen to student discussions and presentations and evaluate student papers and projects take on the role of an audience who provides constructive feedback. Students in a discussion role must prepare carefully and think seriously about the topic under discussion.

The most natural role for teachers is that of instructor, since that is the role which they have seen modeled most often. The usual role for students is that of passive listener, since that is the role they have practiced most often. Taking on other roles requires commitment to learning new methods and procedures, as well as practice for perfecting them. Both teachers and students may feel uncomfortable in new roles until they are practiced enough to become familiar.

CURRICULUM PLANNING

The effective teacher includes resources of all types in the curriculum planning process. He or she should be very familiar with the school library, city/county library, education service center resources, and the library of any college or university in the area. Teachers should have a list of all audiovisual aids which may be borrowed, e.g., kits, films, filmstrips, videos, laser disks, and computer software. Many librarians have keyed their resources to objectives in related subject areas, so the teacher can incorporate them with ease into the lessons. However, resources should never be used with a class unless they have been previewed and approved by the teacher. The list of resources to be used in a lesson or unit should be included in the curriculum guide or the lesson plan for ease of use.

Planning for Resources

The effective teacher determines the appropriate place in the lesson for audiovisual aids. If the material is especially interesting and thought-provoking, he or she may use it to introduce a unit. For example, a travel video on coral reefs or snorkeling might be an excellent introduction to the study of tropical fish and plants. The same video could be used at the end of the study to see how many fish and plants the students can recognize and name. Computer software that "dissects" frogs or worms may be used after a discussion of what students already know about the animals and how their internal organs compare with those of humans. A video of a Shakespearean play could be intermixed with discussion and class reading of scenes from the play.

Videos, films, and filmstrips may be stopped for discussion. Research reveals that students comprehend better and remember longer if the teacher introduces a video or film appropriately, then stops it frequently to discuss what the students have just seen and heard. This method also helps keep students' attention focused and assists them in learning note-taking skills.

Print Resources

The most common print material is the textbook, which has been selected by teachers on the campus from a list of books approved by the state. Textbooks are readily available, economical, and written to match state curriculum requirements. However, the adoption process is a long one, and textbooks (particularly science and history) can become out-dated quickly; therefore, the teacher must use additional contemporary resources.

Local, state, and national newspapers and magazines should not be overlooked. Some newspapers and magazines have special programs to help teachers use their products in the classroom for reading and writing opportunities as well as for sources of information. Local newspapers may be willing to send specialists to work with students or act as special resource persons.

Visual Materials

The most available tools in classrooms are the chalkboard and the overhead projector. There are several principles which apply to both. The teacher must write clearly and in large letters. Overhead transparencies should never be typed on a regular typewriter, because the print is too small. Computers allow type sizes of at least 18 points, which is the minimum legible size for projection. Also, both boards and transparencies should be free of clutter. Old information should be removed before new information is added. These tools work more effectively if the teacher plans ahead of time what she will write or draw on them. Using different colors will emphasize relationships or differences.

Posters and charts can complement lessons, but the walls should not be so cluttered that students are unable to focus on what's important for the current lesson. Posters and charts can be displayed on a rotating basis. Filmstrips, films, and videos are appealing to students because they are surrounded by visual images on television, computers, and video games every day.

Some of the best graphic aids will be those developed by individual students or by groups of students. Along with learning about subject area concepts, students will be learning about design and presentation of information. Students can take pictures of their products to put in a portfolio or scrapbook.

Videodisk and Interactive Video

Videodisks provide a sturdy, compact system of storage for pictures and sound. They can store more than 50,000 separate frames of still images, up to 50 hours of digitized stereo music, or about 325 minutes of motion pictures with sound. An advantage of videodisk over videotape is that each frame can be accessed separately and quickly. The simplest level of use involves commands to play, pause, forward, or reverse. Individual frames can be accessed by inputting their number.

More comprehensive interactive programs can use the computer to present information, access a videodisk to illustrate main points, then ask for responses from the student. A multimedia production run by the computer can include images, text, and sound from a videodisk, CD-ROM, graphics software, word processing software, and a sound effects program. Teachers can develop classroom presentations, but students themselves can also develop learning units as part of a research or inquiry project.

The cost of a multimedia system remains relatively high, but students can use it to develop high-level thought processes, collaborative work, and research skills, as well as content knowledge and understanding.

Computer Software Tools

There are several software tools which are extremely useful for teachers and students alike. Word processing allows teachers and students to write, edit, and polish assignments and reports. Most programs have a spelling-checker or even a grammar-checker to enhance written products. Students in all subjects can use word processors to write term papers or reports of their research. Many word processors allow writers to put the text into columns, so that students can produce newsletters with headlines of varying sizes. For example, an English class could write a series of reviews of Shakespeare's plays or sonnets, add information about Shakespeare and his times, then put everything into a newsletter as a class project. There are also desktop publishing programs which allow text and graphics to be integrated to produce publications, such as a class newsletter and school newspapers and yearbooks.

Databases are like electronic file cards; they allow students to input data, then retrieve it in various ways and arrangements. History students can input data about various countries, e.g., population, population growth rate, infant mortality rate, average income, and average education levels. They then manipulate the database to call up information in a variety of ways. The more important step in learning about databases is dealing with huge quantities of information. Students need to learn how to analyze and interpret the data that they see to discover connections between isolated facts and figures and how to eliminate inappropriate information.

On-line databases are essential tools for research. Most programs allow electronic mail, so that students can communicate over the computer with people from around the world. There are also massive bibliographic databases which help students and teachers to find the resources they need. Many of the print materials can then be borrowed through interlibrary loan. The use of electronic systems can exponentially increase the materials available to students.

Spreadsheets are similar to teacher gradebooks. Rows and columns of numbers can be linked to produce totals and averages. Formulas can connect information in one cell (the intersection of a row and column) to another cell. Teachers often keep gradebooks on a spreadsheet, because of the ease in updating information. Once formulas are in place, teachers can enter grades and have completely up-to-date averages for all students. Students can use spreadsheets to collect and analyze numerical data which can be sorted in various orders. Some spreadsheet programs also include a chart function, so that teachers can display class averages on a bar chart to provide a visual comparison of the classes' performance. Students can enter population figures from various countries, then draw various types of graphs—bars, columns, scatters, histograms, pies—to convey information. This type of graphic information can also be used in multimedia presentations. There are also various stand-alone graph and chart software packages.

Graphics or paint programs allow users to draw freehand to produce any type of picture or use tools to produce boxes, circles, or other shapes. These programs can illustrate classroom presentations or individual research projects. Many word processing programs have some graphic elements.

Computer-Assisted Instruction

Many early uses of computers tended to be drill-and-practice, where students practiced simple skills such as mathematics operations. Many elaborate systems of practice and testing were developed, with management systems so that teachers could keep track of how well the students were achieving. This type of software is useful for skills which students need to practice. An advantage is immediate feedback so students know if they chose the correct answer. Many of these programs have a game format to make the practice more interesting. A disadvantage is their generally low-level nature.

Tutorials are a step above drill-and-practice programs, because they also include explanations and information. Students are asked to make a response, then the program branches to the most appropriate section, based on the students' answer. Tutorials are often used for remedial work, but are also useful for instruction in English as a second language. Improved graphics and sound allow nonspeakers of English to listen to correct pronunciation while viewing pictures of words. Tutorials are used to supplement, not supplant, teacher instruction.

Simulations or problem-solving programs provide opportunities for students to have experiences which would take too long to experience in real-time, would be too costly or difficult to experience, or would be impossible to experience. For example, one of the most popular early simulations allowed students to see if they could survive the Oregon Trail. Users made several choices about food, ammunition, supplies, etc., then the computer moved them along the trail until they reached their goal or died along the way.

Manipulatives and Labs

Other types of materials which can be used effectively are manipulatives. Manipulatives are touchable, movable materials which enhance students' understanding of a concept. They are used particularly in mathematics and science to give students a concrete way of dealing with concepts, but tangible materials are appropriate and helpful in all subject areas. For example social studies and history teachers can use a wealth of cultural artifacts from countries they are studying.

Human Resources

Parents and other members of the community can be excellent local experts from which students can learn about any subject—mathematics from bankers, art and music from artists, English from public relations persons, history from club or church historians or librarians, business from owners of companies. The list can be endless. Effective teachers make sure that any guest who is invited to speak or perform understands the purpose of the visit and the goals or objectives the teacher is trying to accomplish. Preparation can make the class period more focused and meaningful.

Field trips are also excellent sources of information, especially about careers and current issues such as pollution control. One field trip can yield assignments in mathematics, history, science, and English, and often art, architecture, music, or health. Teachers can collaborate with each other to produce thematic assignments for the field trip or simply to coordinate the students' assignments. Often a history report can serve as an English paper as well. Data can be analyzed in math classes and presented with the aid of computers.

Selection and Evaluation Criteria

The effective teacher uses criteria to evaluate audiovisual, multimedia, and computer resources. The first thing to look for is congruence with lesson goals. If the software doesn't reinforce student outcomes, then it shouldn't be used, no matter how flashy or well-done. A checklist for instructional computer software could include appropriate sequence of instruction, meaningful student interaction with the software, learner control of screens and pacing, and motivation. Other factors should be considered, such as ability to control sound and save progress, effective use of color, clarity of text and graphics on the screen, and potential as individual or group assignment.

In addition to congruence with curriculum goals, the teacher considers his or her students' strengths and needs, their learning styles or preferred modalities, and their interests. Students' needs can be determined through formal or informal assessment. Most standardized tests include an indication of which objectives the student did not master. Mastering these objectives can be assisted with computer or multimedia aids.

Evaluation of resources should be accomplished in advance by the teacher, before purchase whenever possible. Evaluation is also conducted during student use of materials. Assessment after student use may be acquired by considering achievement level of the students and/or by surveys which ask for students' responses.

Purposes of Assessment

The effective teacher understands the importance of ongoing assessment as an instructional tool for the classroom and uses both informal and formal assessment measures. Informal measures may include observation, journals, written drafts, and conversations. More formal measures may include teacher-made tests, district exams, and standardized tests. Effective teachers use both formative and summative evaluation. Formative evaluation occurs during the process of learning, when the teacher or the students monitor progress in obtaining outcomes, while it is still possible to modify instruction. Summative evaluation occurs at the end of a specific time period or course, usually by a single grade used to represent a student's performance.

Teacher-Made Tests

The effective teacher uses a variety of assessment techniques. Teacher-made instruments are ideally developed at the same time as the goals and outcomes are planned, rather than at the last minute after all the lessons have been taught. Carefully planned objectives and assessment instruments serve as lesson development guides for the teacher.

Paper and pencil tests are the most common method for evaluation of student progress. There are a number of different types of questions: multiple-choice, true/false, matching, fill-in-the-blank, short answer, and longer essay. The first five tend to test the knowledge or comprehension levels. Essays often test at the lower levels, but are suitable for assessing learning at higher levels. Projects, papers, and portfolios can provide assessment of higher-level thinking skills.

If the purpose is to test student recall of factual information, a short objective test (multiple-choice, true/false, matching, fill-in-the-blank) would be most effective and efficient. The first three types of questions can be answered on machine-scorable scan sheets to provide quick and accurate scoring. Disadvantages are that they generally test lower levels of knowledge and don't provide an opportunity for an explanation of answers.

If the purpose is to test student ability to analyze an event, compare and contrast two concepts, make predictions about an experiment, or evaluate a character's actions, then an essay question would provide the best paper/pencil opportunity for the student to show what he can do. Teachers should make the question explicit enough so that students will know exactly what she expects. For example, "Explain the results of World War II" is too broad; students won't really understand what the teacher expects. It would be more explicit to say, "Explain three results of World War II that you feel had the most impact on participating nations. Explain the criteria you used in selecting these results."

Advantages of an essay include the possibility for students to be creative in their answers, the opportunity for students to explain their responses, and the potential to test for higher-level thinking skills. Disadvantages of essay questions include the time needed for students to formulate meaningful responses, language difficulties of some students, and the time needed to evaluate the essays. Consistency in evaluation is also a problem for the teacher, but this can be alleviated by using an outline of the acceptable answers. Teachers who write specific questions and who know what they are looking for will be more consistent in grading. Also, if there are several essay questions, the effective teacher grades all student responses to the first question, then moves on to all responses to the second, and so on.

Authentic Assessments

Paper and pencil tests or essays are only one method of assessment. Others include projects, observation, checklists, anecdotal records, portfolios, self-assessment, and peer assessment. Although these types of assessment often take more time and effort to plan and administer, they can often provide a more authentic assessment of student progress.

Projects are common in almost all subject areas. They promote student control of learning experiences and provide opportunities for research into a variety of topics, as well as the chance to use visuals, graphics, videos, or multimedia presentations in place of, or in addition to, written reports. Projects also promote student self-assessment because students must evaluate their progress along each step of the project. Many schools have science or history fairs for which students plan, develop, and display their projects. Projects can also be part of business, English, music, art, mathematics, social sciences, health, or physical education courses.

The teacher must make clear the requirements and the criteria for evaluation of the projects before students begin them. He or she must also assist students in selecting projects which are feasible, for which the school has learning resources, and which can be completed in a reasonable amount of time with little or no expense to students.

Advantages of projects are that students can use visual, graphic, art, or music abilities; students can be creative in their topic or research; and the projects can appeal to various learning styles. Disadvantages include difficulty with grading, although this can be overcome by devising a checklist for required elements and a rating scale for quality.

Observations may be made for individual or group work. This method is very suitable for skills or for affective learning. Teachers usually make a list of competencies, skills, or requirements, then check off the ones that are observed in the student or group. An office skills teacher wishing to emphasize interviewing skills may devise a checklist that includes personal appearance, mannerisms, confidence, and addressing the questions that are asked. A teacher who wants to emphasize careful listening may observe a discussion with a checklist which includes paying attention, not interrupting, summarizing another person's ideas, and asking questions of other students.

Anecdotal records may be helpful in some instances, such as capturing the process a group of students uses to solve a problem. This formative data can be useful during feedback to the group. Students can also be taught to write an explanation of the procedures they use for a project or a science experiment. An advantage of an anecdotal record is that it can include all relevant information. Disadvantages include the amount of time necessary to complete the record and difficulty in assigning a grade. If used for feedback, no grade is necessary.

Advantages of checklists include the potential for capturing behavior that can't be accurately measured with a paper and pencil test, i.e., shooting free throws on the basketball court, following the correct sequence of steps in a science experiment, or including all important elements in a speech in class. One characteristic of a checklist that is both an advantage and a disadvantage is its structure, which provides consistency but inflexibility. An open-ended comment section at the end of a checklist can overcome this disadvantage.

Portfolios are collections of students' best work. They can be used in any subject area where the teacher wants students to take more responsibility for planning, carrying out, and organizing their own learning. They may be used in the same way that artists, models, or performers use them to provide a succinct picture of their best work. Portfolios may be essays or articles written on paper, video tapes, multimedia presentations on computer disks, or a combination. English teachers often use portfolios as a means of collecting the best samples of student writing over the whole year. Sometimes they pass on the work to the next year's teacher to help her assess the needs of her new students. Any subject area can use portfolios, since they contain documentation that reflects growth and learning over a period of time.

Teachers should provide or assist students in developing guidelines for what materials should be placed in portfolios, since it would be unrealistic to include every piece of work in one portfolio. The use of portfolios requires the students to devise a means of evaluating their own work. A portfolio should be a collection of the student's own best work, not a scrapbook for collecting handouts or work done by other individuals, although it can certainly include work by a group in which the student was a participant.

Some advantages of portfolios over testing are that they provide a clearer picture of a student's progress, they are not affected by one inferior test grade, and they help develop self-assessment skills in students. One disadvantage is the amount of time required to teach students how to develop meaningful portfolios. However, this time can be well spent if students learn valuable skills. Another concern is the amount of time teachers must spend to assess portfolios. However, as students become more proficient at self-assessment, the teacher can spend more time in coaching and advising students throughout the development of their portfolios. Another concern is that parents may not understand how portfolios will be graded. The effective teacher devises a system which the students and parents understand before work on the portfolio begins.

Self and Peer Assessment

One goal of an assessment system is to promote student self-assessment. Since most careers require employees or managers to evaluate their own productivity as well as that of others, self-assessment and peer assessment are important lifelong skills.

Effective teachers use a structured approach to teach self-assessment, helping students set standards at first by making recommendations about standards, then gradually moving toward student development of their own criteria and application of the criteria to their work.

One method of developing self-assessment is to ask students to apply the teacher's own standards to a product. For example, an English teacher who uses a rating scale for essays might have students use that scale on their own papers, then compare their evaluations with those of the teacher. A science teacher who uses a checklist while observing an experiment might ask students to use the checklist, then compare theirs with the teacher's.

The class can set standards for evaluating group work as well as individual work. Collaborative groups are effective vehicles for practicing the skills involved in assessment.

Standardized Testing

In *criterion-referenced* tests, each student is measured against uniform objectives or criteria. CRTs allow the possibility that all students can score 100 percent because they understand the concepts being tested. Teacher-made tests should be criterion-referenced, because the teacher should develop them to measure the achievement of predetermined outcomes for the course. If teachers have properly prepared lessons based on the outcomes, and if students have mastered the outcomes, then scores should be high. This type of test may be called noncompetitive, because students are not in competition with each other for a high score, and there is no limit to the number of students who can score well. Some commercially developed tests are criterion-referenced; however, the majority are norm-referenced.

The purpose of a *norm-referenced* test is to provide a way to compare the performance of groups of students. This type of test may be called competitive, because a limited number of students can score well. A plot of large numbers of NRT scores will resemble a bell-shaped curve, with most scores clustering around the center and a few scores at each end. The midpoint is an average of data; therefore, by definition, half of the population will score above average and half below average.

The bell-shaped curve was developed as a mathematical description of the results of tossing coins. As such, it represents the chance or normal distribution of skills, knowledge, or events across the general population. A survey of the height of sixth-grade boys will result in an average height, with half the boys above average and half below. There will be a very small number with heights way above average and a very small number with heights way below average, with most heights clustering around the average.

NRT scores are usually reported in percentile scores (not to be confused with percentages), which indicate the percent of the population whose scores fall at or below the score. For example, a group score at the 80th percentile means that the group scored as well as or better than 80 percent of the students who took the test. A student with a score at the 50th percentile has an average score.

Percentile scores rank students from highest to lowest. By themselves the percentile scores do not indicate how well the student has mastered the content objectives. Raw scores indicate how many questions the student answered correctly and are therefore useful in computing the percentage of questions a student answered correctly.

Schools must consider the reliability of a test, or whether the instrument will give consistent results when the measurement is repeated. A reliable bathroom scale, for example, will give identical weights for the same person measured three times in a morning. Teachers evaluate test reliability over time when they give the same, or almost the same, test to different groups of students. Because there are many factors which affect reliability, teachers must be careful in evaluating this factor.

Schools must also be careful to assess the validity of a test, or whether the test actually measures what it is supposed to measure. If students score low on a test because they couldn't understand the questions, then the test is not valid because it measures reading ability instead of content knowledge. If students score low because the test covered material which was not studied, the test is not valid for that situation. A teacher assesses the validity of her own tests by examining the questions to see if they measure what was planned and taught in her classroom.

A test must be reliable before it can be valid. However, measurements can be consistent without being valid. A scale can indicate identical weights for three weigh-ins of the same person during one morning, but actually be 15 pounds in error. A history test may produce similar results each time it is given, but not be a valid measure of what was taught and learned. Tests should be both reliable and valid. If the test doesn't measure consistently, then it can't be accurate. If it doesn't measure what it's supposed to measure, then its reliability doesn't matter.

Commercial test producers perform various statistical measures of the reliability and validity of their tests and provide the results in the test administrator's booklet.

Performance-Based Assessment

Some states and districts are moving toward performance-based testing, which means that students are assessed on how well they perform certain tasks. This allows students to use higher-level thinking skills to apply, analyze, synthesize, and evaluate ideas and data. For example, a biology performance-based assessment may require students to read a problem, design and carry out a laboratory experiment, then write a summary of his or her findings. He or she would be evaluated both on the process used and the output produced.

Performance-based assessment allows students to be creative in solutions to problems or questions, and it requires them to use higher-level skills. This type of assessment can be time-consuming; however, students are working on content-related problems, using skills that are useful in a variety of contexts. This type of assessment requires multiple resources, which can be expensive. It also requires teachers to be trained in how to use this type of assessment. However, many schools consider performance-based testing to be a more authentic measure of student achievement than traditional tests.

Physical Environment

While there are certain physical aspects of the classroom that cannot be changed (size, shape, number of windows, type of lighting, etc.), there are others that can be. Windows can have shades or blinds which distribute light correctly and which allow for the room to be darkened for video or computer viewing. If the light switches do not allow part of the lights to remain on, sometimes schools will change the wiring system. If not, teachers can use a lamp to provide minimum lighting for monitoring students during videos or films.

Schools often schedule maintenance such as painting and floor cleaning during the summer. Often school administrators will accede to requests for a specific color of paint, given sufficient time for planning.

All secondary school classrooms should have a bulletin board used by the teacher and by the students. The effective teacher has plans for changing the board according to units of study. Space should be reserved for display of student work and projects, either on the bulletin board, the wall, or in the hallway. (Secondary teachers who need creative ideas can visit elementary classrooms.)

Bare walls can be depressing; however, covering the wall with too many posters can be visually distracting. Posters with sayings which promote co-operation, study skills, and content ideas should be displayed, but the same ones should not stay up all year, because they become invisible when too familiar.

Most classrooms have movable desks, which allows for varied seating arrangements. If students are accustomed to sitting in rows, this is sometimes a good way to start the year. Once students are comfortable with classroom rules and procedures, the teacher can explain to students how to quickly move their desks into different formations for special activities, then return them to their original positions in the last 60 seconds of class.

The best place for the teacher's desk is often at the back of a room, so there are few barriers between the teacher and the students and between the students and the chalkboards. This encourages the teacher to walk around the classroom for better monitoring of students.

Social and Emotional Climate

The effective teacher maintains a climate which promotes the lifelong pursuit of learning. One way to do this is to practice research skills which will be helpful throughout life. All subject areas can promote the skills of searching for information to answer a question, filtering it to determine what is appropriate, and using what is helpful to solve a problem.

Most English teachers require some type of research project, from middle school through the senior year. Ken Macrorie's books on meaningful research can guide English teachers as they develop a project which can answer a real-life issue for students. For example, a student who is trying to decide which school to attend could engage in database and print research on schools which have the major characteristics he's interested in, telephone or written interviews with school officials and current students, review of school catalogs and other documents, and magazine or journal articles which deal with the school. At the end of the process, students will have engaged in primary as well as secondary research, plus they will have an answer to a personal question.

The English teacher and any other subject area teacher can team up to collaborate on a joint research project. The resulting product satisfies both the need of the English teacher to teach research skills and the need of the subject area teacher to teach content knowledge as well as research skills. Primary research can be done through local or regional resources such as business owners, lawyers, physicians, and the general public.

The effective teacher also facilitates positive social and emotional atmosphere and promotes a risk-taking environment for students. He or she sets up classroom rules and guidelines for how he or she will treat students, how students will treat him or her, and how students will treat each other. In part this means that he or she doesn't allow ridicule or put-downs, either from the teacher or among the students. It also means that the teacher has an accepting attitude toward student ideas, especially when the idea is not what he or she was expecting to hear. Sometimes students can invent excellent ideas which are not always clear until they are asked to explain how they arrived at them.

Students should feel free to answer and ask any questions that are relevant to the class, without fear of sarcasm or ridicule. Teachers should always avoid sarcasm. Sometimes teachers consider sarcasm to be mere teasing, but because some students often interpret it negatively, effective teachers avoid all types and levels of sarcasm.

Routines and Transitions

The effective teacher manages routines and transitions with a minimum of disturbance to students and to learning. Procedures are planned before students come to the first class. A routine is a procedure that has been practiced so that it works automatically. A transition is moving from one activity to another or from one desk arrangement to another.

The teacher needs to consider how he or she wants students to behave in the classroom: how they will ask questions, how they will sharpen pencils, how they will pass in papers, how they will put headings on papers, how they will move to get into groups. Then, the teacher's own behaviors must be considered, including how class will be started, how roll will be taken, how students will be called to attention, how students' tardiness will be dealt with, how materials will be distributed, how resources that can be checked out will be handled, and, of course, how the inevitable late paper or project will be treated.

Effective teachers have the students start class immediately, often by putting instructions for a short activity on the board or the overhead as the class enters the room. He or she teaches the students that they should start work on the activity immediately. While students are completing this activity, the teacher can quickly check roll with a seating chart. The activity can be checked before moving into new activities for the day.

The teacher may decide that all students must raise their hands to be recognized before speaking in the large group. He or she should teach this procedure the first day, then make sure he or she enforces it constantly and consistently, reminding students of the procedure and verbally reinforcing the class for following it. ("I appreciate your remembering to raise your hands to ask a question or make a contribution. That makes the class run more smoothly.")

The teacher who wants students to work collaboratively will also teach procedures for group work. He or she may decide that before a student in a group can ask the teacher a question, he or she must ask everyone else in the group. If no one has an answer, then the group leader for the day can raise his or her hand for teacher assistance. This way, only one-fourth of the class is asking for attention. One member of the group can be assigned the role of materials clerk; only one-fourth of the class is moving around the room.

One method of calling a group back to attention, especially during group work, is for the teacher to raise his or her hand, indicating that all students should raise their own hands, stop talking, and focus attention on the teacher. The reason students raise their hands is that some will have their backs to the teacher, but they will be able to see other students raise hands. This procedure can be taught and practiced in three or four minutes and is effective in a classroom or in a large auditorium. Students should have several opportunities for practice, then the teacher should periodically reinforce the group for following the procedure quickly.

Academic Learning Time

The effective teacher maximizes the amount of time spent for instruction. A teacher who loses five minutes at the beginning of class and five minutes at the end of class wastes ten minutes a day that could have been spent in educational activities. This is equivalent to a whole period a week, four classes a month, and 25 periods a year.

Academic learning time is the amount of allocated time that students spend in an activity at the appropriate level of difficulty with the appropriate level of success. The appropriate level of difficulty is one which challenges students without frustrating them. Students who have typically been low achievers need a higher rate of success than those who have typically been higher achievers.

One way to increase academic learning time is to teach students procedures so they will make transitions quickly. Another is to have materials and resources ready for quick distribution and use. Another is to give students a time limit for a transition or an activity. In general, time limits for group work should be slightly shorter than students need, in order to encourage time on task and to prevent off-task behavior and discipline problems. It is essential for the teacher to have additional activities planned should the class finish activities sooner than anticipated. As students complete group work, they should have other group or individual activities so they can work up until the last minute before the end of class.

Classroom Discipline

The effective teacher realizes that having an interesting, carefully planned curriculum is one of the best ways to prevent most discipline problems. Another way is to have a discipline system of classroom rules, consequences, and rewards, which are applied consistently to every student. All classroom rules, consequences, and rewards must be in compliance with campus requirements. The goals of a classroom system of discipline are that students become self-disciplined and that all but the most serious misbehavior is handled in the classroom by the teacher.

The effective teacher limits rules to four or five essential behaviors by determining the conditions that she must have in order for learning to take place. One might be that students must respect each other by not engaging in sarcasm or cutting remarks. Another might be that students must come to class on time with textbooks, paper, and pencil. (Class rules should not be confused with classroom procedures, such as how to pass in papers.)

The effective teacher knows what the rules will be before students come to the first class, or develops them with the students during the first couple of days. Many teachers choose to have two or three rules, then ask students for input on two more rules for classroom behavior. Others ask for student input for all four or five rules. Most classes will come up with rules that are acceptable to the teacher and to the class. Often teachers will ask students to come up with one or two rules for the teacher (returning tests within two days, making at least one helpful comment on each paper, etc.).

Once the rules have been determined, the teacher makes sure that each student understands each rule, the consequences for breaking a rule, and the rewards for keeping the rules. Consequences should be spelled out in advance, before rules are broken. Some teachers prefer a system of increasingly serious consequences, such as: (1) name on the board, (2) detention after school, (3) call home to parents, (4) visit to the principal. If being sent to the office is a consequence for repeated misbehavior, then the principal must be aware of and approve the consequence. Most principals also have a system of consequences, once students are sent to their office. In general, additional homework should not be assigned as a consequence, because negative feelings transfer to the idea of learning.

Rewards also help maintain discipline. The goal of a discipline system is that students become self-disciplined; however, external rewards can help the classroom run more smoothly. The reward should not be perceived as a bribe, but as a reward for appropriate behavior. They can include verbal praise, stickers, and positive notes home. They can also include class rewards such as ten minutes of free time on Friday or listening to a radio while doing class work, if no more than five misbehaviors have occurred during the week.

After the system of rules, consequences, and rewards has been determined, the teacher should then put them on a poster in the room and give students copies for their notebooks. Often teachers ask students and a parent or guardian to sign a copy and return it for his or her files, to ensure that both the student and parents understand what type of behavior is expected.

One key to effective discipline is consistency. A teacher who has a rule that students must raise their hands to be called on, but who lets students call out questions or answers, will soon find that no one raises his hand. The rule must also be applied to every student. This is one reason that rules must be carefully chosen. A teacher with a rule that states, "Any student who does not turn in homework at the beginning of the period will get a zero," has no room to make allowances for reasonable excuses for not having homework. The rule might be better stated, "Students should turn in homework at the beginning of each class," with a range of consequences that can be chosen by the teacher, based on whether it is a first or repeated infraction.

Correcting Students

The best way to correct students is usually privately. A teacher who reprimands or criticizes a student in front of the rest of the class will often provoke negative or hostile responses from the student. Harry K. Wong and others have described various methods of confronting students privately. The teacher moves close to the student, calls him or her by name, looks the student in the eye, makes a statement of what behavior needs to stop and what behavior needs to begin, thanks him or her, then moves away. If students are accustomed to having the teacher move around the room to monitor achievement, they often will not even know that a student has been corrected.

The effective teacher also perfects "the look," which can be an unobtrusive way to let a student know he or she needs to change their behavior. Effective teachers also avoid falling into the trap of arguing with students. A student who wants to argue with a teacher can be defused if the teacher doesn't respond to the challenge, but restates the change she expects, then continues what she's doing. No one wins in a struggle to defend his or her own position or authority.

Student Ownership

One way of promoting student ownership in the classroom is to provide multiple opportunities for their input. Many teachers do this through allowing students to determine two or three rules for the classroom. Sometimes they also have class meetings where students discuss issues or problems.

Effective teachers also give students choices in what they will study or research, within the parameters of the outcomes for the course. Often this can be accomplished by giving a list of options for assignments, or asking students to brainstorm questions about a topic, then letting them choose from among the ones that are feasible, based on the curriculum and on the available resources. Teachers first determine the overall outcome for the unit, then brainstorm possibilities which would be acceptable.

Collaboration

The effective teacher promotes student ownership of and membership in a smoothly functioning learning community first by modeling positive, cooperative behavior, then by requiring students to exhibit positive behavior to each other. Cooperative learning strategies also promote an environment in which members are responsible, cooperative, purposeful, and mutually supportive. Collaborative activities provide practice in working together and developing social skills necessary to be successful in future classes, vocational or technical school or college, and careers. They allow students to develop leadership ability through the group roles they are assigned.

 Drill Questions

1. Mrs. Rodriguez, a tenth-grade English teacher, has five classes of 25 to 28 students who will begin studying *Julius Caesar* in two weeks. She realizes that today's students may find it difficult to relate to events which took place a long time ago. In previous years, she has asked students to read the play in class, with each student taking different roles. This year she wants to encourage greater student excitement in this unit. Which of the following instructional approaches would be most appropriate for Mrs. Rodriguez to use to encourage students to be self-directed learners?

   (A) Writing a study guide with questions about each act for students to answer in a booklet

   (B) Showing a video of the play and then asking students to role play several scenes

   (C) Developing a list of activities related to the play and having the class vote on which ones they want to do

   (D) Providing a list of objectives and having students develop and carry out two activities to help them meet the objectives

2.   Miss Bailey teaches fifth-grade social studies in a self-contained classroom with 25 students of various achievement levels. She is starting a unit on the history of their local community and wants to stimulate the students' thinking. She also wants to encourage students to develop a project as a result of their study. Which type of project would encourage the highest level of thinking by the students?

(A)   Giving students a list of questions about people, dates, and events, then having them put the answers on a poster, with appropriate pictures, to display in class.

(B)   Giving students questions to use to interview older members of the community, then having them write articles based on the interviews and publish them in a booklet.

(C)   Discussing the influence of the past on the present community, then asking students to project what the community might be like in 100 years.

(D)   Using archived newspapers to collect data, then having them draw a timeline which includes the major events of the community from its beginning to the current date.

3.   Mr. Swenson teaches mathematics in high school. He is planning a unit on fractal geometry, using the computer lab for demonstrations and for exploration for his advanced math students. The students have used various computer programs to solve algebra and calculus problems. As Mr. Swenson plans a unit of study, he determines that a cognitive outcome will be that students will design and produce fractals, using a computer program. An affective outcome is that students will become excited about investigating a new field of mathematics and will show this interest by choosing to develop a math project relating to fractals. The most appropriate strategy to use <u>first</u> would be

(A)   explaining the exciting development of fractal geometry over the past 10 to 15 years.

(B)   demonstrating on the computer the way to input values into formulas to produce fractal designs.

(C)   giving students a few simple fractal designs and asking them to figure out the formulas for producing them.

(D) showing students color pictures of complex fractals and asking them for ideas about how they could be drawn mathematically.

4. Mr. Roberts' sixth-grade social studies class has developed a research project to survey student use of various types of video games. They designed a questionnaire and then administered it to all fourth-, fifth-, and sixth-grade students on their campus. The students plan to analyze their data, then develop a presentation to show at the next parent-teacher meeting. Which types of computer software would be helpful during this class project?

I. Word processing

III. Simulation

II. Database

IV. Graph/chart

(A) I, II, III, and IV

(C) I and III only

(B) I, II, and IV

(D) III and IV only

5. Mrs. Johnson teaches middle school reading. She teaches reading skills and comprehension through workbooks and through reading and class discussion of specific plays, short stories, and novels. She also allows students to make some selections according to their own interests. Because she believes there is a strong connection between reading and writing, her students are required to write their responses to literature in a variety of ways. Some of her students have heard their high school brothers and sisters discuss portfolios, and they have asked Mrs. Johnson if they can use them, also. Which of the following statements are appropriate for Mrs. Johnson to consider in deciding whether to agree to the students' request?

I. Portfolios will develop skills her student can use in high school.

II. Portfolios will make Mrs. Johnson's students feel more mature because they would be making the same product as their older brothers and sisters.

III. Portfolios will assist her students in meeting course outcomes relating to reading and writing.

IV. Portfolios will make grading easier because there will be fewer papers and projects to evaluate.

    (A) I, II, and IV   (C) II and III only

    (B) I and III only   (D) II and IV only

6.   Mr. Deavers, a high school physical education teacher, usually has between 50 and 60 students in each class. He often has difficulty in checking attendance and sometimes doesn't know who is present and who is absent from class. He realizes that he needs to institute a new plan. What would be the best procedure for him to institute?

    (A) Have students gather on the bleachers, call each student's name and have each student respond, then put a check on the roll sheet.

    (B) Divide students into ten groups of five or six, appoint a leader, and have the leaders report absences.

    (C) Design a chart with ten rows, assign each student a specific place to stand or sit at the beginning of class, then check roll visually using the chart.

    (D) Have students start an activity, then visually identify each student and put checks on the roll sheet.

Answers to Drill Questions

1.   **(D)**   The question asks how Mrs. Rodriguez can encourage her students to take control of their own learning. Choice (D) is the best answer because the students are being asked to develop their own learning strategies, which match the goals of the class. This process requires higher-level thinking by the students. The teacher is determining the basic outcomes, but the students will help determine the methods of achieving these outcomes. Choice (A) is a very structured plan which students may complete at their own pace, but it does not allow for choices or innovations by the students. Viewing a video [choice (B)] would be an excellent visual activity to help students understand the play, but the students aren't asked to plan or make decisions. Their role-playing may not be creative because they may tend to imitate the actions from the video. Choice (C) allows students

to choose among several activities, which is a good strategy, but all the planning and goal-setting have been done by the teacher.

2.   **(C)**   The question asks for work on the analysis, synthesis, or evaluation level. Choice (C) is the best choice because it asks the students to analyze how past causes have produced current effects, then to predict what future effects might be based on what they have learned about cause-effect relationships. It requires students to put information together in a new way. Choice (A) may involve some creativity in putting the information on a poster, but in general, answering factual questions calls for lower-level (knowledge or comprehension) thinking. Choice (B) may involve some degree of creativity, but giving students prepared questions requires thinking at a lower level than having students develop their own questions, and then determining which answers to write about. Choice (D) is a lower-level activity, although there may be a great deal of research for factual information. All options may be good learning activities, but (A), (B), and (D) do not require as much deep thinking as choice (C). Depending on the depth of the study, a teacher may want to include several of these activities.

3.   **(D)**   The question relates to appropriate sequencing of activities. Choice (D) is the best introductory activity in order to generate student interest in this new field of mathematics and to get students thinking about how to produce fractals. It would stimulate students to use higher-level thinking skills to make predictions by drawing on their knowledge of how to solve problems mathematically. Choice (A) would be the least appropriate to begin the study. Students who want to learn more could research this topic after they have developed an interest in fractals. Choice (B) would be appropriate as a later step, after students are interested in the process and are ready to learn how to produce fractals. Choice (C) would be appropriate as a subsequent step in the process of learning how to produce fractals. Choice (B) requires students to use preplanned formulas; Choice (C) allows them to develop their own formulas, a very high-level activity.

4.   **(B)**   This question asks for an evaluation of which software programs will help the students achieve their goals of analyzing data and presenting the results. Item I, word processing, would be used in developing and printing the questionnaire, as well as writing a report on the results. Item II, a database, would be used to sort and print out information in various categories so students could organize and analyze their data. Item III, a simulation, would not be appropriate here because the students' ba-

sic purpose is to collect data and analyze it. The project does not call for a program to simulate a situation or event. Item IV, graph or chart, would be very useful in analyzing information and in presenting it to others.

5.   **(B)**   The question asks for appropriate questions for Mrs. Johnson to consider in making an instructional decision. Option I is a valid reason for teaching students how to develop portfolios. Teachers constantly teach students the skills which will be useful in school and in their careers. Although Option II may produce positive affective results, feeling mature because students are imitating older siblings is not a sufficient reason to choose portfolios. Option III is the most appropriate reason to decide whether to use portfolios. Most activities and projects that promote achievement of course outcomes would be considered appropriate strategies. Option IV is not necessarily true; portfolio assessment can result in more written work, which can be more time consuming. Even if it were true, emphasizing student achievement is more important than easing the workload of teachers. Options I and III are appropriate; therefore, the correct answer is choice (B).

6.   **(C)**   The question asks for an effective method of taking attendance that doesn't detract from class. Choice (C) is the best option. By assigning each student a specific place to stand, Mr. Deavers can quickly check attendance, in a method similar to the one he would use in assigning seats in a classroom. If teachers use seating charts in the classroom, this method would be familiar to the students. By requiring students to take this position immediately, he can also assign students to lead warmup exercises while he checks roll, thus making good use of the time. Choice (A) is a poor choice. Although it might increase his awareness of who is absent and who is present, this method wastes instructional time. Also, without organization, one student may answer for another. Choice (B) may be effective, but it assumes that all student leaders will be present each day and that they will all be responsible. A teacher who wants to teach responsibility may use a similar system, but would need to teach responsibility to the student leaders and to have assistant leaders as a backup. Choice (D) is almost impossible if the students are engaged in an activity that requires movement. It would be very time-consuming as well, distracting the teacher's attention from the activity itself.

LAST/ATS-W

Chapter 9

The Professional Environment

Chapter 9

The Professional Environment

How well the teacher performs in the classroom is influenced by a number of factors—content-field preparation, understanding of youth, prior and ongoing personal experiences, and certainly the attitude that's adopted toward the specific teaching assignment. Equally critical to the success of the teacher, however, is his or her ability to fit into the school environment, to be able to relate to the parents and broader community, and to interpret and support the regulations governing New York teachers as well as the ethical concerns associated with the procedures involved in educating youth. The teacher's growth, as a professional, is nurtured by all of these contacts and experiences.

Often individuals are reminded that "no man is an island." Teachers are especially vulnerable to the vital role of interacting positively and successfully with others. The students in the classroom, the teacher across the hall, the principal of the building, the fellow teachers on special assignment committees and teams, the campus technology expert—these are just a few of the immediate continuing contacts the teacher must deal with on a regular basis. Equally important are the interactions with parents and community members. In addition to the teacher's awareness of his or her personal strengths and needs, the varied professional contacts, as well as communications with people in the community, can assist the teacher in selecting the best professional growth opportunities and experiences to reinforce, enrich, and expand the teacher's skills and knowledge.

Even in the days of the one-room school, teachers had to be sensitive to the expectations of parents and community members. Often these expectations focused upon the social behavior of the teacher as much as the effectiveness of the teacher in the classroom. Since teachers often roomed with a family in the community, close observation of personal behavior was a simple matter. Community members generally agreed upon the rather rigid code of behavior deemed suitable for someone to whom the community entrusted its children each day.

Today, such agreement is not as clearly defined. The teacher's role is still often considered the ultimate model of what should be, no matter how unrealistic this notion may be. For this reason, the teacher's skill in communicating with the parents and leaders of the community is vitally important. The success of conducting conferences with parents, of sending response-seeking notes or telephone messages to parents, and of assisting parents in working out positive study support techniques for students are all based upon the parents' trust in the teacher and, therefore, in the teacher's recommendations and referrals.

In addition to this concept of the teacher's personal responsibility and effectiveness in working with parents, the teacher needs to understand the environment students experience when they are not at school. In the home, with friends at neighborhood parks or recreation centers, or "hanging out" at the mall—wherever the student is outside of school hours will affect the student when he or she returns to school. Perhaps no other factor can affect the role of the students more than what goes on in their lives during the hours spent with peers, especially when the students are congregating without parent or other adult supervision.

Other members of the community can become strong allies of the effective teacher. The school today is a focal point of interest to all members of the community—not just those with children or grandchildren attending the school. Patrons of the school district want their "money's worth," be it a school with competitive test scores (equating to a good "product" in the business world), a seat on the school board or at least a voice at the next school board meeting, or a positive contact with a member of the teaching staff—you. This more visible interaction today is two-fold, however, and can bring many benefits to the teacher. The education specialist at the computer store can assist the teacher in understanding the working of established programs and in locating and using software for the classroom. The librarian, always an active friend of the classroom teacher, can share which authors are the popular ones for the summer readers of any age group. Likewise, the video rental clerks will know the hot movies for the various ages. Community workers in specialized fields, such as involvement with drugs or gangs, provide much information for the teacher who has just moved into the community as a workplace.

The teacher, united with the various members of the community, becomes a stronger figure, one who is not only providing classroom instruction but also providing assistance to the students in other ways to be better equipped to meet the demands of life.

Finally, in order to fulfill the role delegated to today's educator, the teacher needs to be aware of the many roles to be enacted while under contract to teach. The local campus and district will have specific expectations for each employee. These expectations will involve matters of legal responsibility as well as ethical considerations. Often the expectations are clearly delineated in a teacher's handbook at the beginning of the school year; however, some expectations are more traditional and can only be learned by observing experienced teachers' behavior. Finding a person who is open and well-informed about the practices and attitudes expected of the professional staff members on the campus is a wise step for a beginner. Such a person may be the teacher across the hall, a counselor, or a secretary.

State rules and regulations associated with education often relate to information that a teacher becomes aware of—matters concerning the privacy of student records, the responsibility to report signs of child abuse, student depression and self-destructive attitudes, special needs of some student populations, equal rights of all children regardless of race, religion, or sexual orientation. The teacher needs to know how to help and how to get help; also, the teacher must be aware of occasions when he or she cannot help but must make referrals for specialized assistance for the student.

Within the work environment, the teacher will constantly be facing decision-making situations that extend well beyond the lesson plans for the day or week. Knowing potential roles, utilizing the various sources of available support services, and exercising communication skills effectively to bring the greatest benefits to the students, the teacher clearly demonstrates an in-depth understanding of the teaching environment.

THE TEACHER'S PERSONAL TRAITS

Knowing one's self is an essential characteristic of a successful person in any area of life. The qualities enabling the teacher to work well in a work situation that is often described by others as stressful or boring are the same qualities that make a businessperson or salesperson successful. The teacher, like the banker or clerk, will never be isolated from others and must use a variety of personal interactive skills on a daily basis. Working with students in the classroom, sharing curriculum ideas in a grade-level meeting, projecting a positive image as a well-trained professional who is planning successfully for his or her assignment, or responding maturely to constructive evaluative comments from a supervisor—in every scenario, the excelling teacher demonstrates certain personal traits that project a strong self image: confidence, competence, dedication, enthusiasm, and a sense of humor. These are all traits that cannot be taught through a teacher education program. They are the result of the experiences of the individual during the developmental stages of his or her life and prepare the individual for a successful career in the area chosen.

Teachers are aware of their personal traits. They feel confident of the skills and content acquired during the years of training to become a teacher. Knowing various ways to modify classwork for a student with special needs or how to bring a highly excited class back to a calmer mode of operation instills a feeling of security in the teacher, a sense of being in control that communicates itself to the students without repetitious reprimand or threat.

The teacher's competence in handling the unexpected as well as the routine is clearly observable, as a professional efficiency of being in control of the situation is demonstrated. Enjoying work with both students and fellow professionals, the self-confident teacher is positive about what is going on in the classroom and meeting with staff members. Enthusiasm is often contagious. When the teacher is excited about the students' work, both younger and older students will respond similarly. Finally, finding laughter a healthy outlet, the teacher shares a sense of humor with the students. Even though students may groan at a teacher's puns, their acceptance of the educator's enjoyment of language will be a further linkage in building a positive working environment in the classroom.

In addition to the personal traits that denote a strong self-image, other traits of the individual identify the person who will have the greatest chance for success in a teaching career. A high energy level is most valuable. The apparently tireless teacher can match, perhaps even surpass, the energy level of the students. A well-organized teacher can achieve equally as much, however, since a plan of accomplishing the endless amount of work also brings about successful outcomes. Teachers described as successful are also understanding. Instead of always doing the talking, they find time to listen to students. In the fine art of communicating, too frequently the vital role of being a good listener is sometimes overlooked. When students have problems, an open attitude and warm responsiveness can help the student to work out the solution needed.

Of course, sometimes students misbehave and do not respond to the initial efforts of the teacher to bring the student back into acceptable behavioral patterns. Consistency in disciplining students assists the teacher in promoting students' positive behavior. When students who have dropped out of the class focus know a teacher's warning will be followed by action, the students are much more likely to join the classwork as requested.

One trait that serves as a valuable adjunct to all other traits listed may elude many teachers. This is the trait of creativity. Although some teacher preparation programs promote training in innovative methodology, many teachers either lack time or the type of thinking skill that brings about fresh ideas for the classroom. Good interpersonal skills can come to the rescue, as the less original teacher can observe and emulate ideas from other teachers who tend to be more innovative.

The preceding discussion has mentioned traits and skills to develop if they are not apparent in a teacher's personality. One other group of traits remains—behaviors to avoid. The negative traits of griping, carelessness, belittling others, or giving up on a student or the job assignment are the special afflictions released from Pandora's box just to plague teachers. These energy-draining traits can also be contagious; therefore, stay away from anyone who exhibits signs of infection. Examine your behaviors and attitudes occasionally, working toward ever greater success in your teaching assignment.

Team Responsibilities in Teaching

A second aspect of this competency concerns the teacher's role in serving as a member of a team. Increasingly, teachers find their work affected by the need to coordinate with other teachers—in planning, in delivering the lessons, and in evaluating students and curriculum. Many of the personal traits that make a successful classroom teacher will also enable a teacher to work well with other professionals on various assignments and in self-developed team projects.

Perhaps the strongest team of teachers is one made up of two or more teachers or support staff members who possess the five basic traits of successful individuals that we discussed: confidence, competence, dedication, enthusiasm, and a sense of humor. The team members complement one another, sharing the responsibility and fully enjoying their work. Humor responds to humor; therefore, each team member especially appreciates his or her teammates' lack of griping and working toward the final goal—the improved learning of the students.

Even if the team members are not equally strong in the personal traits that create a masterful educator, the teachers can learn to share their strengths for the benefit of the students. When a new teacher is assigned to work with a clearly outstanding professional, the opportunity for the less experienced teacher to move along more rapidly in developing successful strategies and polishing skills of instructing occurs.

Teaming Assignments

Teaming assignments may occur for a variety of purposes. Among the more frequently occurring patterns are the following:

1. Classroom instruction—Teachers may be teaching together for the entire day or for specified periods of time. Usually the class section is larger than the class of a single teacher. The teachers may have the same certification or compatible areas of specialization such as social studies, reading, and language arts.

2. Special needs adaptation for the classroom—Since the students who once were placed in special education classes are now integrated into regular classes of study, the classroom teacher becomes a working partner with the specialist. Ways to modify instruction for specific students are discussed and assistance provided by the expert.

3. Curriculum related committees—Teachers and curriculum specialists work together to evaluate the existing curriculum and plan the changes needed. Often, the teacher tries new materials in the classroom and reports to the team about the effectiveness of the new ideas or resources. One annual committee of this nature is the textbook selection committee. Different teachers review and recommend for adoption a specific textbook each year. Teachers may work on a committee for the new textbook in their own subject area or on the district committee, making the final recommendations for all textbook areas to be selected during a single year.

4. Site-based management planning—One of the newer strategies used in schools, committees to assist in making decisions about the management of the school are made up of a variety of staff members. Curriculum, discipline, school regulations, and other concerns affecting the total campus environment become the focus of each meeting, and the teacher's role is often representative of many other teachers on the staff. Meeting time each month may easily total several hours.

5. Special committees—From the calendar committee for the next school year to the cheer committee concerned with providing appropriate contact with ill or bereaved peers, various concerns necessitate that groups of staff members work together. Most of these assignments require only several hours of meeting time, but a demanding issue can extend that time estimate.

In each of the assignments for working together, teachers have the opportunity to demonstrate their positive skills in communicating with others. Often, as in teaching, listening becomes a vital key to the successful outcome of a team meeting.

PROFESSIONAL GROWTH

As a skilled educator, leader, mediator, and listener, the self-aware teacher can identify shaky or worn traits in order to bring about more effective results in work assignments. Some teachers need to develop new traits to provide greater potential for success in certain work-related encounters. Educational practice allows for this improvement in skills through the staff development programs required for all teachers throughout the year. More and more teachers are able to help design these in-service training sessions so that their specific needs are more adequately met. One major committee assignment of teachers is the planning of staff development within a district on specified days. Sessions that enhance the individual's knowledge in a content field are balanced with other opportunities, such as those that work to improve individuals' interpersonal skills, better understanding of technology, or wider knowledge of the available resources within the community.

In addition to required in-service meetings, many teachers continue advanced study at nearby universities. Many of these courses specialize in the needs expressed by the teachers on a campus. For instance, if several teachers are pursuing gifted and talented certification, a university may bring the required courses to a district campus for the teachers' convenience. Individual teachers often belong to the national organizations of their certified area. The reading of the professional magazines of such organizations and the attendance at state and/or national conferences also provide a chance for gaining new content knowledge and strategies of instruction.

The teacher's growth as a professional is never ending. New ideas, new technology, changing roles—all demand continual renewal. The resulting educator, the fully actualized teacher, leads the way.

Developing a Positive Relationship with Parents Early

The teacher will often have a more difficult time getting to know parents today than one or two generations ago. Often parents' attitudes toward becoming involved with the school have changed. This change is not necessarily due to disinterest but to different conditions in life-style. Many parents work outside the community and have less time and energy to develop an interest in the school than formerly. Gone also are the days when many parents, themselves, attended their child's school and even studied under some of the same teachers. Greater mobility in the population and the resulting community instability in both population and shared values have taken their toll as well as have the other factors mentioned. What can the teacher do to establish not only a friendly relationship with the parents but a relationship that has developed a degree of mutual trust and respect?

At the beginning of the school year, before an educational or behavioral problem arises with a student, the teacher can make positive contact with all parents. This contact may be by a written note, telephone call, or even a home visit in the late afternoon if the building administrator is not opposed to such visits. During the visit, the teacher can mention several of the immediate content and skill areas that will be studied during the next five or six weeks. He or she can ask the parent to describe the student's general attitude toward school, the successes of previous years of study, and special interests of the student, and the child's comments about the beginning of the new year. Finally, the teacher can ask the parents about their goals for their children during the coming year.

Parent/Teacher Communication

One of the most helpful resources for the teacher to establish continuing dialogue with the parents is to maintain an informal journal for all parental communications. Recording what the teacher brings to the meeting as well as ideas and attitudes the teacher leaves with can assist the teacher in making each contact non-repetitive and highly personalized.

If the teaching load of the teacher is too great for the one-on-one approach described, the teacher can try to set up meetings of small groups of parents immediately after school or at another convenient time. Working parents sometimes like to come in early before school in the morning; others can come during a lunch break where teacher and parents "brownbag" in the teacher's room at noon if no other place to meet is available. The group of four or five parents, although not as individualized in focus, is still small enough for the teacher to begin building a sense of cooperation and respect with each, essential in problem intervention or solution which may be required later in the school year. The initial attitude of the parents' role is one of a partnership, focused upon the child's well-being and awareness of the classroom objectives and strategies. Any step that avoids future adversarial parental response, almost always a negative base of communication, can only serve as a benefit for the teacher.

One concern of most parents is the quality of instruction occurring in the classroom. When the teacher can share his or her goals and indicate a continuity of study from day to day and week to week, parents respond positively. After the initial parental contact, teachers can begin a pattern of sending home papers for parents to see. A variety of papers—those showing strengths as well as weaknesses of students—should be selected for this step. If a student begins to show repeated weaknesses in work or attitude toward work, calling the parent for a conference is indicated.

Before the conference, the teacher needs to gather all of the materials needed—examples of the student's work to indicate the problem(s) under focus, the record of the student's daily effort if failure to accomplish assignments is the problem or part of it, anecdotes of misbehavior if the problem is one related to discipline, attempts made to change the negative performance of a student, and certainly suggestions for solving the problem. The teacher should always allow time for the parent to present his or her perspective of the situation as well as the child's attitude about the problem. Sometimes, having the student present becomes a useful strategy, especially if the student has been omitting part of the story when talking about it at home.

The end of any conference should include writing down the actions each participant—teacher, parent, and student—will take to help improve the situation. A tentative date for meeting again, or at least communicating between teacher and parent, should also be set before the participants leave. Within a few days, the teacher should try to find opportunity to provide feedback to both the parent and the student about the matter discussed, especially if improvement of a negative situation can be noted.

As students progress through school, their parents generally tend to have less interest in pursuing conferences with teachers. The parent of an elementary child is much more responsive to the teacher's initial overture to meet than the parent of a secondary student. Sometimes the parent has been to countless meetings with educators over the years, and the student is still exhibiting the same undesirable traits. The parent in this case tends to give up on helping the child. The secondary teachers, too, are often not as enthusiastic about contacting and arranging meetings with all students' parents. The secondary teacher, with well over 100 students, has a real scheduling dilemma compared to the elementary teacher. Often limiting meetings to parents of students with difficulty becomes the major effort of the secondary teacher. Whatever effort the teacher makes, however, is to his or her credit.

Responding to Nonresponsive Parents

Parents of some students, invited repeatedly to meet with a teacher, never seem to be able to arrange a time when they can come. The scheduling problem may be a genuine one, since many parents work long hours some distance from the home or hold more than one job. Sometimes when parents do attend a meeting, they are tired or distracted by even more stressful personal problems than the school situation.

When the teacher receives no response to an invitation for parent conferencing, a notation of the effort to make contact on a specific date should be made in the teacher's journal. Another attempt can be made six or eight weeks later. If a parent in this group does come to a school visitation program or is met informally in the community, the teacher should make every effort to show his or her pleasure at meeting the student's parent. Ideally, the teacher will have a recent anecdote about the child or some specific positive learning comment to make to the parent.

Learning about the Community

The first staff development for new teachers in a school district is often based upon providing insight into the make-up of the community. Many larger districts have developed videotapes about their communities. Information to help the teacher adjust to both a new employment situation as well as possibly a new personal residential and shopping area is most vital. Sometimes, the district school busses load up the teachers, and a tour of the immediate neighborhood of the school itself is viewed firsthand, often with helpful commentary by an experienced professional. If such orientation is not provided, the teacher should solicit an informal tour of the community, preferably by someone who has lived there several years. If other new teachers have joined the staff, together they may solicit a guide from the established staff members—a teacher, a secretary, a para-professional. Sometimes a volunteer from the organized parents' group of a campus may have the orientation of new staff members as one of their goals.

Once the students have started school, the teacher may ask the students to talk about their community. Their perceptions, although certainly reflecting their age biases, still provide insights not otherwise available to a new teacher. Perhaps the teacher will find several students who will spend an hour or two one afternoon or Saturday morning touring the community and pointing out special places—the neighborhood library, nearby public parks, shopping areas, any favorite hang-outs of the teenagers. If the teacher is an elementary school teacher, a parent, with one or two of the students, may provide the tour.

Finally, becoming a patron of a few businesses within the community can serve as a source of information about the community as well as its expectations of and attitudes toward the school. The teacher can take cleaning to a local cleaning establishment or shop at a grocery store or drugstore, exchanging a few words about the school with the persons who provide service at such establishments. Visiting the local library and talking with the librarian always will provide help as well. If the teacher attends a local church, certainly talking to church workers can be very informative.

Learning as much as possible about the community that a school serves will assist the teacher in numerous ways throughout the teaching assignment in that community. The teacher, at the same time, may be building allies upon whom to call if a need occurs.

Utilizing Strengths of the Community

Every community will have established sources of support for the school. Parents' groups such as the Parent Teacher Association, the Dads Club, the Band Boosters, the Sports Club, and dozens of other groups have been formed to provide both financial and philosophical support. These groups are often searching for projects to undertake as part of their yearly program of goals.

Using the community as subject matter for writing experiences can provide additional information for the teacher's use while teaching the students to do a variety of activities to gather primary and secondary information about their home area. Students can research the history of the area in several ways. A very young student can interview and tape older members of the community as they talk about the past. Often the elders welcome an invitation to visit a class and talk about their earliest days in the area and retell the stories that their parents may have told them. Gathering letters, photographs, magazines, maps, toys, and other artifacts of days gone by can provide primary documentation that is often quite interesting to students and also to parents when displayed at open house.

Sometimes special interest groups within the community welcome the opportunity to share aspects of their interest with a class. A local story-telling group may visit a class and demonstrate techniques to make a story's retelling truly exciting for the listeners; a writing group may judge creative writing of the students and offer tips for expressive writing. Parents will often attend elementary classes and share work experiences to begin the students' awareness of the world of work. More formal Career Days, frequently planned on secondary campuses, utilize a variety of local people to talk about their vocational choices and respond to students' questions.

Coping with Problems in the Community

Each community, along with the strengths that can be identified, will have deterrents to the educational process. Some of these negative aspects are not merely local problems but symptomatic of many communities today—drug and alcohol abuse, unemployment, heavy mobility within the community, and crime and violence, especially as reflected in gang conflicts. Accompanied by the apparent apathy of adults in regards to the educational process, the toll of these problems upon the effectiveness of the schools can be heavy, for students of any age may be affected adversely by one or more of these conditions of contemporary society.

Often when a school exists in an environment affected by one or more of the societal ills of today, the in-service programs for teachers will focus on the relevant problems obviously affecting the student population. The teacher will learn ways to help students in the classroom and sources of even greater assistance for students through these staff training sessions. The teacher's good judgment will always be required, however, to know to what extent he or she can help with a pervasive problem area. Working at intervention, before a problem area becomes a critical factor affecting the educational process in the classroom, is always a wise course of action.

Any community is now vulnerable to greater crime and violence within its boundaries. Such an atmosphere will affect the youth and, therefore, the school environment. Not uncommon today is the requirement for students to enter a school building by passing through a metal detector, one attempt to keep weapons out of the school building. If the community is unfortunate enough to have gangs attracting the teenagers, the rival attitudes and behaviors cannot be blocked out of the building as easily as knives or guns. Staff training in multicultural understanding will assist the new teachers in understanding the characteristics of different ethnic groups. In the classroom, intervention may be successful by studying literary works based upon prejudice. Class discussion may defuse potentially volatile situations in real life as students read about conflicts between rival groups, as in *Light in the Forest, When the Legends Die, The Chosen, Flowers for Algernon,* or other novels based upon prejudices. The classics can also offer groups in conflict, such as in *Romeo and Juliet, A Tale of Two Cities,* or *Animal Farm.* Actual historical incidents, as well as contemporary news stories, provide other examples to discuss in class. The teacher, making good judgment calls, can successfully intervene before a problem occurs in class.

The effective teacher can make a difference, even when the problems in the community seem insurmountable. Using the time and talent available, the teacher can address the problems that seem to affect his or her students in an appropriate way in the classroom and be familiar with sources of more extensive help available on campus and in the community.

The Teacher as a Curriculum Worker

One job that seems never to be completed is the preparation of curriculum guides for grade level and/or content areas of instruction. Evaluation of the existing curriculum is an on-going process by teachers, and the major revision of curriculum is usually a major focus every four or five years, especially as new textbooks are adopted and other resources purchased or made available. Special concepts often become fashionable trends in education. During the last 20 years, all grade levels and content areas have had major revisions in curricula to include such matters as writing across the content area, reading in the content area, career education, holistic scoring of writing, inquiry study, multicultural concerns, strands of instruction for gifted and talented students, portfolio assessment, and the ever-popular basic skills instruction. One modern buzz phrase is "values training," not to be confused with the values clarification emphasis of the 1970s. Since the home and community may have lost effectiveness as a strong values support system, the school has been automatically selected as the agent to maintain the values for the society. Whatever the reason for curriculum revision, the individual teacher will be affected.

The Teacher as a Specialist

Each teacher has specific certification that defines the areas of assignment he or she expects to receive. This area of specialization will not be addressed at this time. The concern of the teacher as a specialist relates to the teacher's assignment to areas for which he or she is not trained and has little or no interest or skill.

Two generations ago, teachers were often assigned out of their field and frequently stayed in such a teaching assignment for extended periods of time. The current trend is to make teachers' assignments within their certification specialties but to require of every teacher the ability to handle instructional focus for special areas that cross all disciplines. Over the last several years, instructional concepts that overlap subject areas have included drug education, career awareness, reading and writing in the content areas, and values reinforcement. Staff development sessions will focus upon these special expectations of every teacher.

Another specialist area currently affecting teachers concerns students formerly designated as special education students. Currently, many such previously segregated students are being re-entered into mainstream classes. The regular classroom teacher has students, therefore, who have previously been taught primarily by special education teachers. The regular teacher must learn to offer modifications of instruction for these students and maintain a record of the various techniques used to meet the students' special needs. Modification may be as simple as allowing more time on a timed activity or accepting oral testing in place of written assessment. However, the teacher must have several strategies for teaching each unit of work and make available to students the method by which the student best learns.

Other areas of specialization expected of the teacher may concern special responsibilities to accompany the regular teaching assignment. Being offered a job may be contingent on the teacher's acceptance of a coaching assignment, although the teacher had not been seeking a coaching position. Serving as a sponsor or coach of a school organization or activity group may also be expected of many teachers.

Teacher education programs attempt to keep up with the reality of assignments met by new teachers. The diversity of schools and school districts, however, accounts for sometimes surprising job descriptions facing the teacher with a contract offer.

The Teacher and Values in the Classroom

Reference has been made to the emphasis upon values instruction occurring in many schools throughout New York. Not only must the teacher be prepared to support the philosophy of his or her school district in regard to this matter, but also the teacher must be prepared to interact appropriately with the students and parents when certain topics like censorship or sex education become a concern.

Each campus will have an approved approach to values education. The teacher should always work within these guidelines. New York school boards are showing an increased acceptance of character-building strategies and expect the teacher to promote the human qualities deemed as admirable. Generally these qualities, once strongly supported by all facets of communities across the state, especially the home and the church, concern the traits of a good, law-abiding citizen and decent human being. The model of self-discipline and hard work, once traits identified with the head of a family, now may be exhibited as a worthy model for some students only by the teacher.

The teaching of values may be best achieved as students and teacher discuss pertinent events in their everyday lives or in their reading for school. The media's tendency to provide sensational coverage of well-known sports figures, politicians, and business leaders in the news brings the ugliest of human motives and behavior to everyone's attention. Appropriate class discussion, carefully moderated and directed toward a greater depth of understanding human nature, can help students struggle with a public hero's or heroine's fall from grace. The stories read in class, or the events recounted from history, offer equally valid opportunities for discussion.

The whole concept of censorship is another aspect of values interchange that a teacher may meet. Even if a teacher limits reading to the state-adopted textbooks, critics of some materials or ideas within these textbooks may be challenged by some parents. A district committee for dealing with problems of censorship may be in effect, and the teacher's responsibility will end once the problem is submitted to the committee. Complaints from parents are generally sincere, directed by their concerns for their own children. Sometimes, however, organized groups exert pressure to remove certain reading from the classroom. In recent years, censorship hearings in New York have reviewed complaints ranging from Shirley Jackson's short story "The Lottery" to the children's fairy tale "Rumpelstiltskin" to the study of classical Greek mythology. Whenever a matter of censorship arises, the teacher should inform the school administrator promptly and follow the district guidelines for such matters.

Although the problems that are related to sex education are generally limited to teachers of health education or biology, all teachers need to be informed of the district policies regarding this potentially controversial issue. Even very young students are now exposed to early sexual information and even actual experience. Surveys indicate that many middle school students have had intimate relationships of a sexual nature. Each teacher's situation will be different; therefore, teachers need to determine before a situation arises (1) how to handle essays or poems making direct reference to sexual matters, (2) how to help students who have earnest questions of a sexual nature, and (3) how much discussion to allow in the classroom on the subject when it relates to the current study.

The Teacher as a Leader

The current major New York pattern of decision making on school campuses is one based upon site-based management. The individual teacher may, therefore, have a leadership role early in his or her career. In site-based management, a team of professionals on the campus discusses the needs of the campus, makes recommendations to accomplish these needs, and evaluates the resulting actions taken. As a member of the team, the teacher may lead an inquiry or information-gathering committee and report the findings to the other team members—fellow teachers, a school administrator, support staff members, parents, and students. As with many other responsibilities undertaken by the teacher, this leadership role often requires after-hours attendance at meetings and offers no remuneration. The days of the "moonlighting" teacher seem to belong to the past.

Another area of leadership expected of the teacher is as a participant in the professional organizations of the teacher's certification and assignment areas. Area, regional, state, and national organizations service their teachers in various ways, offering displays of new books and other resources for the instructional area as well as workshops and conferences for teachers of the same discipline or teaching interest. Many of these meetings are held on weekends so that teaching responsibilities will not be interrupted.

The Teacher and Legal Issues

A fundamental expectation of the school board hiring a teacher is that this individual will be well-informed on the legal issues affecting teaching and always work in compliance with them. Staff development sessions based upon legal requirements for educators will be offered to teachers, and the teacher's district or campus handbook will itemize these concerns.

One of the major concerns of all teachers should be the safety and welfare of their students. Thus, students are not left without supervision while on the campus during the school day. The daily appearance of a student should be noted. Any indication of child neglect or physical abuse must be reported promptly to the principal. More subtle is the alarm revealed by a child's written or oral language. Such evidence of a disturbed state of mind, especially one that could represent suicidal tendencies, should be reported at once.

The confidentiality of a student's records, including his or her current performance in a teacher's classroom, is protected by law. Since teachers have access to the permanent records of each student, they must be careful to whom they talk about these records. Idle chatter in the teachers' lounge or over lunch with fellow professionals is never appropriate or legal. Likewise, a teacher cannot discuss a student's performance record with adults other than the student's own parents or guardians.

The teacher is often referred to as a professional, a person who has completed advanced study and is deemed worthy of the highest standards of performance. Continually displaying the integrity associated with the teaching of young people, the new teacher can and will easily earn the respect of co-workers, parents, and teachers.

Drill Questions

1.   Jana Davis's eleventh-grade English classes will participate for the first time in a team research project with the American History classes in her high school. (Two teachers in social studies will be working on the project with Mrs. Davis, teaching the same students that she has in her English classes.) The project indicates that the students' pre-writing activities will include reading a novel by an American author, researching the historical accuracy and/or relevance of the setting of the novel (time and place), and planning the paper.

After the paper has been written, each student's social studies teacher will evaluate the content accuracy, focusing upon the historical research. Mrs. Davis will focus her evaluation of the paper upon the analytical aspects of the novel as well as the written expression—style, mechanics, sentence structure, and usage.

During staff development time prior to the implementation of the research project, Mrs. Davis has asked the two American History teachers to meet with her. None of the teachers have ever worked on a team project like this one. Mrs. Davis has prepared a note with questions to initiate the meeting of the teachers on the team.

"I'd like us to plan the calendar for our research project so that we won't run into problems or be rushed in grading the final product. I know the students will need at least two weeks to read their novels. I have some other questions, however, before the project begins.

"What are some of the main points we should use to check progress during the pre-writing and planning stages? Should we all approve the thesis statement of the paper? How will our joint grading be reflected in the evaluation rubric? I know you must have some questions, too. I look forward to our getting together as soon as possible. Will our joint planning period next Tuesday be a good day for us to meet?"

Jane Davis's questions are intended to

(A) show her interest in the team research project.

(B) indicate to the other two teachers her control of the project.

(C) demonstrate her willingness to accomplish the team project successfully.

(D) clarify the problems in the proposed team project.

2. John Kelly, a fifth grade teacher, has been having many behavioral problems with a new student in his class, Bryan Underwood. During the four weeks Bryan has been enrolled, he has been unable to stay in his seat during class activities. He repeatedly speaks out during the middle of class to ask questions unrelated to the work underway. He disturbs other students with his aggressive behavior, often pushing or punching them. Mr. Kelly has called Bryan's mother and talked to her about his behavior. Mrs. Underwood, a single parent, has agreed to come before school to a meeting with Mr. Kelly about her son's behavior.

When Mrs. Underwood arrives for the conference, Mr. Kelly should greet her with which words?

(A) "I just don't know what I'm going to do with your son!"

(B) "Can you tell me why Bryan is so aggressive in my classroom? Has he exhibited these traits before?"

(C) "Mrs. Underwood, I think you have a real problem with your son."

(D) "Mrs. Underwood, let's see what we can come up with to help your son feel happier about his move to a new school."

3. Carla Mendoza has signed a contract to teach in the Davistown Independent School District. She has just started teaching social studies and reading to seventh graders at the middle school. She had never visited Davistown until she went there for her initial

interview. Now, a new resident as well as a new teacher, she is anxious to learn more about her community and the students she has met in her classes. She has driven around the school neighborhood and also shopped in the nearby mall. She has visited three churches but has not decided which one she will join.

Which of the following activities will be most useful in helping Carla Mendoza learn more about her students, school, and community?

(A) Attending a local gathering, such as a church meeting

(B) Visiting the model homes in a new residential area opening soon near the school

(C) Taking walks around the community to visit with community members, such as business owners, the librarian, residents, and policemen

(D) Attending a get-acquainted meeting of new residents in her apartment complex

4. Kate Tillerson is an art teacher at McGregor High School, where she has taught for several years successfully. She is respected by her students as well as her fellow teachers. This year, the new Director of Instruction for the McGregor Independent School District has introduced several curriculum ideas, one of which is the concept of authentic assessment. All curriculum areas have had one or more staff development sessions on this concept. The idea will be incorporated into the curriculum as one of the strategies for assessment in each discipline and at each grade level.

Kate has just received a request from the Fine Arts Department chairperson to submit an example of a lesson involving authentic assessment. A central office form to complete the example accompanies the request, along with a review of the authentic assessment concept, a model of a completed example, and a deadline for submitting teachers' samples.

Kate's general response to the entire focus on authentic assessment has been that all she does in her classroom is based upon authentic assessment philosophy. She really sees no need for making any changes in the curriculum guide or for preparing the assignment sent to her. On the other hand, Kate is an excellent teacher and generally cooperates in the various curriculum tasks requested of her. She has been a leader of staff development sessions within the district and has shared her innovative ideas with fellow professionals at both regional and state meetings of art educators.

Which of the following responses should Kate make to her departmental chairperson's request?

(A)   Kate files the request under things to do and forgets about it.

(B)   Kate writes a passionate letter in response to the Fine Arts Department chairperson's request, explaining how she feels about the proposed example of an authentic assessment in art. She sends a copy of this letter to her chairperson and also to the Director of Curriculum and takes no further action.

(C)   Kate writes a passionate letter in response to the Fine Arts Department chairperson's request, explaining how she feels about the proposed example of an authentic assessment in art. Attached to the letter is a model unit of study Kate has used in her classes, including an authentic assessment project described in detail but not submitted on the form provided by the Director of Curriculum. Kate sends copies of these items to both her chairperson and the Director of Instruction.

(D)   Kate completes an authentic assessment project idea on the form provided by her chairperson. She submits this idea with supplementary photographs of students' projects and a copy of the grading rubric returned to the students for each project photographed. She also sends a videotape of a student discussing the project he has submitted for the unit of study.

Answers to Drill Questions

1.   **(C)**   Jana Davis has asked questions about concerns and decisions that will have a direct impact upon the success of the proposed project. By seeking clarification of these aspects of teaming with two of her teaching colleagues and inviting them to express their ideas and concerns, she will avoid problems and reduce stress associated with working across disciplines. Her pleasant, clearly worded note indicates confidence in working on this team project and a respect for the other two teachers. Her concern about the timing of various stages of the project indicates a good organizational sense and an awareness of the involved nature of the team project.

Incorrect answers for this question are (A), (B), and (D). Answer (A) expresses Mrs. Davis's interest in the project. Her note, however, indicates much more professional forethought than merely expressing an interest. She is ready to get to work in organizing the project and establishing vital points of agreement for the teachers before the students become involved in their research. When she refers to an evaluation rubric, she demonstrates her professional knowledge of creative and meaningful ways to evaluate, especially a way that may be used by more than one evaluator working on the same product. Answer (B) expresses an attitude that is missing in the communication sent by Mrs. Davis. Her message to the teachers is warm and open to input in determining the answers to considerations she mentions. Her capacity to lead is evident, but no strong overtone of seeking control has been expressed in her note. She speaks as an enthusiastic team member, one ready to contribute her time and talent to the joint venture. Answer (D) centers on clarifying problems with the proposed project. Mrs. Davis's questions and her positive tone indicate a willingness to solve potential problems before they actually appear, not accentuate them at this early stage of planning.

2.   **(D)**   Mr. Kelly's response is an opening that establishes the shared responsibility of the teacher and the parent to help Bryan. Recognition of a possible cause of Bryan's behavior is given—his recent move from another school. The basic cause of his aggressive behavior is indicated as a factor not related to the parent's handling of her son. A positive tone has been used and, even though Mr. Kelly may not feel as optimistic about Bryan's change in behavior as his words sound, he is making no promises but is

seeking support from Bryan's mother to help bring about the desired change. Mr. Kelly is inviting Mrs. Underwood to enter into a collaborative working relationship with him, having Bryan's welfare as the focus.

Incorrect answers for this question are (A), (B), and (C). Answers (A) and (C) express a negative tone about Bryan as well as the chances of changing Bryan's aggressive behavior. Mr. Kelly's words do not show the professional confidence that would be expected of an educator truly "in charge" of the situation. Mrs. Underwood, who may well be in need of help in managing her son, cannot be inspired to turn to Mr. Kelly for assistance. Answer (B) immediately places the responsibility upon Mrs. Underwood to explain her son's behavior. Before hearing from the professional educator about the classroom situation, she is asked to tell what is happening. Also, she is asked, rather bluntly, to tell about previous aggressive traits Bryan has exhibited. Of course, we do not know the depth of the telephone conversation between Mr. Kelly and Mrs. Underwood, but if it was only an invitation to a conference, she is hardly ready to compare his current behavior, about which she may know little, to any prior aggressiveness of her son. Again, she cannot view her relationship with Mr. Kelly as a partnership, working to help Bryan. She feels more like a witness being cross-examined at her son's trial in court. All of the wrong answers demonstrate how the lack of communication skills can get a parent conference off to a bad start and possibly doom the session to little positive outcome.

3.   **(C)**   By walking through the community, Carla Mendoza observes first hand the characteristics of the community. She sees the influences which are brought into the classroom. She will also see the resources which can be used in the classroom. By speaking to a wide variety of people, she is better able to create an accurate picture of the community. Answer choice (A) will give Ms. Mendoza a good idea of the church member characteristics but it will not be representative of the entire population. Choice (B) may give Ms. Mendoza an image of the new members of the community but, once again, not a representative image of the entire community. Choice (D), attending a get-acquainted meeting, may be of some personal benefit, but will acquaint her with only a minute portion of the community at large.

4.   **(D)**   Kate, as an effective teacher and respected professional in her school as well as beyond her district, realizes the intent of central office curriculum efforts is to raise the standards of instruction throughout the district. While Kate, as a team player in the educational process, may

be performing at the highest level, other teachers need boosting. The work that Kate submits will probably be used as a model for other teachers throughout the district. The thoroughness of her response indicates that she will be invited to make other presentations at area and state professional meetings, perhaps on the topic of authentic assessment.

Choice (A) is an unprofessional action by Kate. Perhaps she is forgetful or lazy; she is certainly expressing rudeness and lack of cooperation by ignoring the request made of her and all teachers in the district. None of these characteristics represents a teacher who is effective in the classroom and highly respected by her students and peers. Choice (B) indicates that Kate, not forgetful or lazy, is unaware of or resentful of the role she plays as a curriculum developer within her teaching assignment. Her decision to write a "passionate letter in response" to the request is somewhat immature. The professional teacher who seriously questions a curricular approach from central office would discuss the situation reasonably, calmly, and privately with the new Director of Instruction.

Of course, the very fact that Kate feels she has been incorporating authentic assessment ideas in her teaching for some time indicates her valuing the concept. Should her role not be one of support to get other teachers to value authentic assessment as well? Choice (C) is incorrect because Kate, although showing support for the concept of authentic assessment, is still blocking the central office efforts to get some degree of uniformity in preparation of curriculum material. Again, her "passionate letter in response" to the request for an authentic assessment sample indicates poor judgment on Kate's part. Does the strong expression of her feelings indicate an independent nature or a rebel in regards to teamwork? Is her refusal to rewrite her model unit of study to conform to the district format laziness, a rejection of authority, or some other indicator of malcontent? The effective professional would find some other way to communicate her concerns if the provided format for the model of authentic assessment could be improved.

LAST/ATS-W

Chapter 10

Assessment of Teaching Skills-Performance (ATS-P)

Chapter 10

Assessment of Teaching Skills-Performance (ATS-P)

INTRODUCTION

The Assessment of Teaching Skills-Performance (ATS-P) is required of candidates who have received a provisional teaching certificate and need a permanent certificate. Individuals who received a provisional certificate on or after September 2, 1993, for early childhood/elementary education (PreK-6) or secondary (7-12) academic titles are required to attain a passing score on the ATS-P for permanent certification. The teaching performance is to be submitted on video. Candidates must complete the requirements for application and follow specific procedures for proper credit.

The ATS-P is a test used to assess the knowledge and application of teaching skills by an educator. The test was developed by the New York State Education Department (NYSED) and National Evaluation Systems, Inc. (NES), of Amherst, Massachusetts. A candidate for this test must be employed as a regular teacher in a public or nonpublic school with responsibilities between PreK and 12. The test assumes that a standard level of teaching ability is attained before submission of the video. Experience of at least two years is beneficial to the teacher. Candidates are reminded that the tapes should be submitted at least six months prior to the expiration of their provisional certificated to allow proper time for processing.

Candidates who are prepared for the test should register for the ATS-P through the application in the NYSTCE registration bulletin. The registration form can be completed and mailed at any time during the program year. This section of the exam does not adhere to registration or late registration deadlines.

When the registration form is received, NES will forward an ATS-P procedures manual within three weeks. The manual will provide the requirements and instructions for completion of an acceptable videotape. Other documents are also included, such as the Candidate Identification Form and the Content of Instruction Form.

REQUIREMENTS OF THE ATS-P

The ATS-P is a tool used to assess the teacher's knowledge and application of teaching skills. Several guidelines or objectives have been established in order to assess these skills. These skills are encapsulated in five objectives provided by the ATS framework listed here:

1. Comprehend principles and processes for creating and delivering lessons and implement this knowledge to achieve intended outcomes.

2. Comprehend various instructional methods and use this knowledge in various classroom situations.

3. Comprehend how motivational principles and practices can foster learner achievement and active involvement in learning.

4. Comprehend how to use a number of communication methods to foster student achievement and to create a feeling of trust and support in the classroom.

5. Comprehend how to structure and manage a classroom to foster a secure and productive learning environment.

These objectives should be obvious in the instructional procedures of the teacher. The candidate should also be aware of the goals of the New York State Education Department's *A New Compact for Learning,* which states that the teacher should encourage:

1.   Students who are actively engaged in their learning

2.   An environment in which every learner can succeed

3.   Numerous teaching methods that foster student mastery of desired outcomes

When assessing the videotapes, the teacher's ability to effectively incorporate the objectives and goals into a lesson will be expected. The candidates should show instructional strategies which promote learners to achieve. In order to view these situations, the videotape must include a minimum of ten minutes of non-whole-group instruction.

Non-whole-group instruction includes such activities as cooperative learning, small group problem solving and presentations, individual assignments, team-learning activities, and original student ideas. These activities will be used to reinforce the presented material. The environment created will support the active learning of the students. Students must be visible and empower themselves.

Videotape Requirements

Before a candidate starts the tape, he or she should be familiar with the objectives presented by the NYSTCE which were presented earlier. These objectives are the basis of the scoring of the tape.

The ATS-P requires that its procedures and guidelines be followed exactly as prescribed. If any procedure or guideline is not completed to the satisfaction of the ATS-P, the videotape will be considered "unscorable." If a tape is received "unscorable," the candidate will need to re-register and submit a new tape.

The following directions deal with the tape and camera set-up before actual filming begins. First, according to the ATS-P requirements, the tape must contain at least 20 minutes of recorded teaching, but not exceed 30 minutes in length. A tape shorter than twenty minutes will be rated "unscorable." A tape longer than thirty minutes will only have the first thirty minutes scored. All teaching which occurs after the thirty minute period will not be rated. Be sure that when the recording is being made that all teaching begins when the tape begins.

Second, the candidate must choose a class which is representative of his or her certification area. The teaching assignment should be public or nonpublic school PreK through 12 and must be the teacher's regular assignment. It must be a class in which the candidate has applied for permanent certification.

Third, of the 20–30 minutes which are videotaped, at least 10 minutes must represent non-whole group instruction. This includes instructional activities which are for the individual student, team learning, cooperative learning, student presentations, and problem solving.

Fourth, the tape must be a standard, half-inch VHS videotape. The tape must be provided by the candidate and it is recommended that a new tape be used for clarity and accuracy of recording. The scoring will begin at the start of the recorded video.

Fifth, equipment used to make the recording must be provided by the candidate. This can be obtained through the school at which the candidate teaches or the candidate must make necessary arrangements. The recording may only be taken by one VHS recording camera. No extra or additional recording microphones or cameras may be used. The camera should be set on the Standard Play (SP) setting for recording and an AC power source should be used to ensure the quality of the recording.

Sixth, the camera should be set on a camera tripod to ensure the stability of the camera. This will help to ensure the visibility of the recording.

Seventh, at no time should the recording stop. The recording can not be edited. Any breaks or stops in the recording will render the tape "unscorable."

Camera Setup

Before setting up the camera, the candidate should decide if the tape will be self-recorded or camera-operator recorded. A self-recorded video will be set up in a fixed location of the classroom on the tripod. It is recommended that the camera lens be positioned away from windows to ensure proper exposure. The fixed location of the camera will record only the teaching which occurs in the view of the lens. Also, only student activities which are in the field of view will be recorded. However, the microphone will record activities and students' verbal responses in the entire classroom.

With camera-operator recorded videotape, the candidate must have another teacher, teaching intern, a paraprofessional, a student, or member of the staff operate the camera. As in self-recording, the camera must be positioned on a tripod in a fixed location in the classroom. The operator may move the camera lens horizontally and vertically as the lesson evolves. The operator may also use the camera lens to zoom in or out to best record the instructional activities. A camera operator enables the teacher to move about the classroom and record student reaction to the teaching activity. Be aware that at no time may the camera operator stop the recording, not even by accident. All recording must be continual for thirty minutes. If not, the tape will be considered "unscorable."

When setting up the video camera for the recording session the best results will be obtained if the lens is directed away from the windows or any other sources of light. The following paragraphs deal with various positions in which the camera can be positioned. Please consider these possibilities prior to recording the intended lesson.

If the candidate is using a self-recorded videotape, the camera will be set up in a fixed position. The setup should be positioned for the best possible recording of the planned instruction. It may be necessary to make several practice recordings before an accurate recording is produced. The practice recordings will enable the candidate to record the field of view that enhances the instruction and the reaction of the students. The candidate may wish to consider the suggestions below for a fixed camera arrangement.

For a self recording camera arrangement, the candidate may choose to set up the camera in the rear of the classroom with the lens positioned away from the windows. The teacher in front of the classroom should be the center of focus with several students visible. (Fig. 1)

Video Camera Arrangements: Self-recording setup for whole-group instruction

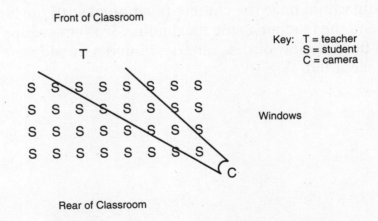

Figure 1. Rear View

A recording may also be set up with the camera arranged for a front view. The camera is set up in the front of the classroom with the lens facing away from the windows. The teacher and several students will be viewed with facial shots. If the classroom seating is arranged in group settings or clusters, a camera's field of view will focus on the teacher and one or more groups of students. These recording arrangements will be beneficial for whole-group instruction. (Fig. 2)

Video Camera Arrangements: Self-recording set up for whole-group instruction

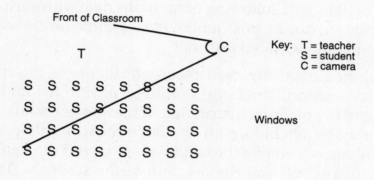

Figure 2. Front View

If the candidate chooses a self-recorded submission, the following positions may be useful for non-whole-group instruction. Position the camera so that the teacher is the focus of attention while the students are in groups. The groups will rotate through the field of view while the teacher monitors the non-whole-group activities. Another alternative for non-whole-group recording would have the camera positioned with the lens away from the windows and the teacher as the focal point. Student groups would be set up within the field of view of the camera. Students outside the field of view would not be recorded. (Fig. 3)

Self-recording setup for non-whole-group instruction

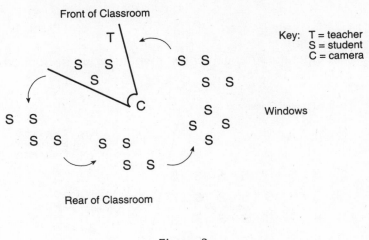

Figure 3a

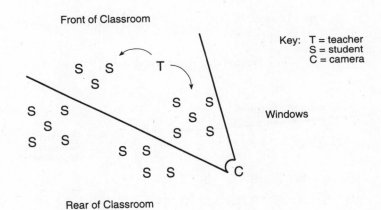

Figure 3b. Groups move through field of view

Candidates who choose to use the camera-operator recording may consider one of the following suggestions. The position of recording will be from a fixed position but the camera-operator may move horizontally or vertically around the classroom. The position of the camera should best represent the instruction of the classroom.

The position of the camera for whole-group instruction with a camera operator may be a rear-view camera position in which the operator can pan the field of view and record the teacher and students. Be sure that the lens is positioned away from the windows for the best recording. The candidate may choose to have a front-view camera position, which will enable the camera operator to record from a fixed location and pan the instruction from side to side. This position would record facial shots of the teacher and students. (Fig. 4)

Camera Operator arrangements for whole-group instruction.

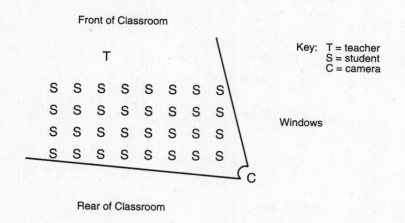

Figure 4a. Rear View

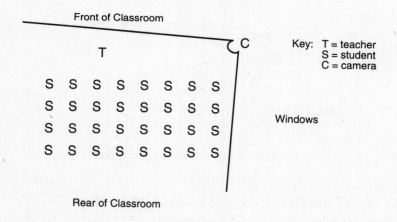

Figure 4b. Front View

When the candidate is recording non-whole-group instruction the camera operator arrangement may be located in the center of the classroom. The students would be set up in small groups around the classroom. The camera operator would pan around the groups as the teacher moves among groups monitoring the students' progress. The camera may also be positioned in the corner of the classroom. The students would be organized in small groups and the camera operator would pan to each group. Groups closer to the lens would appear clearer than other groups. With this setup the teacher would be viewed at all times monitoring the progress of the lesson. (Fig. 5)

Camera Operator non-whole-group arrangement.

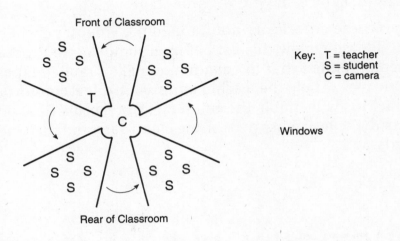

Figure 5a. Central Camera Position

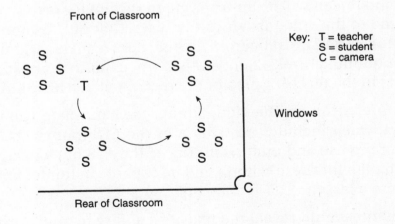

Figure 5b. Corner Camera Position

When positioning the camera it is recommended that the candidate choose the field of view which best records the instruction of the students.

Practice tapes are encouraged so that the candidate may present the best recording for a rating.

In addition to the submission of the videotape, the candidate is reminded to submit the documents sent with the manual. The candidate must complete the Context of Instruction Form. This form will assist the scorers in rating the video. If the form is not completed or if information is incorrect the video will be "unscorable." The Candidate Identification Form needs to be completed by the candidate and a certified teacher. The completed form and signatures must be sent with the videotape.

If any of these criteria are not fulfilled the videotape will be returned "unscorable." Please review this list before attempting to produce a videotape. It is recommended that the candidate make practice tapes of several lessons. Practicing will help the teacher and students feel comfortable in front of the camera. This will enable the candidate to record a final performance which reflects the true atmosphere of the classroom and the true responses of the students.

INSTRUCTIONAL PREPARATION

Once the candidate registers for the ATS-P, he or she is ready to select which class and lesson will be appropriate to submit for review. The subject, date, and time of the video is left to the discretion of the candidate. However, the class selected must be from the teachers regular assignment within a public or nonpublic PreK-12 class. Also, the candidate must videotape a class which is in the teaching area of the requested certification.

When preparing for the videotaping, the candidate should carefully plan a lesson which includes all criteria of the ATS framework. The lesson should reflect the use and understanding of the ATS objectives. The candidate needs to plan for these criteria and be capable of implementing the requirement into a lesson.

The lesson should reveal the teacher's ability to apply principles and procedures for an organized classroom. The procedures used by the teacher should help the learners utilize the presented material and achieve the desired outcome. In order to accommodate all students' learning levels and abilities, the teacher should incorporate a variety of learning techniques. Some of these learning techniques could require visual aides, audio aides, hands-on learning or learning from other students. The teachers must show flexibility and knowledge of various teaching strategies.

A candidate will be successful when the lesson plan can clearly provide the observation of the appropriate level for assessment. A successful teacher will incorporate both whole group and non-whole-group learning. This needs to be accomplished within the time provided. Remember that the ATS-P requires 20-30 minutes of taped instruction, ten minutes of which must be non-whole group.

Non-whole-group instructions would be those outlined by the teacher which the students would follow in small-group activities, individual projects, cooperative learning, peer learning, group discussions, group teaching, presentations, or problem solving activities. It is recommended that these activities be presented in previous lessons so that the students are comfortable with responsibilities such situations require. The students are given the material and framework in which to learn, and it is their responsibility to actively achieve. The teacher remains essential to the lesson by observing groups, offering suggestions, rotating through groups and monitoring activities.

Whole group instruction will involve the remaining time required by the ATS-P outline. This instruction involves the activities and objectives of the teacher being presented to a large group or the entire class. The teacher provides the instructional material and monitors the intended outcome of the activities. The teacher must continually monitor the entire class in order to assess the lesson. An effective teacher will provide a lesson which actively involves the entire class.

When preparing the lesson for submission the candidate is reminded that the ATS-P is an evaluation of his or her ability to teach successfully. Therefore, the candidate should be the primary instructor shown on the video. If you are team teaching, make sure the lesson involves the candidate because recording with others may not meet ATS-P requirements. Limit the use of instructional media such as slides or films. This may not meet the instructional level of the ATS-P. When using instructional media, video, tape recording, or overheads, ensure that the material is being recorded on the videotape. Do not let the use of such devices take away from learning time. Such materials should be set-up prior to recording. Time not spent on instruction may not be acceptable by the ATS-P. Remember, only the first thirty minutes of the tape will be reviewed and scored. If most of this time is wasted setting up equipment, it will lower the candidate's rating. Prepare all lessons and materials before videotaping.

MAKING THE RECORDING

Once the video camera is positioned the taping may begin. The candidate should start taping and immediately begin the lesson. Remember that only the first thirty minutes of the tape will be scored. It would be advisable to have another person set the timer or have the video operator record the time being recorded. This will ensure that a minimum of twenty minutes and a maximum of thirty minutes is recorded.

The quality of the recording will be enhanced if the candidate speaks clearly and conveys instructions and objectives to the class in an organized manner. It is recommended that practice lessons be videotaped. This will help the class and teacher remain comfortable with the notion of being recorded. Actions and responses will appear more natural and the atmosphere will be beneficial to the learning process.

When the focus of instruction goes from whole group to non-whole group or from non-whole group to whole group it is important that the transition is smooth. When working with small groups it may be necessary to position the camera in order to record the lesson or activities. If this is required, the candidate should do so in a manner that is as smooth as possible. Remember, at no time during taping can the video camera be stopped. If the recording is stopped or edited the submission will be considered "unscorable." The candidate will then need to reapply and submit another videotape.

When the lesson has included at least twenty minutes of teaching with the required ten minutes of non-whole group instruction, the videotaping should stop. Only the first thirty minutes of the tape will be viewed. Any material or instruction which occurs after the first thirty minutes will not be scored. If the tape contains less than twenty minutes of instruction, the videotape will be considered "unscorable."

Review of the Recording

Upon completion of the videotaping session, the candidate should view the entire recording using the proper equipment to verify that the submission is accurate. Check for clarity of picture and audio, field of view, and accurate timing of the instructional period. Be certain that the first twenty minutes of the tape include the required instructional material. The tape will be ready for submission if no technical problems have occurred.

After the candidate reviews the recorded lesson it is suggested that the recording be shown to another certified teacher. This will enable the candidate to receive professional feedback and an assessment of the instruction presented. The feedback will assist the candidate in preparation of another video, highlight the positive aspects of the candidate's teaching, and provide a source of instruction or criticism. In addition to the video, show the Context of Instruction Form to a certified teacher. The feedback received on this information will also be beneficial.

After one or more certified teachers have reviewed the videotape, the candidate can decide if the prepared tape is acceptable for submission. If necessary, now is the time to start planning for a new recording. Use the information provided by your associates and your own reaction to the recording.

When you decide that the recorded lesson is acceptable for submission, remove the record-prevention tab located on the spine of the video. The removal of these tabs will prevent the tape from being recorded over. If the you desire, a copy of the tape may be made for your own use. The submitted tape will not be returned to you.

Before mailing the tape, rewind it completely. The Context of Instruction Form must be completed accurately. This form will assist the scorer of the video. The card will not be scored but is essential to submission of the video. Do not include any addition forms or information when submitting the videotape.

The Candidate Identification Form must also include accurate information. This form certifies that the candidate presented on the video is indeed the candidate requesting permanent certification. This also verifies that the class which is being instructed is part of your regular assignment. The form contains a Witness Confirmation of Candidate Identity section, which must be completed by a certified teacher in your school district. The witness's signature confirms that he or she is a certified teacher in New York State, has viewed a segment of the videotaped instruction and that the video and form identify the candidate accurately.

Instructions are provided by the ATS-P test administrators for proper mailing of the video. If all materials are accurate and completed properly once received, the candidate will receive a receipt for the materials. A date will be included for the approximate time of scoring. A score report is usually received within four months of submission of the appropriate materials.

If the video is submitted after June 30 of the program year, the candidate will receive additional procedures to complete. These procedures will not include any additional fees. The video will need to fulfill requirement and policies for the new program year.

SCORING THE RECORDING

This section will provide an overview of how the submitted videotape will be scored by the ATS-P. Once the candidate submits the video, the ATS-P will have the video independently evaluated. The tape will be viewed by at least two teachers with permanent certification in New York State. The scoring will be based on the five Instructional Delivery objectives of the Assessment of Teaching Skills. The score will be an overall judgement of teaching skills. The score will not reflect the quality of the recording. It will be based on the quality of the teaching performance and instructional integrity. The ATS-P has provided a description of the ratings; however, each candidate may not reflect the total description provided. Candidates may receive a "pass," "not pass," "U," or a "B."

To receive a "Pass," the candidate must demonstrate teaching skills which achieve the required level of the ATS Instructional Delivery objectives. The candidate will demonstrate, with a visual performance, a learning environment and atmosphere in which all students are encouraged to succeed. The lesson will be organized and managed in a manner which shows the candidates understanding and implementation of principles and procedures. The candidate will lead learners to develop meaning and produce intended outcomes from the material presented. Communication and teaching techniques will be clear and explained in a variety of strategies. The lesson will be presented in a motivational style which will encourage students to question and become active learners. The lesson will be effective if the learners are provided adequate opportunity to succeed. Positive reinforcement and stimulation should be varied to reach all students. A standard of behavior should be established and maintained during the lesson.

If a candidate should receive a score of "Not Pass," the candidate has not reached a level acceptable to the ATS Instructional Delivery objectives. The submitted lesson reveals that the candidate does not understand and has not implemented the principles and procedures which enable students to achieve, the atmosphere and established behaviors of the classroom do not stimulate the students. A climate of trust and learning has not been maintained or established. The candidate does not utilize motivational techniques and does not provide positive reinforcement for the students. This is reflected by the students not questioning or becoming active learners in the lesson. Communication techniques and teaching strategies are not varied and the teacher does not encourage student involvement. As a result, the environment of the classroom is not conducive to learning.

A rating of "U" means the candidate submitted a video which is "unscorable." An "unscorable" submission is one which does not meet the proper requirements of the ATS. This would include providing a videotaping which does not exceed twenty minutes of instructional information, or submitting a tape which can not be rated because of poor recording quality. If a candidate's videotape is "unscorable," the candidate must obtain another registration bulletin and reapply for the ATS-P. Upon receipt of a new registration application, the candidate should follow the procedures as described in the Procedure Manual provided by the New York State Education Department.

If the candidate receives a rating of "B," the ATS has received a blank videotape. A blank videotape contains no visual image or audio track. The candidate will need to reregister for the ATS-P and submit a new registration fee and video. Once the candidate reapplies and receives a new Procedure Manual, the candidate should follow all procedures as described by the NYSED.

The candidate who prepares properly for the ATS-P will complete a successful video. In order to accomplish this goal, incorporate teaching techniques, discipline techniques, motivational strategies, and a variety of learning activities into everyday instructional procedures. Good luck with the ATS-P!

LAST/A~~TSW~~

LAST PRACTICE TEST

> This test is also on CD-ROM in our interactive TEST*ware*® for the NYSTCE. We strongly recommend that you first take this exam on computer. You will then have the benefits of enforced time conditions, individual diagnostic analysis, and instant scoring.
>
> See page 3 for guidance on how to get the most out of our NYSTCE book and software.

LAST PRACTICE TEST

Time: 4 Hours

80 Multiple-Choice Questions, 1 Essay

SECTION 1

DIRECTIONS: Each of the following questions is accompanied by four answer choices. Select the choice which best answers each question.

1. The floor of a rectangular room is to be covered in two different types of material. The total cost of covering the entire room is $136.00. The cost of covering the inner rectangle is $80.00. The cost of covering the shaded area is $56.00.

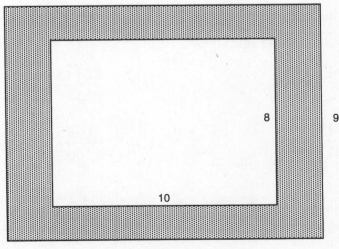

We wish to determine the cost of material per square foot used to cover the shaded area. What information given below is unnecessary for this computation?

I. The total cost of covering the entire room.

II. The cost of covering the inner rectangle

III. The cost of covering the shaded area.

(A) I only   (C) I and II

(B) II only   (D) I and III

2. The distribution of a high school chorus is depicted in the graph below. There is a total of 132 students in the chorus.

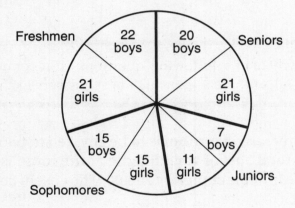

Which of the following expressions represents the percentage of freshman and sophomore girls in the chorus?

(A) $\dfrac{21+15}{132} \times 100$ (C) $\dfrac{21+15}{132}$

(B) $\dfrac{21+15}{132} \div 100$ (D) $\dfrac{21+15}{100} \times 132$

3. Examine the elementary school student's work below. Analyze what the error pattern is that the student is making. If the student worked the problem 88 plus 39, what incorrect answer would the student give (assuming the use of the error pattern exhibited below)?

$$
\begin{array}{r} 74 \\ + \ 56 \\ \hline 1{,}210 \end{array}
\qquad
\begin{array}{r} 35 \\ + \ 92 \\ \hline 127 \end{array}
\qquad
\begin{array}{r} 67 \\ + \ 18 \\ \hline 715 \end{array}
\qquad
\begin{array}{r} 56 \\ + \ 97 \\ \hline 1{,}413 \end{array}
$$

(A)   127

(B)   131

(C)   51

(D)   1,117

4. The needle on the dial points most nearly to which reading?

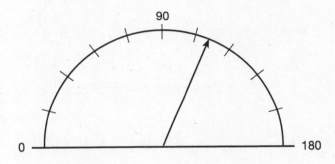

(A)   108

(B)   128

(C)   114

(D)   117

5. How many ten thousands are there in one million?

(A) 100

(B) 10

(C)   1,000

(D)   10,000

6. An owner of twin Siamese cats knows the following data:

    I.   Cost of a can of cat food

    II.   Volume of a can of cat food

    III. Number of cans of cat food eaten each day by one cat

    IV.   The weight of the cat food in one can

Which of the data above can be used to determine the cost of cat food for 7 days for the 2 cats?

(A)   I and II only.

(C)   I and IV only.

(B)   I and III only.

(D)   III and IV only.

7.   The diagram below shows a path for electric flow. As the electrically charged particle flow moves through one complete circuit, it would NOT have to go through

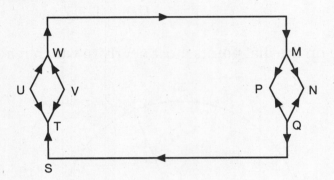

(A)   V to get to W.

(C)   Q to get to T.

(B)   W to get to M.

(D)   T to get to S.

Questions 8–17 refer to the following passage.

Cold is a negative condition, and depends on the absence, or privation, of heat. Intense artificial cold may be produced by the rapid absorption of heat during the conversion of solids into liquids. Dr. Black long since discovered the principle, that when bodies pass from a denser to a rarer state, heat is absorbed and becomes latent in the body so transformed, and consequently cold is produced. And also that when bodies pass from a rarer to a denser state, their latent heat is evolved, and becomes sensible.

It is known to almost everyone, that dissolving common salt in water, particularly if the salt is fine, will render the water so cold, even in summer, as to be painful to the hand. The salt, as it passes from the solid to the liquid state, absorbs caloric from the water, and thus the heat that was before sensible, becomes latent, and cold is produced.

On the contrary, when a piece of lead, or iron, is beaten smartly with a hammer, it becomes hot, because the metal, in consequence of the hammering, has its capacity for caloric reduced, and thus the heat which was before latent, now becomes sensible. For the same reason, when air is compressed forcibly in a tube, or as it is sometimes called, in a *fire-pump*, the heat, which was before latent, becomes sensible, because the condensation lessens its capacity for caloric.

The principle on which all freezing mixtures act is therefore the change of state which one or more of the articles employed undergo, during the process, and this change consists in an enlarged capacity for caloric. The degree of cold will then depend on the quantity of caloric which passes from a free to a latent state, and this again will depend on the quantity of substance liquefied, and the rapidity of the liquefaction.

The substances most commonly employed for this purpose are those originally used by Fahrenheit, to produce the zero of his thermometric scale; viz. common salt and snow, or pounded ice. For this purpose the salt should be fine, and the ice, which must always be used in summer, is to be reduced to small particles in a cold mortar.

The vessel to contain the substance to be frozen may be made of tin. It is simply a tall vessel, holding a few pints, with a close cover, and a rim round the top, for the convenience of handling it. For common purposes, this may be set into any convenient wooden vessel (having first introduced the substance to be frozen) and then surrounded by the freezing mixture. The only care to be taken in this part of the process is to see that the freezing mixture in the outside vessel reaches as high as the contents of the internal one. With two or three pounds of fine common salt, and double this weight of pounded ice, three or four pints of iced cream may be made in this way, during the warmest days of summer. The process requires two or three hours, and while it is going on, the vessel should be set in a cellar, or covered with a flannel cloth, as a bad conductor of the external heat.

From J.L. Comstack, "Elements of Chemistry"

8. After reading the above passage, the reader could correctly infer that dissolving sugar in hot tea will

    (A) lower the temperature of the hot tea.

    (B) cause the temperature of the tea to become even warmer just as beating a piece of lead with a hammer will raise its temperature.

    (C) lower the temperature of hot tea so that if it were placed about cream in a tin container, the cream would freeze within two to three hours.

    (D) reduce the temperature of the hot tea to such a low temperature as to be painful to the hand.

9. The drop in temperature which occurs when sugar is added to coffee is the result of

    I. sugar passing from a solid to a liquid state.

    II. sugar absorbing caloric from the water.

    III. heat becoming latent when it was sensible.

    (A) I only.   (C) I, II, and III.

    (B) I and II.   (D) I and III.

10. Which is the best example of Dr. Black's discovery as outlined in the article?

    (A) To gargle with warm salt water, one should start with water cooler than one desires and then add the salt.

    (B) To gargle in warm salt water, one should start with salt and then pour water which is cooler than that desired over the salt.

    (C) To gargle in warm salt water, one should adjust the temperature of the tap water to the temperature desired and then add fine salt; the fineness of the salt will prevent any change in the water temperature.

    (D) To gargle in warm salt water, one should start with water warmer than desired and then add the salt.

11. The narrator seems to base this article on

    (A)   a sociological study.

    (B)   trial-and-error methods.

    (C)   scientific procedures.

    (D)   historical research.

12. The word "mortar" (Paragraph 5) as used in this article can be best interpreted to mean

    (A)   that which can fix or hold together, as mortar holds bricks.

    (B)   a weapon, a piece of artillery, or a small cannon.

    (C)   a container used for grinding or mixing.

    (D)   a mixture.

13. The writer does not make use of

    (A)   descriptions.   (C)   mathematics.

    (B)   interviews.   (D)   experiments.

14. In pumping up a basketball, one can infer from this article that the metal needle going into the ball

    (A)   will become warm.

    (B)   will not be affected by the process since metal is strong.

    (C)   will become cooler.

    (D)   will quickly reach a freezing temperature.

15. The writer can be best described as

    (A)   concerned with literary form and stylistic devices.

    (B)   subjective in his writing.

    (C)   objective.

(D)   presenting facts which are new to most scientists in the twenty-first century.

16.   A positive condition depending on the absence of cold is

(A)   Fahrenheit.

(B)   intense artificial cold.

(C)   heat.

(D)   a rarer state, according to Black.

17.   Black found that when bodies pass from a rarer to a denser state, their latent heat is evolved and becomes sensible. "Sensible" can be interpreted to mean

(A)   knowledgeable, making sense.

(B)   logical.

(C)   evolving.

(D)   perceptible.

Questions 18–27 refer to the following passage.

Though it is generally recognized from philosophic investigations extending over many years that heat is one manifestation of energy capable of being transformed into other forms such as mechanical work, electricity, or molecular arrangement, and derivable from them through transformations, measurements of quantities of heat can be made without such knowledge, and were made even when heat was regarded as a substance. It was early recognized that equivalence of heat effects proved effects proportional to quantity; thus, the melting of one pound of ice can cool a pound of hot water through a definite range of temperature, and can cool two pounds through half as many degrees, and so on. The condensation of a pound of steam can warm a definite weight of water a definite number of degrees, or perform a certain number of pound-degrees heating effect in water. So that taking the pound-degree of water as a basis the ratio of the heat liberated by steam condensation to that absorbed by ice melting can be found. Other substances such as iron or oil may suffer a certain number of pound-degree changes and affect water by another number of pound-degrees. The unit of heat quantity might be taken as that which is liberated by the condensation of a pound of steam, that absorbed by the freezing of a pound of water, that to raise a pound of iron any number of degrees or any other quantity of heat effect. The heat unit generally accepted is, in metric measure, the calorie, or the amount to raise one kilogram of pure water one degree centigrade, or the B.T.U., that is necessary to raise one pound of water one degree Fahrenheit.

All the heat measurements are, therefore, made in terms of equivalent water heating effects in pound-degrees, but it must be understood that a water pound-degree is not quite constant. Careful observation will show that the melting of a pound of ice will not cool the same weight of water from 200° F to 180° F, as it will from 60° F to 40° F, which indicates that the heat capacity of water or the B.T.U. per pound-degree is not constant. It is, therefore, necessary to further limit the definition of the heat unit, by fixing on some water temperature and temperature change, as the standard, in addition to the selection of water as the substance, and the pound and degree as units of capacity. Here there has not been as good an agreement as is desirable, some using 4° C = 39.4° F as the standard temperature and the range one-half degree both sides; this is the point of maximum water density. Others have used one degree rise from the freezing point 0° C or 32° F. There are good reasons, however, for the most common present-day practice which will probably become universal, for taking as the range and temperatures, freezing-point to boiling-point and dividing by the number of degrees. The heat unit so defined is properly named the mean calorie or mean British thermal unit; therefore,

Mean calorie = (amount of heat to raise 1 Kg. water from 0° C to 100° C)

Mean B.T.U. = (amount of heat to raise 1 lb. water from 32° F to 212° F)

From Charles Edward Lucke, *"Engineering Thermodynamics"*

18. According to the author, which of the following is NOT true?

(A) Heat is capable of being transformed into mechanical work.

(B) Heat is derivable from molecular arrangement.

(C)   Heat should be regarded as a substance.

(D)   Measurements of quantities of heat can be made without knowledge of heat being derivable from mechanical work, electricity, or molecular arrangement.

19.   The calorie and the B.T.U. are similar in that they both relate to

(A)   one pound of water.

(B)   the amount of heat necessary to raise the temperature one degree.

(C)   the metric system.

(D)   a pound of iron.

20.   The author denies which of the following?

(A)   The equivalence of heat effects proves proportional to quantity.

(B)   The melting of one pound of ice can cool a pound of hot water through a definite range of temperature and can cool two pounds through twice as many degrees.

(C)   The melting of one pound of ice can cool a pound of hot water through a definite range of temperature and can cool two pounds through half as many degrees.

(D)   The condensation of a pound of steam can warm a definite weight of water a definite number of degrees.

21.   The author states that

(A)   a water pound-degree is constant.

(B)   the melting of ice will cool the same weight of water from 60° to 40° Fahrenheit as it will from 200° to 180° Fahrenheit.

(C)   the heat capacity of water or the B.T.U. per pound-degree is constant.

(D)   the heat capacity of water or the B.T.U. per pound-degree is not constant.

22. The author indicates a point of disagreement among scientists; this point of contention is

    (A) whether the melting point of ice will not cool the same amount of water from 200° to 180° Fahrenheit as it will from 60° to 40° Fahrenheit.

    (B) whether the heat capacity of water is constant.

    (C) whether the equivalence of heat effects proved effects proportional to quantity.

    (D) how to best limit the definitions of the heat unit.

23. The author appears to

    (A) be a proponent of the metric system.

    (B) be a proponent of the customary system.

    (C) be an opponent of the use of the mean calorie.

    (D) suggest that there are good reasons for taking the freezing-point to boiling-point as the range.

24. The purpose of the passage is to

    (A) advocate mean calories.

    (B) advocate mean British thermal units (B.T.U.).

    (C) oppose mean calories and B.T.U.

    (D) advocate both mean calories and mean B.T.U.

25. The author predicts

    (A) the universal adoption of the B.T.U.

    (B) the universal adoption of the calorie.

    (C) the universal acceptance of the mean B.T.U. and the mean calorie.

    (D) the demise of the calorie and the universal adoption of the mean B.T.U.

26. The author would like to limit the definition of the heat unit by

    I.   fixing on some water temperature.

    II.   fixing on some temperature change.

    III.   selecting water as the substance.

    IV.   using the pound and degree as the units of capacity.

    (A)   I only.   (C)   IV only.

    (B)   II only.   (D)   I, II, III, and IV.

27. The author's argument for limiting the definition of the heat unit is

    I.   to create an agreement within the scientific community regarding the heat unit.

    II.   to explain the inconsistencies found when melting a pound of ice to cool the same weight of water that has been heated to different temperatures.

    III.   not fully explained in this passage.

    (A)   I only.   (C)   I and II only.

    (B)   II only.   (D)   I, II, and III.

28. Which of the following is the correct chronological order for the events in history listed below?

    I.   Puritans arrive in New England

    II.   Protestant Reformation begins

    III.   Columbus sets sail across the Atlantic

    IV.   Magna Carta is signed in England

    (A)   IV, III, II, I   (C)   III, IV, II, I

    (B)   IV, III, I, II   (D)   III, II, I, IV

29. The intellectual movement which encouraged the use of reason and science and anticipated human progress was called the

    (A) American System.   (C) Enlightenment.

    (B) mercantilism.   (D) age of belief.

30. In American government, "checks and balances" were developed to

    (A) regulate the amount of control each branch of government would have.

    (B) make each branch of government independent from one another.

    (C) give the president control.

    (D) give the Supreme Court control.

31. Which of the following groups did not play a role in the settlement of the English colonies in America?

    (A) Roman Catholics   (C) Mormons

    (B) Puritans   (D) Quakers

32. On the map below, which letter represents the Philippines?

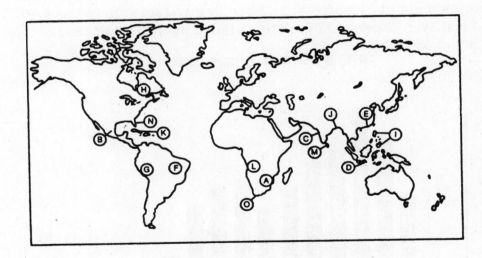

    (A) K   (C) I

    (B) D   (D) M

33. The Bill of Rights

(A) listed the grievances of the colonists against the British.

(B) forbade the federal government from encroaching on the rights of citizens.

(C) gave all white males the right to vote.

(D) specified the rights of slaves.

Questions 34–37 refer to the following passage.

Economic Effects of the Depression

During the early months of the depression most people thought it was just an adjustment in the business cycle which would soon be over. Hoover repeatedly assured the public that prosperity was just around the corner. As time went on, the worst depression in American history set in, reaching its bottom point in early 1932. The gross national product fell from $104.6 billion in 1929 to $56.1 billion in 1933. Unemployment reached about 13 million in 1933, or about 25 percent of the labor force excluding farmers. National income dropped 54 percent from $87.8 billion to $40.2 billion. Labor income fell about 41 percent, while farm income dropped 55 percent from $11.9 billion to $5.3 billion. Industrial production dropped about 51 percent. The banking system suffered as 5,761 banks, over 22 percent of the total, failed by the end of 1932.

UNEMPLOYMENT, 1929–1945

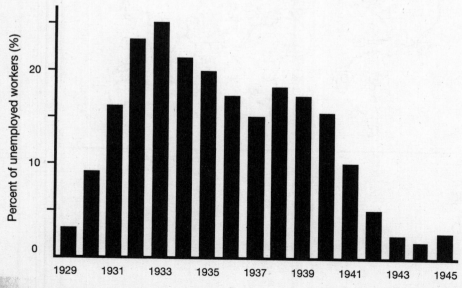

As the depression grew worse, more and more people lost their jobs or had their wages reduced. Many were unable to continue credit payments on homes, automobiles, and other possessions, and lost them. Families doubled up in houses and apartments. Both the marriage rate and the birth rate declined as people put off family formation. Hundreds of thousands became homeless and lived in groups of makeshift shacks called Hoovervilles in empty spaces around cities. Others traveled the country by foot and box-car seeking food and work. State and local government agencies and private charities were overwhelmed in their attempts to care for those in need, although public and private soup kitchens and soup lines were set up throughout the nation. Malnutrition was widespread but few died of starvation, perhaps because malnourished people are susceptible to many fatal diseases.

34. The author's purpose for writing this passage was probably

   (A)   to degrade Hoover's presidency.

   (B)   to track the gross national product.

   (C)   to link Depression statistics to their effects in everyday life.

   (D)   to monitor the effects of the banking system.

35. Which of the following best explains the meaning of the last sentence?

   (A)   Many diseases can make people immune to starvation.

   (B)   Many diseases cause malnutrition.

   (C)   Few malnourished people survived diseases long enough to starve.

   (D)   Few died from the effects of malnutrition.

36. According to the bar graph, the unemployment rate was highest in

   (A)   1929.   (C)   1938.

   (B)   1933.   (D)   1944.

37. According to the graph, the unemployment rate was lowest in

(A) 1929.

(C) 1938.

(B) 1933.

(D) 1944.

38. According to the graph "Households by Income Class" below, which one of the following statements is true?

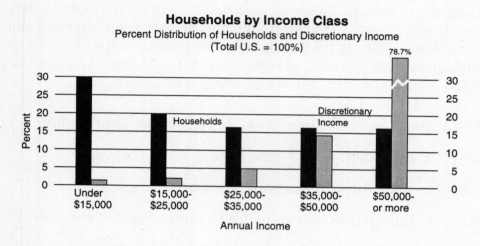

Households by Income Class
Percent Distribution of Households and Discretionary Income
(Total U.S. = 100%)

(A) About 50% of households had under $15,000

(B) Almost 75% of households had $50,000 or more

(C) About 78% of households had $50,000 or more

(D) About 20% of households had between $15,000 and $25,000 annual income

39. According to the graph, "Age of Household Head," which one of the following statements is true?

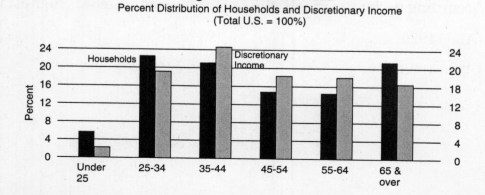

Age of Household Head
Percent Distribution of Households and Discretionary Income
(Total U.S. = 100%)

(A)   Middle age households tend to have greater discretionary income

(B)   The youngest have the most discretionary income

(C)   The oldest have the most discretionary income

(D)   The older one gets, the least discretionary income one has

40.   According to the graph, "Households by Number of Persons," which one of the following is true?

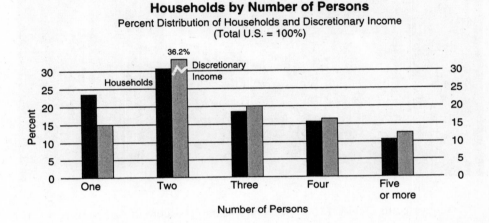

Households by Number of Persons
Percent Distribution of Households and Discretionary Income
(Total U.S. = 100%)

(A)   The larger the number of persons, the greater the percent of discretionary income available

(B)   The smaller the size of the household, the greater the amount of discretionary income available

(C)   Two-person households have the least discretionary income

(D)   None of the above.

41.   Who is the central focus in the picture below and why?

Jacques-Louis David. 1789. The Metropolitan Museum of Art, New York

(A)   The man on the left, with his hands and face pressed against the wall, because he is separate and thus draws attention.

(B)   The man sitting at the foot of the bed, because he is at the lowest elevation.

(C)   The man standing beside the bed, because he is standing alone.

(D)   The man sitting on the bed, because the other men are focused on him.

42.   All of the following can be construed from the print below EXCEPT

Tomb of Nakht, Thebes.

(A)   the three figures portrayed are musicians.

(B)   the art work conveys a strong sense of depth.

(C)   the drawing is representative of Egyptian tomb paintings.

(D)   the artist was not concerned with modeling the figures in three dimensions.

Questions 43–45 refer to the following passage.

It was the best of times, it was the worst of times, it was the age of wisdom, it was the age of foolishness, it was the epoch of belief, it was the epoch of incredulity, it was the season of Light, it was the season of Darkness, it was the spring of hope, it was the winter of despair, we had everything before us, we had nothing before us, we were all going direct to Heaven, we were all going direct the other way—in short, the period was so far like the present period, that some of its noisiest authorities insisted on its being received, for good or for evil, in the superlative degree of comparison only.

There were a king with a large jaw, and a queen with a plain face, on the throne of England; there were a king with a large jaw, and a queen with a fair face, on the throne of France. In both countries it was clearer than crystal to the lords of the State preserves of loaves and fishes, that things in general were settled for ever.

43. The vast comparisons in the above passage indicate that the speaker is describing

   (A)   a placid historical time period.

   (B)   a time of extreme political upheaval.

   (C)   a public event.

   (D)   a time when anything was possible.

44. The last sentence of the passage

   (A)   mocks the self-assuredness of the governments of England and France.

   (B)   comments on the horrible poverty of the two nations.

   (C)   most likely foreshadows an upcoming famine or drought.

   (D)   attacks the two governments for neglecting the poor, hungry masses.

45. The phrase, "some of its noisiest authorities insisted on its being received, for good or for evil, in the superlative degree of comparison only"

   (A)   mocks the arrogance of the governments.

   (B)   mocks the arrogance of the people.

   (C)   compares the attitude of the people to the attitude of the governments.

   (D)   Both (A) and (B).

46. In the example pictured below, which of the following contributes most to an effect of stability and changeless grandeur?

Pylon Temple of Horus, Edfu

(A) The strong horizontal thrust of the architecture

(B) The wealth of elaborate ornamental detail

(C) The vast open courtyard with its surrounding columns

(D) The simplified geometry of the massive forms and the sloping diagonal walls

47. Which of the following seems most true of the sculpture pictured below?

Gianlorenzo Bernini. *David*. 1623.
Galleria Borghese, Rome

(A) The statue is conceived as a decorative work without a narrative function.

(B) The figure seems to be static, passive, and introverted.

(C) The figure is depicted as though frozen in a moment of action.

(D) The figure's garments indicate that he is a soldier or warrior.

48. In the lines below, what does the stage direction "(*Aside*)" mean?

King: Take thy fair hour, Laertes; time be thine,
        And thy best graces spend it at thy will!
        But now, my cousin Hamlet, and my son,—
Hamlet: (*Aside*) A little more than kin, and less than kind.

(A) The actor steps aside to make room for other action on stage.

(B) The actor directly addresses only one particular actor on stage.

(C) The actor directly addresses the audience, while out of hearing of the other actors.

(D) The previous speaker steps aside to make room for this actor.

49. Which of the following is the most important artistic device in the example shown below?

Tawaraya Sotatsu and Hon-Ami Koetsu. *Deer Scroll.*
Early Edo Period. Seattle Art Museum, Seattle

(A) Line   (C) Color

(B) Tone   (D) Volume

50. Which of the following best describes the example pictured below?

Portait of a Roman. c. 80 B.C.E. Palazzo Torlonia, Rome

(A) The subject appears to be poetic, dreamy, and aristocratic.

(B) The sculptor was not concerned with descriptive detail.

(C) The hard material counteracts the effect desired by the sculptor.

(D) The sculpture appears to be hard-bitten, pragmatic, and realistic.

Questions 51–53 refer to the following short passages.

(A)   Once upon a time and a very good time it was there was a moocow coming down along the road and this moocow that was coming down along the met a nicens little boy named baby tuckoo…

(B)   And thus have these naked Nantucketers, these sea hermits, issuing from their ant-hill in the sea, overrun and conquered the watery world like so many Alexanders…

(C)   A large rose tree stood near the entrance of the garden: the roses growing on it were white, but there were three gardeners at it, busily painting them red. Alice thought this a very curious thing, and she went nearer to watch them, and, just as she came up to them, she heard one of them say "Look out now, Five!"

(D)   Emma was not required, by any subsequent discovery, to retract her ill opinion of Mrs. Elton. Her observation had been pretty correct. Such as Mrs. Elton appeared to her on this second interview, such she appeared whenever they met again: self-important, presuming, familiar, ignorant, and ill-bred. She had a little beauty and a little accomplishment, but so little judgement that she thought herself coming with superior knowledge of the world, to enliven and improve a country neighborhood…

51.   Which passage makes use of allusion?

52.   Which passage employs a distinct voice to imitate the speech of a character?

53.   Which passage is most likely taken from a nineteenth-century novel of manners?

54. Which of the following best characterizes the artist's approach in this picture?

Georges Seurat. *A Sunday on La Grand Jatte – 1884*.
1884–1886. The Art Institute of Chicago

(A) Spontaneous and impulsive

(B) Emotionally tormented

(C) Detached and systematic

(D) Passionate and intense

55. In the example pictured below, the four slender columns at the front of the arch do all of the following EXCEPT

Arch of Constantine, Rome

(A) lead the eye from ground level to the upper story.

(B) establish a rhythm across the facade of the arch.

(C) provide structural support for the upper story of the arch.

(D) help to divide the elaborate facade into regular units.

56.   (The veranda of the Voynitzevs' country house. It looks out onto a sunlit garden, with the tall trees of the forest beyond, bisected by a grassy walk.

The whoosh of a rocket taking off. The lights come up to reveal YAKOV in the garden with a large box of assorted fireworks in his arms. Beside him stands DR. TRILETZKY, a match in his hand. They are gazing up into the sky—DR. TRILETZKY with delight, YAKOV with apprehension. There is a smell of sulfur in the air. The rocket bursts, off.)

The above passage is most likely taken from

(A) a Victorian novel.

(B) the stage directions of a play.

(C) the critical notes to a literary work.

(D) the rough draft of a literary work.

57. Which of the following is an important feature of the building pictured below?

Eero Saarinen. Interior of Trans World Airlines Terminal.
John F. Kennedy International Airport, New York

(A)   A dependence on rectilinear lines and angles

(B)   An emphasis on the structural framework of the building

(C)   A traditional interplay of large and small geometric shapes

(D)   The use of curvilinear forms to suggest organic growth or motion

Questions 58–59 refer to the following passage.

Come, now, there may as well be an end of this! Every time I meet your eyes squarely I detect the question just slipping out of them. If you had spoken it, or even boldly looked it; if you had shown in your motions the least sign of a fussy or fidgety concern on my account; if this were not the evening of my birthday and you the only friend who remembered it; if confession were not good for the soul, though harder than sin to some people, of whom I am one,— well, if all reasons were not at this instant converged into a focus, and burning me rather violently in that region where the seat of emotion is supposed to lie, I should keep my trouble to myself.

Bayaro Taylor, Beauty and the Beast, Tales from Home (1872)

58.   The speaker of the above passage feels

(A)   angry.   (C)   ashamed.

(B)   anxious.   (D)   sorrowful.

59.   The speaker feels that confession is

(A)   unnecessary.   (C)   healthy.

(B)   nonsensical.   (D)   impossible.

60. In combining found objects to make the sculpture shown below, the artist sought to create

Pablo Picasso. *Bull's Head*. 1943.
Musée Picasso, Paris

(A) a contrast of line and tone.

(B) a religious symbol.

(C) a visual analogy to a living creature.

(D) a metaphor for human experience.

Questions 61–65 refer to the following passage.

The issue of adult literacy has finally received recognition as a major social problem. Unfortunately, the issue is usually presented in the media as a "women's interest issue." Numerous governors' wives and even Barbara Bush have publicly expressed concern about literacy. As well-meaning as the politicians' wives may be, it is more important that the politicians themselves recognize the seriousness of the problem and support increased funding for literacy programs.

Literacy education programs need to be directed at two different groups of people with very different needs. The first group is composed of people who have very limited reading and writing skills. These people are complete illiterates. A second group is composed of people who can read and write but whose skills are not sufficient to meet their needs. This second group is called function-ally illiterate. Successful literacy programs must meet the needs of both groups.

Instructors in literacy programs have three main responsibilities. First, the educational needs of the illiterates and functional illiterates must be met. Second, the instructors must approach the participants in the program with empathy, not sympathy. Third, all participants must experience success in the program and must perceive their efforts as worthwhile.

61. What is the difference between illiteracy and functional illiteracy?

(A) There is no difference.

(B) A functional illiterate is enrolled in a literacy education program but an illiterate is not.

(C) An illiterate cannot read or write, a functional illiterate can read and write but not at a very high skill level.

(D) There are more illiterates than functional illiterates in the United States today.

62. What does "women's interest issue" mean in the passage?

(A) The issue is only interesting to women.

(B) Many politicians' wives have expressed concern over the issue.

(C) Women illiterates outnumber male illiterates.

(D) Politicians interested in illiteracy often have their wives give speeches on the topic.

63. What is the purpose of the passage?

(A) To discuss the characteristics of successful literacy programs.

(B) To discuss the manner in which literacy programs are viewed by the media.

(C) To discuss some of the reasons for increased attention to literacy as a social issue.

(D)   All of the above.

64.   According to the passage, which of the following is NOT a characteristic of successful literacy programs?

(A)   Participants should receive free transportation.

(B)   Participants should experience success in the program.

(C)   Instructors must have empathy, not sympathy.

(D)   Programs must meet the educational needs of illiterates.

65.   What is the author's opinion of the funding for literacy programs?

(A)   Too much

(B)   Too little

(C)   About right

(D)   Too much for illiterates and not enough for functional illiterates

Questions 66–70 refer to the following passage.

The price of cleaning up the environment after oil spills is on the increase. After the massive Alaskan spill that created miles of sludge-covered beach, numerous smaller spills have occurred along the Gulf Coast and off the coast of California. Tides and prevailing winds carried much of this oil to shore in a matter of days. Workers tried to contain the oil with weighted, barrel-shaped plastic tubes stretched along the sand near the water. They hoped to minimize the damage. Generally, the barriers were successful, but there remained many miles of oil-covered sand. Cleanup crews shoveled the oil-covered sand into plastic bags for removal.

Coastal states are responding to the problem in several ways. California is considering the formation of a department of oceans to oversee protection programs and future cleanups. Some states have suggested training the National Guard in cleanup procedures. Other states are calling for the creation of an oil spill trust fund large enough to cover the costs of a major spill. Still other states are demanding federal action and funding. Regardless of the specific programs that may be enacted by the various states or the federal government, continued offshore drilling and the shipping of oil in huge tankers creates a constant threat to the nation's shoreline.

66. According to the passage, where have oil spills occurred?

    (A) U. S. Gulf Coast   (C) California coast

    (B) Alaskan coast   (D) All of the above.

67. What was the purpose of the barrel-shaped plastic tubes?

    (A) To keep sightseers away from the oil

    (B) To keep oil-soaked animals off the beach

    (C) To force the oil to soak into the sand

    (D) To keep the oil from spreading on the beach

68. Which of the following solutions is NOT discussed in the passage?

    (A) Create an oil cleanup trust fund

    (B) Increase federal funding for cleanups

    (C) Reduce oil production

    (D) Use the National Guard for cleanups

69. According to the passage, which of the following is the largest oil spill?

    (A) Alaskan coastal spill

    (B) Spill off the California coast

    (C) North Sea oil spill

    (D) Spill off the U. S. Gulf Coast

70. What is the author's opinion of the hazards created by oil spills?

    (A) Oil spills must be expected if the present methods of production and shipment continue.

    (B) Oil spills are the result of untrained crews.

    (C) Oil spills would not be a problem if the government was better prepared to cleanup.

    (D) Oil spills are the responsibility of foreign oil producers.

Questions 71–73 refer to the following passage.

Children, young adults, the middle-aged, and retirees all experience some types of stress. Excessive stress, or the inability to cope with normal levels of stress, can lead to high blood pressure, heart disease, mental disorders, infections, and prolonged or aggravated minor illnesses. Although few people can actually eliminate all stress from their lives, the lack of stress can be just as bad as too much stress. Extremely low levels of stress can cause boredom and depression and can contribute to mental illness. Many adults develop strategies for coping with stress. Some of the common strategies, which may include diet and exercise, focus on goal setting, establishing deadlines, and developing contingency plans. Often, adults learn to recognize their own signs of excessive stress. Common symptoms include headaches, stomach upsets, personality changes and chronic tiredness.

71. Boredom, depression, and symptoms of mental illness are the possible result of what condition?

   (A)   High stress levels   (C)   Low stress levels

   (B)   Inability to cope with stress (D)   Insomnia

72. Which of the following are suggested by the passage?

   (A)   Adults can seldom eliminate all stress from daily life.

   (B)   Most adults can learn coping strategies for excessive stress.

   (C)   A certain amount of stress is desirable.

   (D)   All of the above.

73. Which of the following is NOT suggested as a method for coping with stress?

   (A)   Diet   (C)   Goal setting

   (B)   Exercise   (D)   Sleep

Questions 74–76 refer to the following passage.

Reducing the amount of fat in the foods we eat is the goal of an ever increasing number of people. Many restaurants are responding to the demand for low fat foods by adding "Light" or "Good For You" entrees to their menus. These entrees are usually traditional foods prepared without added fat. Cooking methods that require little or no fat include steaming, poaching, broiling and searing. Stir-fried vegetables and chicken dishes are especially popular with diet conscious people. Almost all fried foods should be avoided when eating out, and it is best to avoid foods in cream sauces or gravies. Although salads are very healthful foods, the value of the salad can be ruined by the addition of thick, creamy salad dressings. Desserts based on fresh fruit are usually a better choice than desserts thick with cream, butter, or sugar. If you are concerned about the content or preparation of any food on a restaurant menu, it is best to ask lots of questions about ingredients and methods of preparation in order to make intelligent choices.

74. What is the purpose of the author in this passage?

(A) To warn people of the dangers of fat in the diet

(B) To suggest ways to avoid excessive fat when eating out

(C) To discourage eating in restaurants

(D) To encourage the use of broiling, searing and steaming to cook food

75. Which of the following should be avoided by diet conscious diners?

(A) Salads

(B) Creamy sauces or gravies

(C) Stir-fried vegetables and chicken

(D) Fresh fruit desserts

76. According to the passage, what does "Light" or "Good For You" mean on a restaurant menu?

    (A)   These foods are not deep-fat fried.

    (B)   These foods have reduced salt.

    (C)   These foods are especially good.

    (D)   These foods are prepared without added fat.

Questions 77–80 refer to the following passage.

The pituitary is a very small gland about the size of a marble. Located at the base of the brain, the pituitary produces many different hormones which are released into the blood. Hormones produced by the pituitary control the growth of bones and the function of the kidneys. The pituitary also controls the thyroid, a gland located in the throat, which is essential in regulating metabolism. The parathyroids, four tiny glands at the back of the thyroid, control the amount of calcium and phosphate in the blood. The parathyroids are also controlled by the pituitary. The adrenal glands, also controlled by the pituitary, are located on top of the kidneys. The adrenals have many functions, including controlling the amount of sodium and potassium in the body and producing hormones used in the metabolism of food. Another important function of the adrenal glands is the production of a hormone to help people cope with stress.

77. According to the passage, which of the following is NOT controlled by the pituitary?

    (A)   Growth of bones   (C)   Parathyroids

    (B)   Adrenal glands   (D)   Blood circulation

78. What do the parathyroids control?

    (A)   Metabolism

    (B)   Calcium and phosphate in the blood

    (C)   Sodium and potassium in the blood

    (D)   The kidneys

79. Where are the adrenals located?

    (A) Near the pituitary

    (B) At the back of the thyroid

    (C) Near the liver

    (D) On top of the kidneys

80. If a child is not growing at a normal rate, what glands discussed in the passage might be responsible?

    (A) Adrenals

    (B) Kidneys

    (C) Pituitary

    (D) Parathyroids

SECTION 2

> **DIRECTIONS:** Plan and write an essay on the topic given below. Do not write on any topic other than the one specified. An essay on any other topic is unacceptable.

Essay Topic:

Many leaders have suggested over the last few years that instead of a military draft, we should require all young people to serve the public in some way for a period of time. The service could be military or any other reasonable form of public service.

Assignment:

Do you agree or disagree with the statement? Support your opinion with specific examples from history, current events, literature, or personal experience.

LAST PRACTICE T

ANSWER KEY

1.	(C)	21.	(D)	41.	(D)	61.	(C)
2.	(A)	22.	(D)	42.	(B)	62.	(B)
3.	(D)	23.	(D)	43.	(D)	63.	(D)
4.	(D)	24.	(D)	44.	(A)	64.	(A)
5.	(A)	25.	(C)	45.	(A)	65.	(B)
6.	(B)	26.	(D)	46.	(D)	66.	(D)
7.	(A)	27.	(D)	47.	(C)	67.	(D)
8.	(A)	28.	(A)	48.	(C)	68.	(C)
9.	(C)	29.	(C)	49.	(A)	69.	(A)
10.	(D)	30.	(A)	50.	(D)	70.	(A)
11.	(C)	31.	(C)	51.	(B)	71.	(C)
12.	(C)	32.	(C)	52.	(A)	72.	(D)
13.	(B)	33.	(B)	53.	(D)	73.	(D)
14.	(A)	34.	(C)	54.	(C)	74.	(B)
15.	(C)	35.	(C)	55.	(C)	75.	(B)
16.	(C)	36.	(B)	56.	(B)	76.	(D)
17.	(D)	37.	(D)	57.	(D)	77.	(D)
18.	(C)	38.	(D)	58.	(B)	78.	(B)
19.	(B)	39.	(A)	59.	(C)	79.	(D)
20.	(B)	40.	(D)	60.	(C)	80.	(C)

LAST PRACTICE TEST

Detailed Explanations
of Answers

SECTION 1

1. **(C)** The correct answer is (C). The total area of the larger rectangle is

$$\text{base} \times \text{height} = 12 \times 9 = 108 \text{ sq. ft.}$$

Therefore, the area of the shaded portion surrounding the inner rectangle is

$$108 \text{ sq. ft.} - 80 \text{ sq. ft.} = 28 \text{ sq. ft.}$$

If the total cost of material used to cover the shaded area is $56 and we have 28 sq. ft., the cost per square foot is $\dfrac{\$56}{28 \text{ sq. ft.}} = \$2.00$ per square foot.

Answers (A), (B), and (D) are incorrect. Neither I nor II is necessary to determine the cost per square foot of the shaded area. (D) is incorrect because III is needed to determine the cost per sq foot.

2. **(A)** The correct answer is (A). In order to solve this problem we must first add the number of freshman girls to the number of sophomore girls (21 + 15). In order to find the percentage we divide this sum by the total number of students in the chorus and multiply by 100.

$$\frac{21+15}{132} \times 100 = \% \text{ of freshman and sophomore girls in chorus}$$

Answer (B) is incorrect. In order to find the percentage we need to multiply the fraction by 100, not divide by 100. Answers (C) and (D) are incorrect because the number of freshman and sophomore girls must be divided by the total number of students in the chorus. We then multiply by 100 to get the percent.

3. **(D)** You should note that the student is failing to carry in both the ones and tens places. 56 + 97 is being treated as 5 + 9 and 6 + 7. The two answers are then combined for a total of 1413.

Choice (A) is the standard answer. It is eliminated, since there is no error pattern. Choice (C) exhibits switching from addition to subtraction (9 – 8 = 1) and (8 – 3 = 5). Also, the child subtracts the top number from the bottom one on the first step. In choice (B) the child subtracts 8 from 9, and also 3 from 8, and then adds to the 8 in the tens place. Only choice (D) illustrates the pattern of recording the sum and not carrying. The correct answer is (D).

4. **(D)** You should first count the number of spaces on the dial. There are 10 spaces. Five spaces equals 90 units, and 90 divided by 5 is 18 units. Each space is worth 18 units. The needle points to about halfway between the marks numbered 6 and 7. Thus, one half of 18, plus 6 times 18, is 117. Choice (D) is the correct reading.

5. **(A)** You know that ten thousand contains 4 zeros, or 10^4 in place value. One million contains 10^6, or six zeros. Thus, 10^6 divided by 10^4 is 10^2 or 100. You may divide out 10,000 into one million, but that is the laborious way to solve this. Choice (A) is correct.

6. **(B)** You are challenged to analyze which data you would need to calculate the cost of feeding 2 cats for 7 days. If you calculate the cost for one cat for 7 days, then double the answer, you will have an approximate cost for 2 cats. The total cost for one cat is the cost of a can of food, times the number of cans of food eaten each day by one cat, times 7 days.

7. **(A)** You should note that the particle flow divides at 2 points, T and M. At these points the flow has two paths to reach either point W or point Q. Thus, the correct choice is (A). Particle flow can reach point W by going through point U, rather than V. It would have to flow through all other points listed in order to make a complete circuit or total clockwise path.

8. **(A)** (A) is the best answer since, as stated in the third sentence of the passage, changing the solid to liquid will lower the temperature of the hot tea. Because changing the sugar to liquid will not raise, but rather lower, the temperature of the tea, (B) should not be selected. The temperature of the hot tea will not be lowered to such an extent that it will freeze cream (C) or cause the hand to be painful from the cold (D).

9. **(C)** The best answer is (C) since it includes three correct statements. The sugar does pass from a solid to a liquid state, the sugar does absorb caloric from the water, and the heat does become latent when it is sensible. Since I, II, and III are all causes of the drop of temperature when sugar is added to coffee, all three must be included when choosing an answer. (A) states that sugar passes from a solid to a liquid state (I), but no other information is given. (B) includes two true statements (I and II), but it does not include all the information since there is no mention of heat becoming latent when it was sensible (III). (D) is not a proper answer since it excludes statement II—that sugar absorbs caloric from the water. While (A), (B), and (D) each contain one or more of these statements, none contains all three; subsequently, each of these choices is incorrect.

10. **(D)** The best answer is (D). Answer (D) states that one should take into consideration that dissolving the salt in the water will lower the temperature of the water and that one should start with water that is warmer than is desired. One should not start with water that is cooler than one desires; (A) is not the best answer. The order of adding the salt and the water will make little difference; the temperature will be lowered in both instances; (B) is not the best answer. The salt will lower the temperature of the water; (C) suggests that this will not happen if the salt is fine, so (C) is not an acceptable choice.

11. **(C)** The writing seems scientific since it refers to principles, causes and effects, and measures of heat and cold; (C) is the best answer. The writing is not sociological since there is no description of people and their relationships; consequently, (A) should not be chosen. Because the narrator reports scientific facts and there is no trial-and-error reporting, (B) is not the best answer. Since the information is not reported as historical research with references, footnotes, or dates of previous discoveries, (D) should not be chosen.

12. **(C)** The best choice is (C); paragraph five shows that in this case a mortar is a container used for pounding, pulverizing, and/or mixing. As employed in the last sentence of the fifth paragraph, the use of the mortar is not to fix or hold together; (A) should not be chosen. A mortar can be a weapon (B), but that would not be used to reduce ice to small particles; therefore, (B) is not an acceptable choice. The word "mixture" does not fit into the sentence in this context; choice (D) would not be practical.

13. **(B)** The best choice is (B). The only device that the writer does not record is that of interviews. The other items—descriptions (A), mathematics (C), and experiments (D)—are used.

14. **(A)** One can infer that the metal needle will become warm when the basketball is being pumped up by the air pump. The reason is that the article states, "...air is compressed forcibly in a tube...the heat, which was before latent, becomes sensible..."; (A) is the correct answer. Choice (B) states that the needle will not be affected; (B) should not be chosen since the quotation from the passage states that there will be an effect. (C) is also incorrect because it states that the needle will become cooler, not warmer. (D) is also an incorrect choice; it states that the needle will become freezing cold.

15. **(C)** The writer is objective in his writing and offers no opinions of his own; (C) is the best answer. The writer's main concern is not literary form or stylistic devices; (A) is not acceptable. The writer is objective and does not offer his own opinions; since he is not subjective, (B) is not the best answer. Since the facts presented in the article are not new, (D) is not the best answer.

16. **(C)** Since heat is a positive condition depending on the absence of cold, (C) is the best answer. Fahrenheit is a measure of temperature, not a condition; therefore, (A) is an incorrect choice. Heat is the opposite of intense artificial cold; (B) is not acceptable. Black states that it is "...when bodies pass from a rarer to a denser state that their latent heat is evolved..."; (D) is incorrect.

17. **(D)** In this case, the word "sensible" means perceptible; (D) is the best answer. "Sensible" can mean knowledgeable (A), but the definition does not make sense in this case. The meaning of "sensible" can be logical (B), but that particular meaning does not fit the sentence or passage

here. "Evolving" (C) is not an acceptable answer because it does not seem to fit the context.

18. **(C)** The item that the writer contends is *not* true is (C) because the first sentence of the reading passage uses the words "even when," implying that heat is no longer regarded as a substance. The other items (A), (B), and (D) are all items the writer states as being true in the first paragraph. None of them should be chosen.

19. **(B)** The best answer is (B) because the calorie and B.T.U. both relate to the amount of heat necessary to raise the temperature one degree. Because one unit relates to a kilogram (2.2 pounds) and one relates to a pound of water, (A) should not be chosen; it relates to one pound of water only. One unit relates to the customary system and one to the metric system, not both to the metric system. Thus, (C) cannot be chosen. Only the B.T.U. relates to a pound of iron, so (D) is also incorrect.

20. **(B)** The best answer is (B) because the melting of one pound of ice can cool a pound of hot water through a definite range of temperature and can cool two pounds of water through *half* as many degrees (C). (B) is therefore denied by the author. Neither (A) nor (D) can be the correct answer because they are stated, not denied, by the author in the first paragraph of the reading passage.

21. **(D)** The author states that the heat capacity of water or the B.T.U. per pound-degree is not constant, so (D) is the best answer. The author does not state that a water pound-degree is a constant; therefore, (A) should not be chosen. Because the temperature does make a difference, (B) should not be chosen. (C) is exactly opposite of the correct answer (D) and should not be selected.

22. **(D)** The best choice is (D). The disagreement concerns how to limit and define the heat unit. Since the passage states without any indication of doubt or negation that the melting of a pound of ice will not cool the same weight of water from 200° Fahrenheit to 180° Fahrenheit as it will from 60° Fahrenheit to 40° Fahrenheit, (A) is not the best answer. As the opening sentence of the second and last paragraph states, there is general agreement that a water pound-degree is not quite constant; thus, (B) should not be chosen. There is no point of disagreement among scientists as to whether the equivalence of heat effects proved effects proportional to quantity. Consequently, (C) is not the correct answer.

23. **(D)** The best answer is (D). The author appears to suggest that there are good reasons for taking the freezing-point to the boiling-point as the range by including the words "which will probably become universal"— interesting, but not totally necessary, information that leads the reader to believe the author readily accepts this as a range. Both the metric and the customary systems are mentioned without preference for either system. Therefore, neither (A), which indicates a predilection for the metric system, nor (B), which indicates a predilection for the customary system, is the correct answer. Because the author precedes his mention of the mean calorie with the words "properly named," he is indicating his approval of, rather than his opposition to, the mean calorie; hence, (C) is another incorrect choice.

24. **(D)** The phrase "properly named" is applied to both the mean calorie and the mean British Thermal Unit in the last sentence of the reading passage and makes (D), which includes both mean calories and mean British Thermal Units, the correct choice. Neither (A) nor (B) is correct because each of these answers is only one-half of the correct answer. Because we already know that (D) is the correct answer, we can see that (C) is incorrect; there is no support for such opposition in the passage.

25. **(C)** The author predicts the universal acceptance of the mean B.T.U. and the mean calorie as mentioned toward the end of the reading passage; hence, (C) is the best answer. (A) should not be selected since it mentions the universal adoption of the B.T.U. alone. (B) mentions the universal adoption of the calorie alone and should not be accepted. Because the author predicts not the demise but the universal adoption of the calories, (D) is incorrect.

26. **(D)** Statements I, II, III, and IV are all necessary parts of the definition of the heat unit. Only (D) allows for all these parts. (A), (B), and (C) are all incorrect since each omits some part or parts of the correct four-part answer.

27. **(D)** According to the passage, the author seems to be striving toward a "universality" of the heat unit (I), and would also like to find an explanation for the inconsistencies found when melting a pound of ice to cool the same weight of water when heated to different temperatures (II). The passage does end, however, before the author has completely stated his argument (III). (A), (B), and (C) only allow the reader to choose part of the complete answer and are incorrect. Only (D) allows the reader to select all the correct statements.

28. **(A)** The Magna Carta was signed in 1215. Columbus's voyages began in the fifteenth century. The Protestant Reformation occurred in the sixteenth century. The Puritans came to America in the seventeenth century. Therefore, the best choice is (A).

29. **(C)** Choice (A), as conceived by Henry Clay, referred to the nationalist policy of uniting the three economic sections of the United States in the time following the War of 1812. Choice (B) is an economic theory whose principal doctrine was the belief that the wealth of nations was based on the possession of gold. Choice (D) is tied to tradition and emotion. Choice (C) is the best possible answer.

30. **(A)** Choice (A) is correct; checks and balances provide each of the branches with the ability to limit the actions of the other branches. (B) is incorrect; branches of the federal government do not achieve independence from each other due to checks and balances. Choices (C) and (D) are also incorrect because they deal with only one branch, whereas the system of checks and balances involves the manner in which the three branches are interrelated.

31. **(C)** Choices (A), (B) and (D) all played a role in the early settlements of the English colonies in America. The correct response is item (C), because Mormonism was founded at Fayette, New York, in 1830, by Joseph Smith. *The Book of Mormon* was published in 1830 and it described the establishment of an American colony from the Tower of Babel.

32. **(C)** The letter K represents Cuba, letter D represents Indonesia, and letter M represents Sri Lanka. The correct answer is (C) because letter I represents the Philippine Islands.

33. **(B)** The correct answer is (B), since the document clearly states that Congress may not make laws abridging citizens' rights and liberties. Choices (C) and (D) are incorrect because the Bill of Rights does not talk about voting rights or slaves. A list of grievances (A) is contained in the Declaration of Independence.

34. **(C)** This fits the entire framework of the passage (i.e., first the statistics, then their effects). Though the passage tracks the gross national product (B), this is by no means central to the entire passage. The passage nowhere degrades Hoover's presidency (A) nor does it monitor the actual *effects* of the banking system (D), though it does show how the

banking system was *affected*; yet even so, this is by no means central to the passage.

35. **(C)** Due to the inherent logic of the sentence, (C) is correct. The diseases do make people immune to starvation (A) because the victims of the disease die before they can starve. The sentence nowhere implies that the diseases cause malnutrition (B); rather, it is the malnutrition that creates disease susceptibility. Although few died of starvation, many died of disease, which is indirectly caused by malnutrition; therefore, (D) is incorrect.

36. **(B)** The 1933 bar is highest, and the graph measures the percent of unemployment by the height of the bars. The bars for 1929 (A), 1938 (C), and 1944 (D) are all lower than the bar for 1933, the year in which unemployment was the highest.

37. **(D)** 1944 (the bar between 1943 and 1945) is the lowest bar on the graph. As previously mentioned, the graph measures the percentage of unemployment on the length of the bars. The bars for 1929 (A), 1933 (B), and 1938 (C) are all higher than the bar for 1944.

38. **(D)** Choice (A) is wrong because about 30% of households had under $15,000. Choices (B) and (C) are also incorrect, since slightly more than 15% fell into this category. The correct choice is item (D).

39. **(A)** Graph reading and interpretation is the primary focus of this question. Choice (B) is obviously wrong, since the youngest have the least discretionary income. Items (C) and (D) are also incorrect. The oldest group has less discretionary income than those between 25 and 65, but more than those under 25.

40. **(D)** Since choices (A), (B), and (C) are incorrect, the right answer is (D). (A) is incorrect because the statement is not applicable to all household sizes, such as those with only one person. (B) may at first seem correct, but the statement does not hold true for one-person households. (C) is completely false. Two-person households have the most discretionary income: 36.2%.

41. **(D)** This question tests your ability to determine the central focus in a staged dramatic production and to explain why there is such a focus. The central attraction in this picture is the man on the bed (D). Many eyes are turned to him, and he appears to be speaking. The other men in

the picture are turned away from the viewers, and many are directing their attention towards the man on the bed. Since this character is in a full front position, he will draw more attention than those in profile or full back, which are weaker positions.

42. **(B)** This question asks you to look at the print and come to some conclusions. Since each figure is holding or playing a musical instrument (double aulos, lute and harp), it can be surmised that they are musicians (A). Choice (B) states that the artwork creates the illusion of depth, which means that it has a layered look. This description does not fit the painting, so (B) is the correct choice. The lack of a three-dimensional aspect (D) and the absence of a background against which the figures are placed both point to the deduction that this is an Egyptian tomb painting (C).

43. **(D)** The passage, which opens Charles Dickens's *A Tale of Two Cities*, contains numerous comparisons. By making these comparisons and descriptions of the time period ("we had everything before us, we had nothing before us, we were all going direct to Heaven, we were all going direct the other way," etc.), Dickens is illustrating how during this period (just before the French Revolution) anything was possible: "wisdom," "foolishness," "Light," or "Darkness." This "anything is possible" tone also foreshadows the French Revolution, which the aristocracy never expected. Dickens will, later in the novel, describe extreme political upheaval, but does not here, so (B) is wrong. (A) is wrong because "placid" implies settled and calm; if "anything is possible," then the times are the exact opposite. There is no mention of a public event, so (C) is also incorrect.

44. **(A)** By jokingly suggesting that the two governments contain the positions "lords of the State preserves of loaves and fishes," Dickens mocks their self-assuredness and unflinching certainty that the "preserves" will never be depleted and that "things in general [are] settled for ever." The phrase "clearer than crystal" helps, through its sarcasm, to give this attack more sting. None of the other choices are alluded to or discussed in the passage, and are thus incorrect.

45. **(A)** The "superlative degree" refers to the utmost degree of something being compared (the *hottest* day, the *fastest* runner, the *most beautiful* object, etc.). The phrase indicates that some of the time periods' "noisiest authorities" (a sarcastic euphemism for members of the

governments) wanted time to be remembered as the "most" or "best" of something—"the most evil" or "the most productive." What mattered to these "authorities" was to be at the top of every comparison, regardless of its implications. Thus, (A) is correct. The people are not mentioned here, so (B) and (C) are both incorrect, as is (D).

46. **(D)** The Egyptian Temple of Horus, c. 212 B.C.E., pictured in the example displays elements typical of the monumental architecture which developed during Egypt's Old Kingdom period (c. 2600-2100 B.C.E.) and continued until Egypt became a province of the Roman Empire (c. 31 B.C.E.). This architecture achieved an effect of imposing grandeur and durability through the use of simple, solid geometric forms, constructed on an overwhelming scale and laid out with exacting symmetry. The Temple of Horus avoids any emphasis on horizontal lines (A), and relies instead on the sloping outer walls to visually "pull" the massive building to the ground and make it seem immovable and eternal. Additionally, although the temple carries minor ornamental detail (B), displays huge reliefs of figures, and is set within a large open courtyard (C), all of these elements are secondary to the massive character of the building itself.

47. **(C)** Gianlorenzo Bernini's *David* of 1623 is a perfect example of the Baroque sculptor's wish to express movement and action and to capture a fleeting moment of time. Here, the figure's twisting posture and intense facial expression create a dynamic, not a static, character (B), as David begins the violent twisting motion with which he will hurl the stone from his sling. His gaze is directed outward at an unseen adversary, implying interaction with another character and denying any purely ornamental conception behind this work (A). The figure's meager garments, far from identifying him as a warrior (D), emphasize both his physical vulnerability and his idealized, heroic beauty.

48. **(C)** An aside is a comment spoken directly to the audience that the other actors on stage are supposedly unable to hear. Thus, the correct answer is choice (C).

49. **(A)** The seventeenth-century Japanese ink-on-paper scroll painting shown in the example relies almost exclusively on the qualities of line to convey the graceful forms of two leaping deer. In this painting, called *Deer Scroll,* both the animals and the scripted characters share the same quality of fluid, rhythmic, spontaneous "writing." Gradations of tone (B) and color (C) are unimportant here, since the images are defined by black

line on white, and volume (D), too, is absent, since these forms show no shading or modulation of tone.

50. **(D)** This marble portrait bust of the first century B.C.E. is typical of a style which flourished during the late Roman Republic, and which aimed for a literal, super-realistic depiction of a certain type of individual. The sculptor here avoided any tendency to idealize his subject, and pursued instead an expressive, realistic depiction, in which each particular feature of his subject's face and expression was painstakingly recorded (B). The choice of hard, chiselled marble, rather than modeled clay or incised relief, helped to accentuate the craggy details of his subject's face (C). The sitter here represents not the jaded, effete aristocracy of the later Roman Empire (A), but rather the simple, unsophisticated citizen-farmer of the earlier Republic, whose labor and determination helped to build the Roman state.

51. **(B)** This passage from Melville's *Moby Dick* contains an allusion in the phrase, "like so many Alexanders." Melville is illustrating the strength and power of whalers ("naked Nantucketers") by alluding and comparing them to Alexander the Great, the famous conqueror who died in 323 B.C.E.

52. **(A)** This passage, which opens James Joyce's *A Portrait of the Artist as a Young Man*, is written in "baby talk" ("moocow," "nicens," "baby tuckoo") to convey to readers the age, speech, and mental state of the narrator.

53. **(D)** Nineteenth-century novels of manners employed such themes as the importance (or unimportance) of "good breeding," the elation (and suffocation) caused by society, and the interaction of individuals within the confines of a closed country community (to name just a few). This passage, taken from Jane Austen's *Emma*, mentions "opinions" of other characters, the importance of "beauty" and "accomplishment" (note how Emma sees them as almost saving graces for Mrs. Elton), and the "improvement" of a "country neighborhood."

54. **(C)** In the example, *Sunday Afternoon on the Island of La Grand Jatte*, 1884-86, the French Post-Impressionist painter Georges Seurat developed a systematic, intellectual art in which color values were carefully calculated, composition was rigidly structured, and an overall effect of static, well-ordered design replaced the vibrant spontaneity of the earlier

Impressionists' work. In *La Grand Jatte* the motionless, vertical forms of the human figures are carefully positioned and repeated, and are deftly coordinated with both the diagonal shadows on the ground and with the distant horizon line. The approach overall is detached and scientific (C), and avoids both spontaneous emotional impulse [(A) and (B)] and any poetic, personal content (D).

55. **(C)** The arch pictured in the example is characteristic of much later Roman imperial architecture, in which elaborate combinations of Classical architectural elements were employed in a purely non-structural manner. Although the four columns at the front of the arch appear to lend support to the heavy upper story (C), they in fact serve no functional purpose. They do, however, create a strong vertical thrust which leads the viewer's eye to the sculpted figures above (A), while simultaneously setting off and accenting the three small arches which serve as the monument's basic structural units (D).

56. **(B)** You can tell that this passage is taken from the stage directions of a play because of the visual and auditory descriptions you are given. Also, you are told that "lights come up" and a "rocket bursts, off," here meaning "offstage."

57. **(D)** The architect of the building illustrated was intent on avoiding traditional building forms in the search for a new, expressive use of space. The design pictured, therefore, carefully avoids all reminders of the symmetrical, balanced floor plans of Classical and Renaissance architecture (A). It also dispenses with a conventional structural framework (B) and with the geometric forms and angles of traditional buildings (C). Instead, it exploits fully the potential of a new material—in this case, poured concrete—to create dynamic, curving forms whose arcs and spirals echo both the shape of growing organisms and the motion of wind and water.

58. **(B)** The passage serves to introduce an upcoming story to be told by the narrator. He begins by exclaiming, "there may as well be an end of this!" and then gives a list of reasons why he has finally decided not to "keep my trouble to myself." He is about to relate an event, or series of events, to his friend, because keeping silent has been "burning [him] rather violently." He is very anxious about what he has to say; choice (B) is correct. There is no evidence that the speaker feels angry, ashamed, or sorrowful, so (A), (C), and (D) are all incorrect.

59. **(C)** The speaker gives, as one of the reasons for telling his story, "if confession were not good for the soul, though harder than sin to some people, of which I am one," showing that he regards confession as a healthy, although difficult activity. (C) is the correct answer. He never speaks of confession as being unnecessary, nonsensical, or impossible, so (A), (B), and (D) are all incorrect.

60. **(C)** In the example shown, the *Bull's Head* of 1943, the Spanish artist Pablo Picasso joined a bicycle seat and a set of handlebars in a clever, unexpected combination to produce a sculptural analogy to an actual bull (C). Thus, the artist was concerned here with form and substance, not with a contrast of line and tone (A). Likewise, even though the bull has mythological connotations and figures prominently in many ancient religions, the artist was intent not on creating a religious symbol (B), but in exploring the visual unity of common objects brought together in new ways. The result is a strictly visual, sculptural effect, and in no way provides a metaphor for human experience (D).

61. **(C)** Choice (C) is correct because this is the definition of illiterate and functional illiterate stated in paragraph two. Choice (A) cannot be correct because the passage clearly distinguishes between illiterates and functional illiterates. Choice (B) is not correct because the definition stated is not related to participation in a program. The relative number of illiterates and functional illiterates is not discussed, so choice (D) is incorrect.

62. **(B)** Choice (B) is correct because the passage begins by stating that many politicians' wives have expressed interest in literacy. Choice (A) is incorrect because the author of the passage does not suggest that only women are interested. Choice (C) is incorrect because the passage does not discuss the number of male or female illiterates. Choice (D) is incorrect because there is no discussion in the passage of politicians' wives giving speeches.

63. **(D)** This passage has several purposes. First, the author presents some complaints concerning the way literacy issues are presented in the media (B). The author also discusses the increased attention given to literacy by politicians' wives (C). Third, the author discusses many aspects of successful literacy programs (A). Therefore, choice (D), which includes all of these purposes, is correct.

64. **(A)** This question must be answered using the process of elimination. You are asked to select a statement that names a possible program component which is not characteristic of successful literacy programs. Choice (A) is correct because choices (B), (C), and (D) are specifically mentioned in the passage.

65. **(B)** Choice (B) is correct because the author specifically states that politicians should support increased funding for literacy programs. Choices (A) and (C) are incorrect because the author states that funding should be increased. There is no discussion of funding for different programs, so choice (D) is incorrect.

66. **(D)** Choice (D) is correct because the passage specifically mentions the California coast, the Alaskan coast, and the U. S. Gulf Coast as sites of oil spills.

67. **(D)** Choice (D) is correct because workers were trying to keep the oil in the water and away from the beach. Choices (A) and (B) are incorrect because neither sightseers nor animals are discussed in the passage. Choice (C) is incorrect because the cleanup crews wanted to remove the oil, not let it soak into the sand.

68. **(C)** Choice (C) is correct. This question must be answered using the process of elimination. Cleanup trust funds, increased federal spending, using the National Guard, and creating a department of oceans are all discussed in the passage. Therefore, choices (A), (B), and (D) are incorrect. Only choice (C) names a solution not mentioned in the passage.

69. **(A)** Choice (A) is correct. The passage describes the Alaskan spill as "massive." The spill off the coast of California and the spill off the U.S. Gulf Coast are described as "smaller." Therefore, choices (B) and (D) are incorrect. Spills in the North Sea are not discussed in the passage, so choice (C) is incorrect.

70. **(A)** Choice (A) is correct. The last sentence of the passage specifically states that spills are a constant threat if offshore drilling and the shipment of oil in tankers continues. Choice (B) is incorrect because the passage does not discuss crews or training programs. While the passage does imply that the government should be better prepared to clean up, the author does not state that oil spills would cease to be a problem if the government was better prepared. Therefore, choice (C) is incorrect. Choice (D) is incorrect because foreign oil producers are not mentioned.

71. **(C)** Choice (C) is correct. These symptoms are listed in the fourth sentence as the possible results of low stress levels, so choices (A) and (B) are incorrect. Insomnia is not discussed in relationship to low stress, so choice (D) is incorrect.

72. **(D)** Choice (D) is correct. The passage states that few people can eliminate stress and that people can learn coping strategies so choices (A) and (B) are correct. Although the passage does not state that stress is desirable, the author does state that the lack of stress is harmful, so logically a certain amount of stress must be beneficial. Therefore, choice (C) is also correct.

73. **(D)** Choice (D) is correct because sleep is not mentioned as a technique for coping with stress. This question requires the use of elimination to determine the correct answer. Diet (A), exercise (B), and goal setting (C) in establishing deadlines are all included in the sixth sentence as strategies for eliminating stress.

74. **(B)** Choice (B) is correct because the passage suggests several ways to reduce the total fat in what we eat. Choice (A) is incorrect because the author of the passage does not try to convince readers that too much fat in the diet is bad. The author is assuming that this is the goal of many people, as stated in the first sentence. Choice (C) is incorrect because the author states that you can reduce fat in your diet and still eat in restaurants. Choice (D) is incorrect because, although these cooking methods are recommended, that is not the main purpose of the passage.

75. **(B)** Choice (B) is correct. The suggestion to avoid creamy sauces and gravies is in the seventh sentence. Choice (A) is incorrect because the author states that salads are healthful. Choice (C) is incorrect because stir-frying is listed as a preferred cooking method. Choice (D) is incorrect because the author suggests fresh fruit desserts.

76. **(D)** Choice (D) is correct. The author states this information in the third sentence. Choice (A) is probably a true statement, but the meaning is too narrow. It does not specify what cooking method is used, only that the food is not deep-fat fried.

77. **(D)** This question requires you to use the process of elimination. The passage specifically mentions the growth of bones (A), the adrenal glands (B), and parathyroids (C) as being controlled by the pituitary. Blood circulation is not mentioned, so choice (D) is correct.

78. **(B)** Choice (B) is correct because the fifth sentence specifically states that the parathyroids control the amount of calcium and phosphate in the blood. Choice (A) is incorrect because the thyroid and adrenals control metabolism. Choice (C) is incorrect because the adrenals control sodium and potassium. Choice (D) is incorrect because the pituitary controls the kidneys.

79. **(D)** The correct answer is (D); the adrenal glands are located on top of the kidneys. Choice (A) is incorrect because the passage does not discuss anything that is located near the pituitary. Choice (B) is incorrect because the parathyroids are located at the back of the thyroids. Choice (C) is incorrect because the liver is not mentioned in the passage.

80. **(C)** Choice (C) is correct because the pituitary controls the growth of bones. Choice (A) is incorrect because the adrenals control responses to stress and metabolism. Choice (B) is incorrect because the kidneys function to clean the body of waste products. Choice (D) is incorrect because the parathyroids control the amount of calcium and phosphate in the blood.

SECTION 2

The following essay would receive scores at the highest end of the scale used in LAST essay scoring.

Essay A

The cynic in me wants to react to the idea of universal public service for the young with a reminder about previous complaints aimed at the military draft. These complaints suggest that wars might never be fought if the first people drafted were the adult leaders and lawmakers. Still, the idea of universal public service sounds good to this concerned citizen who sees everywhere—not just in youth—the effects of a selfish and self-indulgent culture.

One reads and hears constantly about young people who do not care about the problems of our society. These youngsters seem interested in money and the luxuries money can buy. They do not want to work from the minimum wage up, but want instead to land a high paying job without "paying their dues." An informal television news survey of high school students a few years ago suggested that students had the well-entrenched fantasy that with no skills or higher education they would not accept a job paying less than $20 an hour. Perhaps universal service helping out in an urban soup kitchen for six months would instill a sense of selflessness rather than selfishness, and provide the perspective necessary to demonstrate the flaw in this perception.

The shiny gleam of a new and expensive sports sedan bought on credit by an accounting student reflects self indulgence that might be toned down by universal service. That self indulgence may reflect merely a lack of discipline, but it also may reflect a lack of purpose in life. Philosophers, theologians and leaders of all types have suggested throughout the ages that money and objects do not ultimately satisfy. Providing service to our fellow human beings often does. Universal public service for that accounting student might require a year helping low income or senior citizens prepare income tax forms. This type of service would dim that self indulgence, give the person some experience in the real world, and also give satisfaction that one's life is not lived only to acquire material things.

Universal service might also help young people restore faith in their nation and what it means to them. Yes, this is the land of opportunity, but it is also a land of forgotten people, and it is a land that faces outside threats. Part of the requisite public service should remind young people of their past and of their responsibility to the future.

Analysis

Essay A uses a traditional structure: the first paragraph states the topic, the second and third present development with specific examples from personal observation, and the fourth ends the essay. It is not as strong a conclusion as it could be, most likely because the writer ran out of time. The essay as a whole is unified and uses pertinent examples to support the opinion stated. The sentence structure varies, and the vocabulary is effective. Generally, it is well done within the time limit.

The following essay would receive scores in the middle of the LAST essay scoring scale.

Essay B

In the U.S. today, when a boy turns 18 he is obligated, by law, to register for the military draft. This is done so that in case of a war or other catastrophic event, these boys and men can be called upon for active duty in the military. It is good to know that we will have the manpower we need in case of a war, but my opinion on the military draft is negative. I don't like the idea of forcing someone to sign up at a certain age for something that they don't want to happen. Of course, I know that we need some sort of military manpower on hand just in case, but it would be so much better if it was left to the individual to decide what area to serve in and at what time.

When a boy turns 18, he's a rebel of sorts. He doesn't want someone telling him what to do and when to do it; he's just beginning to live. In Switzerland, when a boy turns 18, he joins some branch of the military for a time of training. He is given his gun, uniform and badge number. Then, once a year for about two weeks he suits up for retraining. He does this until he is about 65 years old. In a way this is like a draft, but the men love it and feel that it is honorable. I think that they like it because it does not discriminate and their jobs pay them for the time away. Switzerland seems to give the 18 year old some choice regarding what division to join, and whether or not to join at all. They're not as strict on joining as we are so it's more of an honorable thing to do.

Of course, I'd love to see this decision be strictly up to the individual, but it can't be that way. We have too many enemies that we might go to war with and we would need a strong military. Switzerland's neutrality provides more options than we in the United States have.

Analysis

Essay B displays competence in overall thought. It does not state its topic quite as well as Essay A. The extended example of Swiss military conscription is the main strength of the essay. The writer hedges a bit but manages to convey an opinion. Sentences have some variety, and the vocabulary is competent. Some spelling and grammatical errors interfere with the communication.

The following essay would receive scores at the lowest end of the LAST essay scoring scale.

Essay C

I agree with the many leaders who suggest we require young people to serve the public in some way, rather than the military draft.

There are several reasons this could benefit our country. The first being giving the young people, perhaps just out of high school, with no job experience, an opportunity to give something to his community. In return for this, he gains self-respect, pride, and some valuable experience.

Whether it be taking flowers to shut-ins or just stopping for a chat in a rest home, a young person would have gained something and certainly given, perhaps hope, to that elderly person. I can tell from my own experience how enriched I feel when visiting the elderly. They find joy in the simplest things, which in turn, teaches me I should do the same. This type of universal service would also strengthen the bonds between the younger generation and the older generation.

Another thing gained by doing voluntary type work, is a sense of caring about doing the job right-quality! If you can't do it for your country, what else matters? Maybe, if a young person learned these lessons early, our country would be more productive in the global economy.

Analysis

Essay C has major faults, not the least of them the lack of a clear sense of overall organization. The thoughts do have some coherence, but they don't seem to have a plan, except to express agreement with the statement. Examples from personal observation do help, but the paragraphs are not well developed. Several severe grammatical problems interfere with the communication.

LAST/ATS-W

ATS-W ELEMENTARY PRACTICE TEST

This test is also on CD-ROM in our interactive TEST*ware*® for the NYSTCE. We strongly recommend that you first take this exam on computer. You will then have the benefits of enforced time conditions, individual diagnostic analysis, and instant scoring.

See page 3 for guidance on how to get the most out of our NYSTCE book and software.

ATS-W ELEMENTARY PRACTICE TEST

Time: 4 Hours

80 Multiple-Choice Questions, 1 Essay

SECTION 1

DIRECTIONS: Read each scenario carefully, and answer the questions that follow. Mark your responses on the answer sheet provided.

Scenario 1

1. Mr. Drake is a first-grade teacher who is using the whole language method while teaching about animals. Before reading a story to the students, Mr. Drake tells the students what he is expecting them to learn from reading the story. What is his reason for doing this?

   (A) The students should know why the instructor chose this text over any other.

   (B) It is important for teachers to share personal ideas with their students in order to foster an environment of confidence and understanding.

   (C) Mr. Drake wants to verify that all students are on-task before he begins the story.

(D)   Mr. Drake is modeling a vital pre-reading skill in order to teach it to the young readers.

2.   Mr. Drake wants to ensure that the class will have a quality discussion on the needs of house pets. In response to a student who said that her family abandoned their cat in a field because it ate too much, Mr. Drake asks: "What is one way to save pets that are no longer wanted." This exercise involves what level of questioning?

(A)   Evaluation   (C)   Comprehension

(B)   Analysis   (D)   Synthesis

3.   Mr. Drake has a heterogeneously grouped reading class. He has the students in groups of two—one skilled reader and one remedial reader—reading selected stories to one another. The students read the story and question each other until they feel that they both understand the story. By planning the lesson this way, Mr. Drake has

(A)   set a goal for his students.

(B)   condensed the number of observations necessary, thereby creating more time for class instruction.

(C)   made it possible for another teacher to utilize the limited materials.

(D)   utilized the students' strengths and weaknesses to maximize time, materials, and the learning environment.

4.   Mr. Drake is continuing his lesson on the animal kingdom. He wants to ensure that the students learn as much as they can about animals, so he incorporates information they are familiar with into the new information. Knowing that these are first-grade learners, what should Mr. Drake consider when contemplating their learning experience?

(A)   The students will know how much information they can retrieve from memory.

(B)   The students will overestimate how much information they can retrieve from memory.

(C)   The students will be able to pick out the information they need to study and the information which they do not need to study due to prior mastery.

(D)   The students will estimate how much they can learn in one time period.

5.   Before reading a story about a veterinary hospital, Mr. Drake constructs a semantic map of related words and terms using the students' input. What is his main intention for doing this?

(A)   To demonstrate a meaningful relationship between the concepts of the story and the prior knowledge of the students

(B)   To serve as a visual means of learning

(C)   To determine the level of understanding the students will have at the conclusion of the topic being covered

(D)   To model proper writing using whole words

Scenario 2

6.   Mika Felder's sixth-grade class is studying the world of work. She discusses a new idea related to this study with a more experienced teacher. Ms. Felder is planning to invite all parents to visit the class, talk about their own work, and respond to students' questions. She hopes to have three or four parents a day for this activity over a period of two weeks or so. The fellow teacher encourages Ms. Felder to go ahead and make plans for this activity, after receiving approval of the project from the principal. Which of the following reasons would the experienced teacher point out as the major benefit?

(A)   Ms. Felder will have the opportunity to further the career-awareness goals of the curriculum and the relationship she is trying to establish with the families of her students.

(B)   The project will be a free way to have guest speakers for the class.

(C)   The project will introduce students to a variety of careers and help students select the careers they want to follow some day.

(D)   Ms. Felder will be able to see which parents will cooperate with her when she has a need for their help.

Scenario 3

7. Paula Kresmeier teaches sixth-grade language arts classes. One of her curriculum goals is to help students improve their spelling. As one of her techniques, she has developed a number of special mnemonic devices that she uses with the students, getting the idea from the old teaching rhymes like "I before E except after C or when sounding like A as in neighbor or weigh." Her own memory tricks, such as "The moose can't get loose from the noose" or "Spell rhyme? Why me?" have caught the interest of her students. Now, besides Mrs. Kresmeier's memory tricks for better spelling, her students are developing and sharing their own creative ways to memorize more effectively. Mrs. Kresmeier's method of improving her students' spelling has been successful primarily because of which of the following factors related to student achievement?

(A) The students are not relying on phonics or sight words to spell difficult words.

(B) Mrs. Kresmeier has impressed her students with the need to learn to spell.

(C) The ideas are effective with many students and help to create a learning environment that is open to student interaction.

(D) Mrs. Kresmeier teaches spelling using words that can be adapted to mnemonic clues.

Scenario 4

Miss Sharp's fourth-grade class is studying a unit entitled "Discoveries" in social studies and science. Miss Sharp has prepared four learning centers for the class. In Learning Center #1, students use information from their science and social studies textbooks to prepare a time line of discoveries that occurred between 1800 and 1997. In Learning Center #2, students use a variety of resource materials to research one particular discovery or discoverer they have selected from a prepared list. Each student then records what they learned about this discovery or discoverer on an individual chart that will later be shared with the whole class. In Learning Center #3, students add small amounts of five different substances to jars of water and record the results over a period of five minutes. In Learning Center #4, students write a description of the need for a new discovery to solve a problem or answer a question. Then students suggest several possible areas of research that may contribute to this new discovery.

8. Miss Sharp introduces the learning centers by explaining the purpose of each center and giving directions for each activity. Next she divides the class of 22 into four groups and assigns each group to a different center. After 20 minutes, some students are completely finished with one center and want to move on, but other students have only just begun working. What would be the best solution to this situation?

   (A)   Each learning center should be revised so that the activities will require approximately the same amount of time to complete.

   (B)   Students who finish one center early should be given additional work to complete before moving to the next center.

   (C)   Students should be permitted to move from center to center as they complete each activity so long as no more than six students are working at each center.

   (D)   Students should be permitted to work through the activities in each center as quickly as possible so that the class can move on to the next unit.

9. As the students work in the learning centers, Miss Sharp moves from group to group asking questions and commenting on each student's progress. This procedure indicates that Miss Sharp most likely views her role as a (an)

   (A)   facilitator.   (C)   disciplinarian.

   (B)   supervisor.   (D)   evaluator.

10. In selecting resource materials for Learning Center #2, Miss Sharp carefully chooses materials that present information about a variety of discoveries made by both men and women from several different countries. Her purpose in making these selections is most likely to ensure that materials

   (A)   are challenging but written at the appropriate reading level.

(B)   demonstrate the diversity of individuals who have made discoveries.

(C)   contain information about discoveries included in the textbook.

(D)   will be of interest to the majority of the students.

11.   Which of the following would be the most appropriate concluding activity for the Discoveries Unit?

    (A)   Students should have a class party celebrating the birthdays of Marie Curie, Jonas Salk, and Thomas Edison.

    (B)   Each student should be required to prepare a verbal report detailing what they learned about an important medical discovery.

    (C)   Each student should take a multiple-choice test containing questions related to each learning center.

    (D)   Each student should design a concluding activity, or select one from a prepared list, that reflects what they learned about a discovery they studied.

Scenario 5

Mr. Freeman is preparing a year-long unit on process writing for his fifth-grade class. He plans for each student to write about a series of topics over each six-week grading period. At the end of each grading period, students will select three completed writing assignments that reflect their best work. Mr. Freeman will review the assignments and meet with each student. During the conferences, Mr. Freeman will assist the students with preparing a list of writing goals for the next grading term.

12.   Which of the following best describes Mr. Freeman's plan for reviewing student writing assignments, conferencing with each student, and helping each student set specific goals for writing to be accomplished during the next grading period?

    (A)   Summative evaluation

    (B)   Summative assessment

    (C)   Formative assessment

    (D)   Peer assessment

13. Mr. Freeman's goal in planning to conference with each student about his or her writing could be described as

   (A) creating a climate of trust and encouraging a positive attitude toward writing.

   (B) an efficient process for grading student writing assignments.

   (C) an opportunity to stress the importance of careful editing of completed writing assignments.

   (D) an opportunity to stress the value of prewriting in producing a final product.

14. Philip is a student in Mr. Freeman's class who receives services from a resource teacher for a learning disability which affects his reading and writing. Which of the following is the most appropriate request that Mr. Freeman should make of the resource teacher to help Philip complete the writing unit?

   (A) Mr. Freeman should ask the resource teacher to provide writing instruction for Philip.

   (B) Mr. Freeman should excuse Philip from all writing assignments.

   (C) Mr. Freeman should ask the resource teacher for help in modifying the writing unit to match Philip's needs.

   (D) Mr. Freeman should ask the resource teacher to schedule extra tutoring sessions to help Philip with the writing assignments.

Scenario 6

Miss Treen is a kindergarten teacher at Green Valley Elementary. Her students are primarily Hispanic. English is a second language for about one-third of the class.

15. Miss Treen wants to encourage her students to view themselves as successful readers and writers. Which of the following instructional strategies would be *least* effective in accomplishing this goal?

   (A) Providing a reading area in the classroom where students can select books to read in a relaxed and comfortable atmosphere.

(B)   Reading at least two books aloud each day and discussing the story with the students.

(C)   Accepting invented spellings as the students write letters, grocery lists, telephone messages, and describe classroom events.

(D)   Requiring students to copy the alphabet using upper- and lower-case letters at least once each day.

16.   During the first parent conference of the year, Miss Treen should

(A)   keep the conversation light and unemotional, saving any negative comments for the next conference.

(B)   include positive comments about each child and make suggestions for how parents can help the child at home.

(C)   discuss the importance of speaking only English at home at all times and insisting that the child communicate with all family members in English.

(D)   discuss the results of diagnostic testing using technical terms so that parents will understand her desire to help the children.

17.   Miss Treen has just finished teaching a unit on community helpers. She is disappointed because the children did not seem interested in the topic and did not want to discuss the community helpers she had listed on the bulletin board. The best course of action for Miss Treen would be to

(A)   borrow another kindergarten teacher's unit on community helpers for use next year.

(B)   evaluate each lesson in the unit and revise the lessons to make them more meaningful to the students.

(C)   save discussions of community helpers for older children because the topic is too difficult for kindergarten students.

(D)   show a filmstrip about community helpers and invite a policeman to visit the class.

Scenario 7

The fourth-grade students in Mrs. Alvarez's class are studying Native Americans. Mrs. Alvarez wants to strengthen her students' abilities to work independently. She also wants to provide opportunities for the students to use a variety of print and media resources during this unit of study. Mrs. Alvarez plans to begin the unit by leading the class in a brainstorming session to formulate questions to guide their research about Native Americans.

18. Which of the following criteria should guide Mrs. Alvarez as she leads the brainstorming session?

   (A) The questions should emphasize the factual content presented in the available print materials.

   (B) The questions should emphasize higher order thinking skills, such as comparison, analysis, and evaluation.

   (C) The questions should reflect the interests of the students.

   (D) The questions should include all of the fourth-grade objectives for this unit.

19. Mrs. Alvarez has collected a variety of print and media resources for the students to use in their research. Which of the following will probably be the best way to motivate students to research the questions they have prepared?

   (A) The teacher should assign two to three questions to each student so that all the questions are covered.

   (B) The teacher should allow individual students to select the questions they would like to research.

   (C) The teacher should select three key questions and assign them to all the students.

   (D) The teacher should assign one topic to each student, then provide the students with additional information.

20. Mrs. Alvarez is using which of the following instructional delivery systems?

    (A) Direct instruction

    (B) Role playing and simulation

    (C) Exposition and discussion

    (D) Inquiry and problem solving

21. Mrs. Alvarez plans to use contemporary assessment techniques at the conclusion of the unit. She is also concerned about providing sufficient feedback to the students. Which of the following is most likely to meet these assessment goals?

    (A) A teacher-made objective test should be used because questions can be prepared to match the unit's content and the final grades can be computed quickly.

    (B) A variety of formal and informal assessment tests should be used.

    (C) A standardized test with established reliability and validity should be used.

    (D) Individual tests for each student should be used to allow for individual differences.

22. At the conclusion of the unit, Mrs. Alvarez plans to ask her students to present the projects and activities that were prepared for the unit to the other fourth-grade classes in the building. Planning this time for presentation indicates that Mrs. Alvarez

    (A) is concerned about bringing appropriate closure to the unit.

    (B) wants to work collaboratively with other teachers.

    (C) hopes to be appointed grade-level chairperson.

    (D) is concerned about promoting a feeling of student ownership and membership in the class.

23. As part of the presentation of projects and activities, Mrs. Alvarez asks her students to write a narrative explanation of their projects. Then she arranges for the class presentations to be videotaped as the students

read their prepared explanations. A student is appointed "filming director" for each project, and another student is appointed "reporter." All of the students who participated are "writers" and contribute to the written script. This activity is an example of

(A) using a variety of instructional resources to support individual and group learning.

(B) inappropriate use of school video equipment.

(C) providing "directors," "reporters," and "writers" with information about those careers.

(D) a homogeneously grouped cooperative learning exercise.

24. A museum of Native American culture is located about 45 minutes from school. Mrs. Alvarez is considering a field trip to the museum. Which of the following elements should most influence her decision?

(A) The relevance of the current exhibits to the topics her students researched

(B) The cost of admission, the distance from the school, and the availability of transportation

(C) The difficulty in obtaining permission forms from each student

(D) The loss of class time in other subject areas

Scenario 8

Mrs. Gettler teaches 26 third graders in a large inner city school. About one-third of her students participate in the ESL program at the school. Mrs. Gettler suspects that some of the students' parents are unable to read or write in English. Four of the students receive services from the learning resource teacher. At the beginning of the year, none of the students read above 2.0 grade level, and some of the students did not know all the letters of the alphabet.

25. Which of the following describes the instructional strategy that is most likely to improve the reading levels of Mrs. Gettler's students?

(A) An intensive phonics program that includes drill and practice work on basic sight words.

(B)   An emergent literacy program emphasizing pattern books and journal writing using invented spelling.

(C)   An instructional program that closely follows the third-grade basal reader

(D)   Participation by all students in the school's ESL program so they can receive services from the learning resource center.

26.   Mrs. Gettler is selecting books for the classroom library. In addition to student interest, which of the following would be the most important considerations?

(A)   The books should have a reading level that matches the students' independent reading abilities.

(B)   The books should only have a reading level that is challenging to the students.

(C)   The books should include separate word lists for student practice.

(D)   A classroom library is not appropriate for students at such a low reading level.

27.   Which of the following individual and small group learning centers is suitable for Mrs. Gettler's class?

I.   A post office center where students can write letters to friends and family

II.   A restaurant center where students read menus, write food orders, and pay the bill with play money

III.   A weather center where students record current conditions, including temperature, cloud cover and wind direction, and prepare graphs of weather patterns

IV.   A science center where students record the results of experiments with combining liquids such as bleach, vinegar, cooking oil, food coloring, and rubbing alcohol

(A)   I only.

(B)   I and II only.

(C)   I, II, and III only.

(D)   II, III, and IV only.

28. Mrs. Gettler realizes that an individual's preferred learning style contributes to that individual's success as a student. Mrs. Gettler wants to accommodate as many of her students' individual learning styles as possible. Which of the following best describes the way to identify the students' learning styles?

   (A)   Mrs. Gettler should record her observations of each individual student's behavior over a period of several weeks.

   (B)   Each of the students should be tested by the school psychologist.

   (C)   Mrs. Gettler should administer a group screening test for identifying learning styles.

   (D)   Mrs. Gettler should review the permanent file of each student and compare the individual's previous test scores with classroom performance.

29. During the first parent-teacher conference of the year, Mrs. Gettler should

   (A)   stress that it is unlikely that each student in her class will be promoted to the fourth grade.

   (B)   determine the educational background of each parent and recommend the district GED program as needed.

   (C)   emphasize her willingness to work with each student to enable each student to be successful.

   (D)   recommend that parents secure an individual tutor for each student who is reading below grade level.

30. As the school year progresses, Mrs. Gettler includes discussions of holidays of many cultures. She introduces the holiday prior to the actual day of celebration. The children prepare decorations, learn songs, and read stories about children in the countries where the holiday is celebrated. Which of the following best describes the most likely purpose of this activity?

   (A)   It is one way to teach appreciation of human diversity.

   (B)   It is one way to satisfy the demands of political action groups.

(C)   It is one way to encourage students to read aloud to one another.

(D)   It is one way to encourage students to participate in class activities.

_____

Scenario 9

Mr. Dobson teaches fifth-grade mathematics at Valverde Elementary. He encourages students to work in groups of two or three as they begin homework assignments so they can answer questions for each other. Mr. Dobson notices immediately that some of his students chose to work alone even though they had been asked to work in groups. He also notices that some students are easily distracted even though the other members of their group are working on the assignment as directed.

31.   Which of the following is the most likely explanation for the students' different types of behavior?

(A)   Fifth-grade students are not physically or mentally capable of working in small groups; small groups are more suitable for older students.

(B)   Fifth-grade students vary greatly in their physical development and maturity; this variance influences the students' interests and attitudes.

(C)   Fifth-grade students lack the ability for internal control, and therefore learn best in structured settings. It is usually best to seat fifth graders in single rows.

(D)   Mr. Dobson needs to be more specific in his expectations for student behavior.

32.   Mr. Dobson wants to encourage all of his students to participate in discussions related to the use of math in the real world. Five students in one class are very shy and introverted. Which of the following would most likely be the best way to encourage these students to participate in the discussion?

(A)   Mr. Dobson should call on these students by name at least once each day and give participation grades.

(B)   Mr. Dobson should not be concerned about these students because they will become less shy and introverted as they mature during the year.

(C)   Mr. Dobson should divide the class into small groups for discussion so these students will not be overwhelmed by speaking in front of the whole class.

(D)   Mr. Dobson should speak with these students individually and encourage them to participate more in class discussions.

33.   In the same class, Mr. Dobson has two students who are overly talkative. These two students volunteer to answer every question. Which of the following is the best way to deal with these students?

(A)   Mr. Dobson should call on the overly talkative students only once during each class.

(B)   Mr. Dobson should ask these students to be the observers in small group discussions, and take notes about participation and topics discussed.

(C)   Mr. Dobson should place these students in a group by themselves so they can discuss all they want and not disturb the other students.

(D)   Mr. Dobson should recognize that overly talkative students need lots of attention and should be called on to participate throughout the class period.

34.   Mr. Dobson wants his fifth-grade students to serve as tutors for the first graders who are learning addition and subtraction. The main advantage for the fifth graders who participate is

(A)   they will develop proficiency and self-esteem.

(B)   they will be encouraged to view teaching as a possible career.

(C)   they will learn specific tutoring techniques.

(D)   they will have an opportunity to become friends with younger children.

35. Mr. Dobson plans mathematics lessons so that all students will experience at least 70 percent success during independent practice. Considering student success during independent practice reflects Mr. Dobson's understanding that

(A) a student's academic success influences overall achievements and contributes to positive self-esteem.

(B) students who are academically successful have happy parents.

(C) if students are successful when working alone they can finish their homework independently.

(D) if the students are successful they will ask fewer questions, giving Mr. Dobson more time to plan future lessons.

36. Mr. Dobson has just explained a new procedure for solving a particular kind of mathematics problem. He has solved several demonstration problems on the board. Several students raise their hands to ask questions. If a student's question requires more than two or three minutes to answer, then Mr. Dobson knows that

(A) the original explanation was faulty.

(B) the students were not paying attention.

(C) the students are below average in listening skills.

(D) the students have a very poor background in mathematics.

37. Mr. Dobson and Mr. Lowery, a science teacher, are planning a celebration of Galileo's birthday. The students will research Galileo's discoveries, draw posters of those discoveries, and prepare short plays depicting important events in his life. They will present the plays and display the posters for grades 1–4. This is an example of

(A) an end-of-the-year project.

(B) problem solving and inquiry teaching.

(C) working with other teachers to plan instructions.

(D) teachers preparing to ask the PTA for science lab equipment.

38.   Mr. Dobson wants to use a variety of grouping strategies during the year. Sometimes he groups students with others of similar ability; sometimes he groups students with varying ability. Sometimes he permits students to choose their own groupings. Sometimes he suggests that students work with a particular partner; sometimes he assigns a partner. Sometimes he allows students to elect to work individually. This flexibility in grouping strategies indicates Mr. Dobson recognizes that

   (A)   fifth graders like surprises and unpredictable teacher behavior.

   (B)   grouping patterns affect students' perceptions of self-esteem and competence.

   (C)   frequent changes in the classroom keep students alert and interested.

   (D)   it is not fair to place the worst students in the same group consistently.

39.   The principal asks Mr. Dobson and Ms. Gonzalez, another fifth-grade math teacher in the school, to visit the math classes and the computer lab in the middle school that most of the students at Valverde will attend. By asking Mr. Dobson and Ms. Gonzalez to visit the middle school, the principal is most likely encouraging

   (A)   collaboration among the math teachers at Valverde and the middle school.

   (B)   Mr. Dobson and Ms. Gonzalez to consider applying for a job at the middle school.

   (C)   the use of computers in math classes at Valverde.

   (D)   the use of the middle school math curriculum in the fifth-grade classes.

Scenario 10

40.   Mrs. Doe began planning a two-week unit of study of the Native Americans for her fifth-grade class. To begin the unit, she chose a movie on the twenty-first century Native Americans. As Mrs. Doe reflectively listened, key questions were asked.

The following day Mrs. Doe reviewed the use of encyclopedias, indexes, and atlases. The students were divided into groups and taken to the library. Each group was responsible for locating information on their topic. The topics were maps showing the topography of the land, charts illustrating the climate, plants and animals, a map showing migration routes, and a map showing the general areas where the Native Americans settled. The students' involvement in the unit of study is a result of

I.   the teacher's reflective listening during the discussion.

II.   the available resources and materials.

III. careful planning and its relationship to success in the classroom.

IV.   the students' personal acquaintance with Native Americans.

(A)   I only.   (C)   II and III only.

(B)   I and II only.   (D)   I and IV only.

41. Days 3 and 4 were spent with each group being involved in library research. Information was written on index cards. Each group prepared a presentation which included a written explanation of an assigned topic, a shadow box, and a sawdust map or models of Native American clothing. A pictograph was to be used in the telling of a legend or folk story. The presentation was concluded with a collage depicting the Native American way of life. Multiple strategies and techniques were used for

I.   motivation of the group and its effects on individual behavior and learning.

II.   allowing each student regardless of ability to participate in the project.

III. integrating the project with other subjects.

IV.   developing a foundation for teaching American history.

(A)   I, II, and III only.   (C)   III only.

(B)   I and II only.   (D)   IV only.

42. On day 8, Mrs. Doe arranged a display of Native American artifacts and crafts in the hallway. Having collaborated with the music teacher at the onset of her planning and arranging for a general assembly of the entire

student body, she took her students to the auditorium. The general assembly consisted of Native American poetry read by Fawn Lonewolf with Native American music and dance by the school chorus. At the conclusion of the assembly, the class was invited to view the video *The Trail of Tears*. Native American refreshments, including fried bread, were served to the students. As the students ate, *Knots on a Counting Rope* was read orally by the reading teacher. Following the reading, the physical education teacher taught the students several games which had been played by Native American children. The planning of the assembly and the following activities required

I.   the taking of risks by both the teacher and the students.

II.   stimulating the curiosity of the student body.

III.   recognizing individual talents among the students.

IV.   using the collaborative process of working with other teachers.

(A)   I only.

(B)   II only.

(C)   II and III only.

(D)   II, III, and IV only.

43.   Day 10 of the unit was Field Trip Day. The students were given a choice of visiting museums. Whatever the student's choice, he or she was to take notes of what was seen, heard, and experienced. These would be shared with the remainder of the class on the following day. Field Trip Day and its experiences

I.   allowed the student to make connections between their current skills and those that were new to them.

II.   allowed external factors to create a learning environment which would take advantage of positive factors.

III.   allowed a sense of community to be nurtured.

IV.   allowed the students to take responsibility for their own learning.

(A)   I and II only.

(B)   III only.

(C)   IV only.

(D)   III and IV only.

44. The choice of field trip locations

    I.   was to enhance the students' self-concept.

    II.   was to respect differences and enhance the students' understanding of the society in which they live.

    III.   was to foster the view of learning as a purposeful pursuit.

    IV.   was an example of using an array of instructional strategies.

(A)   II only.   (C)   I and II only.

(B)   II and IV only.   (D)   III only.

Scenario 11

Several average classes of fifth graders were found to be inadequately prepared for fifth-grade work. It was important that their problem-solving skills and motivation improve in order to meet the pre-entry criteria for a new middle-school. Most of the students could not comprehend fifth-grade textual material. They lacked enthusiasm for projects and problems. Many of the students had become frightened by their academic failure and were withdrawing in confusion.

Mrs. Sivart is retained to help the classes improve their problem-solving skills and to facilitate motivation and enthusiasm. After reviewing test scores and evaluating daily work, she called for a conference with the concerned teachers.

"Mrs. Dunn, what do you perceive to be the problem?"

"Those students just did not learn the appropriate skills in the lower grades. What can I do when they come to me with deficient skills? After all, I teach social studies, I do not teach basic reading skills."

"Mr. Ellis, what is your perception?"

"I believe, as does Mrs. Dunn, that these students were not taught these skills in the lower grades. They were just promoted along."

"Do you feel a responsibility toward the students to correct this deficiency?" asked Mrs. Sivart.

"Yes, I really do, but my first responsibility is for each student to meet the objectives required by the state each year. I just don't have time to remediate the students."

Mrs. Sivart was reflective for a moment, then gently asked, "What would you say if I told you that at least part of the problem does not lie with the students? What text do you currently use?"

"We use the standard fifth-grade social studies text from Blank Publishing Company."

"May we meet again tomorrow at this same time?" asked Mrs. Sivart. "I have something to show you."

The following day, Mrs. Sivart appeared in the meeting with readability charts, texts, paper, and pencils. Each teacher agreed to do a readability on the text. As they completed the readability, a stunned silence followed. "I certainly did not know I was expecting these students to read materials which are three years above their grade level. No wonder they don't comprehend. Mrs. Sivart, what can we do to remedy this situation?"

45. At this point in the solving of the problem, Mrs. Sivart had

(A) caused the teachers to focus upon reflection and self-evaluation and to recognize their bias.

(B) allowed the teachers to shift part of the blame from the elementary school teachers to the publisher.

(C) allowed the teachers to seek out opportunities to grow professionally by using different sources of support and guidance to enhance their own professional skills.

(D) used informal assessment to understand the learners.

46. Mr. Ellis' statement that he was expected to meet the state objectives each year revealed that he

(A) was refusing to reflect upon his responsibility to the students and was unwilling to change teaching strategies.

(B) understood the requirements and expectations of teaching.

(C) was inflexible in his strategies and the use of collaborative processes.

(D)   probably had a deficiency in using a variety of instructional materials.

At the following planning meeting, Mrs. Sivart agreed to demonstrate a strategy which could be used in each class to make the adopted text appropriate for that class. Following her demonstration, she asked the teachers to develop an exam which would cover the material they had just modified. Each teacher was then to do a readability on the exam. As Mrs. Sivart circulated among the teachers, she saw puzzled expressions and overheard "I have just written a ninth-grade exam for fifth-grade students. I can't believe I did that. What do I do now?" With a smile, Mrs. Sivart responded, "You rewrite the exam until it is on the fifth-grade level. Using your readability chart, check each item on the exam, keep modifying the item until it is written on the correct level." She continued, "What you have done is very common among teachers, but with practice you will soon be writing exams on grade level. By combining modification of the text with writing your exams on grade level and using a few techniques for increasing comprehension, you should see a great change in your students. Nothing breeds success like success."

47.   Through the demonstration, the in-service training of writing exams, and the extra techniques for improving comprehension, Mrs. Sivart had demonstrated that

(A)   the teacher should constantly monitor and adjust strategies in response to student feedback.

(B)   the teacher could promote student learning by designing instruction for different situations.

(C)   the teacher should be able to recognize factors and situations that will either promote or diminish motivation.

(D)   external factors may affect students' performance in school.

48.   The concept that Mrs. Sivart had caused the teachers to focus upon was that

(A)   most of the time when students fail, it is not their fault.

(B)   individualizing instruction does not have to be tedious and time consuming.

(C)   external factors may affect students' performance in class.

(D)   diversity in the classroom may affect learning.

Scenario 12

A traditional elementary school reading program for grades K-6 has been evaluated. The results show that a majority of students are not reading at grade level. Library records reveal the students' lack of interest in reading. The reading coordinator, Mrs. Smith, has been charged with coordinating efforts to improve the reading skills for all grades. The improvement of reading skills on or near grade level is the school objective.

Mrs. Smith's first action was to form a committee of the school psychometrist, the media specialist, and one teacher from each of the seven grades. The psychometrist was to study the test results and determine which of the reading skills were lacking in the students. She reported that only 30 percent of the students were deficient in specific reading skills. The remainder of the students were deficient in no particular area but still had an overall deficiency. She explained that there were developmental progressions and ranges of individual variation in each domain which would account for about 10 percent of the students.

49.   Mrs. Smith asked the teachers to design a plan of study for those students who fell within the 10 percent. The rationale for her request was based upon

(A)   lessening the work load for the teachers.

(B)   obtaining a framework for remediating the other 20 percent of the students.

(C)   facilitating the development of a project plan best suited to address the academic needs of individual students.

(D)   recognizing the benefits of working cooperatively to achieve goals.

50.   Mrs. Smith began to design a plan of study for those students who were deficient in one or more areas of reading skills. She chose a plan which would allow the student to rotate from one teacher to another, remediating one reading skill with each teacher. When the student had

mastered all deficient skills, they would no longer attend the sessions. Mrs. Smith planned her strategy based upon the knowledge that

(A)   students learn faster when they perceive they are learning less.

(B)   teachers would be more receptive to teaching one skill instead of all reading skills.

(C)   parents would be less likely to perceive the remediation as a negative activity.

(D)   assimilation occurs more rapidly for the student when new information is linked to old information.

51.   The media specialist suggested a library reading program which would correlate highly with the teaching program and reward the students as they read. The rewards would be provided by the business community. A pencil carrier would be the reward for having read 25 books, a baseball cap the reward for having read 30 books, a tee shirt for 50 books, and a backpack for having read 100 books. The media specialist's suggestion was based on her knowledge that

(A)   students enjoy doing those things they do well.

(B)   students would read to receive the reward.

(C)   instruction which is planned to enhance students' self-esteem will create an environment where the student feels accepted, competent, and productive.

(D)   library materials which correlate with teaching strategies are more meaningful and help to create an atmosphere which motivates students to continue to read additional books.

52.   Mrs. Smith requested that computers be made available in the small group area of the library. Software would be provided which contained comprehension questions for 500 books. As each student completed reading the book, they could come to the library and take the comprehension quiz. The computer kept a record of those books read and comprehended. If comprehension fell below 80 percent, the student alone knew if he or she needed to reread the book and retake the exam. Mrs. Smith felt that student privacy was important because

(A)   students' self-esteem is easily lowered if others are aware of their failures.

(B)   this strategy would remove the teacher from the role of informing the student if he or she needed to reread and retake the test.

(C)   the use of the computers would prevent the media specialist from having an increased workload.

(D)   the combination of appropriate instructional materials and resources helps students to understand the role of technology as a learning tool.

53.   After yet another brainstorming session with all members of the action committee, the group decided to post and then repost the title of each book every time it was read and comprehended. Publicly displaying the titles of the books was based upon

(A)   understanding the uses of formal and informal assessment to monitor instructional effectiveness.

(B)   facilitating motivation of all the students.

(C)   helping the students to become independent thinkers and problem-solvers.

(D)   varying the role of the teachers in the instructional process.

54.   As the action committee reviewed the design of the curriculum, they recognized that

(A)   the amount of classroom time would be maximized.

(B)   the students would learn a lot about the resources available to them.

(C)   routines and transitions would be managed.

(D)   they had structured a learning environment which not only maintained a positive classroom environment but would promote the lifelong pursuit of learning.

Scenario 13

Mrs. Green, the home economics teacher, was planning a unit on nutrition. Her first task was to identify the performance objectives. She concluded that she wanted the students to master the content of her lecture, but she also wanted them to be able to do independent research in the library on the topic of nutrition. Her second task was to prepare an evaluation tool to be used at the completion of the unit. She decided to have a paper and pencil test as well as a performance exam. Step 3 consisted of choosing resources for the class presentation. She chose a beginning text on foods, the nutrition unit from the curriculum materials, two *Measure Up* games from the media center, teacher-made worksheets covering the appropriate content, a computer program for enhancing the classroom presentation, and the required tools and ingredients for the performance aspect of the unit. The unit would be concluded with a field trip.

55. The presentation of the unit was designed to

   (A)   communicate through verbal, nonverbal, and media resources, thus imparting the expectations and ideas to create a climate of inquiry.

   (B)   present the information by utilizing a variety of materials and techniques.

   (C)   give the students a choice of what they were to learn.

   (D)   integrate with other subjects in the school.

56. The strength of requiring a cognitive objective and a performance objective is that

   (A)   some students are not test takers and do poorly on paper and pencil tests.

   (B)   the score for one objective could offset the score for the other objective.

   (C)   the developmental level in one domain may affect performance in another domain.

   (D)   the teacher is matching the students' learning styles to her teaching style.

57. The multiple resources planned for by Mrs. Green provided for

    (A)   enhancing student achievement.

    (B)   engaging the students in meaningful inquiry.

    (C)   eliciting different levels of thinking from the students.

    (D)   promoting problem solving.

58. To begin the unit, Mrs. Green presented the information through the lecture technique. The students were instructed to add notes to the outline of the lecture which had been provided to them. After the information was presented, the students completed the supplementary activities and planned the activities which would be carried out in the labs. The labs contained recipe ingredients. Some of the students were instructed to deliberately mismeasure one of the key ingredients in the recipe. Later, the recipe was analyzed to determine why the result was a failure. A discussion followed, with various students reporting that while watching their parents cook, many times they had used a "dab," a "dash," or a "pinch" of ingredients, not actually measuring. The demonstration of not accurately measuring the ingredients in a recipe was used to

    I.   show the students what happens when directions are not followed.

    II.   to evaluate the observation techniques used by the students.

    III.   to stimulate curiosity in the students.

    IV.   to illustrate how waste can occur in the kitchen.

    (A)   I only.   (C)   III and IV only.

    (B)   II only.   (D)   I, III, and IV only.

59. The culminating field trip was to the cafeteria where the students were familiarized with special measuring tools, e.g., scales, gallons, and pounds. As the students observed the use of these special tools and amounts, they were asked to try to imagine the quantity that a particular recipe would produce and how many servings it would provide. The field trip was planned as a culminating experience

    (A)   to bring closure to the unit.

    (B)   to promote responsibility for one's own learning.

(C)   to confine the students' learning to the classroom, keeping it in an academic setting.

(D)   to allow the students to make the connection between their current skills and those that are new to them.

Scenario 14

Bill Drayton is a first-year teacher of reading. Bill is an exemplary teacher and is already assuming a leadership role in both the community and the school district. He has started taking classes at a university in order to earn a Master of Teaching credential.

Late in the fall semester, Bill arrived home right as a rental moving truck pulled up in front of the house across the street. The "for sale" sign on the house had recently been taken down, and Bill was eager to meet his new neighbors. He trotted across the street and introduced himself to the man who crawled out of the truck.

As the introductions were taking place, a van pulled up into the driveway and a woman came around the side of the van in order to help a young girl in a wheelchair exit the van. "Come and meet my wife, Rachel, and our daughter, Myra," said the new neighbor, who had introduced himself as Harry Jacobsen.

"Myra is in fourth grade," said her mother.

"Then you'll be in one of my classes," said Bill. "We have two fourth-grade classes. Each one spends half the day in Ms. Wade's room, and the other half of the day in mine. I teach language arts and math, while she teaches social studies, science, and art. We have a lot of fun, because we teach around themes. For example, Ms. Wade's social studies classes are learning about how New York history was influenced by geography, so in my language arts class, we're reading stories about New York history and discussing how the geography contributed to the things that happened in those stories. We also pretend that we are early New Yorkers and write journals and newspapers about the events that shaped our history as those events relate to geography. In my math classes, we're using math to better understand New York geography. Things like lengths of rivers, miles between cities located on the waterways, and so forth."

Myra's eyes lit up. "Can I be in his room, Mama?" she asked.

Rachel shook her head. "No, honey, I'm sorry." Then she explained to Bill that Myra had to go to a private school because the local schools were not wheelchair accessible. "Myra can't get through the outer doors, the inner doors, up the stairs to the classroom, the cafeteria, the gym, or anywhere else. In fact, she can't even get into the toilet stalls," she explained. "These changes would take thousands of dollars, and the district can't spend that kind of money on Myra."

60. What should Bill say?

(A) "I'm sorry. But maybe I can bring home some fun materials from school to share with Myra."

(B) "It is illegal for the school not to make itself accessible to all people with handicaps, regardless of the cost. Let me talk to the principal."

(C) "I'm sorry. If the costs were reasonable, perhaps the district could make changes. But you're right. We can't make changes that expensive for only one student."

(D) "You should sue the school district and force them to make the changes."

61. That evening, Bill and his wife went out to eat to celebrate her birthday. They went to a movie, and then finding that there was a full moon, decided to go for a drive before they went home. As they rounded a corner not far from their home, Bill saw one of his students, Cade Evans, running down the street. Cade was with a group of other boys, one of whom threw something down as they ran. Although Bill did not see the faces of any of the boys except for Cade, judging from their size, he thought that they were probably also fourth graders. Bill stopped his car and looked around. He discovered newly painted graffiti on the side of the building by the corner. What is Bill's best course of action?

I. Chase down the boys with his car and make a citizen's arrest.

II. Call the police and report what he saw.

III. Call the superintendent immediately and report what he saw.

IV. Refer Cade to Big Brothers' as a child in need of a special friend.

(A) I and II only.   (C) II and III only.

(B) II and IV only.   (D) III and IV only.

62. Troubled by what seems to be an increase in gang-type activity among younger and younger children, Bill wants to find out what his students think and know about gangs. He wants to learn the most he can about the students' thinking about this topic in the least amount of time. He wants all students to have the chance to share what they think and know, yet he also wants to maximize interaction among students. The students will spend the entire morning reading, talking, and writing a group report about this subject. Which of the following seating arrangements would best help Bill meet his objectives?

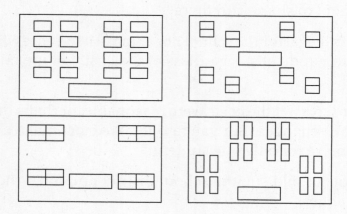

(A)   The upper left-hand diagram

(B)   The lower left-hand diagram

(C)   The upper right-hand diagram

(D)   The lower right-hand diagram

63. One of the activities that Bill decides to employ in his language arts class during the thematic study of the impact of geographic features on the history of New York is storytelling. Bill has studied the art of storytelling and one day aspires to be a master storyteller. What would be the most important reason that Bill learn to be a master storyteller?

(A)   Everyone loves a good story.

(B)   Storytelling is a highly cost-effective method of teaching.

(C)   Storytelling is one of the most effective ways of teaching field dependent students.

(D)   Storytelling is one of the most effective ways of teaching field independent students.

64. Following two days of activities which include Bill's storytelling sessions, Bill tells the children that they are to each write a story to tell to the class. What is most likely the instructional reason that Bill is having the children write a story with the intent of telling it to the class as opposed to merely writing a story?

   (A) Publication is a highly effective tool in motivating people to do their best work.

   (B) Being able to speak in public is a crucial skill for success in a democratic society.

   (C) The students will learn to critique their own work.

   (D) Students' prior exposure to stories is important to their ability to write a story.

65. That afternoon, Bill and Kayla Wade meet after school to begin planning for the next thematic unit of study. Kayla, who is also a first-year teacher, is ready to move into the unit on persons who made contributions to the development of New York. Which strategy for planning for outcome-oriented learning experiences would be the best one with which to start?

   (A) Select desired learning activities.

   (B) Determine time and space constraints.

   (C) Determine desired learner outcomes.

   (D) Solicit input from students.

66. Bill comes to the planning session with a notecard on which he has listed the essential elements that he plans to address during the new unit of study:

   LISTENING
   Distinguish between fact and opinion.

   SPEAKING
   Adapt content and formality of oral language to fit the purpose and audience.

READING
1. Identify multiple causes of characters' actions.
2. Understand the feelings of characters.

WRITING
Use ideas/sources other than personal opinion/experiences.

Which of the following resources are most likely to be of use to Bill?

I.   Computer with word-processing program

II. Laser disk player with laser disk of influential New Yorkers

III. Primary sources

IV. Local expert on ecology

(A) I only.

(B) I and IV only.

(C) II only.

(D) II and III only.

Scenario 15

Gerene Thompson is a first-year teacher who has accepted a position as a first-grade teacher in an inner city school. In college, Gerene's elementary teaching field was science. She is eager to begin working with her first graders so that in addition to teaching them literacy skills, she can teach them to enjoy science and mathematics.

67. In the last week before school starts, Gerene has much to do in order to get ready for the first day of school. Of the many tasks that she must perform, which is likely to have the biggest impact on her students' success in first grade?

(A) Having a wide variety of teaching material ready and available

(B) Making the room look inviting by creating bulletin boards depicting students of many nations

(C) Personally contacting the parents of each child

(D) Coordinating her science activities with her reading activities

68. Of all of her students who do not have documented handicaps, which of her students are most likely to be poor readers?

    (A) Those whose parents seldom read aloud to them

    (B) Those whose parents place them in daycare for more than three hours per day

    (C) Those whose parents allow them to watch more than two hours of television daily

    (D) Those who are being raised by a grandparent

69. In planning her first week's activities, what factors should Gerene consider?

    I.   The interests of first graders

    II.   Her students' prior knowledge

    III. The affective needs of her students

    IV.   The nutritional needs of her students

    (A) I and II only.   (C) I, II, and III only.

    (B) II and IV only.   (D) All of the above.

70. On the first day, Gerene plans to introduce her students to the phoneme/grapheme relationship of the letter M. Which of the following would be the best set of strategies for this objective?

    (A) Gerene should tell her students what sound the letter M makes. She should then provide them with a wide variety of fun paper/pencil and coloring activities as independent work to help them internalize the letter name with its sound. She should schedule the students throughout the day to take turns on the class computer's phonics program.

    (B) Gerene should engage the students in a repetitive, rhythmic oral activity using the letter M phoneme/grapheme relationship. She should use a picture as a cue card and display the cue card where the students can see it at all times. She should not place students at the computer without direct supervision for the first several times.

(C) Gerene should not engage the students in repetitive activity, as repetition will quickly bore them and act as an aversive reinforcer to the reading activity. She should employ paper/pencil activities supplemented with coloring and making M's out of clay, papier-mache, and other manipulative materials. She should also use large-muscle movement activities to reinforce the letter-sound relationship. She should use the interactive laser disk with the entire group to show the students many objects that start with the M sound, but she should not allow students to use the equipment individually.

(D) Gerene should engage the students in repetitive, rhythmic activities using the letter M in its phoneme/grapheme relationship. She should read at least one picture book aloud to the students in a story-circle, and discuss it at length with them as she reads it. She should display a picture cue card for the letter M in a prominent place. She should use a wide variety of paper/pencil and art activities employing the letter M.

71. Gerene wants to teach her students about ways of collecting data in science. This is a skill required by the New York state curriculum for first graders. First graders are also required to learn about living things. Which of the following describes the most appropriate method of teaching Gerene's students about collecting data in science?

(A) Gerene should arrange the students into groups of four. She should then have each group observe while she gently touches the class's pet mouse with a feather. The students should record how many out of ten times the pet mouse moves away from the feather. Then Gerene should gently touch the class's philodendron ten times with a feather. The students should record how many out of ten times the philodendron moves away from the feather.

(B) Gerene should group the students into groups of four. She should give each group five solid balls made of materials that will float and five solid balls made of materials that will not float. She should have the students drop the balls into a bowl of water and record how many float and how many do not.

(C) Gerene should show the students a video about scientific methods of gathering data.

(D)   Gerene should have a scientist come and talk to the class about methods of collecting data. If she cannot get a scientist, she should have a science teacher from the high school come and tell about scientific methods of data collection.

72.   Gerene wants to reinforce the notion of data collection by assigning a homework project which will involve the students' families. Which of the following would be the most appropriate assignment?

(A)   Have the students and their families watch a program on data collection on the Discovery channel

(B)   Have the parents take their students to the exhibit on data collection at the local museum

(C)   Have the students ask their parents to help them count the number of times that their heart beats per minute at rest and after five minutes of exercise

(D)   Have the students ask their parents to read to them about a famous scientist

73.   How can Gerene best teach her students to be lifelong learners and lovers of science?

I.   Give them examples of famous people who were/are lifelong learners.

II.   In an enthusiastic manner, frequently say "Isn't this exciting? Isn't it fun to learn new things!" during science activities.

III.   Employ many hands-on activities that are difficult enough to challenge the students, yet simple enough that the students will succeed.

IV.   Reward students who work hard and punish students who do not perform.

(A)   I and II only.   (C)   III and IV only.

(B)   II and III only.   (D)   III only.

74. In general, how can Gerene best address the learning styles of her female students in science activities?

    (A) Employ cooperative, noncompetitive teaching strategies that utilize many experiences with hands-on activities.

    (B) Employ competitive teaching strategies that utilize many experiences with hands-on activities.

    (C) Employ teaching strategies that require students to work independently on hands-on activities.

    (D) Employ teaching strategies utilizing computer-assisted programmed instruction.

75. In general, when Molly Carter, a student of African-American heritage, makes statements such as "My mama, she works at the store down the block." How should Gerene respond?

    (A) Gerene should tell Molly that it is important that she learn to speak standard English.

    (B) Gerene should not reinforce Molly's speech patterns by interacting with her when she does not speak standard English.

    (C) Gerene should say, "Molly dear, it is not correct to say 'my mama, she works' you should say, 'my mama works' if you want people to understand you."

    (D) Gerene should say, "Tell me what kinds of things your mama does at work."

___

Scenario 16

76. Although Ms. Axtel has two years of experience teaching sixth grade, she has been asked to teach a group of 25 second graders for the new school year. She wants to prepare several units before school begins. Which of the following principles is the most important to consider as she prepares her units?

    (A) The major difference between sixth-grade students and second-grade students is their physical size.

(B)   Second-grade students are very different developmentally from sixth-grade students.

(C)   Some second-grade students read as well as some sixth-grade students.

(D)   Sixth-grade students like to read books on topics that are very different from the topics that second grade students prefer.

77.   When developing a unit about the Erie Canal for elementary-age students, what would you include as an assessment tool?

(A)   Explain to the students that the unit will cover a variety of projects; therefore, you will be using different assessment tools.

(B)   Explain to the students each project in the unit, then describe what they will be asked to do.

(C)   Give a list of new vocabulary words that they will need to know for the final test.

(D)   Explain to the students that they will need to hand in their notebooks at the end of the unit.

78.   When creating student examinations, the teacher needs to consider how reliable the tests will be. With this in mind, which of the following concepts should the teacher reflect upon?

I.   The longer the test, the greater its reliability.

II.   Students should be given ample time to complete each test item.

III.   Time limits ensure the accuracy of responses.

IV.   Introduce new information on the exam, so the students learn new concepts while being tested.

(A)   I and IV

(B)   III and IV

(C)   II and III

(D)   I and II

79. Rubrics are used by many teachers in elementary schools for the purposes of assessment. What criteria should be used when creating a rubric?

   I.   Set clearly defined criteria for each assessment.

   II.   Include a rating scale.

   III. Use only one idea at a time so that students are not confused.

   IV.   Tell students that they can rate themselves.

   (A) IV and III

   (B) III and II

   (C) I and II

   (D) None of these

Use the following excerpt to answer Question 80:

   He walked in the dark world in the mild

   Still guidance of the Light;

   In tearful tenderness a child,

   A strong man in the right

80. This poem most closely reflects which of the following tenets of Christianity?

   (A) Man is a son of God

   (B) Men are equal in the sight of God

   (C) A Christian walks in the real world

   (D) God speaks to all men through his light

SECTION 2

DIRECTIONS: Plan and write an essay on the topic given below. Do not write on any topic other than the one specified. An essay on any other topic is unacceptable.

Essay Topic:

Many schools group students by ability, feeling that this provides the best environment for bright students to excel and remedial students to gain the skills they need to succeed. Many feel, however, that ability grouping prevents some students from reaching their full potential.

Assignment:

Are you in favor of ability grouping? Explain your position by discussing the positive or negative consequences of ability grouping for students and teachers.

ATS-W ELEMENTARY PRACTICE TEST

ANSWER KEY

1.	(D)	21.	(B)	41.	(A)	61.	(B)
2.	(D)	22.	(D)	42.	(D)	62.	(B)
3.	(D)	23.	(A)	43.	(A)	63.	(C)
4.	(B)	24.	(A)	44.	(B)	64.	(A)
5.	(A)	25.	(B)	45.	(C)	65.	(C)
6.	(A)	26.	(A)	46.	(B)	66.	(D)
7.	(C)	27.	(C)	47.	(A)	67.	(C)
8.	(C)	28.	(A)	48.	(C)	68.	(A)
9.	(A)	29.	(C)	49.	(C)	69.	(D)
10.	(B)	30.	(A)	50.	(D)	70.	(D)
11.	(D)	31.	(B)	51.	(C)	71.	(B)
12.	(C)	32.	(C)	52.	(A)	72.	(C)
13.	(A)	33.	(B)	53.	(A)	73.	(B)
14.	(C)	34.	(A)	54.	(D)	74.	(A)
15.	(D)	35.	(A)	55.	(A)	75.	(D)
16.	(B)	36.	(A)	56.	(C)	76.	(B)
17.	(B)	37.	(C)	57.	(A)	77.	(B)
18.	(C)	38.	(B)	58.	(D)	78.	(D)
19.	(B)	39.	(A)	59.	(D)	79.	(C)
20.	(D)	40.	(C)	60.	(B)	80.	(D)

ATS-W ELEMENTARY PRACTICE TEST

Detailed Explanations
of Answers

SECTION 1

1. **(D)** The correct response is (D). Comprehension is shown when the reader questions his or her intent for reading. For example, one may be reading a story to find out what terrible things may befall the main character. The rationale for choosing a book may be an interesting bit of information (A), but it is not a major topic of discussion with the students. Sharing personal information (B) creates a certain bond, but this is not directly relevant to the question. It is also important that all students are on-task before the beginning of a lesson (C), but this is a smaller part of the skill modeled in response (D).

2. **(D)** The correct response is (D). A question testing whether or not a student can synthesize information will include the need to make predictions or solve problems. An evaluation question (A) will require a judgment of the quality of an idea or solution. In order to be real analysis (B), the question would have to ask students to analyze given information to draw a conclusion or find support for a given idea. Comprehension questions (C) require the rephrasing of an idea in the students' own words, and then using this for comparison.

3. **(D)** The correct response is (D). By having a mixed level pair read together, the remedial student receives instruction and the skilled student receives reinforcement. It uses alternate teaching resources, the

students themselves, to enhance the learning environment. A certain goal, comprehension, has been set (A), but this is not the most important outcome. The teacher will need to observe fewer groups (B), but it is unlikely that this will change the time needed to work with all groups as long as quality is to be maintained. Although reading in pairs, each student should have a book, and it would be impractical to permit another teacher to utilize the books while one teacher is using them.

4.   **(B)** The correct response is (B). Students at this age do not have the cognitive skills to realize how much they have actually learned, or how much they will actually be able to retain. For this reason, (A) must be incorrect. Students cannot differentiate material that is completely understood and that which they have not completely comprehended at this stage in their intellectual development (C). Students will generally feel that they are capable of learning much more than they will actually retain (D).

5.   **(A)** The correct response is (A). By mapping out previous knowledge, information already known can be transferred to support new information. Although words on the board are visual (B), this is not the underlying motive. Semantic mapping done at the beginning of a story tests how much knowledge the students have about the topic at the outset, not the conclusion (C). This does model proper use of words (D), but this is not the main intent of the exercise.

6.   **(A)** The correct response is (A). At this grade level, awareness of job roles and developing good attitudes about work ethics related to all forms of employment are major goals of the curriculum. To help accomplish these goals, Ms. Felder's invitation to the parents of children in her class to visit and talk about their careers continues her effort to build a close working relationship with the parents. With three or four parents visiting on a given day, she will have the opportunity to talk with each and strengthen her own communication with each child's family. Even if a parent cannot participate in the project, Ms. Felder will have the opportunity to talk with the parent and perhaps encourage the parent to send some information about his or her career to the class. Having only a few parents a day will enable Ms. Felder to plan her lesson well so that she can focus upon the role each worker plays in benefiting the students in her class. (B) is incorrect because it focuses on an unimportant aspect of the career awareness unit. (C) is incorrect because the teacher is not trying to get 11 year olds to choose a career; she is just trying to make

them aware of the career choices available to them. (D) is incorrect because it places an invalid inference on the parents' being able to speak to the class.

7. **(C)** The correct response is (C). Mrs. Kresmeier uses effective communication strategies to teach the students and encourages them to interact for the same purposes. Mnemonic devices are apparently a new technique for most of the students; at least the teacher's own creative spelling clues are often new ones matching the age level interests and patterns of humor enjoyed by her students. The most success is probably derived from her encouragement to examine the words to find a feature that can be turned into a mnemonic device. (A) is incorrect since there has been no attempt to rule out other techniques of learning to spell. (B) is incorrect because certainly other teachers have impressed upon the students that spelling is important. The creative methodology is the major difference between Mrs. Kresmeier's method and those that students have encountered in the past. (D) is incorrect since no evidence exists to show that Mrs. Kresmeier is especially selective in choosing her spelling lessons.

8. **(C)** The correct response is (C). This response recognizes that children learn at different rates and suggests a structured method to limit the number of children per center. It is impossible for all students to work at the same rate (A). Children who finish early should not be given extra work merely to keep them busy (B). Speed is not the primary goal of this activity (D).

9. **(A)** The correct response is (A). When a teacher provides instruction as a facilitator, he or she adjusts the amount and type of help provided to each student based on their individual needs and abilities. This creates independent learners. A supervisor oversees activities but does not necessarily offer assistance or support independent activities (B). Although a teacher often has to be a disciplinarian, this is not the primary goal of moving from group to group (C). A teacher moving from group to group may also be informally assessing student work (D), but it is not the main goal of the activity.

10. **(B)** The correct response is (B). Materials should represent a wide range of topics and people, thereby fostering an appreciation for diversity in the students. An appropriate reading level (A), related informa-

tion (C), and a majority of interest (D) are all important, but cannot be called the main reason for selecting materials.

11. **(D)** The correct response is (D). A concluding activity should encourage students to summarize what they have learned and share this information with other students. A class party celebrating scientists is a valuable experience but does not allow students to share what they have learned (A). A topic for cumulative reviews should not be limited to only medical discoveries because the unit's topic was much broader (B). A test is considered an evaluation technique and should not be confused with a concluding activity (C).

12. **(C)** The correct response is (C). Formative assessment is continuous and intended to serve as a guide to future learning and instruction. Summative evaluation (A) and summative assessment (B) are both used to put a final critique or grade on an activity or assignment with no real link to the future. Peer assessment would require students to critique each other (D).

13. **(A)** The correct response is (A). Meeting one-to-one to discuss a student's strengths and weaknesses creates a feeling of trust and confidence between the students and the teacher. Grading papers solely on the content of a conference is not an efficient means of grading (B). The student/teacher conference should not focus on only one part of the writing process, such as careful editing (C) or prewriting (D).

14. **(C)** The correct response is (C). The role of the resource teacher is to provide individual instruction for students who qualify for services to work with the classroom teacher through collaborative consultation to adapt instruction to match student needs. A resource teacher should not be entirely responsible for teaching a learning disabled student (A). A learning disabled student should not be totally excused from assignments (B). A resource teacher is not responsible for tutoring outside of the scheduled class meetings (D).

15. **(D)** The correct response is (D). Writing the alphabet simply to write it is an isolated act which will do little to create fluency and self-confidence in reading and writing. Reading in a comfortable atmosphere (A), modeling fluent reading for students (B), and using real-life skills to practice spelling and writing (C) present skills to enhance reading and writing in a manner that is neither threatening nor boring.

16. **(B)** The correct response is (B). All parent conferences should begin and end on a positive note and should avoid technical terms and educational jargon. Any problems should be discussed at once and not left for the second conference (A). Bilingual students should be encouraged to develop fluency in both languages, not exclusively English (C). A teacher is best liked and appreciated if he or she speaks in a way that parents readily understand (D).

17. **(B)** The correct response is (B). By reviewing the lessons, the teacher is reflectively self-evaluating his or her teaching and reviewing ways he or she can improve the lesson to better fit the needs of the students. Although good ideas can be shared, all plans must be modified to fit the class and teacher style (A). "Community helpers" is a topic appropriate for kindergarten (C). Although a class visitor and filmstrip may increase motivation and enthusiasm, (D) does not address the need to evaluate the entire unit.

18. **(C)** The correct response is (C). The use of instructional strategies that make learning relevant to individual student interests is a powerful motivating force that facilitates learning and independent thinking. (A) and (B) are both important factors to consider during a brainstorming session of this type, but both of these factors should influence the teacher only after the students' interests have been included. (D) indicates a misunderstanding of the situation described. The students are setting the objectives for the unit as they brainstorm questions.

19. **(B)** The correct response is (B). Choice is an important element in motivating students to learn. (A) is contradictory with the stated purpose of the activity. The students proposed the questions, so covering all the questions should not be a problem. (C) is incorrect because the students have chosen what they consider to be key questions; the teacher should select different or additional key questions. (D) is a possibility, but only if there is a specific reason why all the students should not research all the questions.

20. **(D)** The correct response is (D). The instructional strategy described is one technique used in inquiry and problem solving. (A) is incorrect because direct instruction requires the teacher to present the content to be learned, frequently asking students questions to monitor comprehension. (B) is incorrect because role playing and simulation are not part of a brainstorming session. (C) is incorrect because exposition and discus-

sion are teacher-led activities using previously established objectives and content.

21. **(B)** The correct response is (B). Ongoing assessment and evaluation, using a variety of formal and informal assessment techniques, is essential to quality instruction. (A) is incorrect because although the teacher may want to use an objective test as part of the overall assessment and evaluation of the unit, an objective test is insufficient assessment without additional instruments. (C) is incorrect because a standardized test is rarely an appropriate tool for an individual unit of instruction. Standardized tests are best used as an end-of-the-year evaluation. (D) is incorrect because every assessment should provide for individual differences. Individual assessments might be part of a total assessment program, but would be inappropriate when used in isolation.

22. **(D)** The correct response is (D). Providing an opportunity to share class projects and activities with other classes will promote a feeling of student ownership and reinforce a feeling of membership in the class as a group. (A) is incorrect because closure refers to that part of a lesson plan that reminds the teacher to conclude the lesson by restating the purpose of the lesson or by summarizing the content of the lesson. (B) is incorrect because although teachers are expected to work collaboratively with other teachers, sharing a class project involves little actual collaboration. (C) is incorrect because although a teacher may be interested in being appointed grade-level chairperson, sharing class projects is a valuable instructional strategy that is not related to a promotion in a school.

23. **(A)** The correct response is (A). Asking students to videotape their project explanations could be highly motivating to the entire class and is an additional way to focus attention and reinforce the significance of the content. (B) is incorrect because this is an appropriate use of video equipment. The value of the equipment and the fact that it is school property is not an issue. (C) is incorrect because the purpose of the activity is to motivate students and does not necessarily accurately represent these careers. (D) is incorrect because nothing is explicitly stated regarding student grouping.

24. **(A)** The correct response is (A). The relevance of the current exhibits to the unit the students are studying is the most important factor in determining if a field trip should be planned. (B) is incorrect because the school should be able to afford the cost of admission for each student or at least for those students who are not able to pay for their own admis-

sion. The distance from the school is simply an element that must be considered when planning the field trip, not a deciding factor in whether or not the trip should be planned. School buses are generally available for field trips, but must be reserved in advance. (C) is incorrect because although obtaining permission slips for each student can be difficult, it should not prevent a teacher from planning a field trip. (D) is incorrect because adjusting the scheduled time for each subject in the following weeks can compensate for any time lost for a particular subject during the field trip.

25. **(B)** The correct response is (B). The best way to teach children to read, regardless of grade level, is to use a program of emergent literacy which includes pattern books and journal writing with invented spelling. (A) is incorrect because although an intensive phonics program that includes drill and practice work may be effective with some students, it is not the most effective way to teach all students to read. (D) is incorrect because an ESL program is intended to provide assistance to only those students who are learning English as a second language. Additionally, the learning resource teacher should provide assistance to only those students who have been identified as having a learning disability that qualifies them to receive services.

26. **(A)** The correct response is (A). By selecting books for the classroom library that match students' independent reading abilities, the teacher is recognizing that each student must improve his or her reading ability by beginning at his or her own level and progressing to more difficult materials. (B) is incorrect because books that are too difficult will most likely be frustrating to many students. (C) is incorrect because the presence or absence of separate word lists should not be a determining factor in selecting books for a classroom library. (D) is incorrect because all children need access to a classroom library regardless of their reading abilities.

27. **(C)** The correct response is (C). A post office center, restaurant center, and a weather center all encourage a variety of reading and writing activities which is what these students need most. (A) and (B) are incorrect because they are incomplete. (D) is incorrect because combining the chemicals in the science center poses an obvious danger to young children.

28. **(A)** The correct response is (A). One of the most reliable ways to identify individual learning styles is to observe the students over a period of time and make informal notes about their work habits and the choices they make within the classroom. (B) is incorrect because although a school psychologist could provide information about each student's learning style, the teacher can identify this information on his or her own. (C) is incorrect because although administering a group screening test will identify learning styles, such a test may be difficult to obtain, and the teacher could gain the same knowledge through simple observation. (D) is incorrect because each student's permanent file may or may not contain this information. In addition, an individual student's learning style may have changed over the years, and there is no guarantee that this change will be noted in the permanent record.

29. **(C)** The correct response is (C). The teacher must make clear that he or she is willing to work with each child and believes that each child can be successful. (A) is incorrect because emphasizing failure early in the year is not appropriate in establishing a feeling of trust with parents. (B) is incorrect because the teacher should emphasize the child during a parent/teacher conference and not discuss the parent's education unless he or she is asked specifically for advice. (D) is incorrect because asking parents to secure an individual tutor may be an unrealistic financial burden. In addition, all children reading below grade level do not necessarily need a tutor.

30. **(A)** The correct response is (A). Celebrating holidays of different cultures teaches appreciation for human diversity. (B) is incorrect because while celebrating different cultures has become a political issue, this should not force or prevent the planning of such a lesson. (C) is incorrect because although celebrating holidays is one way to encourage students to read, this may or may not be related to encouraging students to read aloud. (D) is incorrect because celebrating holidays may encourage all students to participate in class activities, but teaching an appreciation for human diversity is the most significant reason for the activity.

31. **(B)** The correct response is (B). The variance in fifth graders' physical size and development has a direct influence on their interests and attitudes, including their willingness to work with others and a possible preference for working alone. (A) is incorrect because fifth graders do have the physical and mental maturity to work in small groups. (C) is incorrect because not all fifth-grade students lack the ability for internal

control. (D) is incorrect because although Mr. Dobson might need to be more specific in his directions to the students, this is not the main reason for their behavior.

32. **(C)** The correct response is (C). Students who are shy are usually more willing to participate in small groups than in discussions involving the entire class. (A) is incorrect because calling on each student once per day will not necessarily assist shy students to participate in class discussions, even if participation grades are assigned. (B) is incorrect because although students may become less shy as the year progresses, the teacher still has a responsibility to encourage students to participate. Choice (D) is incorrect because although speaking to each student individually may help some students participate, it is likely more students will participate if the procedure outlined in choice (C) is implemented.

33. **(B)** The correct response is (B). Students who are overly talkative are usually flattered to be asked to take a leadership role. Asking these students to take notes also assigns them a task that allows the other students to voice their opinions uninterrupted. Choice (A) is incorrect because calling on these students only once during the class period will most likely frustrate them and create problems. (C) is incorrect because placing overly talkative students in a group by themselves does not teach them to listen to other students' opinions. (D) is incorrect because although overly talkative students usually need attention, they must learn to recognize that other students also have opinions, even though they may not be assertive in voicing them.

34. **(A)** The correct response is (A). Students who tutor peers or younger students develop their own proficiency as a result of assisting other students. Response (B) is incorrect because although some students may view teaching as a possible career, this is not the intended purpose of the tutoring. Choice (C) is incorrect because the goal is helping first graders learn addition and subtraction facts, not teaching fifth graders specific tutoring techniques. Choice (D) is incorrect because although becoming friends with younger children may occur as a result of tutoring, it is not the main goal of the activity.

35. **(A)** The correct response is (A). Planning lessons that will enable students to experience a high rate of success during the majority of their practice attempts is directly related to enhanced student achievement and heightened self-esteem. Choice (B) is incorrect because although

parents are often happy as a result of a student's academic success, this is the result of structuring lessons so students will be successful. Response (C) is incorrect because although students are more likely to complete homework if they are successful in early practice attempts, this is only part of answer (A). Choice (D) is incorrect because students who are successful in independent practice may or may not ask more questions.

36. **(A)** The correct response is (A). As a general rule, if student questions require lengthy responses, then the initial explanation was probably faulty. Choices (B) and (C) are incorrect because there is insufficient information to suggest that the students were not paying attention, or that they have below average listening skills. (D) is incorrect because a teacher should direct all explanations of new information to the level of the students. Even if students did have poor backgrounds in mathematics, the teacher should take that into account when explaining new information.

37. **(C)** The correct response is (C). This is an example of working with other teachers to plan instruction. Response (A) is incorrect because it is incomplete. This activity may complete the school year, but this activity is not necessarily an end-of-the-year project. (B) is incorrect because problem solving and inquiry teaching are only small components of the activity. Choice (D) is incorrect because asking students to research Galileo and asking the PTA to buy science equipment are not necessarily related.

38. **(B)** The correct response is (B). Grouping patterns affect a student's perceptions of self-esteem and competence. Maintaining the same groups throughout the year encourages students in the average group to view themselves as average, students in the above average group to view themselves as above average, and students in the below average group to view themselves as below average. Choice (A) is incorrect because most students do not like unpredictable teacher behavior. Response (C) is incorrect because changes in the classroom often create an atmosphere of mistrust and uneasiness, and do not cause students to be more alert. Choice (D) is incorrect because although the explanation is correct, it is incomplete when compared to the answer (B).

39. **(A)** The correct response is (A). Visiting other teachers in other schools will promote collaboration and cooperation. Choice (B) is incorrect because there is no reason to believe that the principal is encourag-

ing these teachers to apply for a job in the middle school. Response (C) is incorrect because although using computers in math classes may be a topic on which teachers choose to collaborate, choice (A) is more complete. (D) is incorrect because the middle school math curriculum is not intended for use in the fifth grade.

40. **(C)** The correct response is (C). Careful planning includes checking on the availability of resources and materials. (A) Mrs. Doe did reflective thinking during the discussion. However, reflective thinking is only one component of communication and is included in careful planning and its correlation to success in the classroom. (B) Resources and materials were available, but this is a result of careful planning. (D) Personal acquaintance with a Native American would have helped shape the students' attitudes, but it is not necessary for student involvement.

41. **(A)** The correct response is (A). Multiple strategies were planned for the motivation of the students, but a result of the strategies was that each student participated in some way regardless of ability and the unit was integrated into other subjects through library assignments, reading, writing, etc. (C) Ultimately, the unit will be integrated with other subjects; however, it is not the only goal. (D) Developing a foundation for teaching American history is not even a long-range goal, although the attitudes and beliefs developed in the project may become the foundation upon which the students will build their philosophy of American history.

42. **(D)** The correct response is (D). Working collaboratively with other teachers was the avenue through which the talents of the students were identified and the students' curiosity was stimulated. Choice (A) is a false statement. No risks were taken. (B) Curiosity of the student body was stimulated; however, the assembly had other goals. (C) Individual talents were utilized in the assembly, but again that was not the only goal.

43. **(A)** The correct response is (A). The external factors of the field trip could create a positive motivation and would allow the students to make the connection between their old skills and the new skills they were learning. The external factors involved in a field trip are positive; however, Mrs. Doe gave instructions that each student was to take notes on what he or she saw, heard, and experienced. The skill of note taking was founded upon the library assignment which had preceded the field trip. The students were to make the connection. (B) No mention is made of

community involvement in the field trip; the statement is not relevant. (D) The students did not take responsibility for their own learning. They were given instructions concerning what they were to do before they left for the field trip.

44. **(B)** The correct response is (B). Respect was shown to the children by allowing them a choice of field trips. It is an example of the array of instructional strategies used by Mrs. Doe. (A) is incomplete and therefore incorrect. Enhancing students' self-concept and fostering the view of learning as a purposeful pursuit [(C) and (D)] are both incorporated in II, respecting differences and understanding the society in which we live.

45. **(C)** The correct response is (C). The teachers were allowed to seek opportunities to grow professionally by using different sources of support and guidance to enhance their own professional skills. (A) Within the framework of enhancing their own professional skills is the ability to reflect and self evaluate. This statement is implied within the correct response. (B) This statement is not true. (D) The issue is not assessing the learners, but cooperative reflection and self-evaluation.

46. **(B)** The correct response is (B). The teacher is familiar with the various expectations, laws, and guidelines relevant to education. (A) This is a subjective statement and is not the issue. The statement made by the teacher was that he knew of the expectations of the state for his class each year. (C) Again, this is a subjective statement and is not germane to the question. (D) This may or may not be a true statement. It is not relevant to the question.

47. **(A)** The correct response is (A). The teacher should constantly monitor and adjust strategies in response to learner feedback. (B) is a false statement. A teacher does not design instruction for different situations but rather monitors and adjusts instruction as situations change. (C) is a true statement; a teacher should be able to recognize factors that promote or diminish motivation. This skill comes from monitoring and adjusting instructional strategies. (D) is also true; the teacher becomes aware of external factors or internal factors through monitoring and adjusting instructional strategies; however, it is included in the correct response (A).

48. **(C)** The correct response is (C). The teacher should recognize signs of stress in students (e.g., drop in grades) and know how to respond

appropriately to help the student. The teacher should understand that factors outside the classroom may influence students' perceptions of their own self-worth and potential. (A) The statement is generic and cannot be substantiated. (B) Although the statement is true, and individualizing may have occurred, the demonstration by Mrs. Sivart was for modifying the text and tests. (D) Although the statement is true, diversity in the classroom did not cause the text to be written three years above grade level. The statement is not germane to the question.

49. **(C)** The correct response is (C). The teacher uses an understanding of human developmental processes to nurture student growth through developmentally appropriate instruction. (A) The statement is not relevant to the scenario. (B) The framework used in the plan of study designed for the 10 percent could be used for the other 20 percent; however, the framework is a result of the plan of study, not the criteria for a plan. (D) There are intrinsic benefits derived from cooperatively working to achieve goals. The cooperative work called for was not to achieve teacher benefits, but to develop a plan of study.

50. **(D)** The correct response is (D). The teacher understands how learning occurs and can apply this understanding to design and implement effective instruction. (A) The statement is false. (B) This statement may or may not be false, but is an attitude distinctive to each teacher. (C) This statement is subjective; it is an opinion and dependent upon individual parents.

51. **(C)** The correct response is (C). The teacher understands factors inside and outside the classroom that influence students' perceptions of their own potential and worth. (A) This is a true statement; however, it is encompassed within response (C). (B) Some students are extrinsically motivated and some are intrinsically motivated, yet the basic foundation of motivation lies in self-esteem. (D) This is a true statement. Library materials which are highly correlated to instruction are more meaningful, yet this statement is implied in the correct response (C).

52. **(A)** The correct response is (A). Students' self-esteem is easily lowered if others know of their need to reread a book and retake an exam. (B) This strategy would remove the teacher from the role of informing the student; however, teachers fill many roles each day. Filling the role is not the key; the teacher's attitude and communication with the student will be the critical element. (C) This is a true statement, but the work

load of the media specialist is not the issue. The issue is student privacy. The combination of appropriate instructional materials helps students to understand the role of technology as a learning tool. However, this does not affect student privacy.

53. **(A)** The correct response is (A). The instructor understands the uses of informal and formal assessment to monitor instructional effectiveness. The number of books read by each student would be in direct proportion to his or her level of reading skills and interest in reading. (B) This statement is true, but is incorporated in the correct response (A). (C) Becoming independent thinkers and problem-solvers would be a result of higher level reading skills and an interest in books. (D) The teacher's role would be varied and would not be emphasized as much at this phase of the instructional strategy. The issue is not the teacher's role but the effectiveness of instruction and techniques for monitoring it.

54. **(D)** The correct response is (D). The goal of the instructional design was to structure a positive classroom environment which would promote lifelong learning. (A), (B), and (C) are all true statements; however, they are encompassed within the correct response (D).

55. **(A)** The correct response is (A). Choices (B), (C), and (D) are all a part of communicating expectations and ideas, thereby creating a climate of inquiry. (B) Although a variety of materials were presented using several techniques, the goal for the class was to impart teacher expectations to the students and to create a climate of inquiry. (C) The students were not given a choice of what they were to learn. (D) The unit could be integrated across campus into other curricula, but this was not the goal for which many strategies were used.

56. **(C)** The correct response is (C). By requiring both a cognitive and a performance objective, the student was required to show that he or she not only had the knowledge but could apply that knowledge to a life situation. (A) Although this statement is true, it is not the foundation for developing specific objectives. (B) Again, this is an assumption and not relevant to the setting of certain objectives. (D) Teaching style and learning styles are not relevant to the behavioral objectives.

57. **(A)** The correct response is (A). Choices (B), (C), and (D) are components of (A). Active inquiry, eliciting different levels of thinking from the

students, and problem solving are all components of student achievement.

58. **(D)** The correct response is (D). The demonstration was to show what happens when directions are not followed. The result of such actions could be waste in the kitchen. An expected behavioral outcome was curiosity. (A) This is a true statement and is incorporated in the correct answer (D). (B) The terminal goal for the activity was not evaluation, but to gain the knowledge of the importance of correct measurement. (C) The statement is true, and is included in the correct response (D).

59. **(D)** The correct response is (D). The field trip was supposed to extend an academic environment into the community. The students were to see the relationship between what they were taught in the classroom and its practical application in the community. (A) The final activity for the unit will be an evaluation. (B) The field trip did not promote responsibility for one's own learning, because the students were given no instructions prior to arriving in the cafeteria. (C) The field trip was to extend the students' learning beyond the classroom and into the community.

60. **(B)** The correct response is (B). Both federal and state law require that schools be accessible to persons who use wheelchairs. Bill should make the principal aware that Myra resides in the district and that the building is not accessible to her. Disregarding the school's noncompliance with the law by simply offering to share materials with Myra is in no way sufficient (A). The expense to the school posed by making the necessary accommodations does not excuse the school from compliance with the law (C). There is no reason to believe, however, that the school has intentionally failed to comply with the law; proposing a lawsuit (D) is not called for. The school may be eager to comply once the noncompliance is called to their attention.

61. **(B)** The correct response is (B). As a responsible member of the community, Bill should notify the police of the vandalism. He should also make use of community resources by referring Cade to Big Brothers as a child in need of a positive role model. While Bill should call the police and report the vandalism, chasing the boys down himself may place him in great danger, and is therefore not a good solution (A). Calling the superintendent is not an appropriate response. This is a legal issue that does not involve the school in any way [(C) and (D)].

62. **(B)** The correct response is (B). Placing the students in small groups in which they meet face to face will allow Bill to maximize the students' interaction while giving each student the maximum opportunity to speak. Placing students in the traditional rows facing the front discourages student interaction and minimizes each student's opportunities to speak (A). While placing students in pairs maximizes each student's opportunity to speak, it limits the sources of interaction; each student may share thoughts with only one other student (C). In contrast, a group of four allows the student to interact as part of three dyads, two triads, and a quadrat. When placing the students in cooperative groups, it is wise to arrange the desks within the physical space of the classroom in such a way that each group's talking does not distract the members of other groups (D).

63. **(C)** The correct response is (C). Storytelling and other narrative approaches are highly effective ways of teaching field sensitive students. While most people do enjoy a good story, this is not the most important reason why teachers should be good storytellers (A). While storytelling is also a highly cost-effective teaching technique, its cost-effectiveness is only a secondary advantage to its utility in teaching field dependent students (B). Storytelling is not one of the most effective ways of teaching field independent students (D).

64. **(A)** The correct response is (A). People seldom perform to the best of their ability. Knowing that their work will receive public attention, however, is an important way to motivate people to do their best. While being able to speak in public is undoubtedly a crucial skill for success in a democratic society, this choice is not worded in such a way that it would be an instructional reason for having students tell their stories (B). Having students tell their stories to the class does focus on having students learn to critique their own work (C); however, this is encompassed by choice (A). Prior exposure has nothing to do with Bill's instructional reason to have students tell the stories that they write (D).

65. **(C)** The correct response is (C). The first task in developing a unit of study is to determine learner outcomes. Activities are contingent on desired learner outcomes (A). While time and space constraints affect activities, Bill and Kayla must determine desired learner outcomes before they proceed to consider other planning factors (B). Soliciting input from students helps ensure student ownership; however, this step in planning a unit comes after determining learner outcomes (D).

66. **(D)** The correct response is (D). The laser disk and player comprise a superb supplement to primary sources written by the influential New Yorkers themselves. While a computer and word processing program (A) are valuable tools, they are not the most valuable tools for this activity because students must know something about content before they can write. A local expert on ecology is not relevant to a study of persons who make contributions to the development of New York (B). A laser disk player with a laser disk about influential New Yorkers is an important tool for this thematic unit; however, (C) is not the best answer since it is not complete.

67. **(C)** The correct response is (C). Making a personal contact with each child's parents is the most crucial task that Gerene can perform in order to ensure the success of her students. Having a variety of teaching materials ready and available is helpful, but would not have the most important impact on the students' success (A). Using bulletin boards to make the room look inviting and using materials representing the students of many nations will assist in making the new students feel at home; however, the effects of this task are secondary to that of establishing a strong home-school relationship (B). Coordinating science activities with reading activities would not have a significant impact on ensuring the success of first graders (D).

68. **(A)** The correct response is (A). The most important predictor variable of reading success is whether or not a child's parents read to him or her before he or she starts school. An enriched daycare environment can be beneficial to a child's development (B), especially if shared reading and story activities are stressed. While research suggests that excessive television watching by young students may have deleterious effects, the amount of time spent watching television is not as important a predictor of reading success as being read to by a parent (C). Being raised by a grandparent is not a predictor of poor reading ability (D).

69. **(D)** The correct response is (D). Gerene should consider all of the factors listed. Students' basic nutritional needs must be met before they can be efficient learners (B). Students with unmet affective needs will not be able to learn effectively (C). Teaching builds on prior knowledge; experiential deficits must be considered if students are to construct new meaning in their worlds. Employing student interests increases student motivation to learn new material [(A) and (C)].

70. **(D)** The correct response is (D). Gerene should employ a wide variety of instructional strategies and materials in order to teach to the phoneme/grapheme relationship. This is a bottom-up approach to teaching reading. Gerene should also use a top-down approach by reading a story to the students and discussing it at length. The first choice (A) does not include a wide variety of learning activities. In addition, the choice omits the important book reading activity. Like the first choice, the second choice (B) fails to employ a wide variety of learning activities and fails to employ the book reading activity. Whether or not to place students at the computer without direct supervision depends on the students involved and the software employed. Choice (C) employs a wide variety of learning activities; however, it includes the false statement that students dislike repetitive activities and that repetition serves as an aversive reinforcer to reading. Although adults become bored with repetition, young students enjoy repetitive activity, as it gives them a sense of mastery.

71. **(B)** The correct response is (B). The hands-on activity will best help the students learn about data collection. Since choice (B) is the only one that employs a hands-on activity, this is the best answer. The students would learn about direct observation by watching Gerene tickle the mouse and the philodendron (A); however, this method would not be as effective as allowing the students to conduct their own data collection. Research suggests that viewing a video is an inefficient method of learning (C). Having a guest speaker tell the students about data collection is not a good choice for first graders (D).

72. **(C)** The correct response is (C). As in the previous question, the hands-on activity is the best choice; however, another issue should be considered in this question: the child's econiche. Many families cannot afford cable television's premium channels, and therefore do not have access to the Discovery channel (A). Parents may lack transportation, time, or money to take their child to a museum (B). Parents may not have access to books, or they may have work schedules which prevent them from reading to their children. In addition, some parents may be unable to read themselves (D).

73. **(B)** The correct response is (B). By modeling enthusiasm for learning, Gerene will help her students become lifelong learners. In addition, by employing developmentally-appropriate hands-on activities, Gerene will help her students to become enthusiastic learners. Giving students examples of famous people who were lifelong learners is not a strong

instructional technique for helping the students become lifelong learners (A). Punishing students who do not perform will not help students to become lifelong learners (C).

74. **(A)** The correct response is (A). Recent research suggests that girls learn science best in cooperative groups that employ many hands-on experiences. In contrast, competitive teaching strategies are contraindicated in helping girls learn science (B). Independent activities are also not good choices in helping girls learn science (C). Although computer-assisted instruction may be helpful, the key ingredients in developing a successful science program for girls are cooperative and frequent hands-on experiences (D).

75. **(D)** The correct response is (D). By respecting Molly's contribution to class despite its non-standard form of English, Gerene will encourage her to engage in literacy activities and will promote her self-esteem. By criticizing Molly's non-standard grammar (A), Gerene will negatively impact Molly's self-esteem and will discourage her from engaging in literacy activities. By refusing to speak to Molly (B), Gerene will also negatively affect both her self-esteem and her desire to engage in speaking, reading, and writing activities. Telling Molly that people won't understand her (C) would be lying to a student, which a teacher should never do. It is appropriate to encourage Molly to use standard English when engaging in formal language and literacy instruction; however, it is inappropriate to correct her grammar when she engages in casual interaction.

76. **(B)** The correct response is (B). There are many significant developmental differences between second and sixth graders. These differences must be considered when planning instruction. Choice (A) is incorrect because physical size is only one of the ways in which the students differ. Choice (C) is incorrect because reading ability is an issue to consider, but developmental differences include more than just reading ability. Response (D) is incorrect because preferred topics for reading reflect overall development.

77. **(B)** The correct response is (B). This question is designed to demonstrate an understanding that the performance objective should directly tie into the assessment. Students need to know what the expectation is for them to complete the necessary assignments. (A) Students do not understand what assessment tools are. They need clear directions and a

list of explanations. (C) Although the unit may have many new vocabulary words, students need to learn them within the context of the unit rather than from a random list; they should not feel threatened when learning to prepare for a test. (D) There is no connection between notebooks and learning.

78. **(D)** The correct answer is (D). Reliability can be affected by the length of the test and the amount of time allotted to complete the test. In general, a test will be more reliable if it includes a large number of questions; this provides a better representation of the student's knowledge. Setting time limits is good for exams that test only accuracy (option III). Students need to be assessed on the material that has been covered. This type of question would be good for motivating students or assessing their ability to use new information, rather than as an assessment of a course of study (option IV).

79. **(C)** The correct answer is (C). Rubrics are designed to help teachers assess each student's achievement and the quality of his/her responses. Therefore, each criterion needs to have a quality point: Outstanding (5-4), Good (3-2), and/or Fair (1-0). Rubrics need to cover a number of subject areas to allow for a fair assessment of the student's work (option III). Students may rate themselves; however, the teacher needs to work with them as they complete the ratings (option IV).

80. **(D)** The correct response is (D). The term "Light" is used to describe the enlightenment people feel when they are being inspired with an idea. (A) There is no reference to Jesus Christ in this poem. (C) There is no reference to walking in the real world. The author is using the image of darkness to help the reader understand the nature of the Light.

SECTION 2

The following essay would receive scores at the highest end of the scale used in ATS-W essay scoring.

Essay A

The practice of grouping students by ability in the elementary school has negative social and academic consequences for students. The negative effects of ability grouping overshadow the few positive benefits that may be derived from this practice. Grouping by ability may be appropriate for certain subjects, such as reading, within a particular classroom as long as the group membership changes for instruction in other subjects. However, I feel that grouping by ability is an inappropriate practice at the elementary school level if all students remain in that group throughout the day.

One of the negative effects of ability grouping is that it contributes to the development of a poor self-image for many students. Children of all ages are very adept at recognizing and correctly identifying high-, middle- and low-ability groups. Assigning non-threatening names to the groups has no effect on children's ability to identify these groups. This is apparent when observing or talking with students in schools that use ability grouping. It does not matter whether the teacher calls the top group "Red Birds," "Group 3," "Triangles," or "Mrs. Smith's class" — students are keenly aware of their membership in the group and the perceived ability of that group.

Students make comparisons between the ways teachers interact with different groups, the types of assignments groups receive and privileges different groups enjoy. Students in the high-ability group may look down on other students and may refer to students in other groups as "stupid" or "dumb." Name-calling may result. Students in the low-ability group may resent their placement in that group. Students in the middle-ability group may feel ignored or may even resent being labeled "average." The naturally occurring friction between groups creates a climate in which teachers will have difficulty building positive self-images for all students.

Ability grouping also necessarily limits peer interaction, both in and out of the classroom. Elementary students need to interact with many students to develop mature social and intellectual skills.

An additional negative effect of ability grouping is the stilted instructional environment that is created within the classroom. Teachers of high-ability students are encouraged to feel privileged to teach this group and usually prepare creative, challenging lessons. Teachers of the low-ability group usually provide many drill and practice worksheets and seldom assign text materials. Middle-ability students may receive assignments based on the text, but these assignments are often accompanied by drill and practice worksheets. The result of these practices is that only the high-ability students are challenged to work to their capacity.

The negative consequences of ability grouping are experienced by students of all ability levels. For these reasons, the practice of ability grouping in the elementary school should be abandoned.

Analysis

This essay addresses the topic directly. The topic of ability grouping is narrowed in the first sentence to the use of this practice in elementary school. The author's point of view and the focus of the essay (the negative social and academic consequences) are also established in the first sentence. Specific negative effects are named and briefly discussed. The last paragraph restates the author's point of view.

Several sentences in the essay are wordy and seem to ramble. Some of the issues raised (peer interaction) are not fully discussed. The author mentions the "positive benefits" of ability grouping but does not specifically name or discuss the benefits. There are a few errors in punctuation and spelling. However, the author demonstrates the ability to clearly state a topic and present a specific point of view.

The following essay would receive scores in the middle of the ATS-W scoring scale.

Essay B

Most teachers prefer ability grouping. I know I would. Ability grouping allows teachers to plan asignments for specific groups of students. In this way, teachers can make assignments fit the needs of specific groups of students, instead of just making one assignment for everybody. Teachers can spend additional time helping slower students because the advanced group will be able to complete their assignments independantly. Teachers can also give the advanced students extra work or projects to keep them busy. This gave the teachers more time to work with students who really need help.

Schools that group by ability can plan smaller classes for slow students and larger classes for average and advanced students. This is better for the students because those who really need extra help have a better chance of receiving it. Smaller classes for slow students also helps the teachers give more attention to slow students.

Ability grouping is especially important in math and reading because these subjects give many students difficulty.

Analysis

Although the essay is satisfactory given the time limit, it is flawed for several reasons. The major error is the lack of a controlling central idea or theme. The topic stated in the first sentence, that most teachers prefer ability grouping, is never fully developed. Instead of developing this topic, the writer discusses the advantages of small classes for slower students. The last two paragraphs seem tacked on and are not smoothly connected to the first paragraph. In addition, there are several spelling errors and verb tense is inconsistently used.

The following essay would receive scores at the lowest end of the ATS-W scoring scale.

Essay C

Ability grouping is terrible. Its awful to be in the slow group because everybody in the whole school knows it. Average students don't like ability grouping either because teachers don't pay any attention to them. Only the smart kids recieve any attention. Even then it only shows how differant they are. Some kids in the slow class like it because they never have homework and the teachers don't expect them to finish asignments so they get lots of time in class to do everything.

I observed in a school that ability grouping and I would not want to teach there. They would probably assign a new teacher to the slow class.

Analysis

This essay does discuss the topic, but the opinions stated are never developed. Although the writer gives several specific examples to support his point of view (that ability grouping is terrible) he does not develop any of these examples so that the reader can understand the reasons behind his conclusions. There are several punctuation errors. Several words are misspelled, and the writer has left out a word in the second paragraph.

LAST/ATS-W

ATS-W SECONDARY PRACTICE TEST

This test is also on CD-ROM in our interactive TEST*ware*® for the NYSTCE. We strongly recommend that you first take this exam on computer. You will then have the benefits of enforced time conditions, individual diagnostic analysis, and instant scoring.

See page 3 for guidance on how to get the most out of our NYSTCE book and software.

ATS-W SECONDARY PRACTICE TEST

Time: 4 Hours
80 Multiple-Choice Questions, 1 Essay

SECTION 1

> **DIRECTIONS:** Read each scenario carefully, and answer the questions that follow. Mark your responses on the answer sheet provided.

Scenario 1

1. Patrick O'Brien is a high school communications teacher. At the end of the school year, he reviewed the topics he had taught and the assignments he had given. He then used this review to direct his professional development activities over the summer months by

    (A) identifying areas not covered or new topics to study and research over the summer months.

    (B) updating his files on each of the topics.

    (C) assessing the quality of the assignments received from students over the past school year.

    (D) revising student assignments by re-evaluating educational objectives for each.

2.   Mr. O'Brien discovers that he spends virtually no class time discussing the differences in the ways females and males communicate, although he notes that several best-selling books by academic scholars have been written on this topic. Furthermore, he has observed some recurring gender differences among the students he has taught over the years and he wonders if he should add this timely topic to the list of those he now teaches. He decides to discuss this possibility with other teachers at his school to

   (A)   demonstrate for the benefit of his peers his knowledge of current professional and academic topics.

   (B)   solicit their ideas and input on expanding and/or revising the curriculum in communication classes.

   (C)   determine if he should do any additional professional reading on this topic.

   (D)   ascertain any gender differences in communication styles among his colleagues.

3.   When Mr. O'Brien brings up the topic of gender differences in styles of communication, he discovers that two of his colleagues have opposite views. Subsequently, he decides that the best course of action to take is to

   (A)   go immediately to the department chair or curricular supervisor and let that party know about the dissension in the ranks.

   (B)   drop the topic since it is clearly too controversial to pursue.

   (C)   invite both colleagues to help him develop lessons on the topic which would include both viewpoints.

   (D)   argue with both colleagues to clearly state his own view of the topic based on current research findings.

4.   Mr. O'Brien reads Deborah Tannen's book *You Just Don't Understand: Women and Men in Conversation* and decides that he would like to use the book as a reference tool for introducing some gender-related ideas to his students. By selecting a current best-seller as a reference, Mr. O'Brien is

(A)   attempting to locate contemporary and relevant sources of information for his students.

(B)   expecting students to purchase an additional book for his course.

(C)   demonstrating to his colleagues that he is aware of current research in his discipline.

(D)   requiring students to do more outside reading in the course.

5.   The literature Mr. O'Brien surveys reveals that female students are less likely to participate in classroom discussions than are male students. Some researchers cite this behavior as an illustration of females' lower self-esteem. In an effort to boost the self-esteem of female students in his class, Mr. O'Brien

(A)   endeavors to ask the female students easier questions so they will get the answers right.

(B)   develops a question grid to enable him to call on all students in the class, both male and female, an equal number of times.

(C)   does not call on female students if the question is one requiring higher-ordered thinking skills.

(D)   attempts to give no critical feedback to female students who give incorrect answers.

6.   As Mr. O'Brien learns about female students' problems with self-esteem, he recalls a former student, Shonda Harris, who was a very shy, quiet student. Shonda never volunteered to answer questions or participate in class discussions although she made the top grades in his class. Mr. O'Brien never called on her in class and now he wonders if he acted appropriately. In retrospect, he concludes that in the future he should

(A)   continue to call only on those students who raise their hands or otherwise indicate their willingness to respond so as not to unduly pressure students.

(B)   gently tease to provoke shy, quiet students to participate in class discussions.

(C)   require students to participate in class discussions with the result of lowered grades if they fail to do so.

    (D)   meet with the student privately and discuss why he, as the teacher, wants students to participate in class discussions and then listen to his or her reasons for not volunteering to do so.

7.   Mr. O'Brien decides that he will require his students to participate in discussions and that class participation will account for a percentage of students' grades in his communications course. This new requirement will

    (A)   be an effective motivational tool for all students in his classes.

    (B)   motivate only some of the students in the course to participate.

    (C)   result in improved grades for all students in his classes.

    (D)   discourage the majority of students from participating in class discussions.

8.   Before introducing the topic of gender differences in communication styles to his students, Mr. O'Brien asks the class to brainstorm individually ten situations wherein each student would like to improve his or her communication skills. In each situation, students are then asked to identify the gender of their audience (or the receiver of the communication, the other party in the situation). Students next are asked to tally the number of times there is a sex difference between themselves as the sender of the message and the receiver of the message. In this activity, Mr. O'Brien

    (A)   avoids a classroom activity that could deteriorate into an argument.

    (B)   utilizes a strategy to promote student learning.

    (C)   saves classroom time.

    (D)   finds a way to assess who's having trouble communicating and who's not.

9.   As students tally their responses from the brainstorming activity, they indicate that many of the communication problems they routinely encounter involve members of the opposite sex. This discovery allows Mr. O'Brien to

(A)   capitalize on students' self-motivation to learn how to communicate more effectively.

(B)   skip over a formal introduction to the topic of gender differences in communication.

(C)   pinpoint whether male or female students are having greater difficulty communicating.

(D)   dismiss students' concerns about their problems in communicating with others.

10.   Mr. O'Brien asks students to form groups of three or four to describe some of the factors which are commonly associated with the "communication conflicts" involving members of the opposite sex. By asking students to work in groups, Mr. O'Brien's instructional strategy is to

(A)   avoid a tedious lecture.

(B)   encourage students to develop better social skills.

(C)   allow students to structure their own time in class.

(D)   promote collaborative learning.

11.   Mr. O'Brien ends the class by telling students that over the next few weeks they will be required to keep a communications journal. Every time they have an eventful exchange—either positive or negative, they are to record the details of the exchange in their journal. This assignment is given as

(A)   a way to help students improve their composition and rhetorical skills.

(B)   a way of understanding individual students, monitoring instructional effectiveness, and shaping instruction.

(C)   a way of helping students become more accountable for the way they manage their time.

(D)   the basis for giving daily grades to students.

Scenario 2

12.   Joan Jaynes is a secondary special education teacher and reading specialist. Her teaching assignment requires her to provide for the special needs of students who are experiencing difficulties in reading. Among her <u>first</u> actions is to

   (A)   interview the students' previous teachers to solicit their opinions and advice on meeting the educational needs of the students.

   (B)   review school files on each student, including assessment and testing history.

   (C)   meet with students individually and informally to discuss school, reading, and how they feel about each.

   (D)   administer a standardized reading test to determine their current reading performance.

13.   In selecting a test to administer to students, Ms. Jaynes needs to be relatively certain that she has selected a test which is not biased. Test bias refers to whether or not

   (A)   a test measures what it purports to measure.

   (B)   a test consistently measures what it purports to measure.

   (C)   the test discriminates between students who are intelligent or lacking in intelligence.

   (D)   the test discriminates among students on the basis of ideographic characteristics.

14.   Ms. Jaynes gives a standardized reading test to a student in her class on Friday afternoon (Test Time 1). The following Monday morning, Ms. Jaynes is absent and the substitute teacher gives the same form of the test to the student again (Test Time 2). The student's parents are surprised and pleased to learn that their student's grade level score improved significantly from Test Time 1 to Test Time 2. Ms. Jaynes subsequently has to explain the difference in scores to the parents; she explains the difference as a result of test-practice effects. Test-practice effects are the phenomenon of

(A) students' scores improving when they take the same form of a test shortly after the first testing.

(B) students' scores improving as a result of having received adequate instruction and practice time with the skills being tested.

(C) a test not measuring what it claims to measure.

(D) students answering questions the way they think the examiner wants the question answered.

15. Ms. Jaynes wants her students to feel better about themselves and to develop positive attitudes about reading. Therefore, when she gives them a reading assignment she

(A) sends them to the library and lets each student pick whatever he or she would like to read.

(B) tends to guide students in their selection of reading materials, pointing out to them books on topics about which they have expressed an interest.

(C) ensures that students read only worthwhile material, such as literary classics.

(D) makes certain that students do not select books that are written at too high a level so as to result in reading frustration.

16. At the beginning of the semester, Ms. Jaynes has her students read together in class. Initially, she reads a paragraph and then asks the students to find answers to the following questions: "Who... is the paragraph about? What... does the paragraph say about the person, event, or action? When... did it take place? Where... did it occur? Why... did it happen? How... did it happen?" For several weeks, she leads the class through this protocol. After weeks of practice, students are expected to follow this protocol on their own. Ms. Jaynes is attempting to teach her students

(A) an elaboration strategy to help them monitor their reading comprehension.

(B) about the importance of topic sentences in paragraphs.

(C)   about the importance of topic sentences and supporting details in paragraphs.

(D)   important decoding skills.

17.   Ms. Jaynes spends much of her instructional time teaching her students different reading strategies and giving them opportunities to practice these strategies in class. By teaching her students reading strategies they can use on their own, she is

(A)   creating a quiet classroom environment conducive to the learning of all students.

(B)   able to spend more class time on grading students' work.

(C)   stressing to her students the importance of reading as a social activity.

(D)   promoting students' sense of responsibility for their own learning.

18.   Ms. Jaynes determines that she will base students' grades in her class on homework, daily work in class, and informally-constructed (teacher-made) tests. However, the deciding factor as to whether or not students have made sufficient progress to exit her special reading class will be students' performance on standardized reading tests. This decision is based on the proposition that

(A)   standardized tests are easier to grade than informally-constructed tests.

(B)   standardized tests are more subjective than informally-constructed tests.

(C)   statistical procedures used in the construction of standardized tests result in greater test validity and reliability as measures of overall reading achievement.

(D)   standardized tests are more economical in terms of both time and money.

19.   As a special education teacher, Ms. Jaynes has learned that an essential part of her job is to confer with her colleagues who teach core academic

classes. She spends time giving her colleagues weekly reports on students' progress and learning about what the students are doing in their academic classes. Ms. Jaynes believes that this practice is

(A)   an effective way of gaining popularity and respect among her colleagues.

(B)   an effective way to discipline students since they know she has influence among their other teachers.

(C)   an important part of her profession as a member of a community who must work effectively with all members of that community to reach common goals.

(D)   the only way to qualify for merit pay and salary increases.

Scenario 3

20.   Suli Aljuhbar is an ESL teacher. She works with high school-aged students, typically with groups of six to twelve students who possess varying degrees of ability in understanding English. Her primary objective in working with her students is to help them understand the American English spoken in their classes and to help them communicate more effectively in English with their other teachers and classmates. Her secondary objective is to create cultural awareness within her students and expose them to customs of the United States. These objectives are examples of

(A)   behavioral objectives.

(B)   performance objectives.

(C)   instructional objectives.

(D)   outcome-based education.

21.   As Ms. Aljuhbar develops her weekly lesson plans, she identifies specific behavioral objectives for each class session. By doing this, Ms. Aljuhbar

(A)   specifies exactly which instructional methods should be used.

(B)   lists the materials and equipment that will be needed.

(C)   describes what students will be able to do as a result of receiving instruction.

(D)   focuses attention on teacher-centered activities.

22.   Just as Ms. Aljuhbar hopes that her ESL students will learn about the customs and characteristics of people in the United States, she also wants other students at her school to have the opportunity to learn about the culture and practices in the native lands of her ESL students. Thus, to bring about a reciprocal and active learning dynamic, Ms. Aljuhbar

(A)   collaborates with other teachers for ESL students to make presentations in classes.

(B)   gives the ESL students a library research assignment to learn about the United States.

(C)   arranges field trips for the ESL students to visit local points of interest.

(D)   invites a guest speaker to class to talk about how Christmas is celebrated in different countries.

23.   One of Ms. Aljuhbar's students, Lee Zhang, had been enthusiastic in class and eagerly participated in class activities until the end of the fall semester. When the spring semester began, Lee seemed despondent. She no longer participated in class activities and she stopped turning in her homework or even doing assignments in class. The best thing for Ms. Aljuhbar to do to help Lee is to

(A)   contact Lee's family to see if they are having family problems.

(B)   confer with other teachers at the school to determine if Lee is acting the same way in all of her classes.

(C)   ask Lee if something is wrong.

(D)   give Lee extra credit work to help her catch-up and improve her grades.

24.   One activity that Ms. Aljuhbar uses with her ESL students requires that each student choose a fable or folk tale that he or she learned as a child. The student is then videotaped (privately) telling the story in his or her

native language. The student next is given the tape and allowed time to view it, critique it, and then translate it into English. Finally, at a second taping, the student is videotaped telling the story in English. The student is then given the tape with both versions. Ms. Aljuhbar has found that this is an effective instructional strategy because

(A)   it is based on the premise that practice makes perfect.

(B)   it allows the student to make choices and to move from the familiar to the novel or unfamiliar at his or her own pace.

(C)   it permits the student to critique the tape in private.

(D)   it is done in a nonthreatening environment.

25.   When students are satisfied with their tape, they are encouraged to submit it to Ms. Aljuhbar, who compiles the stories for the collection in the elementary school library. ESL students are also invited to participate in story sessions at the public library whereby they tell their folktales to children in the community. These activities

(A)   ensure that student performance on the tapes is standardized.

(B)   are inappropriate for high school-aged students.

(C)   restrict student initiative and creativity.

(D)   motivate ESL students.

Scenario 4

Mr. Reams' science class of ninth graders ranged in abilities from gifted (Joe and Sue) to low-average, (Hank).

The previous day had been recognized as Earth Day. Focusing the students' attention upon the environment, Mr. Reams wanted to extend the text to portray the significant difference one small group could make toward a cleaner environment.

The class reviewed Earth Day and the need for its existence. Mr. Reams followed by asking, "What are some of the pollution problems present in our own school?" Class responses included a tobacco polluted environment, the use of non-biodegradable styrofoam containers and the lack of recycling aluminum soft-drink cans. Forming small groups with a cross-section of abilities, each was charged to determine which offenses could be changed, how they could be changed, the resources needed for the change, and the benefits which could be derived from the change.

While monitoring the groups as they brainstormed, Mr. Reams observed that both Hank and Joe were actively involved in making suggestions as another group member took notes. Mr. Reams paused with each group, listening, reiterating, and encouraging students.

26. Which of the following learning environmental factors was Mr. Reams using for this phase of his class?

    (A)   Small groups are unstructured, therefore he was without a role.

    (B)   By making use of small groups, he had assured the students of success in the classroom.

    (C)   He was modeling effective communication strategies of reflective listening, simplifying, and restating.

    (D)   He had made the instruction relevant to the students' own needs.

27. When Mr. Reams divided the class into cross-sectioned groups he was attempting to

    (A)   select appropriate materials and resources for particular situations and purposes.

    (B)   use observation as an informal assessment.

    (C)   use an array of instructional strategies to actively engage students in learning.

    (D)   prevent any social/emotional atmosphere from developing in the classroom.

Ideas generated in small groups were written on the chalkboard. Each entry was discussed according to the four criteria given by Mr. Reams. It was concluded that a smoke free environment required the legislation of a group with more power than the ninth grade class. The use of non-biodegradable styrofoam containers would require research as to why the school chose to use such containers. Research would also be required to answer why there had been no recycling effort by the school.

Three days later, the students presented their research in class. The school's choice to use non-biodegradable containers was based on economics. Biodegradable containers were more expensive and it was felt that most containers were placed in the trash and hauled to the landfill and posed no problem. Therefore, the school would continue its present policy. Research also revealed that the school had no recycling program because there had been no interest by the students, faculty, or staff for such a program. Hank volunteered to question the soft-drink man concerning the volume of drinks delivered weekly to the school. Sue volunteered to contact Ace Manufacturing Company to find out how they collected the cans, where they recycled them and how much they were paid for them. Other students agreed to interview students, custodians, cafeteria workers, and the administration.

28. As the students conducted the research and began the interview process, Mr. Reams felt he had successfully

    (A)   developed an interdisciplinary activity for the class.

    (B)   maintained class control.

    (C)   almost achieved his goals for the class.

    (D)   helped the students understand the role of technology as a learning tool.

29. One week later, the students reported that collection of the cans would be accomplished by placing receptacles purchased by the administration in strategic places. The custodians would deliver weekly the cans for recycling, and the school would receive $0.023 per pound for them. Mr. Reams was congratulated by the principal for having

    (A)   presented a new and unique problem to the students.

    (B)   made the instruction relevant to the students' own needs.

    (C)   helped the students feel they are members of a community.

    (D)   used an on-going assessment as an instructional tool.

30.   The class began to discuss ways the recycling money could be used. It was concluded that the class would purchase trees to be planted on campus. Mr. Reams ask if the class had considered how the trees were to be cared for. No one had thought of the care that must follow the planting. Hank volunteered that his father was a gardener and knew all about trees. Sue asked if Hank's father could speak to the class about tree care. As the trees were being planted on Arbor Day, several parents and community members were present to encourage the class in their endeavor. Mr. Reams had

(A)   gotten the students to work with members of the community.

(B)   conferenced with parents to explain what the students had yet to do.

(C)   taken advantage of community strengths and resources to foster student growth.

(D)   used a variety of strategies to achieve his goal of trees being planted on campus.

Scenario 5

31.   The Social Studies department of an inner city high school wanted to change to a more relevant curriculum. The department wanted to have units on economics throughout the world instead of only regions of the U.S. Mrs. Dunn was asked to submit a proposal for the new curriculum, related activities, sequencing, themes, and materials. In consultation with the other teachers in the department, a needs assessment was planned. The group felt that the needs assessment would

(A)   help the students make a connection between their current skills and those that will be new to them.

(B)   reveal community problems that may affect the students' lives and their performance in school.

(C)   foster a view of learning as a purposeful pursuit, promoting a sense of responsibility for one's own learning.

(D)   engage students in learning activities and help them to develop the motivation to achieve.

32. When the needs assessment was evaluated, it revealed an ethnically diverse community. Student interests and parental expectations varied, different language backgrounds existed, student exceptionalities were common, and academic motivation was low. The question confronting the teachers was how to bridge the gap from where the students are to where they should be. The available choices were to

    (A) change the text only.

    (B) relate the lessons to the students' personal interests.

    (C) create a positive environment to minimize the effects of the negative external factors.

    (D) help students to learn and to monitor their own performance.

33. It was decided that the students would be administered an interest inventory at the beginning of the semester. The questions would range from "Are you currently working? If so, what is your salary?" to "What salary do you want to earn in ten years? What skills will you need for earning that salary?" and "How are salaries determined?" The results of the interest inventory would allow Mrs. Dunn to

    (A) nurture their academic growth through developmentally appropriate instruction.

    (B) plan instruction which would enhance their self-esteem.

    (C) invite community professionals to speak to the class.

    (D) plan instruction which would lead students to ask questions and pursue problems that are meaningful to them.

34. An activity was planned to follow the interest inventory. Mrs. Dunn contacted various members of the business community. Each agreed to send a representative to the class to discuss those jobs which required the minimally skilled, those which required the semi-skilled, and those requiring the highly skilled. A question-and-answer period would be the format. The above planning reveals that Mrs. Dunn is aware of

    (A) problems facing the students and she understands how these problems may affect their learning.

    (B) the multiplicity of roles that teachers may be called upon to assume.

(C) being a member of a learning community and knowing how to work effectively with all members of the community to solve problems and accomplish educational goals.

(D) the need to establish a relationship of trust with the parents/guardians from diverse backgrounds to develop effective parent-teacher partnerships that foster all students' learning.

35. It was determined that at the end of the question-and-answer period, the students would have an awareness of the correlation between their skills or lack of skills and their salaries. A parent/guardian support group would be established to enhance the students' motivation to master new skills. Strategies for use at home and in the classroom would be developed. Mrs. Dunn felt that with the aid of parents

(A) she could promote her own professional growth as she worked cooperatively with professionals to create a school culture that would enhance learning and result in positive change.

(B) she would be meeting the expectations associated with teaching.

(C) she would be fostering strong home relationships that support student achievement of desired outcomes.

(D) she would be exhibiting her understanding of the principles of conducting parent-teacher conferences and working cooperatively with parents.

Scenario 6

Mrs. Walker is thinking about developing a tenth-grade world history unit. The unit needs to emphasize Virgil's attempt to connect the origins of Rome to the events that followed the destruction of Troy by the Greeks. She wants the unit to be challenging, and yet the students must be able to handle the work. She is aware that this is the semester the students will take their first college entrance exam. The information from a cooperative learning workshop taken during the summer should be included in the unit.

36. What should be Mrs. Walker's first step in planning the unit?

(A) Combining cooperative learning and the content

(B)   Deciding on an evaluation that will be fair to all students

(C)   Developing objectives for the unit

(D)   Finding available materials and resources

37.   Mrs. Walker's understanding of human development is evident because her planning alludes to which statement about cognitive growth?

(A)   Students will learn whatever they need to learn if they are given enough time and proper instruction.

(B)   Students will use higher order thinking skills in real world situations.

(C)   Students will develop a sense of involvement and responsibility in relation to the larger school community.

(D)   Constant difficult schoolwork and demands will cause students to become interested.

38.   Which of the following is an indication that Mrs. Walker is aware of the environmental factors that may affect learning?

(A)   She is developing a tenth-grade world history unit.

(B)   She wants to be sure that the students are challenged.

(C)   She is aware that this is the semester the students will take their first college entrance exam.

(D)   She decides to utilize group work for a large portion of the unit.

39.   In planning for the unit, what information about students is not needed?

(A)   Individual learning style

(B)   Student's cultural background

(C)   Student's grades in previous history courses

(D)   Student's daily class schedule

40. What might Mrs. Walker include in her planning to keep gifted students challenged?

(A)   An extra report on the history of the Greeks

(B)   Let them tutor the students who are unmotivated.

(C)   Encourage students to plan learning activities of their own.

(D)   Create for the student a tightly-organized and well-designed unit.

41. What concepts are always present in cooperative learning?

I.   Team rewards

II.   Individual accountability

III.   Equal opportunities

IV.   Rules

V.   Specific tasks

(A)   I, III, and IV only.

(B)   I, II, and III only.

(C)   II, IV, and V only.

(D)   II, III, and V only.

Scenario 7

Mr. Brown feels very uncomfortable when he has to make decisions about the assessment of students. He has had some difficulty with various types of assessment. He decides it is time to talk to Mr. Williams, the principal.

42. Which of the following would be the most effective way for Mr. Brown to document his teaching in an authentic setting and to be aware of students' efforts, progress, and achievements in one or more areas?

(A)   Standardized tests

(B)   Teacher-made tests

(C)   Observation

(D)   Portfolio

43. Which would be the most effective way to evaluate specific objectives and specific content in Mr. Brown's course?

    (A)   Self and peer evaluation   (C)   Teacher-made test

    (B)   Portfolio   (D)   Observation

44. Mr. Williams asks Mr. Brown what type of test scores are rated against the performance of other students and are reported in terms of percentiles, stanines, and scaled scores. Mr. Brown should give which response?

    (A)   Portfolio   (C)   Observation

    (B)   Teacher-made test   (D)   Standardized test

45. When the teacher's role is that of facilitator who utilizes students' knowledge and understanding of specific evaluation criteria, what type of assessment is being used?

    (A)   Portfolio   (C)   Self and peer assessment

    (B)   Teacher-made test   (D)   Observation

Scenario 8

Tom Jones was asked to improve the remedial reading curriculum for ninth-grade students. He found that the students were continually tested and evaluated on reading, that the current objectives were unclear, and that the teaching materials were inappropriate. Following a lengthy observation of Mrs. Ratu's teaching strategies, Mr. Jones concluded that she was teaching basic reading skills in the same manner as did the lower elementary teachers.✓

The teaching materials used a controlled vocabulary and simple sentences. The students were being taught to rely heavily upon pictures and illustrations for the story. Most of the material was fictional in genre. Rote was Mrs. Ratu's preference for learning.

Mr. Jones analyzed the test results and found that many of the students in Mrs. Ratu's class had average scores in the areas of art, math, and music. He concluded that, with the exception of reading, most were normal students and would be successful when their remediation was complete. Mr. Jones made several decisions: (1) the students would be evaluated annually with an achievement test; (2) reading materials of interest to teenagers would be substituted for elementary materials; (3) each student would be encouraged to read about the subject of his or her choice; (4) roundtable discussions would be developed for each "favorite subject."

46. Mrs. Ratu's method of teaching remedial reading focused upon

   I.   the level at which the students should have learned the basic reading skills.

   II. her own minimal competency in instructional design and evaluation.

   III. her lack of understanding of the learners in her class.

   IV. her desire to make remedial reading easy for the students.

   (A) I only.

   (B) I and IV only.

   (C) II and III only.

   (D) II only.

47. Mr. Jones, having reviewed the students' scores in other classes, knew

   I.   that development in one area would lead to development in another area.

   II. how to use a variety of techniques for creating intrinsic and extrinsic motivation.

   III. that allowing students to have choices in their learning would create camaraderie.

   IV. that roundtable discussions would make class more enjoyable but have no effect on students' grades.

   (A) I and II only.

   (B) II only.

   (C) I, II, and III only.

   (D) IV only.

An interest inventory was conducted with the students to determine those subjects in which they were interested. New materials were ordered. While students were waiting for the new materials, they were instructed to bring to class materials which dealt with the subject of their choice. If there was a deficiency of materials in the home, the student was to go to the library for magazine articles to bring to class.

After some debate the students decided that the first roundtable discussion should be about gun control, an issue about which many students had very strong feelings. Ray was the first student to speak. "Guns have always been a right in this country. Now people are trying to take them away, just when people need them more than ever to protect themselves." Stan supported Ray's opinion but for different reasons. He added "Yeah, every year around this time my father and I take a hunting trip. If we weren't allowed to have guns, we couldn't go." At this point, Tracy entered the discussion. "It's not hunting guns they want to ban, it's machine guns. Nobody needs a machine gun to go hunting." When Tracy was finished speaking, Brian raised his hand. When he was given permission to speak he stated, "But if you take away those guns, then the only people who would have them would be the gangs and the drug dealers." "And the government," Tracy added. As the discussion drew to a close, Mr. Jones asked each student to continue to read about his or her favorite subject.

48.   Mr. Jones' lively roundtable discussion was a success because

   I.   diversity can be used as an advantage by creating an environment that nurtures a sense of community.

   II.   the students had been allowed to discuss their feelings about that which interested them.

   III.   the students had recognized those factors which diminish motivation.

   IV.   the students had begun to respect their differences.

   (A)   I only.   (C)   II and IV only.

   (B)   II only.   (D)   III only.

49.   When Mr. Jones instituted the roundtable discussion, he was using a process which would

   I.   vary his role with the group.

   II.   serve as one form of assessment.

III.   design outcome-oriented learning experiences that foster under-standing.

IV.   structure the learning environment to maintain a lifelong pur-suit of learning.

(A)   I and II only.

(B)   II only.

(C)   I and III only.

(D)   III and IV only.

50.   As the facilitator of the roundtable discussion, Mr. Jones was

I.   able to manage the classroom environment as he chose.

II.   able to model effective communication strategies, thereby shaping the learners into active inquiry.

III.   able to determine the socioeconomic level of the home.

IV.   able to monitor student input on the subject and encourage all students to participate.

(A)   I only.

(B)   II and IV only.

(C)   I and III only.

(D)   I, II, and IV only.

Scenario 9

Phyllis Johnson is a junior high school teacher who has chosen human diversity as the topic for a lesson unit. She has decided to approach the topic by asking students to engage in introspective activities. On the day she introduces the topic to the class, she asks the students to make a list of the things they like about themselves. Then, she asks them to write two paragraphs in class, describing their personal strengths in terms of (a) their classroom behavior and (b) their behavior (or relationships) with others outside class.

51.   By asking her students to make a list of the things they like about themselves, Ms. Johnson is

(A)   giving the class an easy assignment, something that everyone can do.

(B)   making sure that everyone writes something.

(C) stimulating students' thinking and providing the class with a prewriting activity to help students identify ideas to include in their paragraphs.

(D) specifically teaching the students the importance of outlining.

52. By asking her students to think about their own characteristics, Ms. Johnson is promoting her students' cognitive development by helping them to

(A) activate prior knowledge as a basis for understanding new concepts.

(B) demonstrate their ability to write personal narratives.

(C) practice their grammar and sentence structure.

(D) develop positive self-esteem by identifying their assets and skills.

53. In asking her students to think about their behavior both in and outside class, Ms. Johnson is acknowledging that her students

(A) are entitled to their own opinions.

(B) are affected by multiple factors, some which she can control and others she cannot.

(C) are sure to have some strengths they can write about.

(D) can consider themselves successful either inside or outside class.

54. When Ms. Johnson asks the students to write about their behavior in class and their behavior (or relationships) outside class, she is taking into consideration aspects of human development by

(A) stressing that some students are concrete thinkers in adolescence, according to Piaget.

(B) noting that most adolescents are thinking at the stage of formal operations, according to Piaget.

(C) observing that students' cognitive functioning is a product of both their innate intellectual characteristics and their environment.

(D) pinpointing that adolescent students tend to be socially unaware and cognitively insensitive to the thoughts of others.

55. By requiring that students write about themselves, Ms. Johnson is

    (A) fulfilling her responsibilities as an English teacher.

    (B) preparing her class to create autobiographies.

    (C) relying on the Language-Experience-Approach (LEA) for instruction.

    (D) preparing her class to read biographies about great Americans from diverse cultural backgrounds.

56. Ms. Johnson collects the students' papers at the end of class. As she reads the papers, she decides that the best way to give her students positive feedback is to

    (A) not mark errors on the paper so as not to discourage or inhibit their creativity.

    (B) make at least one positive comment about each paragraph.

    (C) begin with one or two positive comments about the paper and then suggest how students could improve their writing.

    (D) give everyone a high grade on the paper for participating in the assignment.

57. After Ms. Johnson finishes reading all the students' papers, she observes that some of the students had difficulty identifying and describing their strengths, whether in class or outside class. She believes that all of her students have strengths and she wants to help them see the assets they possess. She decides that in the next class, students will

    (A) take a learning style assessment to uncover their particular learning strengths and characteristics.

    (B) listen to a lecture about how everyone possesses special skills and strengths.

    (C) read a chapter from a book about Guilford's Structure of Intellect, as a precursor to a discussion about how intelligence is specialized and diverse.

(D)   rewrite their papers, correcting their errors and revising their paragraphs to name at least two additional classroom strengths they possess and at least two additional interpersonal skills they possess.

58.   The next lesson in Ms. Johnson's unit on diversity is a library project. In order to determine what kind of project students will undertake, Ms. Johnson leads the class through a brainstorming activity, allowing the students to generate a list of possible topics for the library project. By doing this, Ms. Johnson

(A)   can determine the students' interests.

(B)   gives everyone a chance to participate in class.

(C)   demonstrates an approach for solving problems creatively.

(D)   avoids giving everyone in class the same assignment which might not appeal to every student and might result in some students cheating.

59.   Students decide that they would like to read about an American they admire. Asking the members of the class to work together in pairs, Ms. Johnson requests that the students select and find a magazine article about the person they have chosen. In order to form pairs so that students can work together in the library, Ms. Johnson decides that the approach which will allow students to be most productive is to assign students to work together so as to ensure that learning preferences and learner characteristics are compatible for the pair of students. In choosing this approach, Ms. Johnson

(A)   avoids having students form their own groups so that the students simply end up working with someone she or he likes.

(B)   takes advantage of the information she has about students' individual learning styles so as to maximize student learning effectiveness and efficiency.

(C)   avoids randomly assigning students to pairs.

(D)   risks having incompatible students working together in pairs.

60. Before the class goes to the library, Ms. Johnson asks the students to predict how they will find the information they will need for the assignment. By doing this, Ms. Johnson is

   (A)   engaging the students in hypothetical thinking and inductive reasoning.

   (B)   saving time so that the students will be able to go straight to work once they get to the library.

   (C)   helping her students acquire good self-management skills.

   (D)   assisting the librarian by covering important information in class.

Scenario 10

Mrs. Gomez teaches a ninth-grade English class. As she, Mrs. Rodriquez, and Mrs. Smith planned for the semester, they designed a "Writers Workshop." The workshop would be both a reading and writing experience for all the ninth graders. The teachers as well as the students would read the works of published authors, as well as the writing of each other. The goal of the workshop was to better one's own writing and to help one's peers become better writers.

The first element of writing to be introduced would be a metaphor. To introduce the concept of a metaphor, an overhead projector would be needed. The definition and examples of a metaphor would be displayed on the overhead. The display would remain visible to the students as the reading of a poem followed. The students' response was to correctly identify the metaphors in the poem. The class further would practice identifying metaphors through a paper and pencil exercise.

Following the paper and pencil exercise, each student would develop their own metaphors and share them with the class. Initially, the metaphors were to be simple while gradually becoming complex. A filmstrip would be viewed and its metaphors identified and discussed.

To stimulate the students in writing their own poetry containing metaphors, brightly colored transparencies of works of art would be displayed. The students would be instructed to write a poem about the art or an object found in the art transparency.

Students will be evaluated through class participation, completion of the steps of the writers' flowchart, special directions given in class, and a poem containing at least three metaphors.

61. The writing workshop was designed in an effort to

I. use a variety of teaching techniques.

II. encourage all students to be creative.

III. promote a sense of responsibility for one's own learning.

IV. develop each student's language and ability.

(A) I only.

(B) II and III only.

(C) I and II only.

(D) I, II, III, and IV.

62. Attention to the details of instruction preceding the creative writing of the poem allowed Mrs. Gomez to

(A) vary her role in the classroom.

(B) enhance the students' understanding of the society in which they live.

(C) identify each students' talents.

(D) engage the students in learning activities which help them to develop the motivation to achieve.

63. The display of brightly colored transparencies of works of art was included to

I. stimulate the creativity of the students.

II. allow students to have choices in their learning.

III. create curiosity and a desire to know more about art.

IV. expose them to art as well as good writing.

(A) I only.

(B) I and II only.

(C) III only.

(D) IV only.

64. The multiple evaluation tools used by Mrs. Gomez exhibited her own competency in

    (A) creative thinking.

    (B) communication through the use of various media.

    (C) being a reflective questioner.

    (D) working with other teachers.

65. Class participation and the completion of the poem containing metaphors allowed for

    I.   respect for the differences among the students.

    II. individual learning styles.

    III. an informal assessment of the students' performance.

    IV. a variety of opinions to be expressed.

    (A) I only.   (C) III only.

    (B) II and IV only.   (D) I and IV only.

Scenario 11

Valley Lake High School is organized as a site-based management campus. The Campus Leadership Council (CLC), after much discussion, has decided to accept the attendance improvement proposal of Lynn Stanford, a librarian serving on the CLC for the first time. The librarian's plan is to solicit support of the community businesses to reward students who are not absent during the spring semester. Businesses wishing to join in the effort to combat an increasing absentee problem at Valley Lake may offer an award. All awards sponsored by the community businesses will be distributed by a random drawing from a list of names of students who have not been absent during the spring semester except for official school business. The principal, expressing appreciation of the idea that originated with Miss Stanford, is ready to implement the plan for the campus during the spring semester.

66. Which of the following does the principal give to the CLC as sound educational strategies, and therefore his primary reasons for approving the plan?

   I.   The financial advantages for the school

   II.   The opportunity to strengthen the working relationship between the school and the community to improve student achievement

   III. The substantial awards some students will receive

   IV.   The favorable publicity the plan will create among other school districts

   (A)   I only.

   (B)   III and IV only.

   (C)   III only.

   (D)   I and II only.

Scenario 12

   Martin Janowsky's Creative Writing class is beginning a study of creative expression and design in advertising. Mr. Janowsky's evaluator has come to visit the class. In his later conference with Mr. Janowsky about the class visit, he discusses the following notations about Mr. Janowsky's lesson:

   Mr. Janowsky used slides of various billboards displayed in the community to stimulate class discussion. He also had taped portions of the Clio Awards (an annual international awards program for advertising) and used these to show differences in various cultures' advertising patterns. Among the samples of individual advertisement methods he brought in for student analysis were three-dimensional magazine ads, endorsement ads using well-known people, and product sample packaging.

67. Which of the following comments will the supervisor make in evaluating Mr. Janowsky's teaching of the class?

   (A)   Mr. Janowsky's understanding of the importance of using multiple resources is clearly evident.

   (B)   Too much clutter used by Mr. Janowsky causes confusion in students' minds about the focus of the lesson.

(C)   Mr. Janowsky should let students participate in gathering materials and resources related to the focus of the lesson.

(D)   The supervisor discusses the varied materials with Mr. Janowsky since he is interested in advertising techniques himself.

Scenario 13

Dominique Woods has two years of teaching experience at a large urban high school. This is her first year teaching at a small, suburban, ethnically-mixed high school.

68.   Ms. Woods wants to take advantage of the week of faculty meetings before school opens to become better acquainted with the school grounds, faculty, curriculum, and available materials. How could she best utilize her time?

(A)   Tour the school while noting the teacher's room, materials room, and other important rooms.

(B)   Talk to the principal about what is expected of her.

(C)   Talk with a willing teacher who has spent several years at the school about community characteristics and available materials as they apply to the curriculum.

(D)   Obtain a copy of the curriculum to take to the materials room where it can be determined what materials are available for classroom use.

69.   Ms. Woods is reviewing her class lists and curriculum guide and wondering what to plan for the first day of school. Taking into account her first-year status at the school, Ms. Woods would most likely

(A)   present the class with a year long outline of the novels they will be reading and when they will be reading them.

(B)   have the class fill out a questionnaire to ascertain what types of literature they like best.

(C)   have each student introduce himself or herself to the class and suggest a favorite book.

(D)   give pairs of students an interview to conduct with one another, asking about their favorite books and their favorite English class activities.

Three months have passed and Ms. Woods is preparing to submit grades and conference request forms. Although students have done well in reading, writing grades seem to be low.

70.   Ms. Woods has come to the conclusion that her students are having trouble assessing their own writing strengths and weaknesses. Which of the following would be appropriate ways of monitoring and improving the students' writing?

I.   Have students submit an original work on the topic of their choice every day to be graded.

II.   Have students identify, with the help of the teacher, one area of writing in which they feel they need improvement, then focus on this area until their goal has been reached and a new area has been identified.

III.   All draft and final copies will be kept in a portfolio from which the student will pick a piece to discuss with the teacher at a teacher-student conference.

IV.   Once a week the teacher will read a quality composition written by a class member.

(A)   II and III only.   (C)   I, III, and IV only.

(B)   I and III only.   (D)   II, III, and IV only.

71.   It is time for parent-teacher conferences. Ms. Woods has prepared a discussion checklist so that she is certain to cover all essential topics during the conference. Which of the following will she need to remember?

(A)   First address the problems and then address the positive aspects with whatever time is remaining.

(B)   Begin with a positive note about the student and then ease into concerns about the negative aspects.

(C) Present as many technical facts as possible so the parents sense an air of confidence and experience in her ability as a teacher.

(D) Present the solutions that she, the teacher, feels are most advantageous and continue to support this issue until the parents have agreed to your recommendations.

72. Ms. Woods attended a seminar on improving the classroom environment. She is looking for more interaction and participation in her classroom. The seminar suggested changing one thing at a time to see what works best. Which of the following would make the fastest change in class participation?

(A) Assigning seats row by row, alternating boys and girls.

(B) Having the industrial arts teacher build new bookshelves for the classroom.

(C) Presenting a new policy where each person must bring one debatable question to class each day.

(D) Arrange the desks into a circle so everyone can see one another.

73. The seminar stressed a multicultural classroom. Every student should be recognized as having important values and ideas. What could Ms. Woods include in her syllabus that would both fit her curriculum and celebrate the cultural diversity in her classroom?

(A) She could have students choose an author to read from their cultural background, or another cultural background that interests them. Then she could have each student present an informal oral report on the cultural aspects found in the book.

(B) Each month she could introduce a new author, focusing on non-American authors.

(C) The students can find their ancestral country on the classroom map during a discussion of a book in which a character takes a journey.

(D) A day will be declared "Cultural Diversity Day" and the teacher will display novels by authors of varied ethnic backgrounds.

74. Ms. Woods uses a seminar suggestion, cooperative grouping, to complete a class project. This project should include chances for the students to do which of the following:

    I.   Demonstrate leadership ability.

    II. Organize and distribute appropriate work for all members of the group.

    III. Self-evaluate the role each has played in the learning activity.

    IV. Be grouped in a way that allows for a high and low learner to be in each group.

    (A) III and IV only.   (C) I, II, III, and IV.

    (B) II only.   (D) I, II, and III only.

75. The cooperative learning exercise is based around a historical novel of the group's choice. They will need to present information to the class about the history that took place in the time around the setting of the novel. Ms. Woods has asked a social studies teacher to demonstrate how the students can prepare a timeline of historical facts simply by reading a novel. In addition, the librarian spoke to the class about the many uses the library serves while students are working on a project such as this. What was Ms. Woods main objective for organizing these speakers?

    (A) Ms. Woods will have a free period to prepare other lessons.

    (B) The students will be acquainted with other faculty members whom they may not have met.

    (C) The students will have to do less work on their own in preparing their projects.

    (D) The students will know what material is at their disposal and how they can gain access to it.

76. While working in their groups, Ms. Woods notices a problem continually surfacing. Ms. Woods would best handle this situation by

    (A) listening to the class as they suggest what they feel the problem is and ways to solve it while she organizes the discussion.

(B)   speaking to the group leaders and telling them to overlook the problem and continue the activity.

(C)   letting the groups work out the problem at their own pace and in their own way.

(D)   stopping the group work, stating that it is not working out as planned and the class will not be finishing the project.

Scenario 14

77.   Mr. Shah teaches middle-school English. His job in the school is both teacher and supervisor. His goal for the marking period is to increase the students' intrinsic motivation to learn and succeed. To accomplish this he should

(A)   reward every good grade with a tangible reward.

(B)   permit students to choose from a teacher generated list of interesting topics, about which they want to read and learn.

(C)   relate lessons to those topics which he, as a teacher, feels interested in teaching.

(D)   provide students with a list of questions on varying topics to answer for each week.

78.   After reading a novel in which a character, having hit hard times, makes a decision to commit a crime, Mr. Shah poses this question for homework: "What would you have the character do such that the story ends in a positive manner?" What was Mr. Shah's purpose for doing this?

(A)   He wanted to develop moral reasoning and problem solving skills.

(B)   He wanted to give the students a creative idea about which to write.

(C)   He wanted to prompt the students to evaluate themselves and their reading skills.

(D)   He wanted to propose a more suitable ending of the story so as not to set a bad example for future citizens.

79.   Mr. Shah has given an assignment in which four students will work together to present a reflection on an author and his or her works. Mr. Shah, through a survey, has realized that many students have not worked in such a group before, so he reviews the rules of participation. Which of the following are vital rules to achieve the desired outcome?

I.   Take turns talking quietly.

II.   Listen to each other's ideas.

III.   Help each other when asked.

IV.   Base the outcome on how each individual participated.

(A)   II and III only.   (C)   I, III, and IV only.

(B)   I and III only.   (D)   I, II, III, and IV.

80.   In order to prepare students for a national writing test, Mr. Shah has created a folder for each student. The folder includes rough drafts, final copies, and a personal checklist of criteria for grading the test samples. Why has Mr. Shah included one check list for every student?

(A)   So the students may conduct an informal assessment of their own work.

(B)   In case the students forgot the requirements and needed a quick reference to use during grading.

(C)   So the teacher will have a means of evaluating their writing samples.

(D)   So that the student is aware of the criteria on which the samples are being graded.

SECTION 2

> **DIRECTIONS:** Plan and write an essay on the topic given below. Do not write on any topic other than the one specified. An essay on any other topic is unacceptable.

Essay Topic:

What specific characteristics do you think a person must possess in order to be an effective teacher? Fully explain each characteristic and show how the absence of each will reduce effectiveness in the classroom.

ATS-W SECONDARY
PRACTICE TEST

ANSWER KEY

1.	(A)	21.	(C)	41.	(B)	61.	(D)
2.	(B)	22.	(A)	42.	(D)	62.	(D)
3.	(C)	23.	(C)	43.	(C)	63.	(B)
4.	(A)	24.	(B)	44.	(D)	64.	(B)
5.	(B)	25.	(D)	45.	(C)	65.	(A)
6.	(D)	26.	(C)	46.	(C)	66.	(D)
7.	(B)	27.	(C)	47.	(C)	67.	(A)
8.	(B)	28.	(A)	48.	(A)	68.	(C)
9.	(A)	29.	(C)	49.	(C)	69.	(D)
10.	(D)	30.	(C)	50.	(D)	70.	(D)
11.	(B)	31.	(A)	51.	(C)	71.	(B)
12.	(C)	32.	(C)	52.	(A)	72.	(D)
13.	(D)	33.	(D)	53.	(B)	73.	(A)
14.	(A)	34.	(C)	54.	(C)	74.	(C)
15.	(B)	35.	(C)	55.	(C)	75.	(D)
16.	(A)	36.	(C)	56.	(C)	76.	(A)
17.	(D)	37.	(A)	57.	(A)	77.	(B)
18.	(C)	38.	(C)	58.	(C)	78.	(A)
19.	(C)	39.	(D)	59.	(B)	79.	(D)
20.	(C)	40.	(C)	60.	(A)	80.	(A)

ATS-W SECONDARY PRACTICE TEST

Detailed Explanations
of Answers

SECTION 1

1.   **(A)** The correct response is (A). Since his goal is his own professional development, the answer is (A). Mr. O'Brien would not assess the quality of students' assignments (C) or revise students' assignments (D) to enhance his own growth and development. Choices (B), (C), and (D) refer to instructional activities, not professional development activities.

2.   **(B)** The correct response is (B). Mr. O'Brien is demonstrating that he is a reflective practitioner who can work cooperatively with others in his school. (A) describes a form of intellectual snobbery that does not lead to collegiality. (C) is a given—independent of others' views, Mr. O'Brien has a professional responsibility to keep pace with developments and issues in his teaching field. Finally, (D) is poor because it would not necessarily help him reach his goal of improving instruction.

3.   **(C)** The correct response is (C). Including both colleagues' viewpoints is an effort to bring students a balanced and fair presentation on the topic and to work effectively with other professionals at his school. Choices (A) and (D) would not promote collegiality or demonstrate Mr. O'Brien's ability to work with other members of the teaching community. Choice (B) would mean that Mr. O'Brien refused to consider the issue carefully simply because it was not an issue with a singular point of view.

4.   **(A)** The correct response is (A). Mr. O'Brien is designing a supportive classroom for all students, both males and females. Using a particular book as a reference work for a course would not result in (B), students having to buy the book, or (D), students having to read the reference book, nor would colleagues necessarily be aware of the practice (C). In sum, Mr. O'Brien would simply have access to Professor Tannen's findings and her interpretation of her data.

5.   **(B)** The correct response is (B). An effective and equitable practice is to give all students an opportunity to participate in class discussions. (A) and (C) are different ways of stating the same practice, which is to treat the female students differently. (D) is incorrect; research already shows that male students tend to receive more feedback when they answer questions, helping to support their self-esteem, whereas female students are seldom given feedback, positive or negative.

6.   **(D)** The correct response is (D). Sensitivity to students' self-esteem means that teachers take an interest in their students, visiting with them privately and trying to understand the reasons for their behavior in class. Taking an interest in the student may provide the encouragement the student needs to start participating in class activities. (B) is a harassing behavior that should be avoided. (A) and (C), although reasonable educational practices, would probably have little direct effect on changing the behavior of the students the teacher is concerned about helping.

7.   **(B)** The correct response is (B). Some students, especially those who respond well to external validators, will be motivated to participate in class when their grades are affected by their participation. (A) is incorrect because this practice will not motivate all students. (C) is incorrect because there is nothing inherent to this practice that would result in all students earning higher grades—only those who participate would improve their grades. This practice of rewarding students for their participation would not be expected to discourage student participation (D).

8.   **(B)** The correct response is (B). Mr. O'Brien's strategy involves everyone in class and encourages each student to discover the practical applications for the information to be learned in class. (A) is incorrect because in a communications class, discourse and discussions are encouraged, not avoided; in communications classes, students learn to argue and disagree in a civil manner. (C) is incorrect because this strategy takes quite a bit of classroom time by allowing all students to be actively involved; it is not a timesaving device. (D) is incorrect because brain-

storming is a creative activity, not an activity aimed at assessing skills or knowledge.

9. **(A)** The correct response is (A). Mr. O'Brien has employed a brainstorming activity to allow students to uncover their own, personal communication problems and needs. Therefore, they will have more motivation and interest in learning about communication differences between men and women. (B) is incorrect; in fact, Mr. O'Brien may choose to introduce the topic formally at the next class meeting. (C) is incorrect because at no point has Mr. O'Brien presented information to pit men and women against each other, nor is that the purpose of presenting this topic. (D) is incorrect as Mr. O'Brien's choice of activities will have the opposite effect of dismissing students' concerns as he recognizes and helps them to identify their problems.

10. **(D)** The correct response is (D). Activities (or group work) allow students to learn cooperatively. (A) is incorrect because it does not specify an instructional goal for the group work. Choice (B) is incorrect because the goal is problem-solving not merely improving social skills. (C) is incorrect because students are not structuring their own time in this example.

11. **(B)** The correct response is (B). Students often disclose more personal information in journals than when speaking in class. The teacher can also check for comprehension of content and the success or failure of class objectives. Journals typically are not graded with consideration to standard usage or grammatical constructions; therefore, (A) is incorrect. The assignment has no direct bearing on time-management skills; therefore, (C) is incorrect. Choice (D) is irrelevant: no mention is made of giving daily grades on the journal writing.

12. **(C)** The correct response is (C). Meeting each student and determining needs individually and informally is the best first step to establish rapport with each student. Subsequently, Ms. Jaynes will want to review school files (B) and administer tests (D). Ms. Jaynes will want to be careful in discussing students with other teachers (A), so as not to be influenced by biased opinions or stereotypes against students with learning disabilities or other special needs.

13. **(D)** The correct response is (D). This choice is a definition of test bias. (A) refers to test validity; choice (B) refers to test reliability. Choice (C) is the objective of intelligence tests.

14. **(A)** The correct response is (A). Practice effects are seen when students are retested with the same instrument shortly after the first testing. It is assumed that students' scores will improve with subsequent exposure to the same material. (B) is not a practice effect, but the desired effect of improved skills or enhanced performance; it, indeed, is the purpose of instruction. Choice (C) pertains to the issue of test validity and choice (D) refers to the issue of social desirability (that is, when students answer the way they believe is desired). Social desirability is an issue with opinion or attitude tests, not achievement or skills tests.

15. **(B)** The correct response is (B). As a reading specialist, Ms. Jaynes understands the important role that motivation plays in reading comprehension. Students are more likely to both read and understand subjects that they enjoy and are interested in, not just literary classics (C). Readability studies reveal that students can comprehend material written at very high levels when they are interested in the material (D). The teacher, certainly, has a responsibility to guide students' choices and not to simply *send* them to the library, choice (A).

16. **(A)** The correct response is (A). Ms. Jaynes has attempted to increase students' metacognitive awareness and fluency by directly teaching them an elaboration strategy to aid and monitor their reading comprehension. This is a holistic approach to teaching reading versus a specific skill or component approach as referred to in choices (B), (C), and (D).

17. **(D)** The correct response is (D). When students are taught effective strategies to use as tools, they can become independent learners. Choice (A), a quiet classroom, is not conducive to the learning of all students; research on learning styles indicates that only some students prefer quiet when reading or studying. Ms. Jaynes must be actively involved in each class, monitoring students' performance, so she does not have any extra time for paperwork in class, choice (B). Although reading can be a social activity, most important reading done by students (in and out of school) is a solitary activity (C).

18. **(C)** The correct response is (C). Statistical procedures used to standardize tests usually result in high validity and reliability; reading tests, in particular, usually are good measures of overall reading achievement as compared to the more specific and narrow purview of most informally-constructed tests. Standardized tests are not always easier to grade (A), nor are they more subjective (B) or more economical (D) than informally-constructed tests.

19. **(C)** The correct response is (C). Although choices (A), (B) and (D) are possible products of Ms. Jaynes' actions, they are not the certain reason she engages in this practice. Popularity, higher salaries, and better-disciplined students do not always accompany involved and caring instruction. However, many intangible rewards are products of being a team member of the learning community.

20. **(C)** The correct response is (C). These broadly-stated goals for instruction are examples of instructional or educational objectives. Behavioral objectives (A) must describe specific skills or knowledge to be acquired and demonstrated by students. Performance objectives (B) include performance standards and other specific performance criteria. The question has nothing to do with outcome-based education (D).

21. **(C)** The correct response is (C). Behavioral objectives describe what students will be able to do as a result of having received appropriate instruction. A variety of teaching methods may be used to reach these objectives (A), and teacher-centered or student-centered (better to use both) activities may be used (D). Materials and equipment lists (B) may or may not be given on lesson plans; if so, they are separate from behavioral objectives.

22. **(A)** The correct response is (A). Ms. Aljuhbar makes use of collaborative processes in planning instruction and designing activities. Choices (B) and (C) would not create reciprocal learning situations; ESL students would only be learning about life in the United States. Choice (D) is poor because it does not include an active role for ESL students, nor does it recognize that some ESL students from non-Christian countries might feel excluded by an activity focusing on a Christian holiday.

23. **(C)** The correct response is (C). This action shows concern for the student and opens the door for dialogue with the student. For high school-aged students, a direct approach which recognizes the student's own responsibility for his or her own learning and behavior is usually the best approach. Choices (A) and (B) are indirect and could exacerbate the student's present problems. (D) fails to get at the cause of Lee's difficulties.

24. **(B)** The correct response is (B). The instructional principle illustrated here is that students can more easily learn new information (English) when linked with the familiar (their native language). Moreover, learning becomes more effective when students are allowed to make choices

about the learning activities in which they engage. Choices (A) and (C) are plausible, but poor choices in comparison with (B). Choice (D) is incorrect because filming one's performance involves some level of risk.

25. **(D)** The correct response is (D). Sharing stories with youngsters allows the older students to instruct younger students, assuming an authority role as teacher; these activities can motivate and reward ESL students. These activities have nothing to do with standardizing student performance (A), nor are they inappropriate for high school-aged students (B); adults routinely engage in such behaviors. Moreover, these activities do not restrict, but rather encourage, student initiative and creativity (C).

26. **(C)** The correct response is (C). Mr. Reams was modeling effective communication techniques. Choice (A) is incorrect because the teacher's role changes from structured to unstructured situations, but it is never minimized. (B) is false because no teaching strategy can ensure success. (D) is incorrect because at this point, students are not aware of environmental needs. They are still in the brainstorming section of the instruction.

27. **(C)** The correct response is (C). The instructor is attempting to vary his instructional strategies to keep students involved. (A) is incorrect because no selection of materials and resources has occurred at this point. (B) is wrong because in a brainstorming situation, assessment is not used and creativity is encouraged. (D) stifles, rather than encourages, the positive social and emotional climate in the classroom that the instructor wishes to create at all times.

28. **(A)** The correct response is (A). Mr. Reams had developed a successful interdisciplinary activity for his class. (B) is incorrect because maintaining class control is not inherently part of brainstorming. (C) is incorrect because promoting problem solving does not allow for a preconceived agenda. (D) is wrong because technology as a learning tool has not been introduced at this point.

29. **(C)** The correct response is (C). The instructor has made the students feel that they are members of a smoothly functioning community. Choice (A) is a false statement. Environmental pollution is not a new or unique problem. (B) expresses only part of the complete answer (C). (D) is incorrect because there has been no assessment thus far.

30. **(C)** The correct response is (C). The instructor has taken advantage of community strengths to foster student growth. (A) is incorrect because the teacher is a role model and has worked cooperatively with the community himself. (B) is incorrect because parent-teacher conferences should begin and end on a positive note. (D) is incorrect because achieving teacher determined personal goals indicates student manipulation rather than student problem solving.

31. **(A)** The correct response is (A). A needs assessment will help students make the connection between their current skills and those that will be new to them. (B) is wrong because a needs assessment focuses on the skills a student currently possesses. (C) is incorrect because the needs assessment is designed to determine what needs to be taught that is not currently in the curriculum. (D) is a false statement. A needs assessment is not designed to motivate students.

32. **(C)** The correct response is (C). A positive environment must be created to minimize the effects of negative external factors. (A) is inappropriate because changing the text but allowing the environment to remain the same only results in maintaining the status quo. (B) is incorrect because relating the students' personal interests to the new material is only a part of creating a positive environment. (D) is wrong because again it is only a small part of maximizing the effects of a positive learning environment.

33. **(D)** The correct response is (D). The instructor should plan instruction that will lead students to ask questions and pursue problems that are meaningful to them. (A) is a part of (D). Meaningful instruction will nurture student growth and the instruction will be developmentally appropriate. (B) is incorrect because it is incomplete. The type of instruction indicated in (D) would enhance students' self-esteem. (C) is incorrect because it may or it may not include an invitation to community professionals to speak in class.

34. **(C)** The correct response is (C). The instructor knows how to work effectively with all members of the community to solve problems and accomplish educational goals. (A) is encompassed in (C). Working with community leaders, identifying community problems and, if possible, solving those problems with the students will motivate students and affect their learning. (B) A teacher's role does change from situation to situation. His or her work within the community would not be one of

teacher/instructor, but rather one of facilitator/helper. (D) is incorrect because although there must be a bond of trust between the parent and the teacher, that bond is not revealed in the planning.

35. **(C)** The correct response is (C). The teacher would be fostering strong home relationships which support student achievement of desired outcomes. Choice (A) is the result of (C). As the teacher interacts with professionals in the community, her own professional growth would be promoted. (B) is also the result of (C). All teachers are expected to interact with the community to help meet the expectations associated with teaching. (D) is incomplete since strong home relationships are developed through the principles of conferences, trust, and cooperation.

36. **(C)** The correct response is (C). This question relates to planning processes to design outcome-oriented learning experiences. Developing objectives is the first step in planning. Cooperative learning and the content are used to reach the objectives (A). Evaluation is the last step in the planning process (B). Finding materials and resources is an important step in planning, but not the first (D).

37. **(A)** The correct response is (A). This question relates to an understanding of human developmental processes. This understanding nurtures student growth through developmentally appropriate instruction. Higher order thinking skills are important instructional strategies, but (B) is not the best answer. Promoting the lifelong pursuit of learning is achieved through structuring and managing the learning environment (C). Understanding how learning occurs would show that constant difficult schoolwork causes students to become disinterested, which renders (D) an incorrect choice.

38. **(C)** The correct response is (C). This question relates to environmental factors. Being aware of external forces will help in the planning and designing of the unit to promote students' learning and self-esteem. (A) relates to the development of the unit which requires choosing lessons and activities that reflect the principles of effective instruction and renders (A) incorrect. Challenging students requires the teacher to be aware of the learners' interests while designing the instruction, which is part of the planning process and incorrect for this situation (B). (D), the grouping of students, is an instructional strategy and is incorrect.

39. **(D)** The correct response is (D). This question relates to how learning occurs and applying this understanding to the design and implementation of effective instruction. A student's daily class schedule is an external factor. Learning styles affect how a student learns; therefore, (A) is incorrect for this question. Cultural background affects how students may develop knowledge and skills and is an important consideration of how learning occurs, which makes (B) incorrect for this question. Previous grades would indicate the ability of a student to learn through linking new information to old, and would make (C) incorrect for this question.

40. **(C)** The correct response is (C). This question relates to human diversity and the knowledge that each student brings to the classroom a constellation of personal and social characteristics related to a variety of factors such as exceptionality. (A) is simply more of the same kind of schoolwork and not an acceptable answer. Being intrinsically motivated, exceptional students often find unmotivated students difficult to tutor, making choice (B) incorrect. Teacher-made, tightly-organized units do not allow the exceptional student the opportunity to experience the learning situation; (D) is incorrect.

41. **(B)** The correct response is (B). Team rewards, individual accountability, and equal opportunities for success are always present in cooperative learning. Rules and specific tasks may be part of the instructions given for cooperative learning groups, but are not required in cooperative learning situations; therefore, choices (A), (C), and (D) are incorrect.

42. **(D)** The correct response is (D). This question relates to enabling teachers to document their teaching and to be aware of students' efforts, progress, and achievements. A portfolio is a purposeful collection of work that exhibits efforts, progress, and achievement of students and enables teachers to document teaching in an authentic setting. Standardized tests are commercially developed and are used for specific events (A). A teacher-made test is used to evaluate specific objectives of the course, so (B) is not the best choice. Observation is used only to explain what students do in classrooms and to indicate some of their capabilities; therefore, (C) is incorrect.

43. **(C)** The correct response is (C). This question relates to evaluating specific objectives and content. Teacher-made tests are designed to evaluate the specific objectives and specific content of a course. (A) is incorrect because self and peer evaluation utilizes students' knowledge according to evaluation criteria that is understood by the students. A

portfolio (B) is a purposeful collection of work that exhibits effort, progress, and achievement of students and enables teachers to document teaching in an authentic setting. Observation (D) is used to explain what students do in classrooms and to indicate to some degree their capabilities.

44. **(D)** The correct response is (D). Standardized tests rate student performance against the performance of other students and report the scores in terms of percentiles, stanines, and scaled scores. A portfolio (A) is a collection of student effort, progress, and achievement. Teacher-made tests evaluate specific objectives and content, so (B) is incorrect. Students' classroom behaviors and capabilities are evaluated through observation, making (C) incorrect.

45. **(C)** The correct response is (C). Self and peer assessment requires that the students be aware of and understand the evaluation criteria. A collection of work that exhibits students' success and enables teachers to document teaching is a portfolio (A). A teacher-made test (B) evaluates specific objectives and content. Observation is used to indicate capabilities and actions of students (D).

46. **(C)** The correct response is (C). Mrs. Ratu's lack of competency is exhibited in her lack of understanding of her students and in her teaching at the elementary level. Mrs. Ratu was not teaching her students at the appropriate level (A). Although she may have desired to make reading easy for her students (B), she was not going about it correctly. When appropriate techniques are used, teaching ninth graders to read is no more difficult than teaching third graders to read.

47. **(C)** The correct response is (C). Mr. Jones knew that development in one area leads to development in other areas. He also knew that using a variety of instructional techniques could lead to inquiry, motivation, and even further development in certain areas. Allowing students to have choices in their learning leads to a positive self-concept and can lead to camaraderie. Roundtable discussions lead to questions and often to the solving of problems and, therefore, to the improvement of grades (D).

48. **(A)** The correct response is (A). Diversity of students was used as an advantage. Similarities and differences need to be discussed in order to create a respect for those differences. Discussions are but one avenue for creating an open, secure environment. Forbidden discussion diminishes motivation. The students had been allowed to discuss their feel-

ings about subjects of interest. However, their feelings were but one element of their diversity (B). Statement (C) is false. The students may have begun to respect their differences, but respect of diversity is only part of the reason for the discussion's success.

49. **(C)** The correct response is (C). Mr. Jones' role was varied. In the discussions he was the facilitator, not the teacher. He had planned the discussion as an outcome-oriented learning experience. Mr. Jones' role did vary, but the activity did not function as an assessment tool (A). Mr. Jones had already made the decision to evaluate the students yearly with an achievement test. The discussion was not a form of assessment (B). Maintaining a lifelong pursuit of learning is the ultimate goal for all education (D). However, the immediate and more pressing goal was to improve the reading skills of the concerned students.

50. **(D)** The correct response is (D). As a facilitator, Mr. Jones listened to and monitored the discussion. His duty as facilitator was to model effective communication strategies, to monitor the students' input, and to encourage all students to participate. Mr. Jones would also be able to manage the classroom environment, which is a part of shaping the learners through effective communication strategies. The amount of information each student had collected could be indicative of the homes' socioeconomic level, but this statement is not an absolute (C). The student could have just forgotten to look for material at home.

51. **(C)** The correct response is (C). A prewriting activity stimulates students' thinking and helps them with the writing process. Choices (A) and (B) are too general and superficial. Choice (D) refers specifically to outlining, something not mentioned in the context of the problem set.

52. **(A)** The correct response is (A). Introspective activities help students to connect new information to previously learned information, an important cognitive process. Choice (B) refers to personal narrative whereas the writing assignment is a personal description. Choice (C) is inappropriate at this point in the learning process. Choice (D) is an affective goal for instruction, but the question specifically asks about cognitive development.

53. **(B)** The correct response is (B). Students are affected by multiple factors, including environmental factors both inside and outside class. Choice (A) is a broad generalization that has no direct application to Ms. Johnson's request that students think about their own behavior inside

and outside class. Choice (C) assumes that students can easily identify their own strengths, even though research shows that students (and adults) often have difficulty identifying their specific strengths and assets. Choice (D) is incorrect because of the same rationale.

54. **(C)** The correct response is (C). One of the central tenets of human development is the constant interaction and precarious balance of nurture and nature. Choices (A) and (B) specifically refer to Piaget's theory of cognitive development, a specific subset of human development theories. Choice (D) is a false statement; theories of human development support the notion that adolescence is a time of increased social cognition and the awareness of the thoughts of others. (Hence, the adolescent phenomena of "personal fable" and "imaginary audience" as identified by Elkind.)

55. **(C)** The correct response is (C). The Language-Experience-Approach (LEA) is a proven method of increasing students' reading and writing proficiency and their overall language competency. It requires that students write about what they know. Choices (A), (B), and (D) are irrelevant. Choice (A) superficially addresses that Ms. Johnson is an English teacher and choice (B) refers to autobiographies, something that is not mentioned in the preceding information. Choice (D) foreshadows the library project, but it has not yet been introduced into the context of these questions.

56. **(C)** The correct response is (C). A basic principle in providing students with appropriate feedback is to first note the student's strengths (or positive aspects of the student's work and/or performance) and then to note specific ways the student can improve his or her work and/or performance. Therefore, the best approach for a teacher to take in providing students with feedback on written work is to first note the good things about students' writing and then to suggest ways to improve. Choices (A) and (B) are in essence the same; both choices indicate that only students' strengths would be acknowledged, omitting the important aspect of addressing ways students can improve. Neither action would enhance students' cognitive skills or their metacognitive skills (or self-awareness). Choice (D) is unacceptable because it denigrates the teacher's responsibility to evaluate students' performance on the basis of individual merit against the standards established by particular disciplines.

57. **(A)** The correct response is (A). This is the best answer of the four options for the following reasons. First, learning style information ac-

knowledges that although learners acquire knowledge in different ways, those differences can lead to effective learning when students are taught cognitive strategies which complement their natural learning tendencies; basically, teaching students about learning styles (and especially about their own learning style) is a recognition of human diversity. Second, beyond mere recognition of human diversity is the legitimacy of different approaches to learning. Every student can perform at a level of proficiency although not every student will attain that level in the same manner; in other words, learning styles validate students as learners and promote high standards for academic achievement. Third, when students are taught not only about learning styles in general, but specifically about their own learning style, they are empowered to take responsibility for their own learning. Fourth, of the four options, only choices (A) and (D) are tasks actively engaging the student. Both choices (B) and (C) are passive activities, and are therefore poor choices. Choice (D) requires that students perform a task without any help (direct instruction) for accomplishing the task; simply asking students to name additional strengths without giving them an opportunity to self-examine, to self-assess, and to explore their strengths will not produce the desired outcome. Only choice (A) gives students the information they need in order to accomplish the task the teacher has identified as being important.

58. **(C)** The correct response is (C). Although brainstorming activities benefit learning by determining students' interests (A) and giving everyone a chance to participate (B), choices (A) and (B) are merely benefits, not the real purpose of the activity. (D) is incorrect because it is irrelevant to the situation described; brainstorming, as an activity, has no direct relationship to honesty or cheating.

59. **(B)** The correct response is (B). Although (A), (C), and (D) are possible choices, the best answer to the question is (B). (A), (C), and (D) are basically restatements of the idea that the teacher forms the groups instead of the students; this was specified in the context of the question. The only option which gives a rationale for the teacher choosing her action is answer (B).

60. **(A)** The correct response is (A). Only choice (A) recognizes the cognitive principle underlying the teacher's assignment. Choices (B) and (D) are essentially the same; although the assignment may result in these timesaving features, they are not the instructional principle guiding the teacher's practice. Choice (C) is irrelevant. Asking students to hypoth-

esize is not directly related to inculcating self-management skills in learners.

61. **(D)** The correct response is (D). I, II, III, and IV were included in the planning. (A) is a true statement but is only one element of the correct response of (D). Both statements are true in (B) and (C), but again are only part of the correct response.

62. **(D)** The correct response is (D). All preceding activities were for the purpose of engaging the students in order to motivate them to achieve. Mrs. Gomez's role (A) is not the issue, it is the students and their learning. The purpose of the workshop was to better each student's writing, not understand the society in which they live (B). The purpose of the workshop was not to identify the talents of the students (C), but to teach them how to creatively write using metaphors.

63. **(B)** The correct response is (B). Bright colors have a stimulating effect. By displaying multiple transparencies of works of art the students could choose the one they wanted to write about. (A) Stimulation of the creativity of the students was not the only goal for using the bright transparencies. The other goal was to allow students to have a choice in their learning. (C) The issue is writing, not art; however, exposure to the art could create a desire to know much more about it. (D) The purpose of the assignment was not just to expose them to art but to stimulate good writing.

64. **(B)** The correct response is (B). In the assessment, Mrs. Gomez had to communicate effectively with the students. To accomplish this she used various media. She was connecting the media to the different learning styles. (A) Evaluation generates divergent thinking but never creative thinking. The statement is false. (C) The evaluation tools were not to evaluate Mrs. Gomez's competency but were designed to evaluate the students' competency in identifying and creating metaphors. (D) Working with other colleagues is not the issue.

65. **(A)** The correct response is (A). The poem was a creative expression, allowing the freedom for each learner to express his or her differences. (B) Statement two is correct but statement four is incorrect. (C) Both class participation and the completion of the poem were included in the formal assessment designed by Mrs. Gomez. (D) Class participation and completion of the poem allowed respect for the differences among students; however, it did not allow for a variety of opinions to be expressed.

66. **(D)** The correct response is (D). Although there may be some value in all of the responses offered, the two strongest strategies are those that will bring about financial advantages and those that will strengthen the relationship between the community and the school. The monetary savings, since school funding is tied into the Average Daily Attendance for a school district, is one way to win favor with members of the community, especially since recent school funding problems in New York have tended to increase taxation supporting the public schools in many communities. Since research also indicates that the better the attendance record, the more likely a student is to achieve success in school, parents and other concerned members of the community will react favorably to the plan. The incentives for the students to attend, derived from the community businesses, may well make the youth more appreciative of their community support structure. Choices (A), (B), and (C) are incorrect. Choice (A) considers only the financial advantage and does not take into account the positive interaction of school and community promoted by the attendance plan. Choice (B) is not the best answer. Some students will be excited about their awards; however, their greatest reward will be the increased opportunity for learning. All schools like positive publicity, but the value of the proposal goes well beyond mere publicity with other school districts. Choice (C) is incorrect because although the students' receiving of awards or prizes may be exciting and motivating to some, the major advantage, as previously stated, is to the students' improved chance to learn.

67. **(A)** The correct response is (A). Mr. Janowsky has enhanced the introductory lesson to the unit of study on advertising by using a variety of materials and resources that pique students' interests and response. The ideas spark the students' own future gathering of advertising ideas for a project during this unit of study. The several primary examples of advertisements and the varied techniques clearly contrasted serve to demonstrate the creativity associated with this area of study. Even cultural differences and preferences are shown by his use of the Clio Awards videotape clippings. (B), (C), and (D) are incorrect. (B)'s negative assessment of the use of varied resources is completely unacceptable in a class of creative thinking and production. Even if Mr. Janowsky has overdone the display of examples, the negative connotation of the word clutter makes the supervisor's comment inappropriate. (C) is not the best answer for this introductory lesson. The examples of materials and resources displayed by Mr. Janowsky serve as a model to stimulate the students' gathering of samples as the unit of study progresses. (D) is incorrect for

a supervisor, no matter how interested in this subject, who is having a conference to evaluate Mr. Janowsky as a professional educator. This focus of evaluation should be the clear purpose of the supervisor's comments. Of course, as an advertising buff, the supervisor may want to meet with Mr. Janowsky again after the formal evaluation conference to discuss their joint interest.

68. **(C)** The correct response is (C). The most efficient way to gain information about a new setting is to speak with someone who is familiar with the circumstances. Orienting oneself with the physical layout (A) would be helpful but cannot tell you about the student population or materials. Although communication with the principal (B) is always a good idea, the principal usually will have little time to have an in-depth discussion and will not be able to tell specifically which books are available for your use. Eventually Ms. Woods will need to match curriculum guidelines to the material available (D), but sitting in a closet will not introduce her to staff and student characteristics.

69. **(D)** The correct response is (D). By having students interact with each other on the first day, the nervousness is broken and Ms. Woods will have quality student profiles to use when preparing suitable lessons. Handing out a syllabus (A), which will change greatly by year's end, does nothing to introduce the students to each other or the teacher to the class. A questionnaire of favorite literature (B) will help the teacher prepare topics around student interests, but the individual questionnaire does nothing to involve students in familiarizing themselves with one another. Individually introducing oneself by name and favorite book (C) puts the students on the spot, which may make a new high school student nervous, and one book will not help the teacher develop a good student profile.

70. **(D)** The correct response is (D). This includes all of the techniques that would be useful in improving and monitoring writing. The students have set goals toward which they will strive (II) bit by bit until they reach them. The teacher and student have an opportunity to discuss good and bad points of the student's writing in a non-threatening atmosphere (III). It is always helpful to have a model of good writing (IV), and by choosing students' papers, self-esteem is enhanced. Forcing a student to write every night will do little to create quality work. Therefore choices (B) and (C) are incorrect.

71. **(B)** The correct response is (B). Parent-teacher communication should always begin and end on a positive note, so as not to offend parents and turn them off to future suggestions. Never leave problems for the end (A) because parents may be put on the offensive if they sense a negative attitude from the teacher. Parents do not want to feel as if they are being put down, which will often occur if the teacher uses too much technical jargon (C). Teachers must gain the parent's cooperation (D) so that both parent and teacher feel comfortable with the plan of improvement at home and at school.

72. **(D)** The correct response is (D). The classroom arrangement can control how the students respond in class. Students tend to respond more openly if they are communicating face to face with each other, which makes a circle the optimal desk arrangement. Putting students in rows by sex does little to stimulate discussion (A). The physical aesthetics of the classroom are important (B), but nice looking book cases will not encourage participation. A new topic each day may spur limited conversation at the time but does little to encourage continual class participation (C).

73. **(A)** The correct response is (A). Many authors include cultural aspects in their books. By reading an author from an appealing culture, a student not only learns about the character, but also the character's culture. By presenting their findings to the class, classmates are exposed to this information as well. Exposure to new authors is important, but highlighting a new author once a month is not enough exposure to be significant (B). Although knowing geographical locations of countries is important (C), cultural diversity encompasses much more. Exposure to varied authors is necessary, but multicultural awareness is meant to be integrated into the entire curriculum, rather than relegated to one day (D).

74. **(C)** The correct response is (C). Cooperative grouping should give the students a chance to display leadership abilities (I), organize and distribute materials so that all members play a vital part in the final product (II), and evaluate for themselves how the group functioned and whether or not they did the best job they could (III). The teacher should have a way to group the students so they are balanced for optimal learning by everyone (IV).

75. **(D)** The correct response is (D). The social studies teacher demonstrates how curricula can cross and how students can use prior knowl-

edge and non-novel resources to aide them in their project. Students new to a school need to know how to gain access to information, which is best done with the help of the librarian. Ms. Woods has used her faculty resources to enhance her teaching and build a good working environment among faculty members. Although Ms. Woods will not be teaching class at the time, it is not necessarily free time, and this was not her main objective (A). The students will become more familiar with these faculty members (B), but they will gain more than just this. If the students listen carefully they will learn time-cutting techniques, but the discussion will not serve as a way to get out of doing work (C).

76. **(A)** The correct response is (A). Ms. Woods will best serve as a facilitator in this situation. She knows how to let the students solve the problem by discussing options while she guides and directs the students. She does this without overtly telling them how to solve the problem. By overlooking the problem (B), the teacher is setting an example that says working problems out is not necessary. By not presenting a model to follow (C) the teacher may be letting the group flounder and waste precious time, even though they may solve the problem in the end. An activity should never be stopped with the only explanation being that it is not working (D).

77. **(B)** The correct response is (B). Intrinsic motivation and the desire to learn is shown to increase when students are given a role to play by choosing their own learning processes and materials. Continuous tangible rewards (A) increase extrinsic motivation but decrease intrinsic motivation. A lesson is usually of high quality if the teacher is interested in the topic (C) but this is not relevant to increasing students' intrinsic motivation. Rote question answering (D) provides little stimulation; it therefore has no positive effect on motivation.

78. **(A)** The correct response is (A). Literature often mimics real life situations, which can be used to discuss how and why people choose what they do. By this age students can and should further their moral reasoning skills. This assignment serves as a prompt to classroom discussion about acceptable and unacceptable conclusions in problem solving. This exercise serves as a way to write creatively (B) but creativity is not the main thrust of this assignment. Improvement in reading skills is always an underlying purpose, but not the most important for this exercise (C). It is not the teacher's place to rewrite the novel's ending (D), but to use it as a catalyst for thought and contemplation.

79. **(D)** The correct response is (D). When working in cooperative groups it is important that members take turns talking quietly, listening to each other and helping each other when asked. To truly assess the outcome it is also necessary to look at each student's performance within the group and individually. Choice (D) is the only answer to contain all four points.

80. **(A)** The correct response is (A). Students can use the checklist to monitor the content and quality of their writing as they go along, thereby making it self-assessment. Although the list may serve as a quick reference during grading (B), this was not the main purpose for it. This list will provide a means of evaluation but this does not address why each student is given one (C). A fair grading system may ensue but this is not the most important reason for using this list individually (D).

SECTION 2

The following essay would receive scores at the highest end of the scale used in ATS-W essay scoring.

Essay A

When I think of what specific characteristics a person must possess in order to be an effective teacher I think of these characteristics: upstanding values, compassion, and a thorough knowledge of their subject matter.

First, a person who becomes a teacher must keep in mind that they are a role model to the children in their midst. Their private and professional life must be beyond reproach. A teacher is responsible for setting values as well as teaching values. A teacher has a big influence on a child's life; therefore, a teacher must be careful about the kinds of signals he sends out to the children in his environment. Today, it is hard to tell teachers from students because they dress alike, wear their hair alike, associate together, and act the same. A teacher should set himself apart if he is to be a positive influence on the students he comes in contact with. Once a teacher loses his credibility and/or self-respect, he is no longer effective in the classroom.

Compassion is a quality that allows a teacher to have a sense of humor, get to know students' qualities, and be supportive of students' efforts. A teacher must be able to laugh with his students. This creates a relationship between learner and teacher, and shows the students that the teacher has a human side, and tells the students that the teacher is approachable. A good teacher will get to know each of his student's learning abilities and styles. This will allow the teacher to get the most from each student. Compassion allows the teacher to empathize with the students who are having problems in school or at home by being supportive and by providing a positive direction. Students can be turned off if they perceive that a teacher does not care.

Finally, if a person is going to be an effective teacher, he must have a thorough knowledge of his discipline. This gives the teacher a sense of confidence and allows the teacher to be well organized. An effective teacher knows and likes what he teaches, and the enthusiasm will show and will become a part of the students. Without a good mastery of the subject matter, a teacher is unable to make well-informed decisions about objectives to be covered.

In conclusion, by possessing and demonstrating upstanding values, showing compassion, and exhibiting a thorough knowledge of his subject area, the right person can make a good teacher. If students are to learn, they must be influenced by persons who have all three of these characteristics.

Analysis

This essay, even though it contains minor errors in punctuation and pronoun-antecedent agreement, is well written, as evidenced by the clarity, organization, and mature language.

The opening sentence is a complex sentence. Therefore, a comma should have been used to separate the dependent clause ("When I think of what specific characteristics a person must possess in order to be an effective teacher,") from the rest of the sentence (the independent clause). Also, in the first sentence, the pronoun *their* (plural) is used to refer to a *person* (singular). This a pronoun-antecedent disagreement. The pronoun *his* or *her* should have been used. This problem disappears later, suggesting that the writer may have been careless. Always save enough time to proof your essay. When writing hurriedly, it's very easy to make careless mistakes: their for there, a for an, no for know.

The writer adequately introduces the topic "Characteristics of an Effective Teacher" by outlining the three characteristics to be discussed. Each of the three paragraphs of the body contains a characteristic as the main idea and details to explain and/or support it. The conclusion is a summary of the essay and an explanation of why these characteristics are important. The reader should have no difficulty understanding the message the writer is conveying.

The following essay would receive scores in the middle of the ATS-W scoring scale.

Essay B

A teacher must have the following characteristics in order to be effective: dedication, knowledge of the subject matter, and versatility. A dedicated teacher is one who is always willing to go that extra mile to help a student to learn. A dedicated teacher is not one who is just looking for a paycheck every other week. This type of teacher will find the students' weaknesses and start building on those points day-by-day. A dedicated teacher is also a caring person who will help build confidence in students' ability to learn. Without this type of dedication, there will be a decrease in effective teaching because if the teacher does not show his dedication and concern for the students to learn the material, then the students will not reflect that initiative to learn.

Teachers must be knowledgeable in the subject areas that they are teaching. Teachers with more formal education, teaching experience, and hours of training are more successful in helping students achieve educational goals. Now, without this knowledge and education, you will have a reduction in the effective teaching method. Teachers who do not know the academic subject that they are teaching cannot make clear presentations or use effective teaching strategies. They cannot answer questions fully and must be very evasive in their answers.

Another characteristic that a teacher must possess is the versatility to teach slower and advanced learners in a manner that both will be able to receive and retain the given information. A teacher must be able to make the subject matter come alive, demanding quality work meeting personal as well as academic needs of students and adding humor to the classroom. With the absence of this versatility, a teacher will only reach a small number of students in the classroom.

All of the above characteristics are important. Teachers who do not possess them will have difficulty reaching their students, and the drop-out rate will continue to climb.

Analysis

The writer of this essay addresses the topic well, and the essay is without major errors in mechanics of grammar. Nevertheless, the essay lacks clarity in organization and presentation of ideas. No introductory paragraph exists. This is very important because the introductory paragraph sets parameters for the remaining parts of the essay. The writer, in this case, combined the introduction and the first paragraph of the body. The introduction should have read: *A teacher must have the following characteristics in order to be effective: dedication, knowledge of subject matter, and versatility.* In earlier years, a one-sentence paragraph was not allowed. That, however, is no longer true; "A dedicated teacher…" should have been the beginning of the next paragraph.

The remaining paragraphs are well organized. Each is introduced by a characteristic (the main idea), and that characteristic is explained and supported by adequate details. However, a bit of ambiguity exists in paragraph three: *A teacher must be able to make the subject matter come alive, demanding quality work meeting personal as well as academic needs of students and adding humor to the classroom.* For clarity purposes, there should have been a comma after work and a comma after students.

Some awkward expressions exist throughout the essay, but considering the time factor, this essay is considered adequate.

The following essay would receive scores at the lowest end of the ATS-W scoring scale.

Essay C

If you pick up a newspaper, turn on your radio, you will hear, see, and read about the declining of education. Discipline is a problem, test scores are down, and the teacher is being slained. Society has asked the perplexing question: What makes an effective classroom teacher?

First, to become an effective classroom teacher, there has to be an internal love within self, along with external love of the art of teaching. Secondly, devotion, dedication, and discipline among self and the environment in which you are entering will demonstrate the first procedure of effectiveness in the classroom and set up the essential elements involved in teaching. Thirdly, carrying the three "P's" in your heart will produce an effective classroom teacher, being "Proud" of what you are, being "Patient" with whom you are teaching, and being "Persistent" in what you are teaching. Finally, living beyond the classroom, I think, is the most effective in an effective classroom teacher, staying beyond your paid time, getting emotionally involved with your students after your paid time and setting up the ability to cope with the stress of the educational process before your paid time. In order to endure effectiveness, there is long-suffering, perservance, and understanding any situation at any given moment to entitle all children to a worthwhile education of an effective classroom teacher.

Analysis

The writer of this essay partially addresses the topic, but the essay itself is totally unacceptable. The initial paragraph, which should have outlined the characteristics to be discussed, leads one to believe that the essay will address "declining of education," "test scores," and "slained teachers." To identify problems that demand effective teachers is an acceptable way to introduce the topic, but the writer of this essay does it very poorly. Additionally, the past participle of *slay* is *slain*, not *slained*.

The writer does present the characteristics of an effective teacher, but these characteristics are all contained in one paragraph, and they are very unclear due to poor word choice, ambiguous expressions (awkward), and poor sentence structure. Three paragraphs should have been used, one for each characteristic, and each should have contained details to explain and support the characteristic.

This essay is filled with awkward expressions that suggest an inability to effectively use the language: "declining of education," "internal love within self," "external love of the art of teaching," "demonstrate the first procedure of effectiveness in the classroom," "set up the essential elements," "Finally, living beyond the classroom, I think, is the most effective in an effective classroom teacher," "staying beyond your paid time," and others.

The writer excessively uses "you" and "your"—second person. Essays should be written in the third person—he, she, or they. For example, the noun *teacher* or *teachers* should have been used as well.

LAST
PRACTICE TEST

1. Ⓐ Ⓑ Ⓒ Ⓓ   21. Ⓐ Ⓑ Ⓒ Ⓓ   41. Ⓐ Ⓑ Ⓒ Ⓓ   61. Ⓐ Ⓑ Ⓒ Ⓓ
2. Ⓐ Ⓑ Ⓒ Ⓓ   22. Ⓐ Ⓑ Ⓒ Ⓓ   42. Ⓐ Ⓑ Ⓒ Ⓓ   62. Ⓐ Ⓑ Ⓒ Ⓓ
3. Ⓐ Ⓑ Ⓒ Ⓓ   23. Ⓐ Ⓑ Ⓒ Ⓓ   43. Ⓐ Ⓑ Ⓒ Ⓓ   63. Ⓐ Ⓑ Ⓒ Ⓓ
4. Ⓐ Ⓑ Ⓒ Ⓓ   24. Ⓐ Ⓑ Ⓒ Ⓓ   44. Ⓐ Ⓑ Ⓒ Ⓓ   64. Ⓐ Ⓑ Ⓒ Ⓓ
5. Ⓐ Ⓑ Ⓒ Ⓓ   25. Ⓐ Ⓑ Ⓒ Ⓓ   45. Ⓐ Ⓑ Ⓒ Ⓓ   65. Ⓐ Ⓑ Ⓒ Ⓓ
6. Ⓐ Ⓑ Ⓒ Ⓓ   26. Ⓐ Ⓑ Ⓒ Ⓓ   46. Ⓐ Ⓑ Ⓒ Ⓓ   66. Ⓐ Ⓑ Ⓒ Ⓓ
7. Ⓐ Ⓑ Ⓒ Ⓓ   27. Ⓐ Ⓑ Ⓒ Ⓓ   47. Ⓐ Ⓑ Ⓒ Ⓓ   67. Ⓐ Ⓑ Ⓒ Ⓓ
8. Ⓐ Ⓑ Ⓒ Ⓓ   28. Ⓐ Ⓑ Ⓒ Ⓓ   48. Ⓐ Ⓑ Ⓒ Ⓓ   68. Ⓐ Ⓑ Ⓒ Ⓓ
9. Ⓐ Ⓑ Ⓒ Ⓓ   29. Ⓐ Ⓑ Ⓒ Ⓓ   49. Ⓐ Ⓑ Ⓒ Ⓓ   69. Ⓐ Ⓑ Ⓒ Ⓓ
10. Ⓐ Ⓑ Ⓒ Ⓓ   30. Ⓐ Ⓑ Ⓒ Ⓓ   50. Ⓐ Ⓑ Ⓒ Ⓓ   70. Ⓐ Ⓑ Ⓒ Ⓓ
11. Ⓐ Ⓑ Ⓒ Ⓓ   31. Ⓐ Ⓑ Ⓒ Ⓓ   51. Ⓐ Ⓑ Ⓒ Ⓓ   71. Ⓐ Ⓑ Ⓒ Ⓓ
12. Ⓐ Ⓑ Ⓒ Ⓓ   32. Ⓐ Ⓑ Ⓒ Ⓓ   52. Ⓐ Ⓑ Ⓒ Ⓓ   72. Ⓐ Ⓑ Ⓒ Ⓓ
13. Ⓐ Ⓑ Ⓒ Ⓓ   33. Ⓐ Ⓑ Ⓒ Ⓓ   53. Ⓐ Ⓑ Ⓒ Ⓓ   73. Ⓐ Ⓑ Ⓒ Ⓓ
14. Ⓐ Ⓑ Ⓒ Ⓓ   34. Ⓐ Ⓑ Ⓒ Ⓓ   54. Ⓐ Ⓑ Ⓒ Ⓓ   74. Ⓐ Ⓑ Ⓒ Ⓓ
15. Ⓐ Ⓑ Ⓒ Ⓓ   35. Ⓐ Ⓑ Ⓒ Ⓓ   55. Ⓐ Ⓑ Ⓒ Ⓓ   75. Ⓐ Ⓑ Ⓒ Ⓓ
16. Ⓐ Ⓑ Ⓒ Ⓓ   36. Ⓐ Ⓑ Ⓒ Ⓓ   56. Ⓐ Ⓑ Ⓒ Ⓓ   76. Ⓐ Ⓑ Ⓒ Ⓓ
17. Ⓐ Ⓑ Ⓒ Ⓓ   37. Ⓐ Ⓑ Ⓒ Ⓓ   57. Ⓐ Ⓑ Ⓒ Ⓓ   77. Ⓐ Ⓑ Ⓒ Ⓓ
18. Ⓐ Ⓑ Ⓒ Ⓓ   38. Ⓐ Ⓑ Ⓒ Ⓓ   58. Ⓐ Ⓑ Ⓒ Ⓓ   78. Ⓐ Ⓑ Ⓒ Ⓓ
19. Ⓐ Ⓑ Ⓒ Ⓓ   39. Ⓐ Ⓑ Ⓒ Ⓓ   59. Ⓐ Ⓑ Ⓒ Ⓓ   79. Ⓐ Ⓑ Ⓒ Ⓓ
20. Ⓐ Ⓑ Ⓒ Ⓓ   40. Ⓐ Ⓑ Ⓒ Ⓓ   60. Ⓐ Ⓑ Ⓒ Ⓓ   80. Ⓐ Ⓑ Ⓒ Ⓓ

ATS-W ELEMENTARY
PRACTICE TEST

1. Ⓐ Ⓑ Ⓒ Ⓓ   21. Ⓐ Ⓑ Ⓒ Ⓓ   41. Ⓐ Ⓑ Ⓒ Ⓓ   61. Ⓐ Ⓑ Ⓒ Ⓓ

2. Ⓐ Ⓑ Ⓒ Ⓓ   22. Ⓐ Ⓑ Ⓒ Ⓓ   42. Ⓐ Ⓑ Ⓒ Ⓓ   62. Ⓐ Ⓑ Ⓒ Ⓓ

3. Ⓐ Ⓑ Ⓒ Ⓓ   23. Ⓐ Ⓑ Ⓒ Ⓓ   43. Ⓐ Ⓑ Ⓒ Ⓓ   63. Ⓐ Ⓑ Ⓒ Ⓓ

4. Ⓐ Ⓑ Ⓒ Ⓓ   24. Ⓐ Ⓑ Ⓒ Ⓓ   44. Ⓐ Ⓑ Ⓒ Ⓓ   64. Ⓐ Ⓑ Ⓒ Ⓓ

5. Ⓐ Ⓑ Ⓒ Ⓓ   25. Ⓐ Ⓑ Ⓒ Ⓓ   45. Ⓐ Ⓑ Ⓒ Ⓓ   65. Ⓐ Ⓑ Ⓒ Ⓓ

6. Ⓐ Ⓑ Ⓒ Ⓓ   26. Ⓐ Ⓑ Ⓒ Ⓓ   46. Ⓐ Ⓑ Ⓒ Ⓓ   66. Ⓐ Ⓑ Ⓒ Ⓓ

7. Ⓐ Ⓑ Ⓒ Ⓓ   27. Ⓐ Ⓑ Ⓒ Ⓓ   47. Ⓐ Ⓑ Ⓒ Ⓓ   67. Ⓐ Ⓑ Ⓒ Ⓓ

8. Ⓐ Ⓑ Ⓒ Ⓓ   28. Ⓐ Ⓑ Ⓒ Ⓓ   48. Ⓐ Ⓑ Ⓒ Ⓓ   68. Ⓐ Ⓑ Ⓒ Ⓓ

9. Ⓐ Ⓑ Ⓒ Ⓓ   29. Ⓐ Ⓑ Ⓒ Ⓓ   49. Ⓐ Ⓑ Ⓒ Ⓓ   69. Ⓐ Ⓑ Ⓒ Ⓓ

10. Ⓐ Ⓑ Ⓒ Ⓓ   30. Ⓐ Ⓑ Ⓒ Ⓓ   50. Ⓐ Ⓑ Ⓒ Ⓓ   70. Ⓐ Ⓑ Ⓒ Ⓓ

11. Ⓐ Ⓑ Ⓒ Ⓓ   31. Ⓐ Ⓑ Ⓒ Ⓓ   51. Ⓐ Ⓑ Ⓒ Ⓓ   71. Ⓐ Ⓑ Ⓒ Ⓓ

12. Ⓐ Ⓑ Ⓒ Ⓓ   32. Ⓐ Ⓑ Ⓒ Ⓓ   52. Ⓐ Ⓑ Ⓒ Ⓓ   72. Ⓐ Ⓑ Ⓒ Ⓓ

13. Ⓐ Ⓑ Ⓒ Ⓓ   33. Ⓐ Ⓑ Ⓒ Ⓓ   53. Ⓐ Ⓑ Ⓒ Ⓓ   73. Ⓐ Ⓑ Ⓒ Ⓓ

14. Ⓐ Ⓑ Ⓒ Ⓓ   34. Ⓐ Ⓑ Ⓒ Ⓓ   54. Ⓐ Ⓑ Ⓒ Ⓓ   74. Ⓐ Ⓑ Ⓒ Ⓓ

15. Ⓐ Ⓑ Ⓒ Ⓓ   35. Ⓐ Ⓑ Ⓒ Ⓓ   55. Ⓐ Ⓑ Ⓒ Ⓓ   75. Ⓐ Ⓑ Ⓒ Ⓓ

16. Ⓐ Ⓑ Ⓒ Ⓓ   36. Ⓐ Ⓑ Ⓒ Ⓓ   56. Ⓐ Ⓑ Ⓒ Ⓓ   76. Ⓐ Ⓑ Ⓒ Ⓓ

17. Ⓐ Ⓑ Ⓒ Ⓓ   37. Ⓐ Ⓑ Ⓒ Ⓓ   57. Ⓐ Ⓑ Ⓒ Ⓓ   77. Ⓐ Ⓑ Ⓒ Ⓓ

18. Ⓐ Ⓑ Ⓒ Ⓓ   38. Ⓐ Ⓑ Ⓒ Ⓓ   58. Ⓐ Ⓑ Ⓒ Ⓓ   78. Ⓐ Ⓑ Ⓒ Ⓓ

19. Ⓐ Ⓑ Ⓒ Ⓓ   39. Ⓐ Ⓑ Ⓒ Ⓓ   59. Ⓐ Ⓑ Ⓒ Ⓓ   79. Ⓐ Ⓑ Ⓒ Ⓓ

20. Ⓐ Ⓑ Ⓒ Ⓓ   40. Ⓐ Ⓑ Ⓒ Ⓓ   60. Ⓐ Ⓑ Ⓒ Ⓓ   80. Ⓐ Ⓑ Ⓒ Ⓓ

ATS-W SECONDARY
PRACTICE TEST

1. Ⓐ Ⓑ Ⓒ Ⓓ
2. Ⓐ Ⓑ Ⓒ Ⓓ
3. Ⓐ Ⓑ Ⓒ Ⓓ
4. Ⓐ Ⓑ Ⓒ Ⓓ
5. Ⓐ Ⓑ Ⓒ Ⓓ
6. Ⓐ Ⓑ Ⓒ Ⓓ
7. Ⓐ Ⓑ Ⓒ Ⓓ
8. Ⓐ Ⓑ Ⓒ Ⓓ
9. Ⓐ Ⓑ Ⓒ Ⓓ
10. Ⓐ Ⓑ Ⓒ Ⓓ
11. Ⓐ Ⓑ Ⓒ Ⓓ
12. Ⓐ Ⓑ Ⓒ Ⓓ
13. Ⓐ Ⓑ Ⓒ Ⓓ
14. Ⓐ Ⓑ Ⓒ Ⓓ
15. Ⓐ Ⓑ Ⓒ Ⓓ
16. Ⓐ Ⓑ Ⓒ Ⓓ
17. Ⓐ Ⓑ Ⓒ Ⓓ
18. Ⓐ Ⓑ Ⓒ Ⓓ
19. Ⓐ Ⓑ Ⓒ Ⓓ
20. Ⓐ Ⓑ Ⓒ Ⓓ

21. Ⓐ Ⓑ Ⓒ Ⓓ
22. Ⓐ Ⓑ Ⓒ Ⓓ
23. Ⓐ Ⓑ Ⓒ Ⓓ
24. Ⓐ Ⓑ Ⓒ Ⓓ
25. Ⓐ Ⓑ Ⓒ Ⓓ
26. Ⓐ Ⓑ Ⓒ Ⓓ
27. Ⓐ Ⓑ Ⓒ Ⓓ
28. Ⓐ Ⓑ Ⓒ Ⓓ
29. Ⓐ Ⓑ Ⓒ Ⓓ
30. Ⓐ Ⓑ Ⓒ Ⓓ
31. Ⓐ Ⓑ Ⓒ Ⓓ
32. Ⓐ Ⓑ Ⓒ Ⓓ
33. Ⓐ Ⓑ Ⓒ Ⓓ
34. Ⓐ Ⓑ Ⓒ Ⓓ
35. Ⓐ Ⓑ Ⓒ Ⓓ
36. Ⓐ Ⓑ Ⓒ Ⓓ
37. Ⓐ Ⓑ Ⓒ Ⓓ
38. Ⓐ Ⓑ Ⓒ Ⓓ
39. Ⓐ Ⓑ Ⓒ Ⓓ
40. Ⓐ Ⓑ Ⓒ Ⓓ

41. Ⓐ Ⓑ Ⓒ Ⓓ
42. Ⓐ Ⓑ Ⓒ Ⓓ
43. Ⓐ Ⓑ Ⓒ Ⓓ
44. Ⓐ Ⓑ Ⓒ Ⓓ
45. Ⓐ Ⓑ Ⓒ Ⓓ
46. Ⓐ Ⓑ Ⓒ Ⓓ
47. Ⓐ Ⓑ Ⓒ Ⓓ
48. Ⓐ Ⓑ Ⓒ Ⓓ
49. Ⓐ Ⓑ Ⓒ Ⓓ
50. Ⓐ Ⓑ Ⓒ Ⓓ
51. Ⓐ Ⓑ Ⓒ Ⓓ
52. Ⓐ Ⓑ Ⓒ Ⓓ
53. Ⓐ Ⓑ Ⓒ Ⓓ
54. Ⓐ Ⓑ Ⓒ Ⓓ
55. Ⓐ Ⓑ Ⓒ Ⓓ
56. Ⓐ Ⓑ Ⓒ Ⓓ
57. Ⓐ Ⓑ Ⓒ Ⓓ
58. Ⓐ Ⓑ Ⓒ Ⓓ
59. Ⓐ Ⓑ Ⓒ Ⓓ
60. Ⓐ Ⓑ Ⓒ Ⓓ

61. Ⓐ Ⓑ Ⓒ Ⓓ
62. Ⓐ Ⓑ Ⓒ Ⓓ
63. Ⓐ Ⓑ Ⓒ Ⓓ
64. Ⓐ Ⓑ Ⓒ Ⓓ
65. Ⓐ Ⓑ Ⓒ Ⓓ
66. Ⓐ Ⓑ Ⓒ Ⓓ
67. Ⓐ Ⓑ Ⓒ Ⓓ
68. Ⓐ Ⓑ Ⓒ Ⓓ
69. Ⓐ Ⓑ Ⓒ Ⓓ
70. Ⓐ Ⓑ Ⓒ Ⓓ
71. Ⓐ Ⓑ Ⓒ Ⓓ
72. Ⓐ Ⓑ Ⓒ Ⓓ
73. Ⓐ Ⓑ Ⓒ Ⓓ
74. Ⓐ Ⓑ Ⓒ Ⓓ
75. Ⓐ Ⓑ Ⓒ Ⓓ
76. Ⓐ Ⓑ Ⓒ Ⓓ
77. Ⓐ Ⓑ Ⓒ Ⓓ
78. Ⓐ Ⓑ Ⓒ Ⓓ
79. Ⓐ Ⓑ Ⓒ Ⓓ
80. Ⓐ Ⓑ Ⓒ Ⓓ

INSTALLING REA'S TEST*ware*®

System Requirements

Pentium 75 MHz (300 MHz recommended), or a higher or compatible processor; Microsoft Windows 98, NT 4 (SP6), ME, 2000, or XP; 64 MB RAM; Internet Explorer 5.5 or higher; minimum 100 MB available hard-disk space; VGA or higher-resolution monitor, 800 x 600 resolution setting; Microsoft Mouse, Microsoft Intellimouse, or compatible pointing device.

Installation

1. Insert the NYSTCE TEST*ware*® CD-ROM into the CD-ROM drive.

2. If the installation doesn't begin automatically, from the Start Menu, choose the RUN command. When the RUN dialog box appears, type d:\setup.exe (where D is the letter of your CD-ROM drive) at the prompt and click OK.

3. The installation process will begin. A dialog box proposing the directory "Program Files\REA\NYSTCE" will appear. If the name and location are suitable, click OK. If you wish to specify a different name or location, type it in and click OK.

4. Start the NYSTCE TEST*ware*® application by double-clicking on the icon.

REA's NYSTCE TEST*ware*® is **EASY** to **LEARN AND USE**. To achieve maximum benefits, we recommend that you take a few minutes to go through the on-screen tutorial on your computer. The "screen buttons" are also explained here to familiarize you with the program.

Technical Support

REA's TEST*ware*® is backed by customer and technical support. For questions about **installation or operation of your software**, contact us at:

Research & Education Association
Phone: (732) 819-8880 (9 a.m. to 5 p.m. ET, Monday–Friday)
Fax: (732) 819-8808
Website: http://www.rea.com
E-mail: info@rea.com

Note to Windows XP Users: In order for the TEST*ware*® to function properly, please install and run the application under the same computer-administrator level user account. Installing the TEST*ware*® as one user and running it as another could cause file access path conflicts.

USING REA'S TESTware®

Exam Directions

The **Exam Directions** button allows you to review the specific exam directions during any part of the test.

Stop Test

At any time during the test or when you are finished taking the test, click on the **Stop** button.

From the dialog box that follows, you can choose to quit the test or return to the last question seen prior to clicking the **Stop** button.

Back / Next Buttons

These two buttons allow you to move successively between questions. The **Next** button moves you to the next question, while the **Back** button allows you to view the previous question.

Mark/Q's List

If you are unsure about an answer to a particular question, the program allows you to mark it for later review. Flag the question by clicking on the **Mark** button. The **Q's List** allows you to navigate through the questions and explanations. This is particularly useful if you want to view marked questions in Explanations Mode.

Change Section

You may freely change between the sections of the exam at any time during the test by clicking on the **Change Section** button.

View Scores

Three score reports are available: Chart, Summary, and Detail (shown below). All are accessed by clicking on the **View Scores** button from the Main Menu.

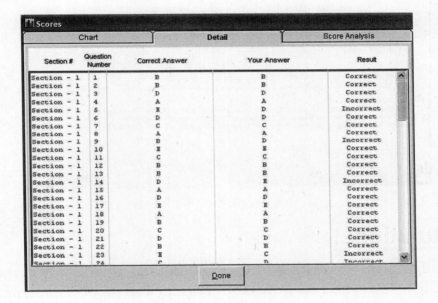

Explanations

In Explanations mode, click on the **Q & A Explanations** button to display a detailed explanation to any question. The split window shown below can be resized for easy reading. To access Explanations Mode from the Main Menu, click Start Test, then the Explanations button.

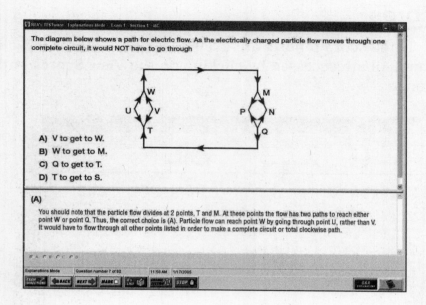

Congratulations!

By studying the reviews in this book, taking the computerized and printed practice tests, and reviewing your correct and incorrect answers, you will be well prepared to succeed on the NYSTCE. Best of luck from everyone at REA.

The ESSENTIALS® of MATH & SCIENCE

Each book in the ESSENTIALS series offers all essential information of the field it covers. It summarizes what every textbook in the particular field must include, and is designed to help students in preparing for exams and doing homework. The ESSENTIALS are excellent supplements to any class text.

The ESSENTIALS are complete and concise with quick access to needed information. They serve as a handy reference source at all times. The ESSENTIALS are prepared with REA's customary concern for high professional quality and student needs.

Available in the following titles:

Advanced Calculus
Algebra & Trigonometry I & II
Anatomy & Physiology
Astronomy
Automatic Control Systems / Robotics II
Biochemistry
Biology I & II
Biology of the Universe
Boolean Algebra
Calculus I, II, & III
Chemistry
Complex Variables I & II
Computer Science I & II
Data Structures I & II
Differential Equations

Electric Circuits
Electromagnetics I & II
Electronic Communications II
Electronics I & II
Fluid Mechanics / Dynamics I
Genetics: Unlocking the Mysteries of Life
Geometry I & II
Group Theory I & II
Heat Transfer II
LaPlace Transforms
Linear Algebra
Math for Computer Applications
Math for Engineers II
Mechanics I, II, & III
Microbiology

Modern Algebra
Numerical Analysis I & II
Organic Chemistry I & II
Physical Chemistry II
Physics I & II
Pre-Calculus
Probability
Real Variables
Set Theory
Statistics I & II
Strength of Materials & Mechanics of Solids II
Thermodynamics II
Topology
Transport Phenomena I & II

If you would like more information about any of these books,
complete the coupon below and return it to us or visit your local bookstore.

Research & Education Association
61 Ethel Road W., Piscataway, NJ 08854
Phone: (732) 819-8880   **website: www.rea.com**

Please send me more information about your Math & Science Essentials® books.

Name _____

Address _____

City_____ State_____ Zip _____

REA's Test Preps
The Best in Test Preparation

- REA "Test Preps" are **far more** comprehensive than any other test preparation series
- Each book contains up to **eight** full-length practice tests based on the most recent exams
- **Every** type of question likely to be given on the exams is included
- Answers are accompanied by **full** and **detailed** explanations

REA publishes over 70 Test Preparation volumes in several series. They include:

Advanced Placement Exams (APs)
Art History
Biology
Calculus AB & BC
Chemistry
Economics
English Language & Composition
English Literature & Composition
European History
French Language
Government & Politics
Latin
Physics B & C
Psychology
Spanish Language
Statistics
United States History
World History

College-Level Examination Program (CLEP)
Analyzing and Interpreting
   Literature
College Algebra
Freshman College Composition
General Examinations
General Examinations Review
History of the United States I
History of the United States II
Introduction to Educational
   Psychology
Human Growth and Development
Introductory Psychology
Introductory Sociology
Principles of Management
Principles of Marketing
Spanish
Western Civilization I
Western Civilization II

SAT Subject Tests
Biology E/M
Chemistry
French
German
Literature
Mathematics Level 1, 2
Physics
Spanish
United States History

Graduate Record Exams (GREs)
Biology
Chemistry
Computer Science
General
Literature in English
Mathematics
Physics
Psychology

ACT - ACT Assessment

ASVAB - Armed Services Vocational
   Aptitude Battery

CBEST - California Basic Educational
   Skills Test

CDL - Commercial Driver License Exam

CLAST - College Level Academic
   Skills Test

COOP & HSPT - Catholic High School
   Admission Tests

ELM - California State University
   Entry Level Mathematics Exam

FE (EIT) - Fundamentals of Engineering
   Exams - For Both AM & PM Exams

FTCE - Florida Teacher Certification
   Examinations

GED - (U.S. Edition)

GMAT - Graduate Management
   Admission Test

LSAT - Law School Admission Test

MAT - Miller Analogies Test

MCAT - Medical College Admission
   Test

MTEL - Massachusetts Tests for
   Educator Licensure

NJ HSPA - New Jersey High School
   Proficiency Assessment

NYSTCE - New York State Teacher
   Certification Examinations

PRAXIS PLT - Principles of Learning
   & Teaching Tests

PRAXIS PPST - Pre-Professional
   Skills Tests

PSAT/NMSQT

SAT

TExES - Texas Examinations of
   Educator Standards

THEA - Texas Higher Education
   Assessment

TOEFL - Test of English as a Foreign
   Language

TOEIC - Test of English for
   International Communication

USMLE Steps 1,2,3 - U.S. Medical
   Licensing Exams

Research & Education Association
61 Ethel Road W., Piscataway, NJ 08854
Phone: (732) 819-8880   **website: www.rea.com**

Please send me more information about your Test Prep books.

Name _____

Address _____

City_____ State_____ Zip _____

REA's Test Prep Books Are The Best!

(a sample of the <u>hundreds of letters</u> REA receives each year)

" I am writing to congratulate you on preparing an exceptional study guide. In five years of teaching this course I have never encountered a more thorough, comprehensive, concise and realistic preparation for this examination. "

Teacher, Davie, FL

" I have found your publications, *The Best Test Preparation...,* to be exactly that. "

Teacher, Aptos, CA

" I used your *CLEP Introductory Sociology* book and rank it 99% – thank you! "

Student, Jerusalem, Israel

" Your GMAT book greatly helped me on the test. Thank you. "

Student, Oxford, OH

" I recently got the French SAT II Exam book from REA. I congratulate you on first-rate French practice tests."

Instructor, Los Angeles, CA

" Your AP English Literature and Composition book is most impressive."

Student, Montgomery, AL

" The REA LSAT Test Preparation guide is a winner! "

Instructor, Spartanburg, SC